The Third International after Lenin

The Third International after Lenin

Leon Trotsky

PATHFINDER
New York London Montreal Sydney

Translated by John G. Wright

Copyright © 1957, 1970, 1996 by Pathfinder Press
All rights reserved

ISBN 0-87348-826-1 paper; 0-87348-827-X cloth
Library of Congress Catalog Card Number 96-68845
Manufactured in the United States of America

First edition, 1936
Second edition, 1957
Third edition, 1970
Fourth edition, 1996

Cover: Eva Braiman. Cover photo: Scene from insurrection in Canton, China, December 1927.

Pathfinder
410 West Street, New York, NY 10014, U.S.A.
Fax: (212) 727-0150 • CompuServe: 73321,414 •
Internet: pathfinder@igc.apc.org

PATHFINDER DISTRIBUTORS AROUND THE WORLD:
Australia (and Asia and the Pacific):
    Pathfinder, 19 Terry St., Surry Hills, Sydney, N.S.W. 2010
    Postal address: P.O. Box K879, Haymarket, N.S.W. 2000
Canada:
    Pathfinder, 4581 rue St-Denis, Montreal, Quebec, H2J 2L4
Iceland:
    Pathfinder, Klapparstíg 26, 2d floor, 101 Reykjavík
    Postal address: P. Box 233, 121 Reykjavík
New Zealand:
    Pathfinder, La Gonda Arcade, 203 Karangahape Road, Auckland
    Postal address: P.O. Box 8730, Auckland
Sweden:
    Pathfinder, Vikingagatan 10, S-113 42, Stockholm
United Kingdom (and Europe, Africa except South Africa, and Middle East):
    Pathfinder, 47 The Cut, London, SE1 8LL
United States (and Caribbean, Latin America, and South Africa):
    Pathfinder, 410 West Street, New York, NY 10014

Contents

Preface / 7

Foreword to 1929 French edition / 13

The Draft Program of the Communist International: A Criticism of Fundamentals / 21

I
The program of international revolution or a program of socialism in one country?
1. The general structure of the program / 23
2. The United States of America and Europe / 26
3. The slogan of the Soviet United States of Europe / 30
4. The criterion of internationalism / 37
5. The theoretical tradition of the party / 43
6. Where is the "social democratic deviation"? / 59
7. The dependence of the USSR on world economy / 62
8. The contradiction between the productive forces and the national boundaries as the cause of the reactionary utopian theory of "socialism in one country" / 70
9. The question can be solved only on the arena of world revolution / 79
10. The theory of socialism in one country as a series of social-patriotic blunders / 84

II
Strategy and tactics in the imperialist epoch

1. The complete bankruptcy of the central chapter of the draft program / *92*
2. The fundamental peculiarities inherent in the strategy of the imperialist epoch and the role of the party / *96*
3. The Third Congress and the question of the permanence of the revolutionary process according to Lenin and according to Bukharin / *103*
4. The German events of 1923 and the lessons of October / *107*
5. The basic strategical mistake of the Fifth Congress / *115*
6. The "democratic-pacifist era" and fascism / *123*
7. The right leaven of ultraleft policy / *131*
8. The period of right-centrist down-sliding / *139*
9. The maneuverist character of revolutionary strategy / *149*
10. The strategy of civil war / *156*
11. The question of the internal party regime / *160*
12. The causes of the defeat of the Opposition and its perspectives / *173*

III
Summary and perspectives of the Chinese Revolution

1. On the nature of the colonial bourgeoisie / *180*
2. The stages of the Chinese revolution / *192*
3. Democratic dictatorship or a dictatorship of the proletariat? / *198*
4. Adventurism as the product of opportunism / *208*
5. Soviets and revolution / *212*
6. The question of the character of the coming Chinese revolution / *218*

7. On the reactionary idea of "two-class workers
     and peasants parties" for the Orient / *223*
  8. The advantages secured from the Peasants International
     must be probed / *234*
     Conclusion / *238*

  ## What Now? / *241*

  1. The aim of this letter / *241*
  2. Why has no congress of the Comintern been
     convoked for more than four years? / *246*
  3. The policy of 1923–1927 / *254*
  4. Radicalization of the masses and questions
     of leadership / *265*
  5. How the current swing toward the left
     in the CPSU was prepared / *273*
  6. One step forward, one-half a step backward / *281*
  7. A maneuver or a new course? / *292*
  8. The social basis of the present crisis / *299*
  9. The party crisis / *306*

  Appendix:
  *Introduction to first edition of
  "The Draft Program of the Communist
  International: A Criticism of Fundamentals"
  by James P. Cannon / 317*

  Explanatory notes / 323

  Index / 372

Preface

IN OCTOBER 1917, IN THE MIDST of a world capitalist economic crisis and the interimperialist world war it engendered, the workers and peasants of Russia threw off the rule of the landlords and capitalists and set out to reorganize society in the interests of the toilers. In so doing they demonstrated that a new epoch in human history had begun—the epoch of the proletarian revolution.

The victory of the Russian revolution in October 1917 and the establishment of the first workers state, under the leadership of the Bolshevik Party led by V.I. Lenin, gave a concrete answer to the decisive question before the working class everywhere: building communist parties, with an internationalist program and perspective, capable of and willing to lead the toilers to take power.

This challenge, which remains decisive for working people today, was taken up by the Bolshevik Party and by the Communist International in the years after the Russian revolution. The fight to continue this course is the central theme of *The Third International after Lenin* by Leon Trotsky.

During the first years after its founding in 1919, the Communist International (Comintern, or Third International*) was a school of Marxist politics. Working-class parties from around the world joined the Comintern, seeking to absorb and apply the lessons of the Russian revolution, discuss how to respond to class

---

* The First International (International Workingmen's Association), led by Karl Marx and Frederick Engels, was active from 1864 to 1872. The Second (Socialist) International, formed in 1889, collapsed in 1914 when the majority of its parties supported their respective capitalist governments in World War I.

battles and revolutionary openings, and build communist parties in their own countries capable of emulating the example of the toilers of Russia.

By the time of Lenin's death in 1924, the working class in Russia was on the defensive. Revolutionary upsurges that broke out throughout Europe in 1918–20 had been defeated. On top of this were the devastating economic and social consequences arising from Russia's defeat in the First World War of 1914–18, followed immediately by the civil war of 1918–20, in which all the major imperialist powers sent troops against the new Soviet state. Under these conditions, the petty-bourgeois and bureaucratic layers within the administration of the state, party, and armed forces—whose leading representative came to be Joseph Stalin—gained the upper hand in their drive to secure a privileged standard of living for themselves. This counterrevolutionary social caste took control of the Communist Party and Soviet state apparatus, using increasingly repressive measures.

Rejecting the revolutionary internationalist outlook that had characterized the Bolshevik Party since its founding, the Stalin-led faction justified its course under the anti-Marxist slogan of building "socialism in one country." At the same time, it began to use the authority of the Communist Party to bureaucratically impose anti-working-class policies and practices on the Communist International and communist parties around the world, which over time became transformed into agencies to advance foreign policy interests of the privileged caste dominating the Soviet Union.

This reversal of course within the Comintern had disastrous consequences for the workers movement internationally, reinforcing the isolation of the working class in the Soviet Union. Working people suffered a series of defeats, ranging from a missed revolutionary opportunity in Germany in October 1923 to the bloody suppression of the Chinese revolution of 1925–27. The lessons of these events are among the subjects discussed in these pages.

The Third International after Lenin contains Trotsky's 1928 defense of the Marxist course that had guided the Communist International in its early years. Its main component is a criticism of the draft program presented by Nikolai Bukharin and Joseph Stalin to the Comintern's Sixth World Congress, held that year in Moscow.

Leon Trotsky had been part of the central leadership team of the Bolshevik Party from the time of the Russian revolution and of the Communist International in its early years. Following Lenin's death, he became the principal leader of the Left Opposition, formed to wage a battle against the social forces led by Stalin and to defend the communist perspective Lenin had fought for. At the time Trotsky wrote this document, he had been expelled from the Russian Communist Party and exiled to Soviet central Asia. In 1929 Trotsky was deported from the Soviet Union. For the next twelve years he worked with revolutionists around the world to reknit the continuity of communism and to prepare the working-class vanguard for the revolutionary opportunities in the face of imperialism's drive toward fascism and imperialist war in the 1930s. He was assassinated in Mexico in 1940 by Stalin's secret police.

Although Trotsky's work was suppressed in the Soviet Union, excerpts were translated and circulated to a small number of delegates attending the sixth Comintern congress. Among these were two members of the congress's Program Commission, James P. Cannon from the United States and Maurice Spector from Canada, who were convinced by Trotsky's criticism. These two communist leaders subsequently smuggled the document out of the Soviet Union and, passing it hand to hand, were able to win over a nucleus of supporters in North America. These working-class cadres were soon expelled from the Communist Party and formed the Communist League of America, forerunner of the Socialist Workers Party. The story of these events is recounted in Cannon's *History of American Trotskyism*, published by Pathfinder.

The expelled communists published the *Militant*, which serialized Trotsky's criticism of the draft program, beginning with its first issue in November 1928. In January 1929 they published it as a small book—the first publication produced by supporters of the *Militant*—under the title *The Draft Program of the Communist International: A Criticism of Fundamentals*. At the time, whole parts of the work were unavailable, including the entire second section. The second section was published as a separate pamphlet in 1930.

Following Trotsky's deportation from the Soviet Union in February 1929, the whole book appeared in French. An English-language edition, under the present title, was produced in 1936, published in collaboration with Trotsky by Pioneer Press, Pathfinder's predecessor. Two items in the French edition of 1929 were not included in the U.S. version. "The Chinese Question after the Sixth Congress" can be found in *Leon Trotsky on China* (Pathfinder, 1976); "Who Is Leading the Comintern Today?" is contained in *The Challenge of the Left Opposition (1928–29)* (Pathfinder, 1981).

The 1936 work, translated by John G. Wright, forms the basis of the present edition, which has been scanned and reset. The explanatory notes prepared for the 1936 edition have been retained and appear at the back. Also included is Trotsky's foreword to the 1929 French version, translated by A.L. Preston for Pathfinder's third edition published in 1970. For this new edition, we have restored, as an appendix, James P. Cannon's introduction to the original 1929 U.S. version. An index has also been added.

When *The Third International after Lenin* was published in 1936, Lenin's *Collected Works* had not yet appeared in English. Quotations from Lenin's writings, cited by Trotsky to the original Russian-language edition of Lenin's *Works*, were therefore translated by John G. Wright directly from the Russian. Wright's translation has been maintained intact in the present edition, but footnotes have been added to indicate where each quotation can be found in the English-language

Collected Works of Lenin. A similar procedure has been followed with citations from other works by Trotsky that are currently available in English.

Michael Taber
MAY 1996

Foreword to 1929 French Edition

THIS BOOK IS MADE UP OF FOUR PARTS independent of each other but having, nevertheless, an indissoluble unity: the whole is devoted to the fundamental problems of the Communist International. The book covers all aspects of the activities of the Communist International: its program, its strategy and tactics, its organization, and the members of its leadership. Since the Soviet Communist Party, the governmental party of the Soviet Union, plays a decisive role in every respect, as the principal party in the Communist International, this book also contains an appreciation of the internal life of the Soviet Communist Party in the most recent period, which began with the illness and death of Lenin. In that way the book constitutes, I hope, a harmonious enough whole.

My work has not been published in Russian. It was written in that period (1928) when Marxist works dealing with contemporary matters had become, in the Soviet Republic, the most prohibited form of literature. To ensure some measure of diffusion for my writings, I made the first two parts of this book into official documents addressed to the Sixth Congress of the Communist International, which met in Moscow during the summer of last year. The third and fourth parts,* written after the congress, passed from hand to hand in manuscript form. The circulation of these manuscripts was, and still is, punished with deportation to the forgotten corners of Siberia and even, most recently, with strict solitary confinement in the prison of Tobolsk.

---

* As explained in the preface, the third and fourth parts of the 1929 French edition are omitted from this volume.

Only the second part,* that is, "The Draft Program of the Communist International—A Criticism of Fundamentals," has been published in German. Till now the book as a whole has lived an embryonic life in the state of manuscripts. It appears for the first time in the form given by the French edition. However, since my manuscripts have penetrated into various countries of Europe and of America and into western China by different ways, I wish to state here that the present French edition is the one and only edition for which I bear responsibility before the readers.

By decision of the Sixth Congress, the draft program criticized in this book has become the official program of the International. But my criticism loses nothing thereby of its relevance. Quite the contrary. All the fatal mistakes in the draft have been retained; they have simply been given a legal basis and consecrated as articles of faith. At the congress, the Program Commission posed the question of what was to be done with a critique whose author had not only been excluded from the Communist International but exiled to Central Asia. Some timid and isolated voices were raised to say that one should also learn from one's opponents and that correct thoughts remained correct, independently of who formulated them. However, another, much stronger group prevailed, almost without resistance or struggle. A respectable old lady—she was formerly Clara Zetkin[1]—said that no ideas emanating from Trotsky could be considered correct. She was merely carrying out a task given her behind the scenes. Assigning dishonorable tasks to people of unchallengeable reputation is the Stalin system. The timid voice of reason was stilled at once; and shutting its eyes, the commission thus passed over my "Criticism." And so, all I said about the draft retains its full force for the present

---

* In the 1929 French edition, "The Draft Program of the Communist International—A Criticism of Fundamentals" was placed after the essay, "What Now?" In the English edition this has been reversed to conform to the chronological order.

1. Numbered explanatory notes begin on page 323.

official program. This program has no theoretical consistency and is politically harmful. It should be changed and it will be.

As usual, the members of the Sixth Congress "unanimously" condemned "Trotskyism" once again. That was what they had been summoned to Moscow to do. The majority of them have come on the political scene only yesterday or the day before. Not a single one of these delegates took part in the founding of the Communist International. Very few present had participated in one or two of the four congresses which took place under Lenin's leadership. All are recruits to the new political course and are agents of the new organizational regime. In accusing me—or more precisely, in signing the accusation made against me—of having violated Leninist principles, the delegates to the Sixth Congress gave proof of docility rather than clarity in theoretical thinking or knowledge of the history of the Communist International.

Till the Sixth Congress, the International had no codified program. Manifestos and resolutions on principles took its place: the First and Second Congresses addressed manifestos to the international working class (the manifesto of the Second Congress, in particular, had in all its aspects the character of a program). I wrote those documents,* they were approved by our Central Committee without any amendment and ratified by the first two congresses—whose importance as constitutive assemblies was noteworthy.

The Third Congress adopted theses on program and tactics which applied to the fundamental problems of the world working-class movement. At the Third Congress I intervened to defend the theses which I had worked out.† The amendments proposed—not in the best faith—were directed as much against Lenin as against me. In struggling firmly against the opposition of that time—represented by Thälmann, Béla Kun, Pepper, and

---

* Reprinted in volume 1 of Trotsky's *The First Five Years of the Communist International* (New York: Pathfinder, 1972).

† *Ibid.*

other confusionists[2]—we, Lenin and I, succeeded in having my theses approved by the congress, almost unanimously.

Lenin shared with me the presentation of the main report to the Fourth Congress, a report on the situation of the Soviet Republic and the perspectives of world revolution. We intervened side by side; and it fell to me to deliver the speeches summing up after each of the two reports.* It is superfluous to add that these documents—the cornerstone of the Communist International—drawn up by me or with my collaboration, presented and applied those very fundamentals of Marxism which the recruits of the Stalin period now condemn as "Trotskyism."

But it is not superfluous to add that the present leader of these recruits took not the slightest part—directly or indirectly—in the work of the Communist International, neither in the congresses nor in the commissions, nor even in the preparatory work which, for the most part, fell on the Russian party. There does not exist one single document which can bear witness to any creative activity by Stalin in the work of the first four congresses or even to any serious interest in that work.

Nor do things stop there. If we examine the lists of the delegates to the first four congresses, that is, the lists of the first and most devoted friends of the October Revolution, of the founders of the Communist International, of Lenin's closest international collaborators, we find that—after Lenin's death—all, with one exception, were not only removed from the leadership but were also expelled from the Communist International. This is as true for the Soviet Union as for France, Germany, Italy, Scandinavia, or Czechoslovakia, for Europe as for America.[3] Accordingly, are we to believe that the Leninist line was attacked by those who had worked it out with Lenin? And accordingly, are we to believe that the Leninist line was defended by those who had fought against it while Lenin was still alive or who joined the Communist International only in the past few years, not knowing what had happened before and not thinking of the morrow?

---

* See *The First Five Years of the Communist International*, volume 2.

The consequences of the changes in policy and in leading personnel are only too well known. From the beginning of 1923, the Communist International suffered only defeats: in Germany, Bulgaria, Britain, and China. In other countries, though not as dramatic, the reverses were as serious. The opportunist blindness of the leadership was the immediate cause everywhere. The most serious of these defeats is what Stalin is preparing in the Soviet Republic: one can believe that he has set himself the goal of going down in history as the great organizer of defeats.

◆◆

In the Soviet Republic, the militants of the Leninist Communist International are exiled, imprisoned, or banished. In Germany and France things have not gone that far, but that is truly not the fault of the Thälmanns or the Cachins.[4] These "leaders" demand of the capitalist police that they not tolerate the presence of Lenin's companions in struggle on the territory of bourgeois democracy.[5] In 1916 Cachin justified my expulsion from France with fiercely chauvinist arguments. Today he demands I be forbidden to enter France. Thus, he is only carrying out his work as I do mine.

As is known, in the period of the first four congresses I was especially involved in French matters. I had often to examine with Lenin the problems of the French workers movement. Sometimes Lenin would ask me, half jocularly but basically quite seriously, "Aren't you treating the parliamentary weathercocks of the Cachin type too indulgently?" I answered that the Cachins were no more than a temporary footbridge allowing access to the French working masses, but when serious revolutionaries arose and were firmly organized they would sweep out of their road the Cachins and their consorts. True, for reasons studied in this book, things have dragged out, but I have no doubt at all that the weathercocks will meet the fate they deserve: the proletariat needs tools made of steel not tin.

The united front of Stalin, the bourgeois police, Thälmann, and Cachin against Lenin's companions is an incontestable and not unimportant fact in the political life of the Europe of today.

❧

What general conclusion is to be drawn from this book? On different sides attempts are being made to attribute to us the project of creating a Fourth International. That idea is entirely false.[6] Communism and democratic "socialism" are two profound historical tendencies with roots deep in class relations. The existence and the struggle of the Second and Third Internationals are a long process intimately bound up with the fate of capitalist society. At certain moments intermediary or "centrist" tendencies can acquire great influence, but never for long. The attempts by Friedrich Adler and Co. to create an intermediary International—the Two-and-a-Half—seemed to promise much at the beginning, but very rapidly it became bankrupt.[7] Stalin's policy, while starting from other bases and other historical traditions, is a variety of the same centrism. With rule and compass in hand, Friedrich Adler tried to construct a political diagonal between Bolshevism and social democracy. Stalin, for his part, has no such doctrinaire views. Stalinist policy is a series of empirical zigzags between Marx and Vollmar,[8] between Lenin and Chiang Kai-shek,[9] between Bolshevism and national socialism. But if we sum up the total of those zigzags in their fundamental expression, we finish with the same arithmetical total: two and a half. After all the mistakes it has made and the cruel defeats it has caused, Stalinist centrism[10] would have been liquidated politically long ago were it not that it could still rely on the ideological and material resources of a state that had emerged from the October Revolution. However, even the most powerful apparatus cannot save a hopeless policy. Between Marxism and social patriotism there is no room for Stalinism. After having gone through a series of tests and crises the Communist International will free itself from the yoke of a bureaucracy without ideological principles, capable only of swinging the helm wildly, of describing zigzags, of repression, and of preparing defeats. We have no need at all to build a Fourth International. We continue and develop the line of the Third International which we prepared during the war and in whose foundation we participated with Lenin after the October Revolution. Not for a moment have we let slip the thread of the ideological heritage. Our judgments and our foresight have been confirmed by facts of great historical importance. Never as much as now, during these years of persecution and exile, have we been so unshakably convinced of the correctness of our ideas and of the inevitability of their victory.

Leon Trotsky
CONSTANTINOPLE
APRIL 15, 1929

The Draft Program of the Communist International

A Criticism of Fundamentals

THE DRAFT PROGRAM, that is, the fundamental document which is to determine the entire activity of the Comintern for many years to come, was published only a few weeks prior to the convocation of the congress that is being held four years after the Fifth Congress. This tardiness in publication cannot be justified by reference to the fact that the first draft[11] had been published even prior to the Fifth Congress, because several years have since elapsed. The second draft differs from the first in its entire structure and it endeavors to sum up the developments of the last few years. Nothing could be more rash and precipitate than to adopt this draft at the Sixth Congress, a draft which bears obvious traces of hasty, even slipshod work, without any preliminary serious and scientific criticism in the press or an extensive discussion in all parties of the Comintern.

During the few days at our disposal between the receipt of the draft and the dispatch of this letter, we could dwell only upon a few of the most vital problems which must be treated in the program.

Due to lack of time, we have been compelled to leave entirely without consideration a number of the most important problems touched upon in the draft which are perhaps less burning today but which may become of exceptional importance tomorrow. This does not at all imply that it is less necessary to criticize them than those sections of the draft to which the present work is devoted.

We must also add that we are compelled to work on the new draft under conditions which make it impossible to obtain indispensable information. Enough to mention the fact that we were unable to procure even the first draft of the program, and in dealing with it, as well as in two or three other cases, we have had to rely upon our memory. It goes without saying that all quotations have been taken from the original sources and checked carefully.

I

The program of the international revolution or a program of socialism in one country?

THE MOST IMPORTANT QUESTION on the agenda of the Sixth Congress is the adoption of a program. The nature of the latter may for a long time determine and fix the physiognomy of the International. The importance of a program does not lie so much in the manner in which it formulates general theoretical conceptions (in the last analysis, this boils down to a question of "codification," i.e., a concise exposition of the truths and generalizations which have been firmly and decisively acquired); it is to a much greater degree a question of drawing up the balance of the world economic and political experiences of the last period, particularly of the revolutionary struggles of the last five years—so rich in events and mistakes. For the next few years, the fate of the Communist International—in the literal sense of the word—depends upon the manner in which these events, mistakes, and controversies are interpreted and judged in the program.

1. THE GENERAL STRUCTURE OF THE PROGRAM

In our epoch, which is the epoch of imperialism, i.e., of *world* economy and *world* politics under the hegemony of finance capital, not a single communist party can establish its program by proceeding solely or mainly from conditions and tendencies of developments in its own country. This also holds entirely for the party that wields the state power within the boundaries of the USSR. On August 4, 1914,[12] the death knell sounded for national programs for all time. The revolutionary party of the proletariat can base itself only upon an international program corresponding to the character of the present epoch, the epoch of the highest development and collapse of capitalism. An international communist program is in no case the sum total of national programs or an amalgam of their common features. The international program must proceed directly from an analysis of the conditions and tendencies of world economy and of the world political system taken as a whole in all its connections and contradictions, that is, with the mutually antagonistic interdependence of its separate parts. In the present epoch, to a much larger extent than in the past, the national orientation of the proletariat must and can flow only from a world orientation and not vice versa. Herein lies the basic and primary difference between communist internationalism and all varieties of national socialism.

Basing ourselves upon these considerations, we wrote in January of this year: "We must begin work to draft a program of the Comintern (Bukharin's program is a bad program of a national section of the Comintern and not a program of a world communist party)." (*Pravda,* January 15, 1928.)*

We have kept insisting upon these considerations since 1923–24 when the question of the United States of America arose in its full scope as a problem of *world* and, in the most direct sense of the term, of *European* politics.

In recommending the new draft, *Pravda* wrote that a communist program "differs radically from the program of the international social democracy not only in the substance of its

---

* "Problems of the International Opposition," in Trotsky, *The Challenge of the Left Opposition (1928–29)* (New York: Pathfinder, 1981), p. 45.

central postulates but also in the characteristic internationalism of its structure." (*Pravda,* May 29, 1928.)

In this somewhat cloudy formulation is obviously expressed the idea which we stated above and which was formerly stubbornly rejected. One can only welcome the break with the first draft program presented by Bukharin, which did not even provoke a serious exchange of opinion; nor, for that matter, did it offer any grounds for one. Whereas the first draft gave a bald schematic description of the development of one abstract country towards socialism, the new draft seeks, unfortunately, and, as we shall see, without consistency or success, to take world economy as a whole as the basis for determining the fate of its individual parts.

Linking up countries and continents that stand on different levels of development into a system of mutual dependence and antagonism, leveling out the various stages of their development and at the same time immediately enhancing the differences between them, and ruthlessly counterposing one country to another, world economy has become a mighty reality which holds sway over the economic life of individual countries and continents. This basic fact alone invests the idea of a world communist party with a supreme reality. Bringing world economy as a whole to the highest phase of development generally attainable on the basis of private property, imperialism, as the draft states quite correctly in its introduction, "aggravates to an extreme tension the contradiction between the growth of the productive forces of world economy and the national state barriers."

Without grasping the meaning of this proposition, which was vividly revealed to mankind for the first time during the last imperialist war, we cannot take a single step towards the solution of the major problems of world politics and revolutionary struggle.

We could only welcome the radical shift of the very axis of the program in the new draft were it not for the fact that the effort to reconcile this, the only correct position, with tendencies of a directly contrary character has resulted in turning the draft into an arena of the cruelest contradictions, which entirely nullify the principled significance of the new manner of approaching the question in its fundamental aspects.

2. THE UNITED STATES OF AMERICA AND EUROPE

To characterize the first, fortunately discarded draft, it suffices to say that, so far as we recall, the name of the United States of America was not even mentioned in it. The essential problems of the imperialist epoch—which, because of the very character of this epoch, must be examined not only in their abstract and theoretical but also in their concrete and historical cross section—were dissolved in the first draft into a lifeless schema of a capitalistic country "in general." However, the new draft—and this, of course, is a serious step forward—now speaks of *"the shift of the economic center of the world to the United States of America";* and of *"the transformation of the 'Dollar Republic' into a world exploiter";* and finally, that the rivalry (the draft loosely says "conflict") between North American and European capitalism, primarily British capitalism, *"is becoming the axis of the world conflicts."* It is already quite obvious today that a program which did not contain a clear and precise definition of these basic facts and factors of the world situation would have nothing in common with the program of the international revolutionary party.

Unfortunately, the essential facts and tendencies of world development in the modern epoch which we have just indicated are merely mentioned by name in the text of the draft, grafted on to it, as it were, by way of theoretical back-writing, without having any internal connection with its entire structure and without leading to any conclusions about perspective or strategy.

America's *new* role in Europe since the capitulation of the German Communist Party, and the defeat of the German proletariat in 1923, has been left absolutely unevaluated. No attempt at all has been made to explain that the period of the "stabilization," "normalization," and "pacification" of Europe as well as the "regeneration" of the social democracy, has proceeded in close material and ideological connection with the first steps of American intervention in European affairs.

Moreover, it has not been shown that the inevitable further development of American expansion, the contraction of the markets of European capital, including the European market itself, entail the greatest military, economic, and revolutionary convulsions, beside which all those of the past fade into the background.

Again, neither has it been made clear that the further inexorable pressure of the United States will reduce capitalist Europe to constantly more limited rations in world economy; and this, of course, implies not a mitigation, but on the contrary, a monstrous sharpening of interstate relations in Europe accompanied by furious paroxysms of military conflict, for states as well as classes fight even more fiercely for a meager and a diminishing ration than for a lavish and growing one.

The draft does not explain that the internal chaos of the state antagonisms in Europe renders hopeless any sort of serious and successful resistance to the constantly more centralized North American republic; and that the resolution of the European chaos through the Soviet United States of Europe is one of the first tasks of the proletarian revolution. The latter (precisely because of the existence of barriers) is immeasurably closer in Europe than in America[13] and will, therefore, most likely have to defend itself from the North American bourgeoisie.

On the other hand, no mention at all has been made of the fact (and this is just as important a phase of the same world problem) that it is precisely the international strength of the United States and her irresistible expansion arising from it, that compels her to include the powder magazines of the whole world into the foundations of her structure, i.e., all the antagonisms between the East and the West, the class struggle in

Old Europe, the uprisings of the colonial masses, and all wars and revolutions. On the one hand, this transforms North American capitalism into the basic counterrevolutionary force of the modern epoch, constantly more interested in the maintenance of "order" in every corner of the terrestrial globe; and on the other hand, this prepares the ground for a gigantic revolutionary explosion in this already dominant and still expanding world imperialist power. The logic of world relations indicates that the time of this explosion cannot lag very far behind that of the proletarian revolution in Europe.

Our elucidation of the dialectics of the interrelations between America and Europe have made us the target in recent years of the most diversified accusations, charging us with the pacifist denial of the existence of European contradictions, with the acceptance of Kautsky's theory of ultra-imperialism, and many other sins. There is no need to dwell here upon these "accusations," which are at best due to a complete ignorance of the real processes and of our attitude toward them. We cannot refrain from observing, however, that it would be hard to waste more effort in confusing and muddling up this most vital world problem than was wasted (incidentally, by the authors of the draft program) in their petty struggle against our formulation of the problem. Our formulation has, however, been entirely confirmed by the course of events.

Even recently, efforts have been made in leading communist organs to minimize—on paper—the significance of American hegemony by alluding to the impending commercial and industrial crisis in the United States. We cannot here enter into an examination of the special problem of the duration of the American crisis and its possible depth. This is a question of conjuncture and not of program. It goes without saying that in our opinion the inevitability of a crisis is entirely beyond doubt; nor, considering the present world scope of American capitalism, do we think it is out of the question that the very next crisis will attain extremely great depth and sharpness. But there is no justification whatsoever for the attempt to conclude from this that the hegemony of North America will be restricted or weakened. Such a conclusion can lead only to the grossest strategical errors.

Just the contrary is the case. *In the period of crisis the hegemony of the United States will operate more completely, more openly, and more ruthlessly than in the period of boom.* The United States will seek to overcome and extricate herself from her difficulties and maladies primarily at the expense of Europe, regardless of whether this occurs in Asia, Canada, South America, Australia, or Europe itself, or whether this takes place peacefully or through war.

We must clearly understand that if the first period of American intervention had the effect of stabilization and pacification on Europe, which to a considerable extent still remains in force today, and may even recur episodically and become stronger (particularly in the event of new defeats of the proletariat), the general line of American policy, particularly in time of its own economic difficulties and crisis, will engender the deepest convulsions in Europe as well as over the entire world.

From this we draw the not unimportant conclusion that there will be no more lack of revolutionary situations in the next decade than in the past decade. That is why it is of utmost importance to understand correctly the mainsprings of development so that we may not be caught unawares by their action. If in the past decade the main source of revolutionary situations lay in the direct consequences of the imperialist war, in the second postwar decade the most important source of revolutionary upheavals will be the interrelations of Europe and America. A major crisis in the United States will strike the tocsin for new wars and revolutions. We repeat: there will be no lack of revolutionary situations. The entire question hinges upon the international party of the proletariat, the maturity and fighting ability of the Comintern, and the correctness of its strategical position and tactical methods.

In the draft program of the Comintern absolutely no expression is to be found of this trend of thought. A fact of such great importance, it would seem, as "the shifting of the world economic center to the United States," is glossed over by a casual journalistic remark. It is, of course, utterly impossible to justify this on the ground of lack of space, for what should be allowed space in a program if not the fundamental questions? Besides, it should be added that too much space is devoted in the program to questions of secondary and tertiary importance, to say nothing of the general literary looseness and innumerable repetitions by elimination of which the program could be reduced at least one-third.

3. THE SLOGAN OF THE SOVIET UNITED STATES OF EUROPE

There is no justifying the omission of the slogan of the Soviet United States of Europe from the new draft program, a slogan which was accepted by the Comintern back in 1923, after a rather protracted internal struggle.[14] Or is it, perhaps, that the authors want to "return" to Lenin's position of 1915 precisely on this question? If that is the case, they must first understand it correctly.

Lenin, as is well known, was hesitant at the beginning of the war in regard to the slogan of the United States of Europe. The slogan was originally included in the theses of the *Sotsial-Demokrat* (the central organ of the party at the time) and then rejected by Lenin. This in itself indicates that the question involved here was not that of the general acceptability of the slogan on principle, but merely a tactical appraisal of it, a question of weighing its positive and negative aspects from the standpoint of the given situation. Needless to say, Lenin rejected the possibility that a *capitalist* United States of Europe could be realized. That was also my approach to the question when I advanced the slogan of the United States of Europe exclusively as a prospective state form of the proletarian dictatorship in Europe.

I wrote at that time: "A more or less complete economic unification of Europe *accomplished from above* through an agreement between capitalist governments is a utopia. Along this road matters cannot proceed beyond partial compromises and half measures. But this alone, an economic unification of Europe, such as would entail colossal advantages both to the producer and consumer and to the development of culture in general, is becoming a *revolutionary task of the European proletariat* in its struggle against imperialist protectionism and its instrument—militarism." (Trotsky, "The Peace Program," *Works,* vol. 3, part 1, p. 85, Russian ed.)

Further: "The United States of Europe represents first of all a form—the only conceivable form—of the dictatorship of the proletariat in Europe." (*Ibid.,* p. 92.)

But even in this formulation of the question Lenin saw *at that time* a certain danger. In the absence of any experience of a proletarian dictatorship in a single country and of theoretical clarity on this question even in the left wing of the social democracy of that period, the slogan of the United States of Europe *might* have given rise to the idea that the proletarian revolution must begin simultaneously, at least on the whole European continent. It was against this very danger that Lenin issued a warning, but on this point there was not a shade of difference between Lenin and myself. I wrote at the time: "Not a single country must 'wait' for the other countries in its struggle. It will be useful and necessary to repeat this elementary idea so that temporizing international inaction may not be substituted for parallel international action. Without waiting for the others, we must begin and continue the struggle on national grounds with the full conviction that our initiative will provide an impulse to the struggle in other countries." (*Ibid.,* pp. 89-90.)

Then follow those words of mine which Stalin presented at the Seventh Plenum of the ECCI as the most vicious expression of "Trotskyism," i.e., as "lack of faith" in the inner forces of the revolution and the hope for aid from without. "And if this [the development of the revolution in other countries—L.T.] were not to occur, it would be hopeless to think (this is borne out both by historical experience and by theoretical considerations) that a revolutionary Russia, for instance, could hold out in face of conservative Europe, or that a socialist Germany could remain isolated in a capitalist world." (*Ibid.*, p. 90.)

On the basis of this and two or three similar quotations is founded the condemnation pronounced against "Trotskyism" by the Seventh Plenum as having allegedly held on this "fundamental question" a position "which has nothing in common with Leninism." Let us, therefore, pause for a moment and listen to Lenin himself.

On March 7, 1918, he said apropos of the Brest-Litovsk peace: "This is a lesson to us because the absolute truth is that without a revolution in Germany, we shall perish." (Lenin, *Works,* vol. 15, p. 132, Russian ed.)*

A week later he said: "World imperialism cannot live side by side with a victorious advancing social revolution." (*Ibid.,* p. 175.)

A few weeks later, on April 23, Lenin said: "Our *backwardness* has thrust us forward and *we will perish* if we are unable to hold out until we meet with the mighty support of the *insurrectionary* workers of other countries." (*Ibid.,* p. 187. Our emphasis.)†

But perhaps this was all said under the special influence of the Brest-Litovsk crisis? No! In March 1919, Lenin again repeated: "We do not live merely in a state but in a system of states and the existence of the Soviet republic side by side with imperialist states for *any length of time is inconceivable.* In the end one or the other must triumph." (*Works,* vol. 16, p. 102.)‡

A year later, on April 7, 1920, Lenin reiterates: "Capital-

---

* "Seventh Congress of the RCP(B): Political Report of the Central Committee," in Lenin, *Collected Works* (hereafter *LCW*), vol. 27, p. 98.

† "Speech in the Moscow Soviet of Workers, Peasants, and Red Army Deputies," in *LCW,* vol. 27, p. 232.

‡ "Eighth Congress of the RCP(B): Report of the Central Committee," in *LCW,* vol. 28, p. 153.

ism, if taken on an international scale, is even now, not only in a military but also in an economic sense, stronger than the Soviet power. We must proceed from this fundamental consideration and never forget it." (*Works,* vol. 17, p. 102.)*

On November 27, 1920, Lenin, in dealing with the question of concessions, said: "We have now passed from the arena of war to the arena of peace and we have not forgotten that war will come again. As long as capitalism and socialism remain side by side we cannot live peacefully—the one or the other will be the victor in the end. An obituary will be sung either over the death of world capitalism or the death of the Soviet republic. At present we have only a respite in the war." (*Ibid.,* p. 398.)†

But perhaps the continued existence of the Soviet republic impelled Lenin to "recognize his mistake" and renounce his "lack of faith in the inner force" of the October Revolution?

At the Third Congress of the Comintern in July 1921, Lenin declared in the theses on the tactics of the Communist Party of Russia: "An equilibrium has been created, which though extremely precarious and unstable, nevertheless enables the socialist republic to maintain its existence within capitalist surroundings, although of course not for any great length of time."‡

Again, on July 5, 1921, Lenin stated point-blank at one of the sessions of the congress: "It was clear to us that without aid from the international world revolution, a victory of the proletarian revolution is impossible. Even prior to the revolution, as well as after it, we thought that the revolution would also occur either immediately or at least *very soon* in other backward countries and in the more highly developed capi-

---

* "Speech Delivered at the Third All-Russia Trade Union Congress," in *LCW,* vol. 30, p. 505.
† Cited in in *LCW,* vol. 31, p. 457.
‡ "Third Congress of the Communist International: Theses for a Report on the Tactics of the RCP," in *LCW,* vol. 32, p. 454.

talist countries, *otherwise we would perish*. Notwithstanding this conviction, we did our utmost to preserve the Soviet system under any circumstances and at all costs, because we know that we are working not only for ourselves but also for the international revolution." (*Works,* vol. 18, part 1, p. 321.)*

How infinitely removed are these words, so superb in their simplicity and permeated with the spirit of internationalism, from the present smug fabrications of the epigones!

In any case, we have the right to ask: wherein do all these statements of Lenin differ from my conviction *in the year 1915* that the coming revolution in Russia or the coming socialist Germany could not hold out alone if "isolated in a capitalist world"? The time factor proved to be different from that posited not only by myself but also in Lenin's forecasts; but the underlying idea retains its full force even today—at the given moment perhaps more so than ever before. Instead of condemning this idea, as the Seventh Plenum of the ECCI has done on the basis of an incompetent and unscrupulous speech, it should be included in the program of the Communist International.

Defending the slogan of the Soviet United States of Europe, we pointed out in 1915, that the law of uneven development is in itself no argument against this slogan, because the *unevenness* of historical development of different countries and continents *is in itself uneven*. European countries develop unevenly in relation to one another. Nevertheless it can be maintained with absolute historical certainty that not a single one of these countries is fated, at least in the historical epoch under review, to run so far ahead in relation to other countries as America has run ahead of Europe. For America there is *one* scale of unevenness, for Europe there is *another*. Geographically and historically, conditions have predetermined such a close organic bond between the countries of Europe that there is no way for them to tear themselves out of

---

* "Third Congress of the Communist International: Report on the Tactics of the RCP," in *LCW*, vol. 32, p. 480.

it. The modern bourgeois governments of Europe are like murderers chained to a single cart. The revolution in Europe, as has already been said, *will in the final analysis* be of decisive importance for America as well. But *directly,* in the immediate course of history, a revolution in Germany will have an immeasurably greater significance for France than for the United States of America. It is precisely from this historically developed relationship that there flows the political vitality of the slogan of the European Soviet federation. We speak of its *relative* vitality because it stands to reason that this federation will extend, across the great bridge of the Soviet Union, to Asia, and will then effect a union of the world socialist republics. But this will constitute a second epoch or a subsequent great chapter of the imperialist epoch, and when we approach it more closely, we will also find the corresponding formulas for it.

It can be proven without any difficulty by further quotations that our difference with Lenin in 1915 over the question of the United States of Europe was of a restricted, tactical, and, by its very essence, temporary character; but it is best proven by the subsequent course of events. In 1923 the Communist International adopted the controversial slogan. Were it true that the slogan of the United States of Europe was inacceptable in 1915 on grounds of principle, as the authors of the draft program now seek to maintain, then the Communist International could not possibly have adopted it. The law of uneven development, one would think, had not lost its effectiveness during these years.

The entire formulation of the questions as outlined above flows from the dynamics of the revolutionary process taken as a whole. The international revolution is regarded as an interconnected process which cannot be predicted in all its concreteness, and, so to speak, its order of occurrence, but which is absolutely clear-cut in its general historical outline. Unless the latter is understood, a correct political orientation is entirely out of the question.

However, matters appear quite differently if we proceed

from the idea of a socialist development which is occurring and is even being completed in one country. We have today a "theory" which teaches that it is possible to build socialism completely in one country and that the correlations of that country with the capitalist world can be established on the basis of "neutralizing" the world bourgeoisie (Stalin). The necessity for the slogan of a United States of Europe falls away, or is at least diminished, if this essentially national-reformist and not revolutionary-internationalist point of view is adopted. But this slogan is, from our viewpoint, important and vitally necessary because there is lodged in it the condemnation of the idea of an isolated socialist development. For the proletariat of every European country, even to a larger measure than for the USSR—the difference, however, is one of degree only—it will be most vitally necessary to spread the revolution to the neighboring countries and to support insurrections there with arms in hand, not out of any abstract considerations of international solidarity, which in themselves cannot set the classes in motion, but because of those vital considerations which Lenin formulated hundreds of times—namely, that without *timely* aid from the international revolution, we will be unable to hold out. The slogan of the Soviet United States corresponds to the dynamics of the proletarian revolution, which does not break out simultaneously in all countries, but which passes from country to country and requires the closest bond between them, especially on the European arena, both with a view to defense against the most powerful external enemies, and with a view to economic construction.

One may, to be sure, try to raise an objection by asserting that following the period of the Ruhr crisis, which provided the latest impulse for the adoption of that slogan, the latter has not played a major role in the agitation for the communist parties of Europe and has, so to speak, not taken root. But this is equally true of such slogans as the workers state, soviets, and so forth, i.e., all the *slogans of the directly prerevo-*

lutionary period. The explanation for this lies in the fact that since the end of 1923, notwithstanding the erroneous political appraisals of the Fifth Congress, the revolutionary movement on the European continent has been on the decline. But that is just why it is fatal to base a program, in whole or in part, upon impressions received only during that period. It was no mere accident that, despite all prejudices, the slogan of a Soviet United States of Europe was adopted precisely in 1923, at a time when a revolutionary explosion was expected in Germany, and when the question of the state interrelationships in Europe assumed an extremely burning character. Every new aggravation of the European and indeed of the world crisis is sufficiently sharp to bring to the fore the main political problems and to invest the slogan of the United States of Europe with attractive power. It is therefore fundamentally wrong to pass over this slogan in silence in the program without rejecting it, that is, to keep it somewhere in reserve, for use "in case of emergency." When questions of principle are involved, the policy of making reservations is futile.

4. THE CRITERION OF INTERNATIONALISM

The draft, as we already know, seeks to proceed in its construction from the standpoint of world economy and its internal tendencies—an attempt which merits recognition. *Pravda* is absolutely correct in saying that herein lies the basic difference in principle between us and the national-patriotic social democracy. A program of the international party of the proletariat can be built only if world economy, which dominates its separate parts, is taken as the point of departure. But precisely in analyzing the main tendencies of world development, the draft not only reveals inadequacies which depreciate its value, as has already been pointed out above, but it also is grossly one-sided, which leads it to commit grave blunders.

The draft refers time and again, and not always in the proper place, to the law of uneven development of capitalism as the main and almost all-determining law of that development. A number of mistakes in the draft, including one fundamental error, are theoretically based on the one-sided and false non-Marxian and non-Leninist interpretation of the law of uneven development.

In its first chapter the draft states that "the unevenness of economic and political development is an unconditional law of capitalism. This unevenness becomes still more accentuated and aggravated in the epoch of imperialism."

This is correct. This formulation in part condemns Stalin's recent formulation of the question, according to which both Marx and Engels were ignorant of the law of uneven development, which was allegedly first discovered by Lenin. On September 15, 1925, Stalin wrote that Trotsky has no reason whatever to refer to Engels because the latter wrote at a time "when there could be no *talk* [!!] about the knowledge of the law of uneven development of capitalist countries." Unbelievable as these words may be, Stalin, one of the authors of the draft, has nevertheless repeated them more than once. The text of the draft, as we have seen, has taken a step forward in this respect. However, if we leave aside the correction of this elementary mistake, what the draft says about the law of uneven development remains in essence one-sided and inadequate.

In the first place, it would have been more correct to say that the entire history of mankind is governed by the law of uneven development. Capitalism finds various sections of mankind at different stages of development, each with its profound internal contradictions. The extreme diversity in the levels attained, and the extraordinary unevenness in the rate of development of the different sections of mankind during the various epochs, serve as the *starting point* of capitalism. Capitalism gains mastery only gradually over the inherited unevenness, breaking and altering it, employing therein its own means and methods. In contrast to the economic systems which preceded it, capitalism inherently and constantly aims at economic expansion, at the penetration of new territories, the surmounting of economic differences, the conversion of self-sufficient provincial and national economies into a system of financial interrelationships. Thereby it brings about their *rapprochement* and equalizes the economic and cultural levels of the most progressive and the most backward countries. Without this main process, it would be impossible to conceive of the relative leveling out, first, of Europe with Great Britain, and then, of America with Europe; the industrialization of the colonies, the diminishing gap between India and Great Britain, and all the consequences arising from the enumerated processes upon which is based not only the program of the Communist International but also its very existence.

By drawing the countries economically closer to one another and leveling out their stages of development, capitalism, however, operates by methods of *its own,* that is to say, by anarchistic methods which constantly undermine its own work, set one country against another, and one branch of industry against another, developing some parts of world economy while hampering and throwing back the development of others. Only the correlation of these two fundamental tendencies—both of which arise from the nature of capitalism—explains to us the living texture of the historical process.

Imperialism, thanks to the universality, penetrability, and mobility and the breakneck speed of the formation of finance capital as the driving force of imperialism, lends vigor to *both these tendencies.* Imperialism links up incomparably more rapidly and more deeply the individual nations and continental units into a single entity, bringing them into the closest and most vital dependence upon each other and rendering their economic methods, social forms, and levels of development more identical. At the same time, it attains this "goal" by such antagonistic methods, such tiger leaps, and such raids upon backward countries and areas that the unification and leveling of world economy which it has effected, is upset by it even more violently and convulsively than in the preceding epochs. Only such a dialectical and not purely mechanical understanding of the law of uneven development can make possible the avoidance of the fundamental error which the draft program, submitted to the Sixth Congress, has failed to avoid.

Immediately after its one-sided characterization of the law of uneven development pointed out by us, the draft program says:

"Hence it follows that the international proletarian revolution must not be regarded as a single, simultaneous, and universal act. Hence it follows that the victory of socialism is at first possible in a few, or even in one isolated capitalist country."

That the international revolution of the proletariat cannot be a simultaneous act, of this there can of course be no dispute at all among grown-up people after the experience of the October Revolution, achieved by the proletariat of a backward country under pressure of historical necessity, without waiting in the least for the proletariat of the advanced countries "to even out the front." Within these limits, the reference to the law of uneven development is absolutely correct and quite in place. But it is entirely otherwise with the second half of the conclusion—namely, the hollow assertion that the victory of socialism is possible "in one isolated capitalist country." To prove its point the draft program simply says: "Hence it follows...." One gets the impression that this follows from the law of uneven development. But this does not follow at all. "Hence follows" something quite the contrary. If the historical process were such that some countries developed not only unevenly but even *independently of each other,* isolated from each other, then from the law of uneven development would indubitably follow the possibility of building socialism in one capitalist country—at first in the most advanced country and then, as they mature, in the more backward ones. Such was the customary and, so to speak, average idea of the transition to socialism within the ranks of the prewar social democracy. This is precisely the idea that formed the theoretical basis of social patriotism. Of course, the draft program does not hold this view. But it inclines towards it.

The theoretical error of the draft lies in the fact that it seeks to deduce from the law of uneven development something which the law does not and cannot imply. Uneven or sporadic development of various countries acts constantly to *upset* but in no case to *eliminate* the growing economic bonds and interdependence between those countries which the very next day, after four years of hellish slaughter, were compelled to exchange coal, bread, oil, powder, and suspenders with each other. On this point, the draft posits the question as if historical development proceeds only on the basis of sporadic leaps, while the economic basis which gives rise to these leaps, and upon which they occur, is either left entirely out of sight by the authors of the draft, or is forcibly eliminated by them. This they do with the sole object of defending the indefensible theory of socialism in one country.

After what has been said, it is not difficult to understand that the only correct formulation of the question should read that Marx and Engels, even prior to the imperialist epoch, had arrived at the conclusion that on the one hand, unevenness, i.e., sporadic historical development, stretches the proletarian revolution through an entire epoch in the course of which nations will enter the revolutionary flood one after another; while, on the other hand, the organic interdependence of the several countries, developing toward an international division of labor, excludes the possibility of building socialism in one country. This means that the Marxian doctrine, which posits that the socialist revolution can begin only on a national basis, while the building of socialism in one country is impossible, has been rendered *doubly and trebly true,* all the more so now, in the modern epoch when imperialism has developed, deepened, and sharpened *both* of these antagonistic tendencies. On this point, Lenin merely developed and concretized Marx's own formulation and Marx's own answer to this question.

Our party program is based entirely upon the international

conditions underlying the October Revolution and the socialist construction. To prove this, one need only transcribe the entire theoretical part of our program. Here we will confine ourselves merely to pointing out that when, during the Eighth Congress of our party, the late Podbelsky inferred that some formulations of the program had reference only to the revolution in Russia, Lenin replied as follows in his concluding speech on the question of the party program (March 19, 1919):

"Podbelsky has raised objections to a paragraph which speaks of the *pending* social revolution.... His argument is obviously unfounded because our *program deals with the social revolution on a world scale.*" (*Works,* vol. 16, p. 131.)*

It will not be out of place here to point out that at about the same time Lenin suggested that our party should change its name from the Communist Party of Russia to the Communist Party, so as to emphasize still further that it is a party of *international* revolution. I was the only one voting for Lenin's motion in the Central Committee. However, he did not bring the matter before the congress in view of the foundation of the Third International. This position is proof of the fact that there was not even an inkling of socialism in one country at that time. That alone is the reason why the party program does *not condemn* this "theory" but merely *excludes it.*

But the program of the Young Communist League, adopted two years later, had to issue a direct warning against home-bred illusions and national narrow-mindedness on the question of the proletarian revolution, in order to train the youth in the spirit of internationalism. We will have more to say on this point later.

The new draft program of the Comintern puts the matter quite differently. In harmony with the revisionist[15] evolution of its authors since 1924, the draft, as we have seen, chooses the directly opposite path. But the manner in which the question of socialism in one country is solved determines the nature of the

---

* "Eighth Congress of the RCP(B): Speech Closing the Debate on the Party Program," in *LCW,* vol. 29, p. 187.

entire draft as a Marxian or a revisionist document.

Of course, the draft program carefully, persistently, and severally presents, emphasizes, and explains the difference between the communist and reformist formulation of questions. But these assurances do not solve the problem. We have here a situation similar to that on board a ship which is equipped and even overloaded with numerous Marxian mechanisms and appliances, while its mainsail is so raised as to be purposely swelled by every revisionist and reformist wind.

Whoever has learned from the experiences of the last three decades and particularly from the extraordinary experience in China during the recent years, understands the powerful dialectical interdependence between the class struggle and the programmatic party documents and will understand our statement that the new revisionist sail can nullify all the safety appliances of Marxism and Leninism. That is why we are compelled to dwell in greater detail upon this cardinal question, which will for a long time determine the development and destiny of the Communist International.

5. THE THEORETICAL TRADITION OF THE PARTY

The draft program, in the foregoing quotation, deliberately uses the expression "victory of socialism in one country" so as to secure an external and purely verbal similarity between its text and Lenin's article of 1915, which has been misused so ruthlessly, not to say criminally, during the discussion on the question of building a socialist society in one country. The draft resorts to the same method elsewhere by "referring" to Lenin's words as a confirmation. Such is the scientific "methodology of the draft."

Of the great wealth of Marxian literature and the treasure of Lenin's works—directly ignoring everything Lenin said and wrote and everything he did, ignoring the party program and the program of the Young Communist League, ignoring the opinions expressed by all party leaders, without exception, during the epoch of the October Revolution, when the question was posed categorically (and how categorically!) ignoring what the authors of the program themselves, Stalin and Bukharin, said up to and including 1924—two quotations all told from Lenin, one from his article on the United States of Europe, written in 1915, and another from his unfinished posthumous work on cooperation, written in 1923, have been used in defense of the theory of national socialism, which was created to meet the exigencies of the struggle against so-called Trotskyism at the end of 1924 or the beginning of 1925. Everything that contradicts these two quotations of a couple of lines each—the whole of Marxism and Leninism—has simply been set aside. These two artificially extracted, and grossly and epigonically misinterpreted quotations are taken as the basis of the new and purely revisionist theory which is unbounded from the viewpoint of its political consequences. We are witnessing the efforts to graft, by methods of scholasticism and sophistry, to the Marxian trunk an absolutely alien branch, which, if grafted, will inexorably poison and kill the whole tree.

At the Seventh Plenum of the ECCI, Stalin declared (not for the first time): "The question of the construction of a socialist economy in one country was for *the first time* advanced in the party by Lenin back in 1915." (*Minutes,* Seventh Plenum of the ECCI, p. 14. Our emphasis.)

Thus an admission is here made that *prior to* 1915 no mention was ever made of the question of socialism in one country. Ergo, Stalin and Bukharin do not venture to encroach upon the entire tradition of Marxism and of the party on the question of the international character of the proletarian revolution. Let us bear this in mind.

However, let us see what Lenin did say "for the first time" in 1915 in contradistinction to what Marx, Engels, and Lenin himself had said previously.

In 1915 Lenin said: "Uneven economic and political development is an unconditional law of capitalism. Hence it follows that the triumph of socialism is, to begin with, possible in a few, or even in a single capitalist country. The victorious proletariat of that country, having expropriated the capitalists and *having organized socialist production* at home, would be up in arms against the rest of the capitalist world, attracting oppressed classes of other countries to its side, causing insurrections in those countries against the capitalists, and acting, in case of need, even with military power against the exploiting classes and their governments." (*Works,* vol. 13, p. 133. August 23, 1915. Our emphasis.)*

What did Lenin have in mind? Only that the victory of socialism in the sense of the establishment of a dictatorship of the proletariat is possible at first in one country, which because of this very fact, will be counterposed to the capitalist world. The proletarian state, in order to be able to resist an attack and to assume a revolutionary offensive of its own, will first have to "organize socialist production at home," i.e., it will have to organize the operation of the factories taken from the capitalists. That is all. Such a "victory of socialism" was, as is shown, first achieved in Russia, and the first workers state, in order to defend itself against world intervention, had first of all to "organize socialist production at home," or to create trusts of "a consistently socialist type." By the victory of socialism in one country, Lenin consequently did not cherish the fantasy of a self-sufficient socialist society, and in a backward country at that, but something much more realistic, namely, what the October Revolution had achieved in our country during the first period of its existence.

Does this, perhaps, require proof? So many proofs can be adduced that the only difficulty lies in making the best choice.

In his theses on war and peace (January 7, 1918) Lenin spoke of the "necessity of a certain period of time, *at least sev-*

---

* "On the Slogan for a United States of Europe," in *LCW,* vol. 21, p. 342.

eral months, for the victory of socialism in Russia. . . . " (*Works,* vol. 15, p. 64.)*

At the beginning of the same year, i.e., 1918, Lenin, in his article entitled "On Left Wing Childishness and Petty-Bourgeois Tendencies," directed against Bukharin, wrote the following: "If, let us say, state capitalism could be established in our country within six months, that would be a tremendous achievement and the surest guarantee that within a year *socialism* will be definitely established and will have become invincible." (*Works,* vol. 15, part 2, p. 263. Our emphasis.)†

How could Lenin have set so short a period for the "definite establishment of socialism"? What material-productive and social content did he put into these words?

This question will at once appear in a different light if we recall that on April 29, 1918, Lenin said in his report to the All-Russia Central Executive Committee of the Soviet government: "It is hardly to be expected that our next generation, which will be more highly developed, will effect a complete transition to socialism." (*Ibid.,* p. 240.)‡

On December 3, 1919, at the Congress of Communes and Artels, Lenin spoke even more bluntly, saying: "We know that we cannot establish a socialist order at the present time. It will be well if our children and perhaps our grandchildren will be able to establish it." (*Works,* vol. 16, p. 398.)§

In which of these two cases was Lenin right? Was it when he spoke of the "definite establishment of socialism" within twelve months, or when he left it not for our children but our grandchildren to "establish the socialist order"?

Lenin was right in both cases, for he had in mind two en-

---

* "Theses on the Question of the Immediate Conclusion of a Separate and Annexationist Peace," in *LCW,* vol. 26, p. 443.

† "'Left-Wing' Childishness and the Petty-Bourgeois Mentality," in *LCW,* vol. 27, pp. 334–35.

‡ "Session of the All-Russia CEC: Report on the Immediate Tasks of the Soviet Government," in *LCW,* vol. 27, p. 301.

§ "Speech Delivered at the First Congress of Agricultural Communes and Agricultural Artels," in *LCW,* vol. 30, p. 202.

tirely different and incommensurable stages of socialist construction.

By the "definite establishment of socialism" in the first case, Lenin meant not the building of a socialist society within a year's time or even "several months," that is, he did not mean that the classes will be done away with, that the contradictions between city and country will be eliminated; he meant the *restoration of production in mills and factories in the hands of the proletarian state,* and thus the assuring of the possibility to exchange products between city and country. The very shortness of the term is in itself a sure key to an understanding of the whole perspective.

Of course, even for this elementary task, too short a term was set at the beginning of 1918. It was this purely practical "miscalculation" that Lenin derided at the Fourth Congress of the Comintern when he said "we were more foolish then than we are now."* But "we" had a correct view of the general perspectives and did not for a moment believe that it is possible to set up a complete "socialist order" in the course of twelve months and in a backward country at that. The attainment of this main and final goal—the construction of a socialist society—was left by Lenin to three whole generations—ourselves, our children, and our grandchildren.

Is it not clear that in his article of 1915, Lenin meant by the organization of "socialist production," not the creation of a socialist society but an immeasurably more elementary task which has already been realized by us in the USSR? Otherwise, one would have to arrive at the absurd conclusion that, according to Lenin, the proletarian party, having captured power, "postpones" the revolutionary war until the third generation.

Such is the sorry position of the main stronghold of the

---

* "Fourth Congress of the Communist International: Five Years of the Russian Revolution and the Prospects of the World Revolution" (November 13, 1922) in *LCW*, vol. 33, p. 419. Also in *Lenin's Final Fight: Speeches and Writings 1922–23* (New York: Pathfinder, 1995).

new theory insofar as the 1915 quotation is concerned. However, what is sadder still is the fact that Lenin wrote this passage not in application to Russia. He was speaking of Europe in contrast to Russia. This follows not only from the content of the quoted article devoted to the question of the United States of Europe, but also from Lenin's entire position at the time. A few months later, November 20, 1915, Lenin wrote specially on Russia, saying:

"The task of the proletariat follows obviously from this actual state of affairs. This task is a bold, heroic, revolutionary struggle against the monarchy (the slogans of the January conference of 1912—the 'Three Whales'[16]), a struggle which would attract all democratic masses, that is, first and foremost the peasantry. At the same time, a relentless struggle must be waged against chauvinism, a struggle *for the socialist revolution* in Europe in alliance with its proletariat. . . . The war crisis has *strengthened* the economic and political factors impelling the petty bourgeoisie, including the peasantry, towards the left. Therein lies the objective basis of the absolute possibility of the victory of the *democratic revolution* in Russia. That the *objective conditions for a socialist revolution have fully matured in Western Europe,* was recognized before the war by all influential socialists of all advanced countries." (*Works,* vol. 13, pp. 212f. Our emphasis.)*

Thus, in 1915, Lenin clearly spoke of a democratic revolution in Russia and of a socialist revolution in Western Europe. In passing, as if speaking of something which is self-evident, he mentions that in Western Europe, distinct from Russia, in contrast to Russia, the conditions for a socialist revolution have "fully matured." But the authors of the new theory, the authors of the draft program, simply ignore this quotation— one of many—which squarely and directly refers to Russia, just as they ignore hundreds of other passages, as they ignore all of Lenin's works. Instead of taking notice of this, they

---

* "On the Two Lines in the Revolution," in *LCW,* vol. 21, pp. 418–19.

snatch, as we have seen, at another passage that refers to Western Europe, ascribe to it a meaning which it cannot and does not contain, attach this ascribed meaning to Russia, a country to which the passage has no reference, and on this "foundation" erect their new theory.

What was Lenin's position on this question immediately before the October period? On leaving Switzerland after the February 1917 revolution, Lenin addressed a letter to the Swiss workers in which he declared:

"Russia is a peasant country, one of the most backward countries of Europe. Socialism cannot be *immediately* triumphant there but the peasant character of the country with the huge tracts of land in the hands of the feudal aristocracy and landowners, can, on the basis of the experience of 1905, give a tremendous sweep to the bourgeois democratic revolution in Russia and make our revolution a *prelude* to the world socialist revolution, a *step* towards it. . . . The Russian proletariat cannot by its own forces *victoriously complete* the socialist revolution. But it can give the Russian revolution dimensions such as will create the most favorable conditions for it, such as will in a certain sense *begin* it. It can facilitate matters for the entrance into a decisive battle on the part of its *main* and most reliable ally, the *European* and American socialist proletariat." (*Works*, vol. 14, part 2, pp. 407f.)*

All the elements of the question are contained in these few lines. If Lenin believed in 1915, in time of war and reaction, as they try to convince us now, that the proletariat of Russia can build socialism by itself so as to be able to declare war on the bourgeois states, after it will have accomplished this work, how could Lenin, at the beginning of 1917, after the February revolution, speak so categorically about the impossibility for backward peasant Russia to build socialism with its own forces? One must at least be somewhat logical and, to put it baldly, have some respect for Lenin.

---

* "Farewell Letter to the Swiss Workers," in *LCW*, vol. 23, p. 371.

It would be superfluous to add more quotations. To give an integral outline of Lenin's economic and political views conditioned by the international character of the socialist revolution would require a separate work that would cover many subjects, but not the subject of building a self-sufficient socialist society in one country, because Lenin did not know this subject.

However, we feel obliged to dwell here on another article by Lenin—"On Cooperation"—since the draft program appears to quote this posthumous article extensively, i.e., utilizes some of its expressions for a purpose which is entirely alien to the article.* We have in mind the fifth chapter of the draft program which states that the workers of the Soviet Republics "possess all the necessary and sufficient *material* prerequisites in the country . . . for the complete construction of socialism" (our emphasis).

If the article dictated by Lenin during his illness and published after his death really did say that the Soviet state possesses all the necessary and *material,* that is, first of all, *productive* prerequisites for an independent construction of complete socialism, one would only have to surmise that either Lenin slipped in his dictation or that the stenographer made a mistake in transcribing her notes. Either conjecture is at any rate more probable than that Lenin abandoned Marxism and his own lifelong teaching in two hasty strokes. Fortunately, however, there is not the slightest need for such an explanation. The remarkable, though unfinished article "On Cooperation," which is bound up by unity of thought with other, no less remarkable articles of his last period, constituting, as it were, a chapter of an unfinished book dealing with *the place occupied by the October Revolution in the chain of revolutions in the West and East*—this article "On Cooperation" does not at all speak of those things which the revisionists of Leninism so lightmindedly ascribe to it.

---

* "On Cooperation" (January 4–6, 1923) in *LCW,* vol. 33, pp. 467–75. Also in *Lenin's Final Fight,* pp. 209–16.

In this article Lenin explains that the "trading" cooperatives can and must entirely change their social role in the workers state and that by a correct policy they may direct the merger of private peasant interests with the general state interests along socialist channels. Lenin substantiates this irrefutable idea as follows:

"As a matter of fact, the state power over all large-scale means of production, state power in the hands of the proletariat, an alliance of that proletariat with the many millions of peasants with small and petty holdings, security of proletarian leadership in relationship to the peasant—is this not all that is necessary for the cooperatives, the cooperatives alone, which we have formerly treated as mere traders, and which, from a certain viewpoint, we still have the right to treat as such even now under the NEP, is this not all that is necessary for the construction of a complete socialist society? It is not yet the construction of a socialist society but it is all that is necessary and sufficient for this construction." (*Works*, vol. 18, part 2, p. 140.)

The text of the passage which includes an unfinished phrase ["the cooperatives alone"] irrefutably proves that we have before us an uncorrected draft which was dictated and not written. It is all the more inadmissible to cling to a few isolated words of the text rather than to try to get a general idea of the article. Fortunately, however, even the *letter* of the cited passage and not only its *spirit* grants no one the right to misuse it as it is being misused by the authors of the draft program. Speaking of the "necessary and sufficient" prerequisites, Lenin strictly limits his subject in this article. In it he deals only with the question as to the ways and means by which we will reach socialism through the atomized and diffused peasant enterprises without new class upheavals, having the prerequisites of the Soviet regime as our basis. The article is entirely devoted to the *socio-organizational forms* of the transition from small private commodity economy to collective economy but not to the *material-productive* conditions of that transition. Were the European proletariat to prove victorious today and come to our assistance with its technology, the question of cooperation raised by Lenin as a socio-organizational method of coordinating private and social interests would still fully retain its significance. Cooperation points the way through which advanced technology, including electricity, can reorganize and unite the millions of peasant enterprises, once a Soviet regime exists. But cooperation cannot be substituted for technology and does not create that technology. Lenin does not merely speak of the necessary and sufficient prerequisites in general, but as we have seen, he definitely enumerates them. They are: (1) "Power of the state over all large-scale means of production" (an uncorrected phrase); (2) "State power in the hands of the proletariat"; (3) "An alliance of that proletariat with millions of . . . peasants"; (4) "Security of proletarian leadership in relation to the peasants." It is only after enumerating these purely political conditions—nothing is said here about material conditions—that Lenin arrives at his conclusion, namely, that "this" (i.e., all the foregoing) "is all that is necessary and sufficient" for the building of a socialist society. "All that is necessary and sufficient" on the *political plane,* but no more. But, adds Lenin right there and then, "it is not yet the construction of a socialist society." Why not? Because political conditions alone, although they be sufficient, do not solve the problem. The cultural question still remains. *"Only"* this, says Lenin, emphasizing the word "only" in order to show the tremendous importance of the prerequisites we lack. Lenin knew as well as we that culture is bound up with technology. "To be cultural"—he brings the revisionists back to earth—"a certain *material* basis is necessary." (*Ibid.,* p. 145.) Suffice to mention the problem of electrification which Lenin, incidentally, purposely linked up with the question of the international socialist revolution. The struggle for culture, given the "necessary and sufficient" political (*but not material*) prerequisites, would absorb all our efforts, were it not for the question of the uninterrupted and irreconcilable economic, political, military, and cultural struggle of the country engaged in the building of a socialist society on a backward basis against world capitalism which is in its decline but is technically powerful.

"I am ready to state," Lenin underscores with particular

emphasis towards the end of this article, "that the center of gravity for us would be transferred to cultural work were it not for our duty to fight for our position on an international scale." (*Ibid.*, p. 144.)

Such is Lenin's real idea if we analyze the article on cooperation, even apart from all his other works. How else, if not as a falsification, can we style the formula of the authors of the draft program who deliberately take Lenin's words about our possession of the "necessary and sufficient" prerequisites and add to them the basic material prerequisites, although Lenin definitely speaks of the material prerequisites in parentheses, saying that it is just what we do not have and what we must still gain in our struggle "for our position on an international scale," that is, in connection with the international proletarian revolution? That is how matters stand with the second and last stronghold of the theory.

We purposely did not deal here with innumerable articles and speeches from 1905 to 1923 in which Lenin asserts and repeats most categorically that without a victorious world revolution we are doomed to failure, that it is impossible to defeat the bourgeoisie economically in one country, particularly a backward country, that the task of building a socialist society is in its very essence an international task —from which Lenin drew conclusions which may be "pessimistic" to the promulgators of the new national reactionary utopia but which are sufficiently optimistic from the viewpoint of revolutionary internationalism. We concentrate our argument here only on the passages which the authors of the draft have themselves chosen in order to create the "necessary and sufficient" prerequisites for their utopia. And we see that their whole structure crumbles the moment it is touched.

However, we consider it in place to present at least one of Lenin's direct statements on the controversial question which does not need any comment and will not permit any false interpretation.

"We have emphasized *in many of our works, in all our*

speeches, and in our entire press that the situation in Russia is not the same as in the advanced capitalist countries, that we have in Russia a minority of industrial workers and an overwhelming majority of small agrarians. The social revolution in such a country can be finally successful only on two conditions: first, on the condition that it is given *timely* support by the social revolution in one or more advanced countries . . . second, that there be an agreement between the proletariat which establishes the dictatorship or holds state power in its hands and the majority of the peasant population. . . .

"We know that *only an agreement with the peasantry can save the socialist revolution in Russia so long as the revolution in other countries has not arrived.*" (*Works,* vol. 18, part 1, pp. 137f. Our emphasis.)*

We hope that this passage is sufficiently instructive. First, Lenin himself emphasizes in it that the ideas advanced by him have been developed "in many of our works, in all our speeches, and in our entire press"; secondly, this perspective was envisaged by Lenin not in 1915, two years prior to the October Revolution, but in 1921, the fourth year after the October Revolution.

So far as Lenin is concerned, we venture to think that the question is clear enough. There remains to inquire: what was formerly the opinion of the authors of the draft program on the basic question now before us?

On this point, Stalin said in November 1926: "The party always took as its starting point the idea that the victory of socialism in one country means the possibility to build socialism in that country, and that this task can be accomplished with the forces of a single country." (*Pravda,* November 12, 1926.)

We already know that the party *never took this as its starting point*. On the contrary, "in many of our works, in all our speeches, and in our entire press," as Lenin said, the party

---

* "Tenth Congress of the RCP(B): Report on the Substitution of a Tax in Kind for the Surplus-Grain Appropriation System" (March 15, 1921) in *LCW,* vol. 32, p. 215.

proceeded from the opposite position, which found its highest expression in the program of the CPSU. But one would imagine that at least Stalin himself "always" proceeded from this false view that "socialism can be built with the forces of one country." Let us check up.

What Stalin's views on this question were in 1905 or 1915 we have absolutely no means of knowing as there are no documents whatever on the subject. But in 1924, Stalin outlined Lenin's views on the building of socialism, as follows:

"The overthrow of the power of the bourgeoisie and the establishment of a proletarian government in one country does not yet guarantee the complete victory of socialism. The main task of socialism—the *organization of socialist production*—still remains ahead. Can this task be accomplished, can the final victory of socialism in one country be attained, without the joint efforts of the proletariat of several advanced countries? *No, this is impossible.* To overthrow the bourgeoisie, the efforts of one country are sufficient—the history of our revolution bears this out. For the final victory of socialism, *for the organization of socialist production, the efforts of one country, particularly of such a peasant country as Russia are insufficient.* For this the efforts of the proletarians of several advanced countries are necessary. . . .

"Such, on the whole, are *the characteristic features of the Leninist theory of the proletarian revolution.*" (Stalin, *Lenin and Leninism,* pp. 40*f.,* Russian ed., 1924.)

One must concede that the "characteristic features of the Leninist theory" are outlined here quite correctly. In the later editions of Stalin's book this passage was altered to read in just the opposite way and the "characteristic features of the Leninist theory" were proclaimed within a year as . . . Trotskyism. The Seventh Plenum of the ECCI passed its decision, not on the basis of the 1924 edition but of the 1926 edition.

That is how the matter stands with Stalin. Nothing could be any sadder. To be sure, we might reconcile ourselves with this if matters were not just as sad with regard to the

Seventh Plenum of the ECCI.

There is one hope left and that is that at least Bukharin, the real author of the draft program, "always proceeded" from the possibility of the realization of socialism in one country. Let us check up.

Here is what Bukharin wrote on the subject in 1917: "Revolutions are the locomotives of history. Even in backward Russia, the irreplaceable engineer of that locomotive can be only the proletariat. But the proletariat can no longer remain within the framework of the property relations of bourgeois society. It marches to power and towards socialism. However, this task which is being 'put on the order of the day' in Russia cannot be accomplished 'within national boundaries.' Here the working class meets with an insurmountable wall [Observe: "an insurmountable wall."—L.T.] which can be broken through only by the battering ram of the *international workers revolution."* (Bukharin, *The Class Struggle and Revolution in Russia,* pp. 3*f.,* Russian ed., 1917.)

He could not have expressed himself more clearly. Such were the views held by Bukharin in 1917, two years after Lenin's alleged "change" in 1915. But perhaps the October Revolution taught Bukharin differently? Again, let us check.

In 1919, Bukharin wrote on the subject of the "Proletarian Dictatorship in Russia and the World Revolution" in the theoretical organ of the Communist International, saying:

"Under existing *world* economy and the connection between its parts, with the mutual interdependence of the various national bourgeois groups, it is *self-evident* [our emphasis] that the struggle in one country cannot end without a decisive victory of one or the other side in *several* civilized countries."

At that time this was even "self-evident." He goes on.

"In the Marxian and quasi-Marxian prewar literature, the question was many times raised as to whether the victory of socialism is possible in one country. Most of the writers replied to this question in the negative [and what about Lenin in 1915?—L.T.] from which one does not at all conclude that it is impossible or impermissible to start the revolution and to seize the power in one country."

Exactly! In the same article we read:

"The period of a rise in the productive forces can begin only with the victory of the proletariat in several major countries. Hence it follows that an all-round development of the world revolution and the formation of a strong economic alliance of the industrial countries with Soviet Russia is necessary." (N. Bukharin, "The Proletarian Dictatorship in Russia and the World Revolution," *Communist International,* no. 5, p. 614, 1919.)

Bukharin's assertion that a rise in the productive forces, that is, *real socialist development,* will begin in our country only after the victory of the proletariat in the advanced countries of Europe is indeed the very same statement that was used as a basis of all acts of indictment against "Trotskyism," including the indictment at the Seventh Plenum of the ECCI. The only thing peculiar is that Bukharin, who owes his salvation to his short memory, stepped forward in the role of accuser. Side by side with this comical circumstance, there is another and a tragic one, namely, that among those indicted was also Lenin, who expressed dozens of times the very same elementary idea.

Finally, in 1921, six years after Lenin's alleged change of 1915, and four years after the October Revolution, the Central Committee headed by Lenin approved the program of the Young Communist League, which was drawn up by a commission directed by Bukharin. Paragraph 4 of this program reads:

"In the USSR state power is already in the hands of the working class. In the course of three years of heroic struggle against world capitalism, the proletariat has maintained and strengthened its Soviet government. Russia, although it possesses enormous natural resources, is, nevertheless, from an industrial point of view, a backward country, in which a petty-bourgeois population predominates. It can arrive at socialism only through the world proletarian revolution, which epoch of development we have now entered."

This single paragraph from the program of the Young Communist League (not a chance article but a program!) renders ridiculous and really infamous the attempts of the authors of the draft to prove that the party "always" held the construction of a socialist society to be possible in one country and, moreover, precisely in Russia. If this was "always" so, then why did Bukharin formulate such a paragraph in the program of the Young Communist League? Where was Stalin looking at the time? How could Lenin and the whole Central Committee have approved such a heresy? How was it that no one in the party noticed this "trifle" or raised a voice against it? Doesn't this look like a sinister joke which is turning into a downright mockery of the party, its history, and the Comintern? Is it not high time to put a stop to this? Is it not high time to tell the revisionists: don't you dare hide behind Lenin and the theoretical tradition of the party!

At the Seventh Plenum of the ECCI, in order to provide the basis for the resolution condemning "Trotskyism," Bukharin, whose safety lies in the shortness of his memory, made the following assertion:

"In Comrade Trotsky's theory of the permanent revolution—and Comrade Trotsky propounds this theory even today—there is also to be found an assertion that because of our economic backwardness we must inevitably perish without the world revolution." (*Minutes,* p. 115.)

At the Seventh Plenum I spoke about the gaps in the theory of the permanent revolution as I had formulated it in 1905–6. But naturally it never even entered my mind to renounce anything in this theory which was fundamental, which tended to and which did bring me close to Lenin, and which made utterly inacceptable to me the present-day revision of Leninism.

There were two fundamental propositions in the theory of the permanent revolution. First, that despite the historical backwardness of Russia, the revolution can transfer the power into the hands of the Russian proletariat before the proletariat of advanced countries is able to attain it. Secondly, that the way out of those contradictions which will befall the proletarian dictatorship in a backward country, surrounded by a world of capitalist enemies, will be found on the arena of world revolution. The first proposition is based upon a correct understanding of the law of uneven development. The second depends upon a correct understanding of the indissolubility of the economic and political ties between capitalist countries. Bukharin is correct in saying that even today I still hold to these two basic propositions of the theory of the permanent revolution. Today, more than ever before. For, in my opinion, they have been completely verified and proven: in theory, by the works of Marx and Lenin; in practice, by the experience of the October Revolution.

6. WHERE IS THE 'SOCIAL DEMOCRATIC DEVIATION'?

The quotations adduced are more than sufficient to characterize Stalin's and Bukharin's theoretical positions of yesterday and today. But in order to determine the character of their political methods one must recall that, having selected from the documents written by the Opposition[17] those statements which are absolutely analogous with those which they themselves made up to 1925 (*in this case* in full agreement with Lenin), Stalin and Bukharin erected on the basis of these quotations the theory of our "social democratic deviation." It appears that in the central question of the relations between the October Revolution and international revolution, the Opposition holds the same views as Otto Bauer, who does not admit the possibility of socialist construction in Russia. One might really think that the printing press was invented only in 1924 and that everything that occurred prior to this date is doomed to oblivion. The stakes are all put on short memory!

Yet, on the question of the nature of the October Revolution, the Comintern settled its accounts with Otto Bauer and other philistines of the Second International at the Fourth

Congress. In my report on the New Economic Policy[18] and the prospects of world revolution, authorized by the Central Committee, Otto Bauer's position was appraised in a manner which expressed the views of our then Central Committee; it did not meet with any objections at the congress and I think it fully holds good today. So far as Bukharin himself is concerned, he declined to clarify the political side of the problem since "many comrades, including Lenin and Trotsky, have already spoken on the subject"; in other words, Bukharin at that time agreed with my speech. Here is what I said at the Fourth Congress about Otto Bauer:

"The social democratic theoreticians, who, on the one hand recognize in their holiday articles that capitalism, particularly in Europe, has outlived its usefulness and has become a brake on historical development, and who on the other hand express the conviction that the evolution of Soviet Russia inevitably leads to the triumph of bourgeois democracy, fall into the most pitiful and banal contradiction of which these stupid and conceited confusionists are entirely worthy. *The New Economic Policy is calculated for certain definite conditions of time and space. It is a maneuver of the workers state which exists in capitalist surroundings and definitely calculates on the revolutionary development of Europe.* . . . Such a factor as time cannot be left out of consideration in political calculations. If we allow that capitalism will really be able to continue existing in Europe for another century or half a century and that Soviet Russia will have to adapt itself to it in its economic policy, then the question solves itself automatically because, by allowing this, we presuppose the collapse of the proletarian revolution in Europe and the rise of a new epoch of capitalist revival. On what grounds is this to be allowed? If Otto Bauer has discovered in the life of present-day Austria any miraculous signs of capitalist resurrection, then all that can be said is that the fate of Russia is predetermined. But thus far we do not see any miracles, nor do we believe in them. From our viewpoint, if the European bourgeoisie is able to maintain itself in power in the course of several decades, it will under the present world conditions signify not a new capitalist bloom, but economic stagnation and the cultural decline of Europe. Generally speaking it cannot be denied that such a process might draw Soviet Russia into the abyss. Whether she would have then to go through a stage of 'democracy,' or decay in some other forms, is a question of secondary importance. But we see no reason whatever for adopting Spengler's philosophy. We definitely count upon a revolutionary development in Europe. *The New Economic Policy is merely an adaptation to the rate of that development.*" (L. Trotsky, "On Social Democratic Criticisms," *Five Years of the Comintern,* p. 491.)*

This formulation of the question brings us back to the point from which we started the evaluation of the draft program, namely, that in the epoch of imperialism it is impossible to approach the fate of one country in any other way but by taking as a starting point the tendencies of world development as a whole in which the individual country, with all its national peculiarities, is included and to which it is subordinated. The theoreticians of the Second International exclude the USSR from the world unit and from the imperialist epoch; they apply to the USSR, as an isolated country, the bald criterion of economic "maturity"; they declare that the USSR is not ripe for independent socialist construction and thence draw the conclusion of the inevitability of a capitalist degeneration of the workers state.

The authors of the draft program adopt the same theoretical ground and take over bag and baggage the metaphysical methodology of the social democratic theoreticians. They too "abstract" from the world entity and from the imperialist epoch. They proceed from the fiction of isolated development. They apply to the national phase of the world revolution a

---

* "Report on the New Soviet Economic Policy and the Perspectives of the World Revolution," in Trotsky, *The First Five Years of the Communist International,* vol. 2 (New York: Pathfinder, 1972), p. 254.

bald economic criterion. But the "verdict" they bring in is different. The "leftism" of the authors of the draft lies in the fact that they turn the social democratic evaluations inside out. Yet, the position of the theoreticians of the Second International, remodel it as you may, remains worthless. One must take Lenin's position which simply *eliminates* Bauer's evaluation and Bauer's prognosis as kindergarten exercises.

That is how matters stand with the "social democratic deviation." Not we but the authors of the draft should consider themselves related to Bauer.

7. THE DEPENDENCE OF THE USSR ON WORLD ECONOMY

The precursor of the present prophets of the national socialist society was no other than Herr Vollmar. Describing in his article entitled "The Isolated Socialist State"[19] the prospect of independent socialist construction in Germany, the proletariat of which country was much further developed than that of advanced Britain, Vollmar, in 1878, refers definitely and quite clearly in several places to the law of uneven development with which, according to Stalin, Marx and Engels were unacquainted. On the basis of that law Vollmar arrived in 1878 at the irrefutable conclusion that:

"Under the prevailing conditions, which will retain their force also in the future, it can be foreseen that a simultaneous victory of socialism in all cultural countries is absolutely out of the question."

Developing this idea still further, Vollmar says: "Thus we have come to the *isolated* socialist state which I hope I have proven to be the *most probable,* although not the only possible way."

Insofar as by the term "isolated state" we may here understand a state under a proletarian dictatorship, Vollmar expressed an irrefutable idea which was well known to Marx and Engels, and which Lenin expressed in the above-quoted article of 1915.

But then follows something which is purely Vollmar's own idea, which, by the way, is by a long shot not so one-sided and wrongly formulated as the formulation of our sponsors of the theory of socialism in one country. In his construction, Vollmar took as a starting point the proposition that socialist Germany will have lively economic relations with world capitalist economy, having at the same time the advantage of possessing a much more highly developed technology and a much lower cost of production. This construction is based on the perspective of a *peaceful coexistence* of the socialist and capitalist systems. But inasmuch as socialism must, as it progresses, constantly reveal its colossal productive superiority, the necessity for a world revolution will fall away by itself: socialism will triumph over capitalism by selling goods more cheaply on the market.

Bukharin, the author of the first draft program and one of the authors of the second draft, proceeds in his construction of socialism in one country entirely from the idea of an isolated self-sufficing economy. In Bukharin's article entitled "On the Nature of Our Revolution and the Possibility of Successful Socialist Construction in the USSR" (*Bolshevik,* no. 19–20, 1926), which is the last word in scholasticism multiplied by sophistry, all the reasoning is done within the limits of isolated economy. The principal and only argument is the following:

"Since we have 'all that is necessary and sufficient' for the building of socialism, therefore, in the very process of building socialism there can be no such point at which its further construction would become impossible. If we have within our country such a combination of forces that, in relation to each past year, we are marching ahead with a greater preponderance of the socialist sector of our economy and the socialized sectors of our economy grow faster than the private capitalist sectors, then we are entering every subsequent new year with a preponderance of forces."

This reasoning is irreproachable: "*Since* we have all that is necessary and sufficient," *therefore* we have it. Starting out from a point which must be proved, Bukharin builds up a complete system of a self-sufficing socialist economy without any entrances to it or exits from it. As to the external milieu, that is, the whole world, Bukharin, as well as Stalin, reminds himself of it only from the angle of intervention. When Bukharin speaks in his article about the necessity of "abstracting" from the international factor, he has in mind not the world market but military intervention. Bukharin does not have to abstract from the world market because he simply forgets about it throughout his construction. In harmony with this schema Bukharin championed the idea at the Fourteenth Congress of the Russian party that if we are not hindered by intervention we will build socialism "even if at the speed of a tortoise." The question of the uninterrupted struggle between the two systems, the fact that socialism can be based only on the highest productive forces; in a word, the Marxian dynamics of the displacement of one social formation by another on the basis of the growing productive forces—all this has been completely blotted out. Revolutionary and historical dialectic has been displaced by a skinflint reactionary utopia of self-sufficient socialism, built on a low technology, developing with the "speed of a tortoise" within national boundaries, connected with the external world only by its fear of intervention. The refusal to accept this miserable caricature of Marx's and Lenin's doctrine has been declared a "social democratic deviation." In the quoted article by Bukharin, this characterization of our views was, for the first time, generally advanced and "substantiated." History will take note that we fell into a "social democratic deviation" because we refused to accept an inferior rehash of Vollmar's theory of socialism in one country.

The proletariat of czarist Russia could not have taken power in October if Russia had not been a link—the *weakest* link, but a link, nevertheless—in the chain of *world economy*. The seizure of power by the proletariat has not at all excluded the Soviet republic from the system of the international division of labor created by capitalism.

Like the wise owl which comes flying only in the dusk, the theory of socialism in one country pops up at the moment when our industry, which exhausts ever greater proportions of the old fixed capital, in two-thirds of which there is crystallized the dependence of our industry on world industry, has given indication of its urgent need to renew and extend its ties with the world market, and at a moment when the problems of foreign trade have arisen in their full scope before our economic directors.

At the Eleventh Congress, that is, at the last congress at which Lenin had the opportunity to speak to the party, he issued a timely warning that the party would have to undergo another test: "... a test to which we shall be put by the Russian and *international market to which we are subordinated, with which we are connected, and from which we cannot escape.*"*

Nothing deals the theory of an isolated "complete socialism" such a death-blow as the simple fact that our foreign trade figures have in most recent years become the keystone of the figures of our economic plans. The "tightest spot" in our economy, including our industry, is our import trade which depends entirely on our export. And inasmuch as the power of resistance of a chain is always measured by its weakest link, the dimensions of our economic plans are made to conform to the dimensions of our imports.

In the journal *Planned Economy* (the theoretical organ of the State Planning Commission[20]) we read in an article devoted to the *system of planning,* that "... in drawing up our control figures for the current year we had to take methodologically our export and import plans as a starting point for the entire plan; we had to orient ourselves on that in our plans for the various branches of industry and consequently for industry in

---

* "Eleventh Congress of the RCP(B): Political Report of the Central Committee" (March 27, 1922) in *LCW,* vol. 33, pp. 276–77. Also in *Lenin's Final Fight,* pp. 23–73.

general and particularly for the construction of new industrial enterprises," etc., etc. (January, 1927, p. 27.)

This methodological approach of the State Planning Commission states flatly, for all who have ears to hear, that the control figures determine the direction and tempo of our economic development but that these control figures are already controlled by world economy; not because having become stronger we have broken free from the vicious circle of isolation.

The capitalist world shows us by its export and import figures that it has other instruments of persuasion than those of military intervention. To the extent that productivity of labor and the productivity of a social system as a whole are measured on the market by the correlation of prices, it is not so much military intervention as the intervention of cheaper capitalist commodities that constitutes perhaps the greatest immediate menace to Soviet economy. This alone shows that it is by no means merely a question of an isolated economic victory over "one's own" bourgeoisie: "The socialist revolution which is impending for the whole world will by no means consist merely in a victory of the proletariat of each country over its own bourgeoisie." (Lenin, *Works,* vol. 16, p. 388, 1919.)* Involved here is a rivalry and a life-and-death struggle between two social systems, one of which has only just begun building on backward productive forces, while the other still rests today on productive forces of immeasurably greater strength.

Anyone who sees "pessimism" in an admission of our dependence on the world market (Lenin spoke bluntly of our *subordination* to the world market) reveals thereby his own provincial petty-bourgeois timorousness in the face of the world market, and the pitiful character of his homebred optimism which hopes to hide from world economy behind a bush and to manage somehow with its own resources.

---

* "Address to the Second All-Russia Congress of Communist Organizations of the Peoples of the East," in *LCW,* vol. 30, p. 159.

The new theory has made a point of honor of the freakish idea that the USSR can perish from military intervention but never from its own economic backwardness. But inasmuch as in a socialist society the readiness of the toiling masses to defend their country must be much greater than the readiness of the slaves of capitalism to attack that country, the question arises: why should military intervention threaten us with disaster? Because the enemy is infinitely stronger in his technology. Bukharin concedes the preponderance of the productive forces only in their military technical aspect. He does not want to understand that a Ford tractor is just as dangerous as a Creusot gun, with the sole difference that while the gun can function only from time to time, the tractor brings its pressure to bear upon us constantly. Besides, the tractor knows that a gun stands behind it, as a last resort.

We are the first workers state, a section of the world proletariat, and together with the latter we *depend* upon world capital. The indifferent, neutral, and bureaucratically castrated word, "connections," is put into circulation only with the object of concealing the extremely onerous and dangerous nature of these "connections." If we were producing at the prices of the world market, our dependence on the latter, without ceasing to be a dependence, would be of a much less severe character than it is now. But unfortunately this is not the case. Our monopoly of foreign trade itself is evidence of the severity and the dangerous character of our dependence. The decisive importance of the monopoly in our socialist construction is a result precisely of the existing correlation of forces which is unfavorable to us. But we must not forget for a moment that the monopoly of foreign trade only regulates our dependence upon the world market, but does not eliminate it.

"So long as our Soviet republic [says Lenin] remains an *isolated borderland* surrounded by the entire capitalist world, so long will it be an absolutely ridiculous fantasy and utopianism to think of our complete economic independence and of the disappearance of any of our dangers." (*Works,* vol. 17,

p. 409. Our emphasis.)*

The chief dangers arise consequently from the objective position of the USSR as the "isolated borderland" in a capitalist economy which is hostile to us. These dangers may, however, diminish or increase. This depends on the action of two factors: our socialist construction on the one hand, and the development of capitalist economy on the other hand. In the last analysis, the second factor, that is, the fate of world economy as a whole, is, of course, of decisive significance.

Can it happen—and in what particular case—that the productivity of our socialist system will constantly lag behind that of the capitalist system—which would unfailingly lead in the end to the downfall of the socialist republic? If we ably manage our economy in this new phase when it becomes necessary to create independently an industrial basis with its incomparably higher demands upon the leadership, then our productivity of labor will grow. Is it, however, inconceivable that the productivity of labor in the capitalist countries, or more correctly, in the predominant capitalist countries, will grow faster than in our country? Without a clear answer to this question, there is no basis whatever for the vapid assertions that our tempo "is in itself" sufficient (let alone the absurd philosophy of the "speed of a tortoise"). But the very attempt to provide an answer to the question of the rivalry of two systems leads us to the arena of world economy and world politics, that is, to the arena of action and decision of the revolutionary International which includes the Soviet republic, but not by any means a self-sufficing Soviet republic which from time to time secures the support of the International.

Speaking of the state economy of the USSR the draft program says that it "is developing large-scale industry at a tempo *surpassing* the tempo of development in capitalist countries." This attempt to juxtapose the two tempos represents, we must

---

* "Eighth All-Russia Congress of Soviets: Report on the Work of the Council of People's Commissars" (December 22, 1920) in *LCW*, vol. 31, p. 493.

allow, a principled step forward in comparison to that period when the authors of the program categorically rejected the very question of the comparative coefficient between our development and world development. There is no need of "intruding the international factor," said Stalin. Let us build socialism "even if at the speed of a tortoise," said Bukharin. It was precisely along this line that the principled controversies occurred over a period of several years. *Formally*—we have won along this line. But if we do not merely insert into the text comparisons between the tempos of economic development, but penetrate to the root of the matter, it will become apparent that it is impermissible to speak in another section of the draft about "a sufficient minimum of industry," without any relation to the capitalist world, taking as a starting point only the internal relations; and that it is equally impermissible not only to pass a decision on but even to pose the question of whether it is "possible or impossible" for any given country to build socialism independently. The question is decided by the dynamics of the struggle between the two systems, between the two world classes; and in this struggle, regardless of the high coefficients of growth of our *restoration period,* one incontestable and basic fact remains, namely, that:

"Capitalism, if taken on an international scale, is even now, not only in a military but also in an economic sense, stronger than the Soviet power. *We must proceed from this fundamental consideration and never forget it.*" (Lenin, *Works,* vol. 17, p. 102.)*

The question of the interrelation between the different tempos of development remains an *open* question for the future. It depends not only upon our capacity to really achieve the *smychka*,[21] to assure the grain collections, and to increase our export and import; in other words, not only upon our internal successes which, of course, are extremely important

---

* "Speech Delivered at the Third All-Russia Trade Union Congress" (April 7, 1920) in *LCW,* vol. 30, p. 505.

factors in this struggle but also upon the fate of world capitalism, upon its stagnation, upsurge, or collapse, that is to say, upon the course of world economy and world revolution. Consequently, the question is decided not within the national framework but on the arena of world economic and political struggle.

8. THE CONTRADICTION BETWEEN THE PRODUCTIVE FORCES AND THE NATIONAL BOUNDARIES AS THE CAUSE OF THE REACTIONARY UTOPIAN THEORY OF 'SOCIALISM IN ONE COUNTRY'

The basis for the theory of socialism in one country, as we have seen, sums up to sophistic interpretations of several lines from Lenin on the one hand, and to a scholastic interpretation of the "law of uneven development" on the other. By giving a correct interpretation of the historic law as well as of the quotations in question we arrive at a directly opposite conclusion, that is, the conclusion that was reached by Marx, Engels, Lenin, and all of us, including Stalin and Bukharin, up to 1925.

From the uneven sporadic development of capitalism flows the nonsimultaneous, uneven, and sporadic character of socialist revolution; from the extreme tensity of the interdependence of the various countries upon each other flows not only the political but also the economic impossibility of building socialism in one country.

Let us examine once again from this angle the text of the program a little closer. We have already read in the introduction that:

"Imperialism . . . aggravates to an exceptional degree the contradiction between the growth of the national productive forces of world economy and national state barriers."

We have already stated that this proposition is, or rather was meant to be, the keystone of the international program.

But it is precisely this proposition which excludes, rejects, and sweeps away a priori the theory of socialism in one country as a reactionary theory because it is irreconcilably opposed not only to the fundamental *tendency* of development of the productive forces but also to the *material results* which have already been attained by this development. The productive forces are incompatible with national boundaries. Hence flow not only foreign trade, the export of men and capital, the seizure of territories, the colonial policy, and the last imperialist war, but also the economic impossibility of a self-sufficient socialist society. The productive forces of *capitalist* countries have long since broken through the national boundaries. Socialist society, however, can be built only on the most advanced productive forces, on the application of electricity and chemistry to the processes of production including agriculture; on combining, generalizing, and bringing to maximum development the highest elements of modern technology. From Marx on, we have been constantly repeating that capitalism cannot cope with the spirit of new technology to which it has given rise and which tears asunder not only the integument of bourgeois private property rights but, as the war of 1914 has shown, also the national hoops of the bourgeois state. Socialism, however, must not only take over from capitalism the most highly developed productive forces but must immediately carry them onward, raise them to a higher level and give them a state of development such as has been unknown under capitalism. The question arises: how then can socialism drive the productive forces back into the boundaries of a national state which they have violently sought to break through under capitalism? Or, perhaps, we ought to abandon the idea of "unbridled" productive forces for which the national boundaries, *and consequently also the boundaries of the theory of socialism in one country,* are too narrow, and limit ourselves, let us say, to the curbed and domesticated productive forces, that is, to the technology of economic backwardness? If this is the case, then in many branches of industry we should stop making progress right now and decline to a level even lower than our present pitiful technical level which managed to link up bourgeois Russia with world economy in an inseparable bond and to bring it into the vortex of the imperialist war for an *expansion of its territory for the productive forces* that had outgrown the state boundaries.

Having inherited and restored these productive forces the workers state is *compelled* to import and export.

The trouble is that the draft program injects mechanically into its text the thesis of the incompatibility of modern capitalist technology with the national boundaries, and then the argument proceeds as if there were no question at all of this incompatibility. Essentially the whole draft is a combination of ready-made revolutionary theses taken from Marx and Lenin and of opportunist or centrist conclusions which are absolutely incompatible with these revolutionary theses. That is why it is necessary *without becoming allured by the isolated revolutionary formulas contained in the draft* to watch closely *whither its main tendencies lead.*

We have already quoted that part of the first chapter which speaks of the possibility of the victory of socialism "in one isolated capitalist country." This idea is still more crudely and sharply formulated in the fourth chapter, which says that:

"The dictatorship [?] of the world proletariat . . . can be realized only as a result of the victory of socialism [?] in individual countries when the newly formed proletarian republics will establish a federation with those already in existence."

If we are to interpret the words "victory of socialism" merely as another expression for the dictatorship of the proletariat, then we will arrive at a general statement which is irrefutable for all and which should be formulated less equivocally. But this is not what the authors of the draft have in mind. By a victory of socialism, they do not mean simply the capture of power and the nationalization of the means of production but the building of a socialist society in one country. If we were to accept this interpretation then we would obtain not a world socialist economy based on an international division of labor but a federation of self-sufficing socialist communes in the spirit of blissful anarchism, the only difference being that these communes would be enlarged to the size of the present national states.

In its uneasy urge to cover up eclectically the new formulation by means of old and customary formulas, the draft program resorts to the following thesis:

"Only after the complete world victory of the proletariat and the consolidation of its world power will there ensue a prolonged epoch of intense construction of world socialist economy." (Chapter 4.)

Used as a theoretical shield, this postulate in reality only serves to expose the basic contradiction. If we are to interpret the thesis to mean that the epoch of genuine socialist construction can begin only after the victory of the proletariat, at least in several advanced countries, then it is simply a rejection of the theory of building socialism in one country, and a return to the position of Marx and Lenin. But if we are to take our point of departure from the new theory of Stalin and Bukharin which is lodged in the various sections of the draft program, then we obtain the following perspective: up to the complete world victory of the world proletariat a number of individual countries build complete socialism in their respective countries, and subsequently out of these socialist countries there will be built a world socialist economy, after the manner in which children erect structures with ready-made blocks. As a matter of fact, world socialist economy will not at all be a sum total of national socialist economies. It can take shape in its fundamental aspects only on the soil of the worldwide division of labor which has been created by the entire preceding development of capitalism. In its essentials, it will be constituted and built not after the building of "complete socialism" in a number of individual countries, but in the storms and tempests of the world proletarian revolution which will require a number of decades. The economic successes of the first countries of the proletarian dictatorship will be measured not by the degree of their approximation to a self-sufficing "complete socialism" but by the political stability of the dictatorship itself and by the successes achieved in preparing the elements of the future world socialist economy.

This revisionist idea is still more definitely and therefore still more grossly expressed, if that is possible, in the fifth chapter where, hiding behind one and a half lines of Lenin's posthumous article they have distorted, the authors of the draft declare that the USSR ". . . possesses the necessary and sufficient *material* prerequisites within the country not only for the overthrow of the feudal landlords and the bourgeoisie but also for the complete construction of socialism."

Thanks to what circumstances have we obtained such extraordinary historical advantages? On this point we find a reply in the second chapter of the draft:

"The imperialist front was broken [by the revolution of 1917] at its *weakest link,* czarist Russia." (Our emphasis.)

This is Lenin's splendid formula. Its meaning is that Russia was the most backward and economically weakest of all the imperialist states. That is precisely why her ruling classes were the first to collapse as they had loaded an unbearable burden on the insufficient productive forces of the country. Uneven, sporadic development thus compelled the proletariat of the most backward imperialist country to be the first to seize power. Formerly we were taught that it is precisely for this reason that the working class of the "weakest link" will encounter the greatest difficulties in its progress towards socialism as compared with the proletariat of the advanced countries, who will find it more difficult to seize power but who, having seized power long before we have overcome our backwardness, will not only surpass us but will carry us along so as to bring us towards the point of real socialist construction on the basis of the highest world technology and international division of labor. This was our idea when we ventured upon the October Revolution. The party has formulated this idea tens, nay, hundreds and thousands of times in the press and at meetings, but since 1925 attempts have been made to substitute just the opposite idea. Now we learn that the fact that the former czarist Russia was "the weakest link" gives the proletariat of the USSR, the inheritor of czarist Russia with all its weaknesses, an inestimable advantage, to wit, of possessing no more and no less than its own national prerequisites for the "complete construction of socialism."

Unfortunate Britain does not possess this advantage because of the *excessive* development of her productive forces which require almost the whole world to furnish the necessary raw materials and to dispose of her products. Were the productive forces of Great Britain more "moderate" and had they maintained a relative equilibrium between industry and agriculture, then the British proletariat would apparently be able to build complete socialism on its own "isolated" island, protected from foreign intervention by its navy.

The draft program, in its fourth chapter, divides the capitalist states into three groups: (1) "Countries of highly developed capitalism (United States, Germany, Great Britain, etc.)" (2) "Countries of a middle level of capitalist development (Russia prior to 1917, Poland, etc.)" (3) "Colonial and semicolonial countries (China, India, etc.)."

Despite the fact that "Russia prior to 1917" was far closer to present-day China than to the present-day United States, one might refrain from any serious objections to this schematic division were it not for the fact that, in relation to other parts of the draft, it serves as a source of false conclusions. Inasmuch as the countries "of middle level" are declared in the draft to possess "sufficient industrial minimums" for independent socialist construction, this is all the more true of countries of high capitalist development. It is *only* the colonial and semicolonial countries that need outside assistance. As we shall see later, that is precisely how they are characterized in another chapter of the draft program.

If, however, we approach the problems of socialist construction only with this criterion, abstracting from other conditions, such as the natural resources of the country, the correlation between industry and agriculture within it, its place in the world economic system, then we will fall into new, no less gross errors and contradictions. We have just spoken about Great Britain. Being no doubt a highly developed capitalist country, it has *precisely because of that* no chance for successful socialist construction within the limits of its own island. Great Britain, if blockaded, would simply be strangled in the course of a few months.

To be sure, all other conditions being equal, the more highly developed productive forces are of enormous advantage for the purposes of socialist construction. They endow economic life with an exceptional flexibility even when the latter is hemmed in by a blockading ring, as was evidenced by bourgeois Germany during the war. But the building of socialism on a national basis would imply for these advanced countries a general decline, a wholesale cutting down of productive forces, that is to say, something directly opposed to the tasks of socialism.

The draft program forgets the fundamental thesis of the incompatibility between the present productive forces and the national boundaries, from which it follows that highly developed productive forces are by no means a lesser obstacle to the construction of socialism in one country than low productive forces, although for the reverse reason, namely, that while the latter are insufficient to serve as the basis, it is the basis which will prove inadequate for the former. The law of uneven development is forgotten precisely at the point where it is most needed and most important.

The problem of building socialism is not settled merely by the industrial "maturity" or "immaturity" of a country. This immaturity is itself *uneven*. In the USSR, some branches of industry are extremely inadequate to satisfy the most elementary domestic requirements (particularly machine construction), other branches on the contrary cannot develop under present conditions without extensive and increasing exports. Among the latter are such branches of major importance as timber, oil, and manganese, let alone agriculture. On the other hand, even the "inadequate" branches cannot seriously develop if the "superabundant" (relatively) are unable to export. The impossibility of building an isolated socialist society, not in a utopia or an Atlantis but in the concrete geographical and historical conditions of our terrestrial economy, is determined for various countries in different ways—by the insufficient development of some branches as well as by the "excessive" development of others. On the whole, this means that the modern productive forces are incompatible with national boundaries.

"What was the imperialist war? It was the revolt of the productive forces not only against the bourgeois forms of property, but also against the boundaries of capitalist states. The imperialist war expressed the fact that the productive forces are unbearably constrained within the confines of national states. We have always maintained that capitalism is incapable of controlling the productive forces it itself develops and that only socialism is capable of incorporating the productive forces which have outgrown the boundaries of capitalist states within a higher economic entity. All roads that lead back to the isolated state have been blocked. . . ." (*Minutes,* Seventh Plenum of the ECCI, Trotsky's speech, p. 100.)*

Endeavoring to prove the theory of socialism in one country the draft program commits a double, triple, and quadruple mistake: it exaggerates the productive forces in the USSR; it shuts its eyes to the law of uneven development of the various branches of industry; it ignores the international division of labor; and, finally, it forgets the most important contradiction inherent in the imperialist epoch, the contradiction between the productive forces and the national barriers.

In order not to leave a single argument unanalyzed, there

---

* "Speech to the Seventh (Enlarged) Plenum of the ECCI," in Trotsky, *The Challenge of the Left Opposition (1926–27)* (New York: Pathfinder, 1980), p. 181.

remains for us to recall another and, moreover, a generalized proposition of Bukharin's in defense of the new theory.

On a world scale, says Bukharin, the correlation between the proletariat and the peasantry is not any more favorable than that existing in the USSR. Consequently, if due to reasons of backwardness it is impossible to build socialism in the USSR, then it would be equally impossible of realization on the scale of world economy.

This argument deserves being included in all the textbooks on the dialectic, as a classic example of scholastic thinking.

In the first place, it is quite probable that the correlation of forces between the proletariat and the peasantry on the world scale is not very much different from the correlation within the USSR. But the world revolution is not at all accomplished in accordance with the method of the arithmetical mean, and, incidentally, neither is the national revolution. Thus the October Revolution occurred and entrenched itself first of all in the proletarian Petrograd, instead of choosing such a region where the correlation between the workers and peasants would correspond to the average for the whole of Russia. After Petrograd and later Moscow had created the revolutionary government and the revolutionary army, they had to overthrow the bourgeoisie in the outlying country, in the course of several years; and only as a result of this process, called revolution, was there established within the boundaries of the USSR the present correlation between the proletariat and the peasantry. The revolution does not occur in accordance with the method of the arithmetical mean. It can begin in a less favorable sector, but until it entrenches itself in the decisive sectors of both the national and the world frontiers, it is impermissible to speak about its complete victory.

Secondly, the correlation between the proletariat and the peasantry, given an "average" level of technology, is not the only factor for the solution of the problem. There exists in addition the class war between the proletariat and the bourgeoisie. The USSR is surrounded not by a workers and peasants world but by a capitalist world. If the bourgeoisie were overthrown throughout the entire world, then this fact, by itself, would still change neither the correlation between the proletariat and the peasantry, nor the average level of technology within the USSR and in the entire world. But, nevertheless, the socialist construction in the USSR would immediately acquire entirely different possibilities and different proportions, which are absolutely incomparable with the present possibilities and proportions.

Thirdly, if the productive forces of every advanced country have to some degree outgrown national boundaries, then according to Bukharin, it should hence follow that the productive forces of all countries taken together have outgrown the limits of our planet, and that consequently socialism must be built not otherwise than on the scale of the solar system.

We repeat that the Bukharinistic argument from the average proportion of workers and peasants must be included in all political primers, naturally not as it is now included in order to defend the theory of socialism in one country, but as proof of the utter incompatibility between scholastic casuistry and Marxist dialectics.

9. THE QUESTION CAN BE SOLVED ONLY ON THE ARENA OF WORLD REVOLUTION

The new doctrine proclaims that socialism can be built on the basis of a national state *if only there is no intervention*. From this there can and must follow (notwithstanding all pompous declarations in the draft program) a collaborationist policy towards the foreign bourgeoisie with the object of averting intervention, as this will guarantee the construction of socialism, that is to say, will solve the main historical question. The task of the parties in the Comintern assumes, therefore, an auxiliary character; their mission is to protect the USSR from intervention and not to fight for the conquest of power. It is, of course, not a question of the subjective intentions but of the objective logic of political thought.

"The difference in views lies in the fact," says Stalin, "that the party considers that these [internal] contradictions and possible *conflicts can be entirely overcome* on the basis of the inner forces of our revolution, whereas Comrade Trotsky and the Opposition think that these contradictions and conflicts can be overcome 'only on an international scale, on the arena of the worldwide proletarian revolution.'" (*Pravda,* no. 262, November 12, 1926.)

Yes, this is precisely the difference. One could not express better and more correctly the difference between national reformism and revolutionary internationalism. If our internal difficulties, obstacles, and contradictions, which are fundamentally a reflection of world contradictions, can be settled merely by "the inner forces of our revolution" without entering "the arena of the worldwide proletarian revolution" then the International is partly a subsidiary and partly a decorative institution, the congress of which can be convoked once every four years, once every ten years, or perhaps not at all.[22] Even if we were to add that the proletariat of the other countries must protect our construction from military interventions, the International according to this schema must play the role of a *pacifist* instrument. Its main role, the role of an instrument of world revolution, is then inevitably relegated to the background. And this, we repeat, does not flow from anyone's deliberate intentions (on the contrary, a number of points in the program testify to the very best intentions of its authors), but it does flow from the internal logic of the new theoretical position which is a thousand times more dangerous than the worst subjective intentions.

As a matter of fact, even at the Seventh Plenum of the ECCI, Stalin became so bold as to develop and defend the following idea:

"Our party has no right to fool [!] the working class; it should declare openly that the *lack of assurance* [!] in the possibility of building socialism in our country leads to the abdication of power and to the passing of our party from its position as a ruling party to the position of an opposition party." (*Minutes,* vol. 2, p. 10. Our emphasis.)

This means that we have only the right to place assurance on the scanty resources of national economy but that we must not dare to place any assurance upon the inexhaustible resources of the international proletariat. If we cannot get along without an international revolution, then give up the power, give up that October power which we conquered in the interests of the international revolution. Here is the sort of ideological debacle we arrive at if we proceed from a formulation which is false to the core!

The draft program expresses an incontrovertible idea when it says that the economic successes of the USSR constitute an inseparable part of the worldwide proletarian revolution. But the political danger of the new theory lies in the false comparative evaluation of the two levers of world socialism—the lever of our economic achievements and the lever of the worldwide proletarian revolution. Without a victorious proletarian revolution, we will not be able to build socialism. The European workers and the workers the world over must clearly understand this. The lever of economic construction is of tremendous significance. Without a correct leadership, the dictatorship of the proletariat would be weakened; and its downfall would deal a blow to the international revolution from which the latter would not recover for a good many years. But the conclusion of the main historical struggle between the socialist world and the world of capitalism depends on the second lever, that is, the world proletarian revolution. The colossal importance of the Soviet Union lies in that it is the disputed base of the world revolution and not at all in the presumption that it is able to build socialism independently of the world revolution.

In a tone of supreme superiority, entirely unfounded, Bukharin has asked us more than once:

"If there already exist preconditions, and starting points,

and a sufficient base, and even certain successes in the work of building socialism, then where is the limit beyond which everything 'turns topsy-turvy'? There is no such limit." (*Minutes,* Seventh Plenum of the ECCI, p. 116.)

This is bad geometry but not historical dialectics. There can be such a "limit." There can be several such limits, internal as well as international, political as well as economic, as well as military. The most important and dire "limit" could turn out to be a serious and prolonged stabilization of world capitalism and a new boom. Consequently, the question shifts politically and economically over to the world arena. Will the bourgeoisie be able to secure for itself a new epoch of capitalist growth and power? Merely to deny such a possibility, counting on the "hopeless position" in which capitalism finds itself would be mere revolutionary verbiage. "There are no absolutely hopeless situations" (Lenin).* The present unstable class equilibrium in the European countries cannot continue indefinitely precisely because of its instability.

When Stalin and Bukharin maintain that the USSR can get along without the "state" aid of the proletariat of the other countries, that is, without its victory over the bourgeoisie, because the present active sympathy of the working masses protects us from intervention, they betray the same blindness as is revealed in the entire ramification of their principled mistake.

It is absolutely incontestable that after the social democracy had sabotaged the postwar insurrections of the European proletariat against the bourgeoisie, the active sympathy of the working masses saved the Soviet republic. During these years, the European bourgeoisie proved unable to wage war against the workers state on a large scale. But to think that this corre-

---

* "Second Congress of the Communist International: Report on the International Situation and the Fundamental Tasks of the Communist International," in *LCW*, vol. 31, p. 227. Also in *Workers of the World and Oppressed Peoples Unite! Proceedings and Documents of the Second Congress, 1920* (New York: Pathfinder, 1991).

lation of forces will continue for many years, say, until socialism is built in the USSR, is to be so utterly shortsighted as to judge the entire curve of development by one of its tiny segments. A situation so unstable that the proletariat cannot take power while the bourgeoisie does not feel firmly enough the master of its own home, must sooner or later be abruptly resolved in one way or another, either in favor of the proletarian dictatorship or in favor of a serious and prolonged capitalist stabilization on the backs of the popular masses, on the bones of the colonial peoples and . . . perhaps on our own bones. "There are no absolutely hopeless situations!" The European bourgeoisie can find a lasting way out of its grave contradictions only through the defeats of the proletariat and the mistakes of the revolutionary leadership. But the converse is equally true. There will be no new boom of world capitalism (of course, with the prospect of a new epoch of great upheavals) only in the event that the proletariat will be able to find a way out of the present unstable equilibrium on the revolutionary road.

"It is necessary to 'prove' now by the practical work of the revolutionary parties," said Lenin on July 19, 1920, at the Second World Congress, "that they are sufficiently conscious and organized, and that they have sufficient contact with the exploited masses, and determination and ability to utilize the crisis for a successful and victorious revolution." (*Works,* vol. 17, p. 264.)*

Our internal contradictions, however, which depend directly on the trend of the European and world struggle, may be rationally regulated and abated by a correct internal policy based on Marxian foresight. But they can be finally overcome only when the class contradictions will be overcome, which is out of the question without a victorious revolution in Europe. Stalin is right. The difference lies precisely on

---

* "Second Congress of the Communist International: Report on the International Situation and the Fundamental Tasks of the Communist International," in *LCW,* vol. 31, p. 227.

this point and this is the fundamental difference between national reformism and revolutionary internationalism.

10. THE THEORY OF SOCIALISM IN ONE COUNTRY AS A SERIES OF SOCIAL-PATRIOTIC BLUNDERS

The theory of socialism in one country inexorably leads to an underestimation of the difficulties which must be overcome and to an exaggeration of the achievements gained. One could not find a more antisocialist and antirevolutionary assertion than Stalin's statement to the effect that "socialism has already been 90 percent realized in the USSR."[23] This statement seems to be especially meant for a smug bureaucrat. In this way one can hopelessly discredit the idea of a socialist society in the eyes of the toiling masses. The Soviet proletariat has achieved grandiose successes, if we take into consideration the conditions under which they have been attained and the low cultural level inherited from the past. But these achievements constitute an extremely small magnitude on the scales of the socialist ideal. Harsh truth and not sugary falsehood is needed to fortify the worker, the agricultural laborer, and the poor peasant, who see that in the eleventh year of the revolution, poverty, misery, unemployment, breadlines, illiteracy, homeless children, drunkenness, and prostitution have not abated around them. Instead of telling them fibs about having realized 90 percent socialism, we must say to them that our economic level, our social and cultural conditions, approximate today much closer to capitalism, and a backward and uncultured capitalism at that, than to socialism. We must tell them that we will enter on the path of *real* socialist construction only when the proletariat of the most advanced countries will have captured power; that it is necessary to work unremittingly for this, using both levers—the short lever of our internal economic efforts and the long lever of the international proletarian struggle.

In short, instead of the Stalinist phrases about socialism which has already been 90 percent accomplished, we must speak to them the words of Lenin:

"Russia (the land of poverty) will become such a land (the land of plenty) if we cast away all pessimism and phrasemongering; if clenching our teeth, we gather all our might, strain every nerve and muscle, if we understand that salvation is possible *only* along the road of international socialist revolution that we have entered." (*Works,* vol. 15, p. 165.)*

From prominent leaders of the Comintern we have had to hear such an argument as: the theory of socialism in one country, of course, is unfounded, but it provides the Russian workers with a perspective in the difficult conditions under which they labor and thus gives them courage. It is difficult to plumb the depths of the theoretical debacle of those who seek in a program not for a scientific basis for their class orientation but for moral consolation. Consoling theories which contradict facts pertain to the sphere of religion and not science; and religion is opium for the people.

Our party has passed through its heroic period with a program which was entirely oriented on the international revolution and not on socialism in one country. Under a programmatic banner on which was inscribed that backward Russia alone, with her own forces, will not build socialism, the YCL has passed through the most strenuous years of civil war, hunger, cold, hard Saturday-ings and Sunday-ings, epidemics, studies on hunger rations, and the numberless sacrifices which were paid for every forward step taken. The members of the party and the YCL fought at the front or lugged logs to the railroad stations, not because they hoped to build national socialism out of those logs, but because they served in the cause of international revolution which made it essential that the Soviet fortress hold out—and every additional log is important for the Soviet fortress. That is how we used to

---

* "The Chief Task of Our Day" (March 11, 1918) in *LCW,* vol. 27, p. 161.

approach the question. Times have changed, things have altered (yet, not so very radically), but the principled approach retains its full force even now. The worker, the poor peasant and partisan, and the young communist, have previously shown by their entire conduct up to 1925, when the new gospel was for the first time proclaimed, that they have no need of it. But in need of it is the functionary who looks down on the masses from above; the petty administrator who does not want to be disturbed; the apparatus retainer who seeks to dominate under cover of an all-saving and consoling formula. It is they who think that the ignorant people need the "good tidings," and that there is no dealing with the people without consoling doctrines. It is they who catch up the false words about "90 percent socialism," for this formula sanctions their privileged position, their right to dominate and command, their need to be rid of criticisms on the part of "skeptics" and men of "little faith."

Complaints and accusations to the effect that the denial of the possibility of building socialism in one country dampens the spirit and kills enthusiasm are theoretically and psychologically closely related to those accusations which the reformists have always hurled at the revolutionists, notwithstanding the entirely different conditions under which they originate. Said the reformists: "You are telling the workers that they cannot really improve their lot within the framework of capitalist society; and by this alone you kill their incentive to fight." It was, indeed, only under the leadership of revolutionists that the workers really fought for economic gains and for parliamentary reforms.

The worker who understands that it is impossible to build a socialist paradise, like an oasis in the hell of world capitalism; that the fate of the Soviet republic and therefore his own fate depend entirely on the international revolution, will fulfill his duties toward the USSR much more energetically than the worker who is told that what we already possess is presumably 90 percent socialism. "If so, is it worth while to strive toward socialism?" Here, too, the reformist orientation works as always not only against revolution but also against reform.

In the article written in 1915 dealing with the slogan of the United States of Europe, which has already been quoted, we wrote:

"To approach the prospects of a social revolution within national boundaries is to fall victim to the same national narrowness which constitutes the substance of social patriotism. Vaillant to his dying day considered France the promised land of social revolution; and it is precisely from this standpoint that he stood for national defense to the end. Lensch and Co. (some hypocritically and others sincerely) consider that Germany's defeat means first of all the destruction of the basis of social revolution. . . . In general it should not be forgotten that in social patriotism there is, alongside of the most vulgar reformism, a national revolutionary messianism which deems that its own national state, whether because of its industrial level or because of its 'democratic' form and revolutionary conquests, is called upon to lead humanity towards socialism or towards 'democracy.' If the victorious revolution were really conceivable within the boundaries of a single more developed nation, this messianism together with the program of national defense would have some relative historical justification. But as a matter of fact this is inconceivable. To fight for the preservation of a national basis of revolution by such methods as undermine the international ties of the proletariat, actually means to undermine the revolution itself, which can begin on a national basis but which cannot be completed on that basis under the present economic, military, and political interdependence of the European states, which was never before revealed so forcefully as during the present war. This interdependence which will directly and immediately condition the concerted action on the part of the European proletariat in the revolution is expressed by the slogan of the United States of Europe." (*Works,* vol. 3, part 1, pp. 90f.)

Proceeding from a false interpretation of the polemics of 1915, Stalin has many times endeavored to show that under "national narrowness" I was here alluding to Lenin. No greater absurdity could be imagined. In my polemic with Lenin I always argued openly because I was guided only by ideological considerations. In the given case Lenin was not involved at all. The article mentions by name the people against whom these accusations were hurled—Vaillant, Lensch, and others. One must recall that the year 1915 was a year of social-patriotic orgy and the crushing of our struggle against it. This was our touchstone for every question.

The fundamental question raised in the foregoing passage was undoubtedly formulated correctly: *the conception of the building of socialism in one country is a social-patriotic conception.*

The patriotism of the German social democrats began as a legitimate patriotism to their own party, the most powerful party of the Second International. On the basis of the highly developed German technology and the superior organizational qualities of the German people, the German social democracy prepared to build its "own" socialist society. If we leave aside the hardened bureaucrats, careerists, parliamentary sharpers, and political crooks in general, the social patriotism of the rank-and-file social democrat was derived precisely from the belief in building German socialism. It is impossible to think that hundreds of thousands of rank-and-file social democrats (let alone the millions of rank-and-file workers) wanted to defend the Hohenzollerns or the bourgeoisie. No. They wanted to protect German industry, the German railways and highways, German technology and culture, and especially the organizations of the German working class, as the "necessary and sufficient" national prerequisites for socialism.

A similar process also took place in France. Guesde, Vaillant, and thousands of the best rank-and-file party members with them, and hundreds of thousands of ordinary workers believed that precisely France with her revolutionary traditions, her heroic proletariat, her highly cultured, flexible, and talented people, was the promised land of socialism. Old Guesde and the Communard Vaillant, and with them hundreds of thousands of sincere workers, did not fight to protect the bankers or the rentiers. They sincerely believed that they were defending the soil and the creative power of the future socialist society. They proceeded entirely from the theory of socialism in one country and in the name of this idea they sacrificed international solidarity, believing this sacrifice to be "temporary."

This comparison with the social patriots will, of course, be answered by the argument that patriotism to the Soviet state is a revolutionary duty whereas patriotism to a bourgeois state is treachery. Very true. Can there be any dispute on this question among grown-up revolutionists? But, as we proceed, this incontrovertible postulate is turned more and more into a scholastic screen for a deliberate falsehood.

Revolutionary patriotism can only have a class character. It begins as patriotism to the party organization, to the trade union, and rises to state patriotism when the proletariat seizes power. Whenever the power is in the hands of the workers, patriotism is a revolutionary duty. But this patriotism must be an inseparable part of revolutionary internationalism. Marxism has always taught the workers that even their struggle for higher wages and shorter hours cannot be successful unless waged as an international struggle. And now it suddenly appears that the ideal of the socialist society may be achieved with the national forces alone. This is a mortal blow to the International.

The invincible conviction that the fundamental class aim, even more so than the partial objectives, cannot be realized by national means or within national boundaries, constitutes the very heart of revolutionary internationalism. If, however, the ultimate aim is realizable within national boundaries through the efforts of a national proletariat, then the backbone of internationalism has been broken. The theory of the possibility of realizing socialism in one country destroys the inner connection between the patriotism of the victorious proletariat and the defeatism of the proletariat of the bourgeois countries. The proletariat of the advanced capitalist countries is still traveling on the road to power. How and in what manner it marches towards it depends entirely upon whether it considers the task of building the socialist society a national or an international task.

If it is at all possible to realize socialism in one country, then one can believe in that theory not only *after* but also *before* the conquest of power. If socialism can be realized within the national boundaries of backward Russia, then there is all the more reason to believe that it can be realized in advanced Germany. Tomorrow the leaders of the Communist Party of Germany will undertake to propound this theory. The draft program empowers them to do so. The day after tomorrow the French party will have its turn. It will be the beginning of the disintegration of the Comintern along the lines of social patriotism. The communist party of any capitalist country, which will have become imbued with the idea that its particular country possesses the "necessary and sufficient" prerequisites for the independent construction of a "complete socialist society," will not differ in any substantial manner from the revolutionary social democracy which also did not begin with a Noske but which stumbled decisively on August 4, 1914, over this very same question.

When the statement is made that the very existence of the USSR is a guarantee against social patriotism because in relation to a workers republic patriotism is a revolutionary duty, then in this one-sided application of a correct idea there is expressed national narrow-mindedness. Those who say so have in mind only the USSR, closing their eyes to the entire world proletariat. It is possible to lead the proletariat to the position of defeatism in relation to the bourgeois state only by means of an international orientation in the program on this central question and by means of a ruthless rejection of the social-patriotic contraband which is masked as yet but which seeks to build a theoretical nest for itself in the program of Lenin's International.

It is not yet too late to return to the path of Marx and Lenin.

It is this return that opens up the only conceivable road to progress. We address this criticism of the draft program to the Sixth Congress of the Comintern, in order to make possible the realization of this turn in which salvation lies.

II

Strategy and tactics in the imperialist epoch

1. THE COMPLETE BANKRUPTCY OF THE CENTRAL CHAPTER OF THE DRAFT PROGRAM

THE DRAFT PROGRAM of the Comintern contains a chapter devoted to the questions of revolutionary *strategy*. It must be acknowledged that its intention is quite correct and corresponds to the aim and spirit of an international program of the proletariat in the imperialist epoch.

The conception of revolutionary strategy took root only in the postwar years, and in the beginning undoubtedly under the influence of military terminology. But it did not by any means take root accidentally. Prior to the war we spoke only of the tactics of the proletarian party; this conception conformed adequately enough to the then-prevailing trade union, parliamentary methods which did not transcend the limits of the day-to-day demands and tasks. By the conception of tactics is understood the system of measures that serves a single current task or a single branch of the class struggle. Revolutionary strategy on the contrary embraces a combined system of actions which by their association, consistency, and growth must lead the proletariat to the conquest of power.

The basic principles of revolutionary strategy were naturally formulated since the time when Marxism first put before the revolutionary parties of the proletariat the task of the conquest of power on the basis of the class struggle. The First International,[24] however, succeeded in formulating these principles, properly speaking, only theoretically, and could test them only partially in the experience of various countries. The epoch of the Second International[25] led to methods and views according to which, in the notorious expression of Bernstein, "the movement is everything, the ultimate goal nothing." In other words, the strategical task disappeared, becoming dissolved in the day-to-day "movement" with its partial tactics devoted to the problems of the day. Only the Third International[26] reestablished the rights of the revolutionary strategy of communism and completely subordinated the tactical methods to it. Thanks to the invaluable experience of the first two Internationals, upon whose shoulders the Third rests, thanks to the revolutionary character of the present epoch and the colossal historic experience of the October Revolution, the strategy of the Third International immediately attained a full-blooded militancy and the widest historical scope. At the same time, the first decade of the new International reveals to us a panorama not only of great battles but also of the greatest defeats of the proletariat, beginning with 1918. That is why the questions of strategy and tactics should have constituted, in a certain sense, the central point in the program of the Comintern. As a matter of fact, however, the chapter in the draft program devoted to the strategy and tactics of the Comintern, bearing the subtitle "The Road to the Dictatorship of the Proletariat," is one of the weakest chapters, almost devoid of meaning. The section of this chapter that deals with the East really consists only of a generalization of the mistakes made and the preparation of new ones.

The introductory section of this chapter is devoted to a criticism of anarchism, revolutionary syndicalism, constructive socialism, Guild Socialism,[27] etc. Here we have a purely literary imitation of the *Communist Manifesto* which in its time inaugurated the era of the scientifically established policy of the proletariat through an ingeniously terse characterization of the most important varieties of utopian socialism. But to engage now, on the tenth anniversary of the Comintern, in a desultory and anemic criticism of the "theories" of Cornelissen, Arturo Labriola, Bernard Shaw, or lesser known Guild Socialists, means that instead of answering political needs one becomes a victim of purely literary pedantry. This ballast could easily be transferred from the program to the field of propaganda literature.

So far as the strategical problems are concerned, in the proper sense of the word, the draft program limits itself to such ABC wisdom as:

"The extension of its influence over the majority of its own class. . . .

"The extension of its influence over the broad section of the toiling masses in general. . . .

"The day-to-day work of conquering the trade unions is of an especially high importance. . . .

"The winning of the broadest section of the poorest peasantry is also [?] of enormous importance. . . ."

All these commonplaces, indisputable enough in themselves, are merely set down in rotation here, that is to say, they are brought in without any connection with the character of the historical epoch and, therefore, in their *present* abstract, scholastic form, could be introduced without difficulty into a resolution of the Second International. Quite dryly and sketchily the central problem of the program is considered here in a single schematic passage which is much shorter than the passage dealing with "constructive" and "Guild" socialism. This means that the strategy of the revolutionary overturn, the conditions and the roads to the armed insurrection itself, and the seizure of power—all this is presented abstractly and pedantically, and without the slightest regard to the living experience of our epoch.

We find here mention made of the great struggles of the proletariat in Finland, Germany, Austria, the Hungarian soviet republic, the September days in Italy, the events of 1923 in

Germany, the general strike in England, and so forth, only in the form of a bald, chronological enumeration. Yet even this is to be found not in the sixth chapter, which deals with the strategy of the proletariat, but in the second on "The General Crisis of Capitalism and the First Phase of Development of the World Revolution." In other words, the great struggles of the proletariat are approached here only as objective occurrences, as an expression of the "general crisis of capitalism" but not as strategical experiences of the proletariat. It is sufficient to refer to the fact that the rejection, necessary in itself, of revolutionary adventurism (putschism) is made in the program without any attempt to answer the question whether, for example, the uprising in Estonia, or the bombing of the Sofia cathedral in 1924, or the last uprising in Canton[28] were heroic manifestations of revolutionary adventurism or, on the contrary, planned actions of the revolutionary strategy of the proletariat. A draft program which in dealing with the problem of "putschism" gives no answer to this burning question is only a diplomatic office job and not a document of communist strategy.

Obviously, this abstract, suprahistorical formulation of the questions of the revolutionary struggle of the proletariat is no accident for this draft. In addition to the Bukharinistic manner of treating questions in general in a literary, pedantic, didactic, and not in an actively revolutionary way, there is another reason for it: the authors of the draft program, for reasons easily understood, prefer generally not to deal too closely with the strategical lessons of the last five years.

But a program of revolutionary action naturally cannot be approached as a bare collection of abstract propositions without any relation to all that has occurred during these epoch-making years. A program cannot, of course, go into a description of the events of the past, but it must proceed from these events, base itself upon them, encompass them, and relate to them. A program, by the position it takes, must make it possible to understand all the major facts of the struggle of the proletariat and all the important facts relating to the ideological struggle inside the Comintern. If this is true with regard to the program as a whole, then it is all the truer with regard to that part of it which is specifically devoted to the question of strategy and tactics. Here, in the words of Lenin, in addition to what has been *conquered* there must also be registered that which has been lost, that which can be transformed into a "conquest," if it has been understood and assimilated. The proletarian vanguard needs not a catalog of truisms but a manual of action. We will, therefore, consider here the problems of the "strategic" chapter in closest connection with the experiences of the struggles of the postwar period, especially of the last five years, the years of tragic mistakes of the leadership.

2. THE FUNDAMENTAL PECULIARITIES INHERENT IN THE STRATEGY OF THE REVOLUTIONARY EPOCH AND THE ROLE OF THE PARTY

The chapter devoted to strategy and tactics does not so much as give a "strategical" characterization, coherent to any degree, of the imperialist epoch as an epoch of proletarian revolutions in contradistinction to the prewar epoch.

To be sure, the period of industrial capitalism as a whole is characterized in the first chapter of the draft program as a "period of relatively continuous evolution and propagation of capitalism over the whole terrestrial globe through the division of still unoccupied colonies and the armed seizure of them."

This characterization is certainly quite contradictory and it obviously idealizes the whole epoch of industrial capitalism, which was an epoch of colossal convulsions, of wars and revolutions by far surpassing in this sphere the entire preceding history of mankind. This idyllic characterization was apparently necessary so as to provide at least a partial justification for the recent absurd contention of the authors of the draft program that at the time of Marx and Engels "there could not be any talk as yet" of the law of unequal development.[29] But while it is false to characterize the entire history of industrial capitalism as a "continuous evolution," it is extremely important to demarcate a special European epoch which comprises the years 1871 to 1914, or at least to 1905. This was an epoch of the organic accumulation of contradictions which, so far as the internal class relations of Europe are concerned, almost never overstepped the bounds of legal struggle and so far as international relations are concerned, adjusted themselves to the framework of an armed peace. This was the epoch of the origin, the development, and the ossification of the Second International, whose progressive historical role completely terminated with the outbreak of the imperialist war.

Politics, considered as a mass historical force, always lags behind economics. Thus, while the reign of finance capital and trust monopolies already began towards the end of the nineteenth century, the new epoch in international politics which reflects this fact, first begins in world politics with the imperialist war, with the October Revolution, and the founding of the Third International.

The explosive character of this new epoch, with its abrupt changes of the political flows and ebbs, with its constant spasmodic class struggle between fascism and communism, is lodged in the fact that the international capitalist system has already spent itself and is no longer capable of progress *as a whole*. This does not mean to imply that individual branches of industry and individual countries are incapable of growing and will not grow any more, and even at an unprecedented tempo. Nevertheless, this development proceeds and will have to proceed to the detriment of the growth of other branches of industry and of other countries. The expenditures incurred by the productive system of world capitalism devour its world income to an ever increasing degree. And inasmuch as Europe, accustomed to world domination, with the inertia acquired from its rapid, almost uninterrupted growth in the prewar period, now collides more sharply than the other continents with the new relation of forces, the new division of the world market, and the contradictions deepened by the war, it is precisely in Europe that the transition from the "organic" epoch to the revolutionary epoch was particularly precipitous.

Theoretically, to be sure, even a new chapter of a *general* capitalist progress in the most powerful, ruling, and leading countries is not excluded. But for this, capitalism would first have to overcome enormous barriers of a class as well as of an inter-state character. It would have to strangle the proletarian revolution for a long time; it would have to enslave China completely, overthrow the Soviet republic, and so forth. We are still a long way removed from all this. Theoretical eventualities correspond least of all to political probabilities. Naturally, a great deal also depends upon us, that is, upon the revolutionary strategy of the Comintern. In the final analysis, this question will be settled in the struggle of international forces. Still, in the present epoch for which the program was created, capitalist development as a whole is faced with insurmountable obstacles and contradictions and beats in frenzy against them. It is precisely this that invests our epoch with its revolutionary character and the revolution with its permanent character.

The revolutionary character of the epoch does not lie in that it permits of the accomplishment of the revolution, that is, the seizure of power at every given moment. Its revolutionary character consists in profound and sharp fluctuations and abrupt and frequent transitions from an immediately revolutionary situation; in other words, such as enables the communist party to strive for power, to a victory of the fascist or semifascist counterrevolution, and from the latter to a provisional regime of the golden mean (the "Left Bloc," the inclusion of the social democracy into the coalition, the passage of power to the party of MacDonald, and so forth), immediately thereafter to force the antagonisms to a head again and acutely raise the question of power.

What did we have in Europe in the course of the last decades before the war? In the sphere of economy—a mighty advance of productive forces with "normal" fluctuations of the conjuncture. In politics—the growth of social democracy at the expense of liberalism and "democracy" with quite insignificant fluctuations. In other words, a process of systematic intensification of economic and political contradictions, and in this sense, the creation of the prerequisites for the proletarian revolution.

What have we in Europe in the postwar period? In economy—irregular, spasmodic curtailments and expansions of production, which gravitate in general around the prewar level despite great technical successes in certain branches of industry. In politics—frenzied oscillations of the political situation towards the left and towards the right. It is quite apparent that the sharp turns in the political situation in the course of one, two, or three years are not brought about by any changes in the basic economic factors, but by causes and impulses of a purely superstructural character, thereby indicating the extreme instability of the entire system, the foundation of which is corroded by irreconcilable contradictions.

This is the sole source from which flows the full significance of revolutionary strategy in contradistinction to tactics. Thence also flows the new significance of the party and the party leadership.

The draft confines itself to purely formal definitions of the party (vanguard, theory of Marxism, embodiment of experiences, and so forth) which might not have sounded badly in a program of the left social democracy prior to the war. Today it is utterly inadequate.

In a period of growing capitalism even the best party leadership could do no more than only accelerate the formation of a workers party. Inversely, mistakes of the leadership could retard this process. The objective prerequisites of a proletarian revolution matured but slowly, and the work of the party retained a preparatory character.

Today, on the contrary, every new sharp change in the political situation to the left places the decision in the hands of the revolutionary party. Should it miss the critical situation, the latter veers around to its opposite. Under these circumstances the role of the party leadership acquires exceptional importance. The words of Lenin to the effect that two or three days can decide the fate of the international revolution would have been almost incomprehensible in the epoch of the Second International. In our epoch, on the contrary, these words have only too often been confirmed and, with the exception of the October Revolution, always from the negative side. Only out of these general conditions does that exceptional position become understandable which the Comintern and its leadership occupy with respect to the whole mechanics of the present historical epoch.

One must understand clearly that the initial and basic cause—the so-called stabilization—lies in the contradiction between the general disorganization of the economic and social position of capitalist Europe and the colonial East on the one hand, and the weaknesses, unpreparedness, irresolution of the communist parties and the vicious errors of their leadership on the other.

It is not the so-called stabilization, arriving from nowhere, that checked the development of the revolutionary situation of 1918–19, or of the recent years, but on the contrary, the unutilized revolutionary situation was transformed into its opposite and thus guaranteed to the bourgeoisie the opportunity to fight with relative success for stabilization. The sharpening contradictions of this struggle for "stabilization" or rather of the struggle for the further existence and development of capitalism prepare at each new stage the prerequisites for new international and class upheavals that is, for new revolutionary situations, the development of which depends entirely upon the proletarian party.

The role of the subjective factor in a period of slow, organic development can remain quite a subordinate one. Then diverse proverbs of gradualism arise, as: "slow but sure," and "one must not kick against the pricks," and so forth, which epitomize all the tactical wisdom of an organic epoch that abhorred "leaping over stages." But as soon as the objective prerequisites have matured, the key to the whole historical process passes into the hands of the subjective factor, that is, the party. Opportunism, which consciously or unconsciously thrives upon the inspiration of the past epoch, always tends to underestimate the role of the subjective factor, that is, the importance of the party and of revolutionary leadership. All this was fully disclosed during the discussions on the lessons of the German October, on the Anglo-Russian Committee, and on the Chinese revolution. In all these cases, as well as in others of lesser importance, the opportunistic tendency evinced itself in the adoption of a course that relied solely upon the "masses" and therefore completely scorned the question of the "tops" of the revolutionary leadership. Such an attitude, which is false in general, operates with positively fatal effect in the imperialist epoch.

The October Revolution was the result of a particular relation of class forces in Russia and in the whole world and their particular development in the process of the imperialist war. This general proposition is ABC to a Marxist. Nevertheless, there is no contradiction whatever between Marxism and posing, for instance, such a question as: would we have seized power in October had not Lenin arrived in Russia in time? There is much to indicate that we might not have been able to seize power. The resistance of the party heads—for the most part, incidentally, they are the same people who determine policies today—was very strong even under Lenin. And without Lenin it would undoubtedly have been infinitely stronger. The party might have failed to adopt the necessary course in time, and there was very little time left at our disposal. During such periods, a few days sometimes decide. The working masses would indeed have pressed upwards from below with great heroism but without a leadership certain of itself and leading consciously to the goal, victory would have been little probable. In the meantime, however, the bourgeoisie could have surrendered Petrograd to the Germans and after a suppression of the proletarian uprising could have reconsolidated its power most probably in the form of Bonapartism, by means of a separate peace with Germany and through other measures. The entire course of events might have taken a different direction for a number of years.

In the German revolution of 1918, in the Hungarian revolution of 1919, in the September movement of the Italian proletariat in 1920, in the English general strike of 1926, in the Vienna uprising of 1927, and in the Chinese revolution of 1925–27—everywhere, one and the same political contradiction of the entire past decade, even if at different stages and in different forms, was manifested. In an objectively ripe revolutionary situation, ripe not only with regard to its social bases but not infrequently also with regard to the mood for struggle of the masses, the subjective factor, that is, a revolutionary mass party, was lacking or else this party lacked a farsighted and intrepid leadership.

Of course, the weaknesses of the communist parties and of their leadership did not fall from the sky, but are rather a product of the entire past of Europe. But the communist parties could develop at a swift pace in the present existing maturity of the objectively revolutionary contradictions provided, of course, there was a correct leadership on the part of the Comintern speeding up this process of development instead of retarding it. If contradiction is, in general, the most important mainspring of progress then the clear understanding of the contradiction between a general revolutionary maturity of the objective situation (despite ebbs and flows) and the immaturity of the international party of the proletariat ought now to constitute the mainspring for the forward movement of the Comintern, at least of its European section.

Without an extensive and generalized dialectical comprehension of the present epoch as an epoch of abrupt turns, a real education of the young parties, a correct strategical leadership of the class struggle, a correct combination of tactics, and, above all, a sharp and bold and decisive rearming at each successive breaking point of the situation is impossible. And it is just at such an abrupt breaking point that two or three days sometimes decide the fate of the international revolution for years to come.

The chapter of the draft program devoted to strategy and tactics speaks of a struggle of the party for the proletariat *in general,* and of a general strike, and of the armed insurrection *in general.* But it does not at all dissect the peculiar character and the inner rhythm of the present epoch. Without comprehending these theoretically and "sensing" them politically, a real revolutionary leadership is impossible.

That is why this chapter is so pedantic, so thin, so bankrupt from beginning to end.

3. THE THIRD CONGRESS AND THE QUESTION OF THE PERMANENCE OF THE REVOLUTIONARY PROCESS ACCORDING TO LENIN AND ACCORDING TO BUKHARIN

Three periods can be established in the political development of Europe after the war. The first period runs from 1917 to 1921, the second from March 1921 to October 1923, and the third from October 1923 up to the English general strike, or even up to the present moment.

The postwar revolutionary movement of the masses was strong enough to overthrow the bourgeoisie. But there was no one to bring this to a consummation. The social democracy, which held the leadership of the traditional organizations of the working class, exerted all its efforts to save the bourgeois regime. When we looked forward at that time to an immediate seizure of power by the proletariat, we reckoned that a revolutionary party would mature rapidly in the fire of the civil war. But the two terms did not coincide. The revolutionary wave of the postwar period ebbed before the communist parties grew up and reached maturity in the struggle with the social democracy so as to assume the leadership of the insurrection.

In March 1921, the German Communist Party made the attempt to avail itself of the declining wave in order to overthrow the bourgeois state with a single blow. The guiding thought of the German Central Committee in this was to save the Soviet republic (the theory of socialism in one country had not yet been proclaimed at that time). But it turned out that the determination of the leadership and the dissatisfaction of the masses do not suffice for victory. There must obtain a number of other conditions, above all, a close bond between the leadership and the masses and the confidence of the latter in the leadership. This condition was lacking at that time.

The Third Congress of the Comintern was a milestone demarcating the first and second periods. It set down the fact that the resources of the communist parties, politically as well as organizationally, were not sufficient for the conquest of power. It advanced the slogan: "To the masses!" that is, to the conquest of power through a *previous conquest of the masses*, achieved on the basis of the daily life and struggles. For the mass also continues to live its daily life in a revolutionary epoch, even if in a somewhat different manner.

This formulation of the problem met with a furious resistance at the congress which was inspired theoretically by Bukharin. At that time he held a viewpoint of his own permanent revolution and not that of Marx. "Since capitalism had exhausted itself, *therefore* the victory must be gained through an uninterrupted revolutionary offensive." Bukharin's position always reduces itself to syllogisms of this sort.

Naturally, I never shared the Bukharinist version of the theory of the "permanent" revolution, according to which no interruptions, periods of stagnation, retreats, transitional demands, or the like, are at all conceivable in the revolutionary process. On the contrary, from the first days of October, I fought against this caricature of the permanent revolution.

When I spoke as did Lenin of the incompatibility between Soviet Russia and the world of imperialism, I had in mind the great strategical curve and not its tactical windings. Bukharin, on the contrary, prior to his transformation into his own antipode, invariably expounded a scholastic caricature of the Marxian conception of a continuous revolution. Bukharin opined in the days of his "Left Communism,"[30] that the revolution allows neither of retreats nor temporary compromises with the enemy. Long after the question of the Brest-Litovsk peace, in which my position had nothing in common with Bukharin's, the latter together with the entire ultraleft wing of the Comintern of that time advocated the line of the March 1921 days[31] in Germany, being of the opinion that unless the proletariat in Europe was "galvanized," unless there were ever new revolutionary eruptions, the Soviet power was threatened with certain destruction. The consciousness that real dangers actually threatened the Soviet power did not prevent me from waging an irreconcilable struggle shoulder to shoulder with Lenin at the Third Congress against this putschistic parody of a Marxian conception of the permanent revolution. During the Third Congress, we declared tens of times to the impatient leftists: "Don't be in too great a hurry to save us. In that way you will only destroy yourselves and, therefore, also bring about our destruction. Follow systematically the path of the struggle for the masses in order thus to reach the struggle for power. We need your victory but not your readiness to fight under unfavorable conditions. We will manage to maintain ourselves in the Soviet republic with the help of the NEP and we will go forward. You will still have time to come to our aid at the right moment if you will have gathered your forces and will have utilized the favorable situation."

Although this took place after the tenth party congress which prohibited factions, Lenin nevertheless assumed the initiative at that time to create the top nucleus of a new faction for the struggle against the ultraleftists who were strong at that time. In our intimate conferences, Lenin flatly put the question of how to carry on the subsequent struggle should the Third World Congress accept Bukharin's viewpoint. Our "faction" of that time did not develop further only because our opponents "folded up" considerably during the congress.

Bukharin, of course, swung further to the left of Marxism than anybody else. At this same Third Congress and later, too, he led the fight against my view that the economic conjuncture in Europe would inevitably rise; and that despite a whole series of defeats of the proletariat I expected after this inevitable rise of the conjuncture not a blow at the revolution, but, on the contrary, a new impetus to revolutionary struggle. Bukharin, who held to his standpoint of the scholastic permanence of both the economic crisis and the revolution as a whole, waged a long struggle against me on this viewpoint, until facts finally forced him, as usual, to a very belated admission that he was in error.

At the third and fourth congresses Bukharin fought against the policy of the united front and the transitional demands, proceeding from his mechanical understanding of the permanence of the revolutionary process.

The struggle between these two tendencies, the synthesized, Marxian conception of the continuous character of the proletarian revolution and the scholastic parody of Marxism which was by no means an individual quirk of Bukharin's, can be followed through a whole series of other questions, big as well as small. But it is superfluous to do so. Bukharin's position today is essentially the selfsame ultraleft scholasticism of the "permanent revolution," only, this time, turned inside out. If, for example, Bukharin was of the opinion until 1923 that without a permanent economic crisis and a permanent civil war in Europe the Soviet republic would perish, he has today discovered a recipe for building socialism without any international revolution at all. To be sure, the topsy-turvy Bukharinist permanency has not improved any by the fact that the present leaders of the Comintern far too frequently combine their adventurism of yesterday with their opportunist position of today, and vice versa.

The Third Congress was a great beacon. Its teachings are still vital and fruitful today. The Fourth Congress only concretized these teachings. The slogan of the Third Congress did not simply read: *"To the masses!"* but: *"To power through a previous conquest of the masses!"* After the faction led by Lenin (which he characterized demonstratively as the "right" wing) had to curb intransigently the entire congress throughout its duration, Lenin arranged a private conference toward the end of the congress in which he warned prophetically: "Remember, it is only a question of getting a good running start for the revolutionary leap. The struggle for the masses is the struggle for power."

The events of 1923 demonstrated that this Leninist position was not grasped, not only by "those who are led" but also by many of the leaders.

4. THE GERMAN EVENTS OF 1923 AND THE LESSONS OF OCTOBER

The German events of 1923 form the breaking point that inaugurates a new, post-Leninist period in the development of the Comintern. The occupation of the Ruhr by French troops early in 1923 signified Europe's relapse into war chaos. Although the second attack of this disease was incomparably weaker than the first, violent revolutionary consequences were nevertheless to be expected from the outset, since it had seized the already completely debilitated organism of Germany. The leadership of the Comintern did not take this into consideration at the right time. The German Communist Party still continued to follow its one-sided interpretation of the slogan of the Third Congress which had firmly drawn it away from the threatening road to putschism. We have already stated above that in our epoch of abrupt turns the greatest difficulty for a revolutionary leadership lies in being able to feel the pulse of the political situation at the proper moment, so as to catch the abrupt contingency and to turn the helm in due time. Such qualities of a revolutionary leadership are not acquired simply by swearing fealty to the latest circular letter of the Comintern. They can be acquired, if the necessary theoretical prerequisites exist, by personally acquired experience and genuine self-criticism. It was not easy to achieve the sharp turn from the tactics of the March days of 1921 to a systematic revolutionary activity in the press, meetings, trade unions, and parliament. After the crisis of this turn had been weathered, there arose the danger of the development of a new one-sided deviation of a directly opposite character. The daily struggle for the masses absorbs all attention, creates its own tactical routine, and diverts attention away from the strategical tasks flowing from changes in the objective situation.

In the summer of 1923, the internal situation in Germany, especially in connection with the collapse of the tactic of passive resistance, assumed a catastrophic character. It became quite clear that the German bourgeoisie could extricate itself from this "hopeless" situation only if the Communist Party failed to understand in due time that the position of the bourgeoisie was "hopeless" and if the party failed to draw all the necessary revolutionary conclusions. Yet it was precisely the Communist Party, holding the key in its hands, that opened the door for the bourgeoisie with this key.

Why didn't the German revolution lead to a victory? The reasons for it are all to be sought in the tactics, not in the existing conditions. Here we had a classic example of a missed revolutionary situation. After all the German proletariat had gone through in recent years, it could be led to a decisive struggle only if it were convinced that this time the question would be decisively resolved and that the Communist Party was ready for the struggle and capable of achieving the victory. But the communist party executed the turn very irresolutely and after a very long delay. Not only the Rights but also the Lefts, despite the fact that they had fought each other very bitterly, viewed rather fatalistically the process of revolutionary development up to September–October 1923.

Only a pedant and not a revolutionist would investigate now, after the event, how far the conquest of power would have been "assured" had there been a correct policy. We confine ourselves here to quoting a remarkable testimonial from *Pravda* bearing on this point, a testimonial which is purely accidental and unique because it is contradictory to all the other pronouncements of this organ:

"If in May 1924, when the mark was comparatively stabilized and the bourgeoisie had achieved a certain degree of consolidation, after the middle class and the petty bourgeoisie went over to the Nationalists, after a deep crisis in the party, and after a heavy defeat of the proletariat, if after all this the communists are able to rally 3.7 million votes, then it is clear that in October 1923, during the unprecedented economic crisis, during the complete disintegration of the middle classes, during a frightful confusion in the ranks of the social democracy resulting from the powerful and sharp contradictions within the bourgeoisie itself and an unprecedented militant mood of the proletarian masses in the industrial centers, the Communist Party had the majority of the population on its side; it could and should have fought and had all the chances for success." (*Pravda,* May 25, 1924.)

And here are the words of a German delegate (name unknown) at the Fifth World Congress:

"There is not a single class-conscious worker in Germany who is unaware that the party should have engaged in a battle and not have shunned it.

"The leaders of the CPG forgot all about the independent

role of the party; this was one of the main reasons for the October defeat." (*Pravda,* June 24, 1924.)

A great deal has already been related in discussions concerning what took place in the upper leadership of the German party and the Comintern in 1923, particularly during the latter part of the year, even though many of the things said did not correspond by far to what really took place. Kuusinen in particular has brought much confusion into these questions; the same Kuusinen whose job from 1924 to 1926 was to prove that salvation lay only in the leadership of Zinoviev, just as he applied himself from a certain date in 1926 to prove that the leadership of Zinoviev was ruinous. The necessary authority to pass such responsible judgments is probably conferred upon Kuusinen by the fact that he himself in 1918 did everything that lay in his modest resources to doom the revolution of the Finnish proletariat to destruction.[32]

There have been several attempts, after the event, to attribute to me a solidarity with the line of Brandler. In the USSR these attempts were camouflaged because too many of those on the scene knew the real state of affairs. In Germany this was done openly because no one knew anything there. Quite accidentally, I find in my possession a printed fragment of the ideological struggle that occurred at that time in our Central Committee over the question of the German revolution. In the documents of the January 1924 conference, I am directly accused by the Political Bureau of a hostile and distrustful attitude towards the German Central Committee in the period prior to its capitulation. Here is what we find said there:

". . . Comrade Trotsky, before leaving the session of the Central Committee [September 1923 plenum], made a speech which profoundly disturbed all the members of the Central Committee and in which he alleged that the leadership of the German Communist Party was worthless and that the Central Committee of the German CP was permeated with fatalism, sleepy-headedness, etc. Comrade Trotsky then declared that the German revolution was doomed to failure. This speech had a depressing effect on all those present. But the great majority of the comrades were of the opinion that this phillipic was called forth by an episode [?!], in no way connected with the German revolution, which occurred during the plenum of the Central Committee and that this speech *did not correspond to the objective state of affairs.*" (*Documents of the Conference of the CPSU,* January 1924, p. 14. Our emphasis.)

No matter how the members of the Central Committee may have sought to explain my warning, which was not the first one, it was dictated only by concern over the fate of the German revolution. Unfortunately, events fully confirmed my position; in part because the majority of the Central Committee of the leading party, according to their own admission, did not grasp in time that my warning fully "corresponded to the objective state of affairs." Of course, I did not propose hastily to replace Brandler's Central Committee by some other (on the eve of decisive events such a change would have been sheerest adventurism), but I did propose from the summer of 1923 that a much more timely and resolute position be taken on the question of the preparation of the armed insurrection and of the necessary mobilization of forces for the support of the German Central Committee. The latter-day attempts to ascribe to me a solidarity with the line of the Brandlerite Central Committee, whose mistakes were only a reflection of the general mistakes of the Comintern leadership, were chiefly due to the fact that *after the capitulation* of the German party, I was opposed to making a scapegoat of Brandler, *although,* or more correctly, *because* I judged the German defeat to be much more serious than did the majority of the Central Committee. In this case as in others, I fought against the inadmissible system which only seeks to maintain the infallibility of the central leadership by periodic removals of national leaderships, subjecting the latter to savage persecutions and even expulsions from the party.

In the *Lessons of October,* written by me under the influence of the capitulation of the German Central Committee, I developed the idea that under the conditions of the present epoch, a revolutionary situation can be lost for several years in the course of a few days. It may be hard to believe, but this opinion was stamped as "Blanquism"[33] and "individualism." The innumerable articles written against the *Lessons of October* reveal how completely the experiences of the October Revolution have been forgotten and how little its lessons have penetrated the consciousness. It is a typical Menshevist dodge to shift responsibility for the mistakes of the leaders on the "masses" or to minimize the importance of leadership *in general,* in order thus to diminish its guilt. It arises from the total incapacity to arrive at the dialectic understanding of the "superstructure" in general, of the superstructure of the class which is the party, and the superstructure of the party in the shape of its central leadership. There are epochs during which even Marx and Engels could not drive historical development forward a single inch; there are other epochs during which men of much smaller caliber, standing at the helm, can check the development of the international revolution for a number of years.

The attempts made recently to represent the matter as though I had repudiated the *Lessons of October* are entirely absurd. To be sure, I have "admitted" one "mistake" of secondary importance. When I wrote my *Lessons of October,* that is, in the summer of 1924, it seemed to me that Stalin held a position further to the left (i.e., left centrist) than Zinoviev in the autumn of 1923. I was not quite abreast of the inner life of the group that played the role of the secret center of the majority faction apparatus. The documents published after the split of this factional grouping, especially the purely Brandlerist letter of Stalin[34] to Zinoviev and Bukharin, convinced me of the incorrectness of my estimation of these personal groupings, which, however, had nothing to do with the essence of the problems raised. But even this error as to personalities is not a major one. Centrism is quite capable, it is true, of making big zigzags to the left but as the "evolution" of Zinoviev has once again demonstrated, it is utterly incapable of conducting a revolutionary line in the least systematic.

The ideas developed by me in the *Lessons of October* retain their full force today. Moreover, they have been confirmed over and over again since 1924.

Among the numerous difficulties in a proletarian revolution, there is a particular, concrete, and specific difficulty. It arises out of the position and tasks of the revolutionary party leadership during a sharp turn of events. Even the most revolutionary parties run the risk of lagging behind and of counterposing the slogans and measures of struggle of yesterday to the new tasks and new exigencies. And there cannot, generally, be a sharper turn of events than that which creates the necessity for the armed insurrection of the proletariat. It is here that the danger arises that the policy of the party leadership and of the party as a whole does not correspond to the conduct of the class and the exigencies of the situation. During a relatively languid course of political life, such incongruities are remedied, even if with losses, but without a catastrophe. But in periods of acute revolutionary crisis, it is precisely *time* that is lacking to eliminate the incongruity and to redress the front, as it were, under fire. The periods of the maximum sharpening of a revolutionary crisis are by their very nature transitory. The incongruity between a revolutionary leadership (hesitation, vacillation, temporizing in the face of the furious assault of the bourgeoisie) and the objective tasks, can lead in the course of a few weeks and even days to a catastrophe and to a loss of what took years of work to prepare.

Of course, the incongruity between the leadership and the party or between the party and the class can also be of an opposite character, that is to say, in cases when the leadership runs ahead of the development of the revolution and confounds the fifth month of pregnancy with the ninth. The clearest example of such an incongruity was to be observed in Germany in March 1921. There we had in this party the extreme manifestation of the "infantile disease of leftism," and as a consequence of it—putschism (revolutionary adventurism). This danger is quite actual for the future as well. That is why the teachings of the Third Congress of the Comintern retain their full force. But the German experience of 1923 brought before us the opposite danger in harsh reality: the situation is ripe and the leadership lags behind. By the time the leadership succeeds in accommodating itself to the situation, the latter has already changed; the masses are in retreat and the relationship of forces worsens abruptly.

In the German defeat of 1923, there were, of course, many national peculiarities but there also were profoundly typical features which indicate a general danger. This danger may be termed as *the crisis of the revolutionary leadership on the eve of the transition to the armed insurrection.* The rank and file of the proletarian party are by their very nature far less susceptible to the pressure of bourgeois public opinion. But certain elements of the party tops and the middle stratum of the party will unfailingly succumb in larger or smaller measure to the material and ideological terror of the bourgeoisie at the decisive moment. To dismiss this danger is not to cope with it. To be sure, there is no panacea against it suitable for all cases. But the first necessary step in fighting a peril is to understand its source and its nature. The inevitable appearance or development of a right-wing grouping in every communist party during the "pre-October" period reflects on the one hand the immense objective difficulties and dangers inherent in this "leap" and on the other hand the furious pressure of bourgeois public opinion. Herein lies the gist and the import of the right-wing grouping. And this is precisely why hesitations and vacillations arise inevitably in the communist parties at the very moment when they are most dangerous. In our party, only a minority of the party tops was seized by vacillations in 1917, and they were overcome, thanks to the harsh energy of Lenin. In Germany, the leadership as a whole vacillated and this irresolution was transmitted to the party and through it to the class. The revolutionary situation was thereby missed. In China, where the workers and poor peasants were fighting for the seizure of power, *the central leadership worked against this struggle*. All these, of course, are not the last crises of the leadership in the most decisive historical moments. To reduce these inevitable crises to a minimum is one of the most important tasks of each communist party and of the Comintern as a whole. This cannot be achieved except by arriving at a complete understanding of the experiences of October 1917 and the political content of the then Right Opposition inside our party in contrast to the experiences of the German party in 1923.

Herein precisely is the gist of the *Lessons of October*.

5. THE BASIC STRATEGICAL MISTAKE OF THE FIFTH CONGRESS

We have had, beginning with the end of 1923, a whole series of documents of the Comintern as well as declarations of its leaders on the subject of the "mistake in tempo" committed in the autumn of 1923, all accompanied by the invariable references to Marx, who, you see, also had miscalculated in his dates. At the same time, they passed in deliberate silence over the question whether the "mistake in tempo" of the Comintern consisted in underestimating or, on the contrary, overestimating the proximity of the critical moment of the seizure of power. In conformity with the regime of double bookkeeping that has become traditional for the leadership in recent years, a blank space was left for either the former or latter construction.

It is not difficult, however, to draw the conclusion from the entire policy of the Comintern during this period that throughout 1924 and for the greater part of 1925 the leadership of the Comintern held the view that the high point of the German crisis was still ahead. The reference to Marx was, therefore, hardly in place. For while Marx, owing to his foresight, occasionally perceived the impending revolution closer than it really was, he never had the occasion of failing to recognize the lineaments of revolution when it stood directly before him or of subsequently stubbornly accepting the backside for the face of the revolution, after the latter had already turned its rear.

At the Thirteenth Conference of the CPSU, Zinoviev, upon putting in circulation the equivocal formula on the "mistake in tempo," declared:

"The Executive Committee of the Communist International must say to you that should similar events repeat themselves, we would do the very same thing in the very same situation." (*Pravda,* January 25, 1924.)

This promise had the earmarks of a threat.

On February 20, 1924, Zinoviev declared at a conference of the International Red Aid that the situation in the whole of Europe was such that "we must not expect there a period now, no matter how brief, of even an external pacification, any lull whatever. . . . Europe is entering into the phase of decisive events. . . . Germany is apparently marching towards a sharpened civil war. . . ." (*Pravda,* February 2, 1924.)

Early in February 1924, the Presidium of the ECCI said in its resolution on the lessons of the German events:

"The Communist Party of Germany must not remove from the agenda the question of the uprising and the seizure of power. *On the contrary* [!] this question must stand before us in all its concreteness and urgency. . . ." (*Pravda,* February 7, 1924.)

On March 26, 1924, the ECCI wrote to the German Communist Party:

"The mistake in the evaluation of the tempo of events [what kind of a mistake?—L.T.] made in October 1923, caused the party great difficulties. Nevertheless, it is *only an episode.* The fundamental estimate remains the same as before." (*Pravda,* April 20, 1924. Our emphasis.)

From all this the ECCI drew the following conclusion:

"The German Communist Party must continue as hitherto to exert all its forces in the work to arm the working class. . . ."

(*Pravda,* April 19, 1924.)

The great historical tragedy of 1923—the surrender without a struggle of the great revolutionary position—was appraised six months later as an episode. "Only an episode!" Europe is still suffering today from the gravest consequences of this "episode." The fact that the Comintern did not have to convoke a congress for four years, like the fact that the left wing was crushed in one party of the Comintern after the other, is in the same measure a result of this "episode" of 1923.

The Fifth Congress met eight months after the defeat of the German proletariat, when all the consequences of this catastrophe were already manifest. Here it was not even the case of having to forecast something coming but to see that which is. The fundamental tasks of the Fifth Congress were: first, to call this defeat clearly and relentlessly by its name, and to lay bare its "subjective" cause, allowing no one to hide behind the pretext of objective conditions; secondly, to establish the beginning of a new stage during which the masses would temporarily drift away, the social democracy grow, and the communist party lose in influence; thirdly, to prepare the Comintern for all this so that it would not be caught unawares and to equip it with the necessary methods of defensive struggle and organizational consolidation until the arrival of a new change in the situation.

But in all these questions the congress adopted a directly opposite attitude.

Zinoviev defined the import of the German events at the congress in the following manner: "We expected the German revolution but it did not come." (*Pravda,* June 22, 1924.)

In reality, however, the revolution had the right to answer: "I did come but you, gentlemen, arrived too late at the rendezvous."

The leaders of the congress reckoned together with Brandler that we had "overestimated" the situation, when, in reality, "we" had estimated it far too lightly and too late. Zinoviev reconciled himself very easily with this so-called "overestimation" of his. He saw the chief evil elsewhere.

"Overestimating the situation was not the worst thing. What is much worse, as the example of Saxony showed, is the fact that there are still many social democratic survivals left in the ranks of our party." (*Pravda,* June 24, 1924.)

Zinoviev did not see the catastrophe, and he was not alone. Together with him the whole Fifth Congress simply passed over this greatest defeat of the world revolution. The German events were analyzed principally from the angle of the policies of the communists . . . in the Saxon Landtag.[35] In its resolution, the congress lauded the ECCI for having ". . . condemned the opportunistic conduct of the German Central Committee and, *above all,* its perverted application of the united front tactic during the Saxon government experiment." (*Pravda,* June 29, 1924.)

This is somewhat like condemning a murderer "above all" for failing to take off his hat upon entering the home of his victim.

"The Saxon experience," insisted Zinoviev, "created a new situation. It carried a threat of beginning the liquidation of the revolutionary tactic of the Communist International." (*Pravda,* June 24, 1924.)

And inasmuch as the "Saxon experience" was condemned and Brandler deposed, nothing else remained except to pass on to the next business on the agenda.

"The general political perspectives," said Zinoviev, and the congress with him, "remain essentially as before. The situation is pregnant with revolution. New class struggles are already unfolding again. A gigantic struggle is on the march. . . ." etc. (*Pravda,* June 24, 1924.)

How flimsy and unreliable is a "leftism" that strains at a gnat and cooly swallows a camel.

Those who were wide awake to the situation and pushed the significance of the October defeat to the foreground, those who pointed out the inevitable subsequent lengthy period of revolutionary ebb and temporary consolidation ("stabilization") of capitalism (with all the ensuing political consequences), the leadership of the Fifth Congress endeavored to brand as opportunists and liquidators of the revolution. This is what Zinoviev and Bukharin set as their main task. Ruth Fischer, who together with them underestimated the defeat of the previous year, saw in the Russian Opposition *"the loss of the perspective of world revolution, the lack of faith in the proximity of the German and European revolution,* a hopeless pessimism and the liquidation of the European revolution, etc." (*Pravda,* June 25, 1924.)

It is needless to explain that those who were most directly to blame for the defeat howled loudest against the "liquidators," that is, against those who refused to label defeats as victories. Thus Kolarov thundered against Radek who had the audacity to consider the defeat of the Bulgarian party[36] as a decisive one:

"The defeats of the party were decisive neither in June nor in September. The CP of Bulgaria stands firm and is preparing itself for new battles." (Speech of Comrade Kolarov at the Fifth Congress.)

Instead of a Marxian analysis of the defeats—irresponsible bureaucratic bluster triumphing all along the line. Yet Bolshevik strategy is incompatible with smug and soulless Kolarovism.

A good deal of the work of the Fifth World Congress was correct and necessary. The struggle against the right tendencies, which sought to raise their head, was absolutely urgent. But this struggle was sidetracked, confused, and distorted by the radically false estimate of the situation, as a result of which everything was jumbled and those were classed in the camp of the right who were able to see better and more clearly the events of yesterday, today, and tomorrow. Had the Lefts of that time triumphed at the Third World Congress, Lenin would have been classed together with Levi, Clara Zetkin, and others in the right wing on the same grounds. The ideological muddle engendered by the false political orientation of the Fifth Congress became subsequently the source of new great misfortunes.

The estimate adopted by the congress in the political sphere was likewise carried over completely to the economic field. The symptoms of the economic consolidation of the German bourgeoisie, which were already manifest, were either denied or ignored. Varga, who always dishes up the economic facts to conform with the current reigning political tendency, brought in a report this time, too, that ". . . there are no perspectives of the recovery of capitalism." (*Pravda*, June 28, 1924.)

But a year later, after the "recovery" had been *belatedly* rechristened "stabilization," Varga painstakingly made the discovery after the event. By that time, the Opposition had already to bear up under the accusation of not recognizing the stabilization because it had the audacity to establish the commencement of it a year and a half before, while in 1925 it already discerned tendencies undermining this stabilization (*Where Is Britain Going?*).[37]

The Fifth Congress perceived political processes and ideological groupings as they were reflected in the distorted mirror of a false orientation; and this also gave birth to its resolution classifying the Russian Opposition as a "petty-bourgeois deviation." History has corrected this mistake in its own fashion by forcing Zinoviev, the chief prosecuting attorney at the Fifth Congress, to admit publicly[38] two years later that the central nucleus of the Opposition in 1923 had been correct in all the fundamental questions at issue.

From the basic strategical mistake of the Fifth Congress necessarily had also to arise a lack of understanding of the processes occurring within the German and the international social democracy. At the congress there were speeches only of its decay, disintegration, and collapse. Zinoviev had the following to say with regard to the last Reichstag elections in which the Communist Party of Germany received 3.7 million votes:

"If on the parliamentary field in Germany, we have a proportion of 62 communists to 100 social democrats, then this should serve as proof to every one of *how close we are to win-*

ning the majority of the German working class." (*Pravda,* June 22, 1924.)

Zinoviev understood absolutely nothing of the dynamics of the process; the influence of the CPG during that year and the following years did not grow but declined. The 3.7 million votes represented only an impressive *remnant* of the decisive influence that the party had had over the majority of the German proletariat towards the end of 1923. This number would undoubtedly diminish in the subsequent elections.

In the meantime, the social democracy which was going to pieces in 1923 like a rotted mat of straw, began to recover systematically after the defeat of the revolution at the end of 1923, to start up and to grow, and chiefly at the expense of communism. Inasmuch as we had foreseen this—and how could one have failed to forsee it?—our forecast was attributed to our "pessimism." Is it still necessary now, after the last elections in May 1928 in which the social democrats received more than 9 million votes, to prove that we were correct when at the beginning of 1924 we spoke and wrote that there must inevitably follow a revival of the social democracy for a certain period, while the "optimists" who were already chanting the requiem over the social democracy were grossly mistaken? Above all, the Fifth Congress of the Comintern was grossly mistaken.

The second youth of the social democracy, exhibiting all the traits of doddering senility, is naturally not lasting. The demise of the social democracy is inevitable. But how long it will be before it dies is nowhere established. This, too, depends on us. To bring it closer, we must be able to face the facts, to recognize in due time the turning points of a political situation, to call a defeat a defeat, and to learn to foresee the coming day.

If the German social democracy still represents a force of many millions today, and this, too, within the working class, then there are two immediate causes for it. First, the defeat of the German party which capitulated in the fall of 1923, and second, the false strategical orientation of the Fifth Congress.

In January 1924 the ratio between the communists and the social democratic voters was almost 2 to 3, but four months later this proportion fell badly to slightly more than 1 to 3; in other words, during this period, taken as a whole, we did not draw closer to the conquest of the majority of the working class but drew further away from it. And this despite an indubitable strengthening of our party during the past year which, with a correct policy, can and must become the point of departure for a real conquest of the majority.

We shall take the occasion later to dwell on the political consequences of the position adopted by the Fifth Congress. But isn't it already clear that there cannot be serious talk of Bolshevik strategy without the ability to survey both the basic curve of our epoch as a whole, and its individual segments which are at every given moment of the same importance for the party leadership as railway curves are for the locomotive engineer? To open wide the throttle on a steeply banked curve is surely to run the train over the embankment.

Yet, only a few months ago *Pravda* had to acknowledge more or less distinctly the correctness of the estimate we made as early as the end of 1923. On January 28, 1928, *Pravda* wrote:

"The phase of a certain [!] apathy and depression which set in after the defeat of 1923 and permitted German capital to strengthen its positions, is *beginning* to pass."

A "certain" depression which set in the fall of 1923 is first beginning to pass only in 1928. These words published after a delay of four years are a ruthless condemnation of the false orientation established by the Fifth Congress and also of that system of leadership which does not lay bare and illumine the errors committed but covers them up and thereby extends the radius of the ideological confusion.

A draft program which passes by without evaluating either the events of 1923 or the basic mistake of the Fifth Congress simply turns its back on the real questions of a revolutionary strategy of the proletariat in the imperialist epoch.

6. THE 'DEMOCRATIC-PACIFIST ERA' AND FASCISM

The capitulation of German communism in the autumn of 1923, which removed the threatening proletarian danger with a minimum of civil war, inevitably had to weaken the position not only of the Communist Party but also of fascism. For even a civil war in which the bourgeoisie is victorious undermines the conditions of capitalist exploitation. Already at that time, that is, at the end of 1923, we fought against the exaggeration of the strength and the danger of German fascism. We insisted that fascism would be relegated to the background while the political stage in the whole of Europe would be occupied for a certain period by the democratic and pacifist groupings: the Left Bloc in France, the Labour Party in England. And the strengthening of these groupings would in turn provide an impetus for a new growth of the German social democracy. Instead of understanding this inevitable process and organizing the struggle against it along a *new* front, the official leadership continued to identify fascism with the social democracy and to prophecy their joint collapse in an imminent civil war.

The problem of the interrelations between the United States and Europe was very intimately bound up with the question of fascism and the social democracy. Only the defeat of the German revolution in 1923 made it possible for American capital to begin with the realization of its plans for the (momentarily) "peaceful" subjugation of Europe. Under these circumstances, the American problem should have been considered in its full magnitude. Instead, the leadership of the Fifth Congress simply passed it by. It proceeded entirely from the internal situation in Europe without even noticing that the long postponement of the European revolution had immediately shifted the axis of international relations towards the side of an American offensive upon Europe. This offensive assumed the shape of an economic "consolidation" of Europe, its normalization and pacification, and a "recovery" of democratic principles. Not only the ruined petty bourgeoisie but also the average worker said to himself: since the Communist Party failed to achieve victory, then maybe the social democracy will bring us not victory (nobody expects that of it), but a piece of bread through a revival of industry with the aid of American gold. It was necessary to understand that the vile fiction of American pacifism with the dollar lining—after the defeat of the German revolution—would and did become the most important factor in the life of Europe. Not only did the German social democracy rise again, thanks to this leaven, but to a great extent also the French Radicals and the English Labour Party.

As a counterpoise to this new enemy front, it should have been pointed out that bourgeois Europe will be able to exist and maintain itself only as a financial vassal of the United States and that the pacifism of the latter is tantamount to an endeavor to put Europe on hunger rations. Instead of making this very perspective the point of departure of the new struggle against the social democracy with its new religion of Americanism, the leadership of the Comintern turned its fire in the opposite direction. It imputed to us the asinine theory of a normalized imperialism, without wars and revolutions, placed on American rations.

During the very same February sessions at which the Presidium of the ECCI—four months prior to the congress—declared that the armed insurrection "stood concretely and urgently" on the order of the day for the German party, it also gave the following estimation of the situation in France, which was just at that time approaching the "left" parliamentary elections:

"This pre-election fever also affects only the most insignificant and weakest parties and *dead political groupings. The Socialist Party* has been aroused and stirred back to life under the rays of the approaching elections. . . ." (*Pravda,* February 7, 1924.)

At a time when a wave of petty-bourgeois pacifist leftism was quite obviously ascending in France, carrying away broad sections of the workers and weakening both the party of the proletariat and the fascist detachments of capital; in a word, in face of the victory of the "Left Bloc," the leadership of the Comintern proceeded from a directly opposite perspective. It flatly denied the possibility of a pacifist phase and, on the eve of the May 1924 elections, spoke of the French Socialist Party, the left banner-bearer of petty-bourgeois pacifism, as an already "dead political grouping." At that time we protested against this lightminded estimation of the social-patriotic party in a special letter addressed to the delegation of the CPSU. But all in vain. The leadership of the Comintern stubbornly persisted in considering as "leftism" its disregard of these facts. Hence arose that distorted and sordid polemic, as always in recent years, over democratic pacifism which brought so much confusion into the parties of the Comintern. The spokesmen of the Opposition were accused of pacifist prejudices only because they did not share the prejudices of the leadership of the Comintern and foresaw at the right time that the defeat suffered by the German proletariat without a struggle (after a brief strengthening of the fascist tendencies), would inevitably bring the petty-bourgeois parties to the fore and strengthen the social democracy.

We have already mentioned above that Zinoviev, at a conference of the International Red Aid some three or four months before the victory of the Labour Party in England and the Left Bloc in France, declared in an obvious polemic against me:

"In practically the whole of Europe the situation is such that we need expect no period now, no matter how brief, of even an external pacifism, or any kind of lull. . . . Europe is entering into the stage of decisive events. . . . Germany is apparently heading towards a violent civil war. . . ." (*Pravda,* February 2, 1924.)

Zinoviev, to all appearances, had completely forgotten that back at the Fourth Congress in 1922 I was successful, despite rather stubborn opposition by Zinoviev himself and Bukharin, in introducing at a commission an amendment (considerably modified, it is true) to the resolution of the congress; this amendment speaks of the impending approach of a "pacifist-democratic" era as a probable stage on the road of the political decline of the bourgeois state and as a first step to the rule of communism or—fascism.

At the Fifth Congress, which met already after the rise of the "left" governments in England and France, Zinoviev recalled—very appropriately—this amendment of mine and proclaimed loudly as follows:

"At the present moment the international situation is characterized by fascism, by martial law, and by a rising wave of the white terror against the proletariat. But this does not exclude the possibility that in the near future the open reaction of the bourgeoisie will be replaced in the most important countries by a 'democratic-pacifist era.'"

And Zinoviev went on to add with satisfaction:

"This was said in 1922. Thus the Comintern, a year and a half ago, definitely predicted a democratic-pacifist era." (*Pravda*, June 22, 1924.)

It's the truth. The prognosis which had so long been held against me as a "pacifist" deviation (as *my deviation* and not that of the historical course of development) came in very handy at the Fifth Congress during the honeymoon weeks of the MacDonald and Herriot ministries. That is how, unfortunately, matters stood with prognoses in general.

We ought to add that Zinoviev and the majority of the Fifth Congress construed too literally the old perspective of the "democratic-pacifist era" as a stage on the road of capitalist decay. Thus Zinoviev declared at the Fifth Congress: "The democratic-pacifist era is a symptom of capitalist decay."

And in his conclusion he said again: "*I repeat that precisely the democratic-pacifist era is a symptom of the decay and the incurable crisis* [of capitalism]." (*Pravda,* July 1, 1924.)

This would have been correct had there been no Ruhr crisis and if evolution had proceeded more smoothly without such a historical "leap." This would have been doubly and trebly correct had the German proletariat achieved the victory in 1923. In that case, the regimes of MacDonald and Herriot would only have meant an English and French "Kerensky period." But the Ruhr crisis did break out and posed point-blank the question of who was to be the master in the house. The German proletariat did not achieve the victory but suffered a decisive defeat and in such a way as was bound to encourage and consolidate the German bourgeoisie to the highest degree. Faith in the revolution was shattered throughout Europe for a number of years. Under such conditions the governments of MacDonald and Herriot by no means implied either a Kerensky period or generally the decay of the bourgeoisie. On the contrary, they would and could become only the ephemeral precursors of more serious, more solid, and more self-assured bourgeois governments. The Fifth Congress failed to understand this because by failing to estimate the extent of the German catastrophe and by reducing the latter merely to a question of the comedy in the Saxon Landtag, it remained unaware of the fact that the proletariat of Europe was already in a political retreat all along the front, and that our task consisted not in an armed insurrection but in a new orientation, in rearguard engagements, and in the strengthening of the party's organizational positions, above all in the trade unions.

In connection with the question of the "era," a polemic arose over fascism, no less distorted and unscrupulous. The Opposition maintained that the bourgeoisie advances its fascist shoulder only at the moment when an immediate revolutionary danger threatens the foundations of its regime and when the normal organs of the bourgeois state prove inadequate. In this sense, active fascism signifies a state of civil war on the part of capitalist society waged against the rebelling proletariat. Contrariwise, the bourgeoisie is forced to advance its left, the social democratic shoulder, either in a period that precedes that of the civil war, so as to deceive, lull, and demoralize the proletariat, or in a period following upon a serious and lasting victory over the proletariat, i.e., when it is forced to lay hold of the broad masses of the people parliamentarily, among them also the workers disappointed by the revolution, in order to reestablish the normal regime. In opposition to this analysis, which is absolutely irrefutable theoretically and which was confirmed by the entire course of the struggle, the leadership of the Comintern set up the senseless and oversimplified contention of the *identity* of the social democracy with fascism. Proceeding from the incontestable fact that the social democracy is no less servile towards the foundations of bourgeois society than fascism and is always ready to volunteer its Noske at the moment of danger, the leadership of the Comintern entirely expunged the political difference between the social democracy and fascism, and together with that also the difference between a period of open civil war and the period of the "normalization" of the class struggle. In a word, everything was turned on its head, entangled and muddled up, only in order to maintain the sham of an orientation upon the immediate development of the civil war. Just as though nothing out of the ordinary had happened in Germany and Europe in the fall of 1923; an episode—and that was all!

In order to show the course and the level of this polemic we must quote from the article by Stalin "On the International Situation" (*Pravda,* September 20, 1924):

"Many believe," Stalin said, polemizing against me, "that the bourgeoisie came to "pacifism" and "democracy" not out of necessity but of its own free will, of free choice, so to speak."

This basic historico-philosophical thesis which it is positively embarrassing to dwell upon, is followed by two principal conclusions:

"First, it is false that fascism is only a combat organization of the bourgeoisie. Fascism is not merely a military-technical category [?!]."

It is incomprehensible why the combat organization of bourgeois society must be considered a technical and not a political "category." But what is fascism? Stalin's indirect answer reads: "The social democracy is objectively a moderate wing of fascism."

One might say that the social democracy is the left wing of bourgeois society and this definition would be quite correct if one does not construe it so as to oversimplify it and thereby forget that the social democracy still leads millions of workers behind it and within certain limits is constrained to reckon not only with the will of its bourgeois master but also with the interests of its deluded proletarian constituency. But it is absolutely senseless to characterize the social democracy as the "moderate wing of fascism." What becomes of bourgeois society itself in that case? In order to orient oneself in the most elementary manner in politics, one must not throw everything into a single heap but instead distinguish between the social democracy and fascism, which represent two poles of the bourgeois front—*united at the moment of danger*—but two *poles,* nevertheless. Is it still necessary to emphasize this now, after the May 1928 elections, characterized at one and the same time by the decline of fascism and the growth of the social democracy, to which, incidentally, the Communist Party in this case, too, proposed a united front of the working class?

"Secondly," the article continues, "it is false that the decisive battles have already occurred; that the proletariat has suffered a defeat in these battles; and the bourgeoisie has become consolidated as a result. The decisive struggles have not yet taken place at all, even if [?] only because there have not been real Bolshevik mass parties as yet."

So, the bourgeoisie could not consolidate itself because there have been no struggles as yet, and there have been no struggles "even if only" because there has not yet been a Bolshevik party. Thus what hinders the bourgeoisie from consolidating itself is . . . the absence of a Bolshevik party. In reality, however, it was precisely the absence—not so much of the party as of a Bolshevik leadership—that helped the bourgeoisie to consolidate itself. If an army capitulates to the enemy in a critical situation without a battle, then this capitulation completely takes the place of a "decisive battle," in politics as in war. Back in 1850 Engels taught that a party which has missed a revolutionary situation disappears from the scene for a long time. But is there anybody still unaware that Engels, who lived "before imperialism," is obsolete today? So, Stalin writes as follows: "Without such [Bolshevik] parties no struggles for the dictatorship are possible under the conditions of imperialism."

One is, therefore, compelled to assume that such struggles were quite possible in the epoch of Engels, when the law of uneven development had not yet been discovered.

This whole chain of thought is crowned, appropriately enough, by a political prognosis:

"Finally, it is also false . . . that out of this "pacifism" must arise the consolidation of the power of the bourgeoisie and a postponement of the revolution for an indeterminate period of time."

Nevertheless, such a postponement did result, not according to Stalin, it is true, but according to Engels. A year later, when it became clear even to the blind that the position of the bourgeoisie had become stronger and that the revolution was adjourned for an indefinite time, Stalin set himself to accuse us of refusing to recognize stabilization. This accusation became particularly insistent in the period when the "stabilization" already began to crack anew, when a new revolutionary wave drew near in England and China. And this whole hopeless muddle served to fulfill the functions of a leading line! It should be remarked that the definition of fascism and its relations to the social democracy contained in the draft (Chapter 2), despite the ambiguities deliberately introduced (so as to tie up the past), is far more rational and correct than the schema of Stalin quoted above, which was essentially the schema of the Fifth Congress. But this insignificant step forward does not solve the question. A program of the Comintern, after the experiences of the last decade, cannot be left without a characterization of the revolutionary situation, of its origin and disappearance, without pointing out the classic mistakes committed in the evaluation of such a situation, without explaining how the locomotive engineer must act at the curves, and without inculcating into the parties the truth that there are such situations in which the success of the world revolution depends upon two or three days of struggle.

7. THE RIGHT LEAVEN OF ULTRALEFT POLICY

After the period of turbulent high tide in 1923, began the period of a long-lasting ebb. In the language of strategy this meant an orderly retreat, rearguard battles, the strengthening of our positions within the mass organizations, the reinspection of our own ranks, and the cleansing and sharpening of our theoretical and political weapons. This position was branded as liquidationism. The latter concept, as well as other concepts of the Bolshevik lexicon in late years, met with the grossest abuse; there was no longer any teaching and training but only the sowing of confusion and error. Liquidationism is the renunciation of the revolution, the attempt to substitute the roads and methods of reformism for the roads and methods of revolution. The Leninist policy has nothing in common with liquidationism; but it has just as little to do with a disregard of the changes in the objective situation and with maintaining verbally the course towards the armed insurrection after the revolution has already turned its back upon us, and when it is necessary to resume the long, stubborn, systematic, and laborious work among the masses in order to prepare the party for a new revolution ahead.

On ascending the stairs a different type of movement is required from that which is needed to descend. Most dangerous is such a situation as finds a man, with the lights out, raising his foot to ascend when the steps before him lead downward. Falls, injuries, and dislocations are then inevitable. The leadership of the Comintern in 1924 did everything in its power to suppress both the criticism of the experiences of the German October and all criticism in general. And it kept stubbornly repeating: the workers are heading directly for the revolution—the stairs lead upward. Small wonder that the directives of the Fifth Congress, applied during the revolutionary ebb, led to cruel political falls and dislocations!

Number 5-6 of the *Information Bulletin of the German Opposition*,[39] March 1, 1927, stated:

"The greatest mistakes of the Lefts at this party congress [the Frankfurt congress in the spring of 1924, when they took over the leadership], consisted in their *not speaking relentlessly enough to the party of the gravity of the defeat of 1923; in their not drawing the necessary conclusions, in not explaining to the party, soberly and without embellishment, the tendencies of relative stabilization of capitalism, and in not formulating a corresponding program for the impending period with its struggles and slogans*. It was entirely possible to do this and to underscore sharply the theses of the program, as was correct and absolutely necessary." (Our emphasis.)

These lines were to us an indication at that time that a section of the German left, who participated during the Fifth Congress in the struggle against our alleged "liquidationism," had seriously understood the lessons of 1924–25. And this brought us subsequently closer on the basis of principle.

The key year of the *sharp turn in the situation was the year 1924*. Yet the recognition that this sharp turn had occurred ("stabilization") followed only a year and a half later. It is hardly astonishing, therefore, that the years 1924–25 were the years of left mistakes and putschist experiments. The Bulgarian terrorist adventure, like the tragic history of the Estonian armed uprising of December 1924, was an outburst of despair resulting from a false orientation. The fact that these attempts to rape the historical process by means of a putsch were left without a critical investigation led to a relapse in Canton towards the end of 1927. In politics not even the smallest mistakes pass unpunished, much less the big ones. And the greatest mistake is to cover up mistakes, seeking mechanically to suppress criticism and a correct Marxian evaluation of the mistakes.

We are not writing a history of the Comintern for the last five years. We bring here only a factual illustration of the two strategical lines at the fundamental stages of this period, and at the same time an illustration of the lifelessness of the draft program for which all these questions do not even exist. We cannot, therefore, give here a description, however general, of the inextricable contradictions which befell the parties of the Comintern, placed between the directives of the Fifth Congress on the one hand and political reality on the other. Of course, not everywhere were the contradictions resolved by such fatal convulsions as was the case in Bulgaria and Estonia in 1924. But always and everywhere the parties felt themselves bound, failed to respond to the aspirations of the masses, went about with eye flaps, and stumbled. In the purely party propaganda and agitation, in the work in the trade unions, on the parliamentary tribune—everywhere the communists had to drag the heavy ball and chain of the false position of the Fifth Congress. Each party, to a lesser or greater degree, fell a victim of the false points of departure. Each chased after phantoms, ignored the real processes, transformed revolutionary slogans into noisy phrases, compromised itself in the eyes of the masses and lost all the ground under its feet. To crown all this, the press of the Comintern was, then as now, deprived of every possibility of assembling, arranging, and publishing facts and figures on the work of the communist parties in recent years. After the defeats, mistakes, and failures, the epigone leadership prefers to execute the retreat and to deal with opponents with all lights turned out.

Finding itself in a cruel and constantly growing contradiction with real factors, the leadership has had to cling ever more to fictitious factors. Losing the ground under its feet the ECCI was constrained to discover revolutionary forces and signs where there were no traces of any. To maintain its balance, it had to clutch at rotten ropes.

In proportion as obvious and growing shifts to the right were going on in the proletariat, there began in the Comintern the phase of idealizing the peasantry, a wholly uncritical exaggeration of every symptom of its "break" with bourgeois society, an embellishment of every ephemeral peasant organization and a downright adulation of "peasant" demagogues.

The *task* of a long and stubborn struggle of the proletarian vanguard against the bourgeoisie and pseudopeasant demagoguery for influence over the most disinherited strata of the peasant poor was being more and more displaced by the *hope* that the peasantry would play a direct and an independent revolutionary role on a national as well as on an international scale.

During 1924, i.e., in the course of the basic year of the "stabilization," the communist press was filled with absolutely fantastic data on the strength of the recently organized Peasants International. Dombal, its representative, reported that the Peasants International, six months after its formation, already embraced several million members.

Then there was enacted the scandalous incident with Radić, who was the leader of the Croatian "Peasants" Party and who, en route from Green Zagreb, thought it advisable to show himself in Red Moscow in order to strengthen his chances to become minister in White Belgrade. On July 9, 1924, Zinoviev in his report to the Leningrad party workers on the results of the Fifth Congress, told of his new "victory":

"At this moment important shifts are taking place within the peasantry. You have all probably heard of the Croatian Peasants Party of Radić. Radić is now in Moscow. He—is a real leader of the people. . . . Behind Radić stands united the entire poor and middle peasantry of Croatia. . . . Radić now has decided in the name of his party to join the Peasants International. We consider this a very important event. . . . The formation of the Peasants International is an event of the greatest importance. Certain comrades did not believe that a large organization would grow out of it. . . . Now we are getting a great auxiliary mass—the peasantry. . . ." (*Pravda,* July 22, 1924.)

And so forth and so on, and more of it.

The leader, La Follette, corresponded, on the other side of the ocean, to the "genuine people's leader," Radić. The representative of the Comintern, Pepper, in order to set the "auxiliary mass"—the American farmers—into motion at an accelerated tempo, drew the young and weak American Communist Party onto the senseless and infamous adventure of creating a "farmer-labor party" around La Follette in order to overthrow quickly American capitalism.

The glad tidings of the proximity of the revolution in the United States based on the farmers filled the speeches and articles of the official leaders of the ECCI at that time. At a session of the Fifth Congress, Kolarov reported:

"In the United States the small farmers have founded a farmer-labor party, which is becoming ever more radical, drawing closer to the communists, and becoming permeated with the idea of the creation of a workers and peasants government in the United States." (*Pravda,* July 6, 1924.)

No more, no less!

From Nebraska came Green—one of the leaders of La Follette's organization—to the Peasants Congress in Moscow. Green also "joined" something or other, and then, as is customary, he later assisted at the St. Paul conference[40] in laying low the Communist Party when it made a feeble attempt to proceed to the realization of Pepper's great plans—the same Pepper who was counsellor to Count Karolyi, an extreme left-winger at the Third Congress, a reformer of Marxism, one of those who slit the throat of the revolution in Hungary.

In its issue of August 29, 1924, *Pravda* complained:

"The American proletariat en masse has not even risen to the level of consciousness of the need for even so collaborationist a party as the English Labour Party is."

And about a month and a half previously, Zinoviev reported to the Leningrad party workers:

"Several million farmers are being voluntarily or involuntarily pushed by the agrarian crisis all at once [!] to the side of the working class." (Pravda, July 22, 1924.)

"And to a workers and peasants government!" immediately added Kolarov.

The press kept repeating that a farmer-labor party would soon be formed in America, "not a purely proletarian, but a class" farmer-labor party for the overthrow of capitalism. What the "not a proletarian, but class" character was supposed to mean, no astrologist on either side of the ocean could possibly explain. In the long run it was only a Pepperized edition of the idea of a "two-class workers and peasants party," of which we will have occasion to speak again in greater detail in connection with the lessons of the Chinese revolution. Suffice here to remark that this reactionary idea of nonproletarian but class parties arose entirely from the pseudo-"left" policy of 1924 which, losing the ground from under its feet, clutched at Radić, La Follette, and the inflated figures of the Peasants International.

"We are now witnessing," retailed the academician of commonplaces, Milyutin, "an extraordinarily important and significant process of the splitting away of the peasant masses from the bourgeoisie, of the peasantry on march against the bourgeoisie, and of the increasing strengthening of the united front between the peasantry and the working class in the capitalist countries in struggle against the capitalist system." (*Pravda,* July 27, 1924.)

In the course of the whole year of 1924, the press of the Comintern did not weary of telling about the universal "radicalization of the peasant masses," as though something independent could be expected from this, in most cases, only imaginary radicalization of the peasants in a period when the workers were obviously moving to the right, when the social democracy grew in strength and the bourgeoisie consolidated its position!

We encounter the same failing in political vision towards the end of 1927 and the beginning of 1928 with regard to China. After every great and deep-going revolutionary crisis, in which the proletariat suffers a decisive and long lasting defeat, the spurts of ferment still continue for a long time among the semiproletarian urban and rural masses, as the circles spread in the water after a stone has fallen in. Whenever a leadership ascribes an independent significance to these circles and, contrary to the processes within the working class, interprets them as symptoms of an approaching revolution, bear well in mind that this is an infallible sign that the leadership is heading towards adventures, similar to those in Estonia or Bulgaria in 1924 or Canton in 1927.

During the same period of ultraleftism, the Chinese Communist Party was driven for several years into the Kuomintang, which was characterized by the Fifth Congress as a "sympathizing party" (*Pravda,* June 25, 1924) without any serious attempt to define its class character. As we proceed, we find that the idealization of "the national revolutionary bourgeoisie" became greater and greater. Thus, in the Orient, the false left course, with its eyes shut and burning with impatience, laid the foundation for the subsequent opportunism. It was Martynov himself who was called upon to formulate the opportunist line. Martynov was all the more reliable a counsellor of the Chinese proletariat for having himself tailed behind the petty bourgeoisie during the three Russian revolutions.

In the hunt after an artificial acceleration of the periods, not only were Radić, La Follette, the peasant millions of Dombal, and even Pepper clutched at, but a basically false perspective was also built up for England. The weaknesses of the English Communist Party gave birth at that time to the necessity of replacing it as quickly as possible with a more imposing factor. Precisely then was born the false estimate of the tendencies in English trade unionism. Zinoviev gave us to understand that he counted upon the revolution finding an entrance, not through the narrow gateway of the British Communist Party, but through the broad portals of the trade unions. The struggle to win the masses organized in the trade unions through the Communist Party was replaced by the hope for the swiftest possible utilization of the ready-made apparatus of the trade unions for the purposes of the revolution. Out of this false position sprang the later policy of the Anglo-Russian Committee,[41] which dealt a blow to the Soviet Union as well as to the English working class; a blow surpassed only by the defeat in China.

In the *Lessons of October,* written as early as the summer of 1924, the idea of an accelerated road—accelerated through friendship with Purcell and Cook, as the further development of this idea showed—is refuted as follows:

"Without the party, independently of the party, skipping over the party, through a substitute for the party, the proletarian revolution can never triumph. That is the principal lesson of the last decade. To be sure, the English trade unions can become a powerful lever of the proletarian revolution. They can, for example, under certain conditions and for a certain period, even replace the workers soviets. But they cannot play such a role without the Communist Party and certainly not against it, but only provided that communist influence in the trade unions becomes decisive. We have paid too dearly for this conclusion as *to the role and significance of the party for the proletarian revolution to renounce it so lightly or even to have it weakened.*" (Trotsky, *Works,* vol. 3, part 1, p. 9.)*

The same problem is posed on a wider scale in my book *Where Is Britain Going?*† This book, from beginning to end, is devoted to proving the idea that the English revolution, too,

---

* "The Lessons of October," in Trotsky, *The Challenge of the Left Opposition (1923–25)* (New York: Pathfinder, 1975), p. 252.

† In *Leon Trotsky on Britain* (New York: Pathfinder, 1973).

cannot avoid the portals of communism and that with a correct, courageous, and intransigent policy which steers clear of any illusions with regard to detours, the English Communist Party can grow by leaps and bounds and mature so as to be equal in the course of a few years to the tasks before it.

The left illusions of 1924 rose thanks to the right leaven. In order to conceal the significance of the mistakes and defeats of 1923 from others as well as from oneself, the process of the swing to the right that was taking place in the proletariat had to be denied and revolutionary processes within the other classes optimistically exaggerated. That was the beginning of the downsliding from the proletarian line to the centrist, that is, to the petty-bourgeois line which, in the course of the increasing stabilization, was to liberate itself from its ultraleft shell and reveal itself as a crude collaborationist line in the USSR, in China, in England, in Germany, and everywhere else.

8. THE PERIOD OF RIGHT-CENTRIST DOWNSLIDING

The policy of the most important communist parties, attuned to the Fifth Congress, very soon revealed its complete inefficacy. The mistakes of pseudo-"leftism" which hampered the development of the communist parties, later gave an impetus to new empirical zigzags: namely, to an accelerated sliding down to the right. A cat burned by hot milk shies away from cold water. The "left" central committees of a number of parties were deposed as violently as they had been constituted prior to the Fifth Congress.[42] The adventurist leftism gave way to an open opportunism of the right-centrist type. To comprehend the character and the tempo of this organizational rightward swing, it must be recalled that Stalin, the director of this turn, back in September 1924 appraised the passing of party leadership to Maslow, Ruth Fischer, Treint, Suzanne Girault, and others, as the expression of the Bolshevization of the parties and an answer to the demands of the Bolshevik workers who are marching toward the revolution and "want revolutionary leaders."

Stalin wrote, "The last half year is remarkable in the sense that it presents a radical turning point in the life of the communist parties of the West, in the sense that the social democratic survivals were decisively liquidated, the party cadres Bolshevized, and the opportunist elements isolated." (*Pravda*, September 20, 1924.)

But ten months later the genuine "Bolsheviks" and "revolutionary leaders" were declared social democrats and renegades, ousted from leadership, and driven out of the party.

Despite the panicky character of this change of leaders, frequently effected by resorting to rude and disloyal mechanical measures of the apparatus, it is impossible to draw any rigorous ideological line of demarcation between the phase of ultraleft policy and the period of opportunistic downsliding that followed it.

In the questions of industry and the peasantry in the USSR, of the colonial bourgeoisie, of "peasant" parties in the capitalist countries, of socialism in one country, of the role of the party in the proletarian revolution, the revisionist tendencies already appeared in fullest bloom in 1924–25, cloaked with the banner of the struggle against "Trotskyism," and they found their most distinctly opportunist expression in the resolutions of the conference of the CPSU in April 1925.

Taken as a whole, the course to the right was the attempt at a half-blind, purely empirical, and belated adaptation to the setback of revolutionary development caused by the defeat of 1923. Bukharin's initial formulation, as has already been mentioned, was based on the "permanent" development of the revolution in the most literal and the most mechanical sense of the term. Bukharin granted no "breathing spaces," interruptions, or retreats of any kind; he considered it a revolutionary duty to continue the "offensive" under all circumstances.

The above-quoted article of Stalin, "On the International Situation," which is a sort of program and which marks Stalin's debut on international questions, demonstrates that the second author of the draft program also professed the very same purely mechanical "left" conception during the initial period of the struggle against "Trotskyism." For this conception there existed always and unalterably only the social democracy that was "disintegrating," workers who were becoming "radicalized," communist parties that were "growing," and the revolution that was "approaching." And anybody who looked around and tried to distinguish things was and is a "liquidator."

This "tendency" required a year and a half to sense something new after the break in the situation in Europe in 1923 so as to transform itself panic-stricken, into its opposite. The leadership oriented itself without any synthesized understanding of our epoch and its inner tendencies, only by groping (Stalin) and by supplementing the fragmentary conclusions thus obtained with scholastic schemas renovated for each occasion (Bukharin). The political line as a whole, therefore, represents a chain of zigzags. The ideological line is a kaleidoscope of schemas tending to push to absurdity every segment of the Stalinist zigzag.

The Sixth Congress would act correctly if it decided to elect a special commission in order to compile all the theories created by Bukharin and intended by him to serve as a basis, say, for all the stages of the Anglo-Russian Committee; these theories would have to be compiled chronologically and arranged systematically so as to draw a fever chart of the ideas contained in them. It would be a most instructive strategical diagram. The same also holds for the Chinese revolution, the economic development of the USSR, and all other less important questions. *Blind empiricism multiplied by scholasticism*—such is the course that still awaits merciless condemnation.

The effects of this course showed themselves most fatally in the three most important questions: in the internal policy of the USSR; the Chinese revolution; and in the Anglo-Russian Committee. The effects were in the same direction, but less obvious and less fatal in their immediate consequences, in all the other questions of the policies of the Comintern in general.

As regards the internal questions of the USSR, a sufficiently exhaustive characterization of the policy of downsliding is given in the *Platform of the Bolshevik-Leninists (Opposition)*.[43] We must limit ourselves here merely to this reference to the latter. The *Platform* now receives an apparently most unexpected confirmation in the fact that all the attempts of the present leadership of the CPSU to escape from the consequences of the policy of the years 1923 to 1928 are based upon almost literal quotations from the *Platform,* the authors and adherents of which are dispersed in prisons and exile. The fact, however, that the present leaders have recourse to the *Platform* only in sections and bits, without putting two and two together, makes the new left turn extremely unstable and uncertain; but at the same time it invests the *Platform* with a greater value than ever as the generalized expression of a real Leninist course.

In the *Platform,* the question of the Chinese revolution is dealt with very insufficiently, incompletely, and in part positively falsely by Zinoviev. Because of the decisive importance of this question for the Comintern, we are obliged to subject it to a more detailed investigation in a separate chapter. (See section 3.)

As to the Anglo-Russian Committee, the third most important question from the strategical experiences of the Comintern in recent years, there only remains for us, after all that has already been said by the Opposition in a series of articles, speeches, and theses, to make a brief summary.

The point of departure of the Anglo-Russian Committee, as we have already seen, was the impatient urge to leap over the young and too slowly developing Communist Party. This invested the entire experience with a false character even prior to the general strike.

The Anglo-Russian Committee was looked upon not as an episodic bloc at the tops which would have to be broken and which would inevitably and demonstratively be broken at the very first serious test in order to compromise the General Council. No, not only Stalin, Bukharin, Tomsky, and others, but also Zinoviev saw in it a long-lasting "copartnership"—an instrument for the systematic revolutionization of the English working masses, and if not the gate, at least an approach to the gate through which would stride the revolution of the English proletariat. The further it went, the more the Anglo-Russian Committee became transformed from an episodic alliance into an inviolable principle standing above the real class struggle. This became revealed at the time of the general strike.

The transition of the mass movement into the open revolutionary stage threw back into the camp of the bourgeois reaction those liberal labor politicians who had become somewhat left. They betrayed the general strike openly and deliberately; after which they undermined and betrayed the miners' strike. The possibility of betrayal is always contained in reformism. But this does not mean to say that reformism and betrayal are one and the same thing at every moment. Not quite. Temporary agreements may be made with the reformists whenever they take a step forward. But to maintain a bloc with them when, frightened by the development of a movement, they commit treason, is equivalent to criminal toleration of traitors and a veiling of betrayal.

The general strike had the task of exerting a united pressure upon the employers and the state with the power of the five million workers, for the question of the coal mining industry had become the most important question of state policy. Thanks to the betrayal of the leadership, the strike was broken in its first stage. It was a great illusion to continue in the belief that an isolated economic strike of the mineworkers would alone achieve what the general strike did not achieve.

That is precisely where the power of the General Council lay. It aimed with cold calculation at the defeat of the mineworkers, as a result of which considerable sections of the workers would be convinced of the "correctness" and the "reasonableness" of the Judas directives of the General Council.

The maintenance of the amicable bloc with the General Council, and the simultaneous support of the protracted and isolated economic strike of the mineworkers, which the General Council came out against, seemed, as it were, to be calculated beforehand to allow the heads of the trade unions to emerge from this heaviest test with the least possible losses.

The role of the Russian trade unions here, from the revolutionary standpoint, turned out to be very disadvantageous and positively pitiable. Certainly, support of an economic strike, even an isolated one, was absolutely necessary. There can be no two opinions on that among revolutionists. But this support should have borne not only a financial but also a revolutionary-political character. The All-Russia Central Council of Trade Unions should have declared openly to the English mineworkers union and the whole English working class that the mineworkers strike could seriously count upon success only if by its stubbornness, its tenacity, and its scope, it could prepare the way for a *new outbreak of the general strike.* That could have been achieved only by an open and direct struggle against the General Council, the agency of the government and the mine owners. The struggle to convert the economic strike into a political strike should have signified, therefore, a furious political and organizational war against the General Council. The first step to such a war had to be the break with the Anglo-Russian Committee, which had become a reactionary obstacle, a chain on the feet of the working class.

No revolutionist who weighs his words will contend that a victory *would have been guaranteed* by proceeding along this line. But a victory was *possible* only on this road. A defeat on this road was a defeat on a road that could lead *later* to victory. Such a defeat educates, that is, strengthens the revolutionary ideas in the working class. In the meantime, mere financial support of the lingering and hopeless trade union strike (trade union strike—in its methods; revolutionary-political—in its aims), only meant grist to the mill of the General Council, which was biding calmly until the strike collapsed from starvation and thereby proved its own "correctness." Of course, the General Council could not easily bide its time for several months in the role of an open strikebreaker. It was precisely during this very critical period that the General Council required the Anglo-Russian Committee as its political screen from the masses. Thus, the questions of the mortal class struggle between English capital and the proletariat, between the General Council and the mineworkers, were transformed, as it were, into questions of a friendly discussion between allies in the same bloc, the English General Council and the All-Russia Central Council of Trade Unions, on the subject of which of the two roads was better at that moment: the road of an agreement, or the road of an isolated economic struggle. The inevitable outcome of the strike led to the agreement, that is, tragically settled the friendly "discussion" in favor of the General Council.

From beginning to end, the entire policy of the Anglo-Russian Committee, because of its false line, provided only aid to the General Council. Even the fact that the strike was long sustained financially by the great self-sacrifice on the part of the Russian working class, did not serve the mineworkers or the English Communist Party, but the selfsame General Council. As the upshot of the greatest revolutionary movement in England since the days of Chartism, the English Communist Party has hardly grown while the General Council sits in the saddle even more firmly than before the general strike.

Such are the results of this unique "strategical maneuver."

The obstinacy evinced in retaining the bloc with the General Council, which led to downright servility at the disgraceful Berlin session in April 1927, was explained away by the ever recurring reference to the very same "stabilization." If there is a setback in the development of the revolution, then, you see, one is forced to cling to Purcell. This argument, which appeared very profound to a Soviet functionary or to a trade unionist of the type of Melnichansky, is in reality a perfect example of blind empiricism—adulterated by scholasticism at that. What was the significance of "stabilization" in relation to English economy and politics, especially in the years 1926–27? Did it signify the development of the productive forces? The improvement of the economic situation? Better hopes for the future? Not at all. The whole so-called stabilization of English capitalism is maintained only upon the conservative forces of the old labor organzations with all their currents and shadings in the face of the weakness and irresoluteness of the English Communist Party. On the field of the economic and social relations of England, the revolution has already fully matured. The question stands purely politically. The basic props of the stabilization are the heads of the Labour Party and the trade unions, which, in England, constitute a single unit but which operate through a division of labor.

Given such a condition of the working masses as was revealed by the general strike, the highest post in the mechanism of capitalist stabilization is no longer occupied by MacDonald and Thomas, but by Pugh, Purcell, Cook, and Co. They do the work and Thomas adds the finishing touches. Without Purcell, Thomas would be left hanging in midair and along with Thomas also Baldwin. The chief brake upon the English revolution is the false, diplomatic masquerade "leftism" of Purcell which fraternizes sometimes in rotation, sometimes simultaneously with churchmen and Bolsheviks and which is always ready not only for retreats but also for betrayal. *Stabilization is Purcellism*. From this we see what depths of theoretical absurdity and blind opportunism are expressed in the reference to the existence of "stabilization" in order to justify the political bloc with Purcell. Yet, precisely in order to shatter the "stabilization," Purcellism had first to be destroyed. In such a situation, even a shadow of solidarity with the General Council was the greatest crime and infamy against the working masses.

Even the most correct strategy cannot, by itself, always lead to victory. The correctness of a strategical plan is verified by whether it follows the line of the actual development of class forces and whether it estimates the elements of this development realistically. The gravest and most disgraceful defeat which has the most fatal consequences for the movement is the typically Menshevist defeat, due to a false estimate of the classes, an underestimation of the revolutionary factors, and an idealization of the enemy forces. Such were our defeats in China and in England.

What was expected from the Anglo-Russian Committee for the USSR?

In July 1926, Stalin lectured to us at the joint plenum of the Central Committee and the Central Control Commission as follows:

"The task of this bloc [the Anglo-Russian Committee] consists in organizing a broad movement of the working class against new imperialist wars and generally against an intervention in our country (especially) on the part of the mightiest of the imperialist powers of Europe, on the part of England in particular."

While he was instructing us, Oppositionists, to the effect that "care must be taken to defend the first workers republic of the world against intervention" (we, naturally, are unaware of this), Stalin added:

"If the reactionary trade unions of England are ready to conclude a bloc with the revolutionary trade unions of our country against the counterrevolutionary imperialists of their own country, then why should we not hail such a bloc?"

If the "reactionary trade unions" were capable of conducting a struggle against their own imperialists they would not be reactionary. Stalin is incapable of distinguishing any longer between the conceptions *reactionary* and *revolutionary*. He characterizes the English trade unions as reactionary as a matter of routine but in reality he entertains miserable illusions with regard to their "revolutionary spirit."

After Stalin, the Moscow Committee of our party lectured to the workers of Moscow:

"The Anglo-Russian Committee can, must, and will undoubtedly play an enormous role in the struggle against all possible interventions directed against the USSR. It will become the organizing center of the international forces of the proletariat for the struggle against every attempt of the international bourgeoisie to provoke a new war." (Theses of the Moscow Committee.)

What did the Opposition reply? We said:

"The more acute the international situation becomes, the more the Anglo-Russian Committee will be transformed into a weapon of British and international imperialism."*

This criticism of the Stalinist hopes in Purcell as the guardian angel of the workers state was characterized by Stalin at the very same plenum as a deviation "from Leninism to Trotskyism."

Voroshilov: "Correct."

A voice: "Voroshilov has affixed his seal to it."

Trotsky: "Fortunately all this will be in the minutes."

Yes, all this is to be found in the minutes of the July plenum at which the blind, rude, and disloyal opportunists dared to accuse the Opposition of "defeatism."

This dialogue, which I am compelled to quote briefly from my earlier article, "What We Gave and What We Got,"† is far more useful as a strategical lesson than the entire sophomoric chapter on strategy in the draft program.[44] The question—*what we gave (and expected) and what we got?*—is in general the principal criterion in strategy. It must be applied at the Sixth Congress to all questions that have been on the agenda in recent years. It will then be revealed conclusively

---

* "The Struggle for Peace and the Anglo-Russian Committee," in *Leon Trotsky on Britain*, p. 278.

† In *Leon Trotsky on Britain*, p. 285.

that the strategy of the ECCI, especially since the year 1926, was a strategy of imaginary sums, false calculations, illusions with regard to the enemy, and persecutions of the most reliable and unwavering militants. In a word, it was the rotten strategy of right centrism.

9. THE MANEUVERIST CHARACTER OF REVOLUTIONARY STRATEGY

At first sight, it appears incomprehensible why the "maneuvering" and "flexibility" of Bolshevik strategy are passed over in complete silence in the draft. Out of this entire vast question only a single point is taken—the point on agreements with the colonial bourgeoisie.

Yet, the opportunism of the recent period, zigzagging ever more deeply to the right, has advanced primarily under the banner of *maneuver* strategy. The refusal to concur with unprincipled compromises which, because of this very fact, were harmful in practice, was characterized as lack of "flexibility." The majority declared its basic principle to be the maneuver. Zinoviev maneuvered back in 1925 with Radić and La Follette. Stalin and Bukharin thereafter maneuvered with Chiang Kai-shek, with Purcell, and with the kulaks. The apparatus continually maneuvered with the party. Zinoviev and Kamenev are now maneuvering with the apparatus.

A whole corps of specialists in maneuvers for bureaucratic requirement arose which consists predominantly of people who never were revolutionary fighters, and who now bow all the more ardently before the revolution after it has already conquered power. Borodin maneuvers in Canton, Rafes in Peking, D. Petrovsky maneuvers around the English Channel, Pepper maneuvers in the United States, but Pepper can maneuver in Polynesia, too; Martynov maneuvers from a distance, but to make up for it he does it in every corner of the globe. Whole broods of young academicians in maneuvers have been brought up who approach Bolshevik flexibility mainly by the elasticity of their own spines. The task of this school of strategy consists in obtaining through maneuvers what can be won only through revolutionary class forces. Just as every alchemist of the Middle Ages hoped, in spite of the failure of others, to make gold, so the present-day strategists in maneuvers also hope, each in his place, to deceive history. In the nature of things, of course, they are not strategists but only bureaucratic combinationists of all statures, save the great. Some of them, having observed how the Master settled petty questions, imagine that they have mastered the secrets of strategy. That is precisely the essence of epigonism. Others, again, obtained the secrets of combinationism at second and third hand, and after becoming convinced that with them wonders are sometimes achieved in small matters, they concluded that these methods are all the more applicable to great matters. Yet, all attempts to apply the method of bureaucratic combinations as being "more economic" in comparison with the revolutionary struggles in order to solve great questions, have led invariably to disgraceful failures, in addition to which, combinationism, armed with the apparatus of the party and of the state, each time broke the spine of the young parties and the young revolutions. Chiang Kai-shek, Wang Ching-wei, Purcell, the kulaks—all these have up to now emerged as victors from the attempts to deal with them by means of "maneuvers."

Naturally, this does not mean to say that maneuvers are impermissible in general, that is, incompatible with the revolutionary strategy of the working class. But it must be clearly understood that maneuvers can bear only a subordinated, auxiliary, and expedient character in relation to the basic methods of revolutionary struggle. Once and for all it must be grasped that a maneuver can never decide anything in great matters. If combinations appear to solve something in small affairs, it is always at the expense of great matters. A correct maneuver can only facilitate the solution by providing the possibility of gaining time or of attaining greater results with smaller forces. It is impossible to escape from fundamental difficulties by means of a maneuver.

The contradiction between the proletariat and the bourgeoisie is a fundamental one. That is why the attempt to bridle the Chinese bourgeoisie by means of organizational and personal maneuvers and to compel it to submit to combinationist plans is not a maneuver but contemptible self-deception, even though it be colossal in scope. Classes cannot be tricked. This applies, considered historically, to all the classes and it is particularly and immediately true of the ruling, possessing, exploiting, and educated classes. The world experience of the latter is so great, their class instinct so refined, and their organs of espionage so varied that an attempt to deceive them by posing as somebody else must lead in reality to trapping, not the enemy, but one's own friends.

The contradiction between the USSR and the capitalist world is a fundamental one. There is no escape from it by way of maneuvers. By means of clear and candidly acknowledged concessions to capital, and by utilizing the contradictions between its various sections, the breathing spell can be extended and time gained, but even this, only under certain historical conditions, and by no means under any and all circumstances. It is gross self-deception to believe that the international bourgeoisie can be "neutralized" until the construction of socialism, that is, that the fundamental contradictions can be overcome with the aid of a maneuver. Such self-deception may cost the Soviet republic its head. Only the international proletarian revolution can liberate us from the fundamental contradiction.

A maneuver can consist either of a concession to the enemy, or an agreement with a temporary and, therefore, always dubious ally, or a well-timed retreat calculated to keep the enemy from our throat, or, finally, the raising of partial demands and slogans in such succession as to split the enemy camp. These are the principal varieties of maneuvers. Others might be mentioned, secondary ones. But every maneuver is by its nature only an episode in relation to the fundamental strategical line of the struggle. In maneuvering with the Kuomintang and the Anglo-Russian Committee, these must always be kept in mind as the perfect examples of a Menshevik and not a Bolshevik maneuver. What occurred was just the reverse. What should have been only a tactical episode developed there into a strategical line and the real strategic task (the struggle against the bourgeoisie and the reformists) was atomized into a series of second-rate and petty tactical episodes which, moreover, were only decorative in character.

In a maneuver, one must always proceed from the worst and not the best assumptions with regard to the adversary to whom concessions are made, or the unreliable ally with whom an agreement is concluded. It must be constantly borne in mind that the ally can become an enemy on the morrow. This applies even to such an ally as the peasantry:

"We must be distrustful towards the peasantry, always organize ourselves separately from it, and be ready for a struggle against it, insofar as the peasantry shows itself to be reactionary or antiproletarian." (Lenin, *Works,* vol. 6, p. 113.)*

This does not at all contradict the great strategical task of the proletariat which Lenin worked out for the first time theoretically as well as practically with such gifted profundity, the task of tearing the exploited layers of poor peasants away from the influence of the bourgeoisie and leading them after us. But the alliance between the proletariat and the peasantry is by no means given ready-made by history and it cannot be created by means of oily maneuvers, contemptible attempts at wheedling, and pathetic declamations. The alliance between the proletariat and the peasantry is a question of the political relation of forces and consequently of the complete independence of the proletariat in relation to *all* other classes. The ally must first be edu-

---

* "The Proletariat and the Peasantry" (March 1905) in *LCW,* vol. 8, p. 234.

cated. This can be achieved, on the one hand, by paying great attention to all its progressive and historical needs, and, on the other hand, by displaying an organized distrust towards the ally, and fighting tirelessly and relentlessly against its every antiproletarian tendency and custom.

The import and the limits of a maneuver must always be clearly considered and demarcated. A concession must be called a concession, and a retreat a retreat. It is infinitely less dangerous to exaggerate one's own concessions and retreats than to underestimate them. The vigilance of the class and the organized distrust of our own party must be maintained and not lulled.

The essential instrument of a maneuver, as in every historical action of the working class in general, is the party. But the party is not simply a tractable instrument in the hand of the "masters" of the maneuver, but a conscious and self-acting instrument, the highest expression of proletarian self-action in general. Therefore, every maneuver must be clearly grasped by the party itself throughout its application. In question here are, of course, not diplomatic, military, or conspiratorial secrets, that is, not the *technique* of the struggle of the proletarian state or of the proletarian party under capitalist conditions. In question here is the *political* content of the maneuver. That is why the whispered explanations to the effect that the course of 1924 to 1928 towards the kulaks was a great maneuver, are absurd and criminal. There is no deceiving the kulak. He does not judge by words but by deeds, by taxes, prices, and net profit. However, one's own party—the working class and the peasant poor—can very well be deceived. Nothing is so calculated to disintegrate the revolutionary spirit of the proletarian party as unprincipled maneuvering and combinationism behind its back.

The most important, best established, and most unalterable rule to apply in every maneuver reads: you must never dare to merge, mix, or combine your own party organization with an alien one, even though the latter be most "sympathetic" today. Undertake no such steps as lead directly or indirectly, openly or maskedly, to the subordination of your party to other parties, or to organizations of other classes, or constrict the freedom of your own agitation, or your responsibility, even if only in part, for the political line of other parties. You shall not mix up the banners, let alone kneel before another banner.

It is the worst and most dangerous thing if a maneuver arises out of the impatient opportunistic endeavor to outstrip the development of one's own party and to leap over the necessary stages of its development (it is precisely here that no stages must be leaped over), by binding, combining, and uniting superficially, fraudulently, diplomatically, through combinations and trickery, organizations and elements that pull in opposite directions. Such experiments, always dangerous, are fatal to young and weak parties.

In a maneuver, as in a battle, what decides is not strategical wisdom alone (still less, the cunning of combinationists), but the relationship of forces. Even a correctly contrived maneuver is, generally speaking, all the more dangerous for a revolutionary party, the younger and weaker the latter is in relation to its enemies, allies, and semi-allies. That is why—and we arrive here at a point which is of paramount importance for the Comintern—the Bolshevik Party did not at all begin with maneuvering as a panacea but came to it, grew into it in the measure that it sunk its roots deeply into the working class, became strong politically and matured ideologically.

The misfortune lies precisely in the fact that the epigones of Bolshevik strategy extol maneuvers and flexibility to the young communist parties as the quintessence of this strategy, thereby tearing them away from their historical axis and principled foundation and turning them to unprincipled combinations which, only too often, resemble a squirrel whirling in its cage. It was not flexibility that served (nor should it serve today) as the basic trait of Bolshevism but rather *granite hardness*. It was precisely of this quality, for which its enemies and opponents reproached it, that Bolshevism was always justly proud. Not blissful "optimism" but intransigence, vigilance, revolutionary distrust, and the struggle for every hand's breadth of independence—these are the essential traits of Bolshevism. This is what the communist parties of both the West and the East must begin with. They must first gain the right to carry out great maneuvers by preparing the political and material possibility for realizing them, that is, the strength, the solidity, the firmness of their own organization.

The Menshevik maneuvers with the Kuomintang and the General Council are tenfold criminal because they were flung upon the still-frail shoulders of the communist parties of China and England. These maneuvers not only inflicted a defeat upon the revolution and the working class but also crushed, weakened, and undermined for a long time to come the fundamental instrument of future struggle, the young communist parties. At the same time they have also introduced elements of political demoralization into the ranks of the oldest party of the Comintern, the CPSU.

The chapter of the draft dealing with strategy remains obstinately silent about maneuvering—that hobby horse of late years—as if its mouth were filled with water. Indulgent critics may say: silence is good enough. But such rationalizing would be a great mistake. The misfortune lies in the fact that the draft program itself, as we have already shown in a number of examples and as we will show later on, also bears the character of a maneuver in the bad, that is, the combinationist sense of the word. The draft maneuvers with its own party. Some of its weak spots it masks with the formula "according to Lenin"; others, it evades by silence. That is the manner in which it deals with the strategy of maneuvers today. It is impossible to speak on this subject without touching upon the fresh experiences in China and England. But the very mention of maneuvers would conjure up the figures of Chiang Kai-shek and Purcell. The authors do not want this. They prefer to remain silent on the favorite theme and to leave the leadership of the Comintern a free hand. And this is precisely what must not be permitted. It is necessary to tie the hands of the combinationists and their candidates. This is precisely the purpose the program should serve. Otherwise, it would be superfluous.

A place must be found in the chapter on strategy for the fundamental rules which determine and delimit maneuvering as an auxiliary method of the revolutionary struggle against the class enemy which can be only a life-and-death struggle. The rules noted above and based upon the teachings of Marx and Lenin can undoubtedly be presented in a more concise and precise form. But they must by all means be brought into the program of the Communist International.

10. THE STRATEGY OF CIVIL WAR

In connection with the question of the armed insurrection, the draft program remarks casually:

"This struggle is subject to the rules of the art of war. It presupposes a military plan, an offensive character of the fighting operations, and unlimited sacrifice and heroism on the part of the proletariat."

Here the draft does not go beyond a terse repetition of a few casual remarks once made by Marx. In the meantime, we have had, on the one hand, the experiences of the October Revolution, and on the other, the experiences of the defeat of the Hungarian and Bavarian revolutions, of the struggle in Italy in 1920, the uprising in Bulgaria in September 1923, the German movement of 1923, Estonia in 1924, the English general strike of 1926, the uprising of the Viennese proletariat in 1927, and the second Chinese revolution of 1925–27. A program of the Comintern must contain an infinitely more lucid and concrete characterization of both the social and political prerequisites of the armed insurrection as well as of the military and strategical conditions and methods that can guarantee the victory. Nothing exposes the superficial and literary character of this document so much as the fact that the chapter devoted to revolutionary strategy occupies itself with Cornelissen and the Guild Socialists (Orage, Hobson, G.D.H. Cole, all specified by name), but gives neither a general characterization of the strategy of the proletariat in the imperialist epoch nor a definitive exposition of the methods of the struggle for power on the basis of living historical material.

In 1924, after the tragic experiences in Germany, we raised that question anew, demanding that the Comintern place on the agenda and work out the questions of strategy and tactics of the armed insurrection and of civil war in general.

"It is necessary to say bluntly that the question of the duration of the armed insurrection frequently has the character of litmus paper with which to test the revolutionary consciousness of very many Western European communists who have not liberated themselves to this day from their passive, fatalistic approach to the fundamental tasks of the revolution. Such an approach found its most profound and talented expression in Rosa Luxemburg. Psychologically, this is perfectly comprehensible. Her formative period was spent mainly in struggle against the bureaucratic apparatus of the German social democracy and the trade unions. She demonstrated tirelessly that this apparatus stifled the initiative of the masses and she saw the way out and salvation in a spontaneous movement from below that was to overthrow all social democratic obstructions and barriers. A revolutionary general strike that inundates all the banks of bourgeois society became for Luxemburg a synonym for the proletarian revolution. But a general strike, be it ever so distinguished by mass strength, does not decide the question of power as yet, but only raises it. For the seizure of power, it is necessary to organize the armed insurrection on the basis of the general strike. To be sure, the entire development of Rosa Luxemburg tended in this direction: she departed from the stage before she had said her last words, or even her penultimate words. However, up to the very latest period, very strong tendencies towards revolutionary fatalism have prevailed within the German Communist Party. The revolution is on the way, the revolution is nigh, the revolution will bring with it the armed insurrection and give us power and the party . . . will, in the meantime, carry on revolutionary agitation and await the results. Under such conditions, to put point-blank the question of the date of the insurrection is to awake the party out of fatalistic passivity and to turn it towards the basic revolutionary task, that is, to the conscious organization of the armed insurrection in order to tear the power out of the hands of the enemy." (Trotsky's speech at the session of the Board of Military Science Society, July 29, 1924—*Pravda,* September 6, 1924.)*

"We devote considerable time and theoretical labor to the Paris Commune of 1871 but completely neglect the struggle of the German proletariat which has already acquired precious experiences in civil war; for example, we hardly occupy ourselves at all with the experience of the Bulgarian uprising of last September; and finally, what is most astonishing, we have completely relegated the experiences of October to the archives. . . .

"The experiences of the October Revolution, the only victorious proletarian revolution up to now, must be painstakingly studied. A strategical and tactical calendar of the October must be compiled. It must be shown, wave by wave, how events developed and how they were reflected in the party, the soviets, the Central Committee, and the military organization. What did the vacillations inside the party mean? What was their specific weight in the general sweep of events? What was the role of the military organization? That would be a work of inestimable importance. To defer it still further would be positively criminal." (*Ibid.*)

"What then is the task properly speaking? The task is to compile a universal reference book, or a guide book, or a manual, or a book of statutes on the question of the civil war and, therefore, above all on the armed insurrection as the highest point of the revolution. A balance must be drawn

---

* "Problems of Civil War," in *Challenge of the Left Opposition (1923–25),* pp. 182–83.

from the experiences, the preliminary conditions thoroughly analyzed, the mistakes examined, the most correct operations selected, and the necessary conclusions drawn. Will we thereby enrich science, that is, the knowledge of the laws of historical development, or art as the totality of rules of action drawn from experience? The one as well as the other, I believe. For our aim is a strictly practical one; namely, to enrich the military art of revolution." (*Ibid.*)

"Such 'statutes' will necessarily be very complex in structure. First of all, there must be given a characterization of the fundamental premises for the seizure of power by the proletariat. Here we still remain on the field of revolutionary politics; for the uprising is the continuation of politics—only by special means. The analysis of the premises for the armed uprising must be adapted to the varying types of countries. There are countries with a proletarian majority of the population and also countries with an insignificant minority of the proletariat and with an absolute predominance of the peasantry. Between these two extremes lie the countries of the transitional type. As a basis for the analysis, therefore, at least three 'typical' countries must be taken: the industrial country; the agrarian country; and the intermediate country. The introduction (treating the premises and the conditions for the revolution) must contain the characterization of the peculiarities of each of these types from the standpoint of the civil war. We consider the insurrection from a twofold angle. On the one hand, as a definite stage of the historical process, as a definite reflection of the objective laws of the class struggle; and on the other, from the subjective or active standpoint: how to prepare and carry out the insurrection in order best to guarantee its victory." (*Ibid.*)*

In 1924, a collective work on the elaboration of the directives of civil war, that is, a Marxian guide to the questions of the open clashes of the classes and the armed struggle for the dictatorship, was begun by a large circle of individuals grouped

---

* *Challenge of the Left Opposition (1923–25)*, pp. 175–98.

around the Military Science Society. But this work soon encountered opposition on the part of the Comintern—this opposition was a part of the general system of the struggle against so-called Trotskyism; and the work was later liquidated altogether. A more lightminded and criminal step can hardly be imagined. In an epoch of abrupt turns, the rules of the civil war in the sense presented above must be part of the iron inventory of the entire revolutionary cadre, let alone the leaders of the party. These "statutes" would have to be studied constantly and augmented from the fresh experiences in one's own country. Only such a study can provide a certain guarantee against steps of panic and capitulation at moments when supreme courage and decisiveness are required, as well as against adventurist leaps in periods which require prudence and patience.

Had such regulations been incorporated in a number of books, the serious study of which is as much the duty of every communist as the knowledge of the basic ideas of Marx, Engels, and Lenin, we might well have avoided such defeats as were suffered during recent years, and which were by no means inevitable, especially the Canton uprising contrived with such puerile lightmindedness. The draft program treats these questions in a few lines, almost as charily as it speaks of Gandhiism in India. Of course, a program cannot become engrossed in details. But it must pose a problem in its full scope and give its basic formulas, citing the most important achievements and mistakes.

Quite independently of this, the Sixth Congress, in our opinion, must instruct the ECCI in a special resolution to elaborate the rules of the civil war into a manual based on the past experiences of victory and defeat.

11. THE QUESTION OF THE INTERNAL PARTY REGIME

The organizational questions of Bolshevism are inseparably bound up with questions of program and tactics. The draft program touches this subject only in passing by referring to the necessity of "maintaining the strictest revolutionary order of democratic centralism." This is the sole formula defining the internal party regime, and, besides, it is quite a new formula. We were aware that the party regime rests upon the principles of democratic centralism. This presupposed in theory (and was also carried out in practice) that the regime of democratic centralism implied a full opportunity for the party to discuss, criticize, express dissatisfaction, elect, and depose, just as it involved an iron discipline in action under the fully empowered leadership of the elective and removable directing organs. If, by *democracy* was understood the sovereignty of the party over all its organs, then *centralism* meant a correctly established, conscious discipline that guaranteed the fighting ability of the party. Now, however, to this formula of the internal party regime which has stood the tests in the whole past, an entirely new criterion has been added, that of *"the strictest revolutionary order."* It appears that mere democratic centralism no longer suffices for the party but that it now requires a certain *revolutionary order* of democratic centralism. This formula simply puts the new self-sufficing idea of "revolutionary order" above democratic centralism, i.e., above the party.

What is the meaning of this idea of revolutionary order—and a "strictest" order at that—which stands *above* the ideas of democracy and centralism? It implies a party apparatus completely independent of the party or aspires to such an independence—a self-sufficing bureaucracy which is supposed to preserve "order" independently of the party masses and able to suspend or violate the will of the party, trample its statutes underfoot, postpone party conventions or turn them into mere fictions whenever "order" requires it.

The apparatus has aimed for a long time and by devious routes for such a formula as a "revolutionary order" raised above democracy and centralism. During the last two years we have had offered us a whole series of definitions of party democracy by the most responsible representatives of the party leadership which in essence reduced it to mean that democracy and centralism are simply submission to higher organs. Everything done in practice went far in this direction. But centralism accompanied by strangled and hollow democracy is bureaucratic centralism. Of course, such an "order" must, of necessity, be camouflaged by the forms and rites of democracy; it must be whipped by means of circular letters emanating from above, and commanded to "self-criticize" under the threat of Article 58;[45] and it must continually prove that violations of democracy proceed not from the leading center but from the so-called executants, but there is no proceeding against the latter because every "executant" turns out to be a leader of all his inferiors.

Thus, the new formula is theoretically completely absurd. It demonstrates by its newness and absurdity that it was engendered only in order to satisfy certain matured wants. It sanctifies the bureaucratic apparatus that created it.

This question is indissolubly bound up with the question of factions and groupings. In every controversial question and every difference of opinion, the leadership and the official press, not only of the CPSU but also of the Comintern and all its sections, has immediately shifted the debate over to the question of factions and groupings. *Without temporary ideological groupings, the ideological life of the party is unthinkable.* Nobody has yet discovered any other procedure. And those who have sought to discover it have only shown that their remedy was tantamount to strangling the ideological life of the party.

Naturally, groupings as well as differences of opinion are an "evil." But this evil constitutes as necessary an integral part of the dialectic of party development as do toxins in the life of the human organism.

The transformation of groupings into organized and, moreover, closed factions is a much greater evil. The art of party leadership consists precisely in preventing such a development. It is impossible to achieve this by a mere prohibition. The experience of the CPSU testifies best to it.

At the tenth party congress, under the reverberations of the Kronstadt uprising and the kulak mutinies, Lenin had a resolution adopted prohibiting factions and groupings. By groupings were understood not temporary tendencies that inevitably arise in the process of party life, but those selfsame factions that passed themselves off as groupings. The party masses understood clearly the mortal danger of the moment and supported their leader by adopting the resolution, harsh and inflexible in its form: the prohibition of factions and factionalism. But the party also knew very well that this formula would be interpreted by the Central Committee under the leadership of Lenin; that there would be neither rude nor disloyal interpretation, and still less, any abuse of power (see the "Testament" of Lenin[46]). The party knew that, exactly one year later, or, should one-third of the party request it, even a month later, it could examine the experiences at a new party congress and introduce any necessary qualifications. The decision of the tenth party congress was a very severe measure, evoked by the critical position of the ruling party at the most dangerous turn from war communism to the NEP. This severe measure proved to be fully justified for it only supplemented a correct and farsighted policy and cut the ground from under the groupings that had arisen prior to the transition to the New Economic Policy.

But the decision of the tenth party congress on factions and groupings, which even then required judicious interpretation and application, is in no case an absolute principle that stands above all other requirements of the party development, independent of the country, the situation, and the time.

Insofar as the party leadership after the departure of Lenin, in order to protect itself from all criticism, based itself formally upon the decisions of the tenth party congress on factions and groupings, it did so in order to stifle party democracy ever more and at the same time was less able to accomplish its real purpose, i.e., the elimination of factionalism. For the task does not consist of prohibiting factions but of doing away with them. Meanwhile, never have factions so devastated the party and disintegrated its unity as has been the case since Lenin's departure from leadership. At the same time, never before has there prevailed in the party such a hundred percent monolithism, utterly fraudulent and serving only to cover up the methods of strangling the party life.

An apparatus faction kept secret from the party arose in the CPSU even before the twelfth party congress. Later it assumed the character of a conspirative organization with its own illegal Central Committee (the "Septumvirate"[17]), with its own circular letters, agents, codes, and so forth. The party apparatus handpicks from its ranks a closed order which is uncontrolled and which disposes of the extraordinary resources not only of the party but also of the state apparatus and transforms the party masses into a mere cover and an auxiliary instrument for its combinatory maneuvers.

But the more boldly this closed intra-apparatus faction detaches itself from the control of the party masses—ever more diluted by all sorts of "drives"—the deeper and more sharply does the process of faction division proceed, not only below but also within the apparatus itself. Under the complete and unlimited domination of the apparatus over the party, already accomplished at the time of the thirteenth party congress, the differences arising within the apparatus itself find no way out, for to appeal to the party for a real decision would mean to subject the apparatus to it again. Only that apparatus grouping which is assured of a majority in advance is inclined to decide a disputed question by resorting to the methods of *apparatus democracy,* that is, to balloting the members of the secret faction. The result is that inside the ruling apparatus faction, antagonistic factions arise that do not strive so much to capture the majority within the common faction as to seek for support in the institutions of the state apparatus. As regards the majority at the party congress, the latter is automatically assured, for the congress can be convoked whenever it is most convenient and prepared to suit. That is how the usurpation of the apparatus develops, which constitutes the most terrible danger both to the party and to the dictatorship of the proletariat.

After the first "anti-Trotskyist" campaign in 1923–24 was carried through with the aid of this apparatus faction, a deep schism[48] took place within the underground faction headed by the Septumvirate. The fundamental reason for this was the class dissatisfaction of the Leningrad proletarian vanguard with the incipient downsliding in questions of internal as well as international policy. The advanced Leningrad workers continued in 1925 the work begun by the advanced workers of Moscow in 1923. But these deep class tendencies could not manifest themselves openly in the party. They were reflected in the muffled struggle within the apparatus faction.

In April 1925, the Central Committee sent out a circular letter to the whole party which denied the rumors allegedly spread by the "Trotskyists" (!!) that differences of opinion on the peasantry existed within the nucleus of the "Leninists," that is, within the factional Septumvirate. It was only from this circular letter that broader party cadres learned that such differences of opinion actually existed; but this did not at all prevent the leading cadre from continuing to deceive the party membership with the assertion that the "Opposition" was allegedly disrupting the monolithism of the "Leninist Guard." This propaganda was pounding away at full speed when the fourteenth party congress precipitated upon the party the amorphous and confused differences between the two sections of the reigning faction, differences that were, nevertheless, profound in their *class sources*. At the very last moment before the party congress, the Moscow and the Leningrad organizations, that is, the two main fortresses of the party, adopted resolutions at their district conferences of a *directly opposite character*. It is self-understood that both were adopted *unanimously*. Moscow explained this miracle of "revolutionary order" by charging use of force by the apparatus in Leningrad, and Leningrad reciprocated by accusing Moscow. As though there existed some sort of impenetrable wall between the Moscow and Leningrad organizations! In both cases the party apparatus always decided, demonstrating with its hundred percent monolithism that in all the fundamental questions of party life there is no party.

The fourteenth party congress found itself compelled to settle new differences of opinion on various basic questions and to determine a new composition of the leadership *behind the back of the unconsulted party*. The congress was left no alternative other than to leave this decision immediately to a scrupulously handpicked hierarchy of party secretaries. The fourteenth party congress was a new milestone on the road to the liquidation of party democracy by the methods of "order," that is, the arbitrary power of the masked apparatus faction. The next stage of the struggle took place only a little while ago. The art of the reigning faction consisted of always confronting the party with an already adopted decision, an irreparable situation, an accomplished fact.

This new and higher stage of "revolutionary order," however, did not by any means signify the liquidation of factions and groups. On the contrary, they attained an extreme development and sharpness within the party masses as well as within the party apparatus. So far as the party was concerned, the bureaucratic chastisement of the "groupings" became ever sharper and here demonstrated its impotence, descending to the infamy of the Wrangel officer[49] and Article 58. At the same time, a process of *new split* within the reigning faction itself took place and this process is even now developing further. Certainly, even now there is no lack of mendacious demonstrations of monolithism and of circular letters vouching for the complete unanimity of the tops. As a matter of fact, all indications are that the muffled struggle within the closed apparatus faction, violent because of its impassability, has assumed an extremely tense character and is driving the party to some new explosion.[50]

Such is the theory and practice of "revolutionary order" which is being inevitably transformed into the theory and practice of usurpation.

These things, however, have not been confined to the Soviet Union. In 1923, the campaign against factionalism proceeded mainly from the argument that factions represent the embryos of new parties; and that in a country with an overwhelming peasant majority and surrounded by capitalism, the dictatorship of the proletariat cannot allow freedom of parties. In itself, this postulate is absolutely correct. But it also requires a correct policy and a correct regime. It is clear, however, that such a formulation of the question signified the discarding of any extension to the communist parties in the bourgeois states of the resolution adopted at the Tenth Congress of the ruling CPSU. But a bureaucratic regime has a devouring logic of its own. If it tolerates no democratic control within the Soviet party, then it tolerates it all the less within the Comintern which stands formally above the CPSU. That is why the leadership made a universal principle out of its rude and disloyal interpretation and application of the resolution of the tenth party congress—which met the specific requirements at the time in the USSR—and extended it over all the communist organizations on the terrestrial globe.

Bolshevism was always strong because of its historical concreteness in elaborating organizational forms. No arid schemas. The Bolsheviks changed their organizational structure radically at every transition from one stage to the next. Yet, today, one and the same principle of "revolutionary order" is applied to the powerful party of the proletarian dictatorship as well as to the German Communist Party which represents a serious political force, to the young Chinese party which was immediately drawn into the vortex of revolutionary struggles, and to the party of the USA which is only a small propaganda society. In the latter, no sooner did doubts arise as to the correctness of the methods foisted upon it by a Pepper, in command at the time, than the "doubters" were subjected to chastisement for factionalism. A young party representing a political organism in a completely embryonic stage, without any real contact with the masses, without the experience of a revolutionary leadership, and without theoretical schooling, has already been armed from head to foot with all the attributes of a "revolutionary order," fitted with which it resembles a six-year-old boy wearing his father's accoutrement.

The CPSU has the greatest wealth of experience in the domain of ideology and revolution. But as the last five years showed, even the CPSU has been unable to live with impunity for a single day on the interest of its capital alone, but is obliged to renew and expand it constantly, and this is possible only through a collective working of the party mind. And what, then, need be said of the communist parties in other countries which were formed a few years ago and are just passing through the initial stage of accumulating theoretical knowledge and practical ability? Without a real freedom of party life, freedom of discussion, and freedom of establishing their course collectively, and by means of groupings, these parties will never become a decisive revolutionary force.

Prior to the tenth party congress which prohibited the formation of factions, the CPSU had existed two decades without such a prohibition. And precisely these two decades so trained and prepared it that it was able to accept and endure the harsh decisions of the tenth party congress at the time of a most difficult turn. The communist parties of the West, however, proceed from this point at the very outset.

Together with Lenin, we feared most of all that the CPSU, armed with the mighty resources of the state, would exert an excessive and crushing influence upon the young parties of the West that were just being organized. Lenin warned tirelessly against premature strides along the road of centralism, against the excessive tendencies of the ECCI and the Presidium in this direction and, especially, against such forms and methods of assistance as transform themselves into direct commands from which there is no appeal.

The change began in 1924 under the name of "Bolshevization." If by Bolshevization is understood the purging of the party of alien elements and habits, of social democratic functionaries clinging to their posts, of freemasons, pacifist-democrats, idealistic muddleheads, etc., then this work was being performed from the very first day of the Comintern's existence; at the Fourth Congress, this work with regard to the French party even assumed extremely sharp combat forms. But previously this genuine Bolshevization was inseparably connected with the individual experiences of the national sections of the Comintern, grew out of these experiences, and had as its touchstone questions of national policy which grew to the point of becoming international tasks. The "Bolshevization" of 1924 assumed completely the character of a caricature. A revolver was held at the temples of the leading organs of the communist parties with the demand that they adopt immediately a final position on the internal disputes in the CPSU without any information and any discussion; and besides they were aware in advance that on the position they took depended whether or not they could remain in the Comintern. Yet, the European communist parties were in no sense equipped in 1924 for a rapid-fire decision on the questions under discussion in Russia where, just at that time, two principled tendencies were in the formative stage, growing out of the new stage of the proletarian dictatorship. Of course, the work of purging was also necessary after 1924 and alien elements were quite correctly removed from many sections. But taken as a whole, the "Bolshevization" consisted in this: that with the wedge of the Russian disputes, driven from above with the hammer blows of the state apparatus, the leaderships being formed at the moment in the communist parties of the West were disorganized over and over again. All this went on under the banner of struggle against factionalism.

If a faction which threatens to paralyze its fighting ability for a long time does crystallize inside the party of the proletarian vanguard, the party will then naturally always be confronted with the necessity to decide whether to allot more time for a supplementary reexamination or to recognize immediately that the split is unavoidable. A fighting party can never be the sum of factions that pull in opposite directions. This is incontestably true, if taken in this general form. But to employ the split as a preventive measure against differences of opinion and to lop off every group and grouping that raises a voice of criticism, is to transform the internal life of the party into a chain of organizational abortions. Such methods do not promote the continuation and the development of the species but only exhaust the maternal organism, that is, the party. The struggle against factionalism becomes infinitely more dangerous than the formation of factions itself.

At the present time, we have a situation in which the actual initiators and founders of almost all the communist parties of the world have been placed outside of the International, not excepting even its former chairman. The leading groups of the *two* consecutive stages in party development are either expelled or removed from leadership in almost all the parties. In Germany the Brandler group today still finds itself in the position of semi–party membership. The Maslow group is outside the party. In France are expelled the old groups of Rosmer, Monatte, Loriot, Souvarine, as well as the leading group of the subsequent period, Girault-Treint. In Belgium, the basic group of Van Overstraeten has been expelled. If the Bordiga group, the founder of the Communist Party in Italy, is only half expelled that is to be accounted for by the conditions of the fascist regime. In Czechoslovakia, in Sweden, in Norway, in the United States, in a word, in almost all the parties of the world we perceive more or less similar phenomena which arose in the post-Leninist period.[51]

It is incontestable that many of the expelled committed the greatest mistakes; and we have not been behindhand in pointing them out. It is equally true that many of the expelled, after they were cut off from the Comintern, have to a great extent returned to their former points of departure, to the left social democracy or syndicalism. But the task of the leadership of the Comintern by no means consists in driving the young leaderships of the national parties into a blind alley every time, and thus dooming their individual representatives to ideological degeneration. The "revolutionary order" of the bureaucratic leadership stands as a terrible obstacle in the path of the development of all the parties of the Communist International.

❖

Organizational questions are inseparable from questions of program and tactics. We must take clearly into account the fact that one of the most important sources of opportunism in the Comintern is the bureaucratic regime of the apparatus in the Comintern itself as well as in its leading party. There cannot be any doubt after the experience of the years 1923–28 that bureaucratism in the Soviet Union is the expression and the instrument of the pressure exerted by the nonproletarian classes upon the proletariat. The draft program of the Comintern contains a correct formulation on this score when it says that bureaucratic perversions "arise inevitably on the soil of an insufficient cultural level of the masses and of class influences alien to the proletariat." Here we have the key to the understanding not only of bureaucratism in general but also of its extraordinary growth in the last five years. The cultural level of the masses, while remaining insufficient, has been rising constantly in this period (and this is incontestable); therefore, the cause for the *growth* of bureaucratism is to be sought only in the *growth* of class influences alien to the proletariat. In proportion as the European communist parties, i.e., primarily their directing bodies, aligned themselves organizationally with the shifts and regroupings in the apparatus of the CPSU, the bureaucratism of the communist parties abroad was for the most part only a reflection and a supplement of the bureaucratism within the CPSU.

The selection of the leading elements in the communist parties has proceeded and still proceeds mainly from the standpoint of their readiness to accept and approve the very latest apparatus grouping in the CPSU. The more independent and responsible elements in the leadership of the parties abroad who refused to submit to shuffling and reshuffling in a purely administrative manner, were either expelled from the party altogether or they were driven into the right (often the pseudoright) wing, or, finally, they entered the ranks of the Left Opposition. In this manner, the organic process of the selection and welding together of the revolutionary cadres, on the basis of the proletarian struggle under the leadership of the Comintern was cut short, altered, distorted, and in part even directly replaced by the administrative and bureaucratic sifting from above. Quite naturally, those leading communists who were the readiest to adopt the ready-made decisions and to countersign any and all resolutions, frequently gained the upper hand over those party elements who were imbued with the feeling of revolutionary responsibility. Instead of a selection of tested and unwavering revolutionists, we have frequently had a selection of the best-adapted bureaucrats.

All questions of internal and international policy invariably lead us back to the question of the internal party regime. Assuredly, deviations away from the class line in the questions of the Chinese revolution and the English labor movement, in the questions of the economy of the USSR, of wages, of taxes, etc., constitute in themselves a grave danger. But this danger is increased tenfold because the bureaucratic regime binds the party hand and foot and deprives it of any opportunity to correct the line of the leading party tops in a normal manner. The same applies to the Comintern as well. The resolution of the fourteenth party congress of the CPSU on the necessity of a more democratic and more collective leadership in the Comintern has been transformed in practice into its antithesis. A change in the internal regime of the Comintern is becoming a life-and-death question for the international revolutionary movement. This change can be achieved in two ways: either hand in hand with a change in the internal regime in the CPSU or in the struggle against the leading role of the CPSU in the Comintern. Every effort must be made to assure the adoption of the first way. The struggle for the change of the internal regime in the CPSU is a struggle for regenerating the regime in the Comintern and for the preservation of the leading ideological role of our party in the Comintern.

For this reason, it is necessary to expunge ruthlessly from the program the very idea that living, active parties can be subordinated to the control of the "revolutionary order" of an irremovable governmental party bureaucracy. The party itself must be restored its rights. The party must once again become a party. This must be affirmed in the program in such words as will leave no room for the theoretical justification of bureaucratism and usurpatory tendencies.

12. THE CAUSES OF THE DEFEAT OF THE OPPOSITION AND ITS PERSPECTIVES

The left, proletarian wing of the party which set down its views in a number of documents, the principal of which is the *Platform of the Bolshevik-Leninists (Opposition)*, has been subjected, beginning with the fall of 1923 to systematic, organizational campaigns of extermination. The methods of repression were conditioned upon the character of the internal party regime which became more bureaucratic to the degree that the pressure exerted by the nonproletarian classes upon the proletariat grew stronger. The possibilities for the success of such methods were created by the general political character of the period in which the proletariat suffered the greatest defeats, the social democracy came to life again, while in the communist parties the centrist-opportunist tendencies grew stronger, in addition to which centrism systematically slid to the right up to the recent months. The first onslaught against the Opposition was perpetrated immediately after the defeat of the German revolution and served, as it were, as a supplement of this defeat. This onslaught would have been utterly impossible with a victory of the German proletariat, which would have raised extraordinarily the self-confidence of the proletariat of the USSR and therefore also its power of resistance to the pressure of the bourgeois classes, internally as well as externally, and to the party bureaucracy which transmits this pressure.

To render clearer the meaning of the regroupings that took place in the Comintern since the end of 1923 it would be highly important to examine step by step how the leading group explained its organizational "victories" over the Opposition at the various stages of its downsliding. We are not in a position to do so within the framework of a criticism of the draft program. But it is sufficient for our purposes to examine how the first "victory" over the Opposition in September 1924 was viewed and explained. In his debut article on the question of international policy, Stalin said the following:

"The decisive victory of the revolutionary wing in the communist parties is the surest indication *of the deepest revolutionary processes that are now taking place within the working class*...."

And in another place in the same article:

"If we add to this the fact of the complete isolation of the opportunist currents in the CPSU, the picture is complete. The Fifth Congress only consolidated the victory of the revolutionary wing in the basic sections of the Communist International." (*Pravda*, September 20, 1924. Our emphasis.)

Thus, the defeat of the Opposition in the CPSU was proclaimed to be the result of the fact that the European proletariat was going to the *left*, was marching directly towards the revolution and was giving the revolutionary wing the ascendancy over the opportunists in all the sections of the Comintern. Today, some five years later, after the greatest defeat of the international proletariat in the fall of 1923, *Pravda* finds itself compelled to admit that "the wave of a certain apathy and dejection which set in after the defeat of 1923 and which permitted German capital to consolidate its position" is only now beginning to disappear. (*Pravda,* January 28, 1928.)

But, in that case, a question arises which is new for the present leadership of the Comintern but not for us: should not, then, the defeat of the Opposition in 1923 and the years that followed be explained not by a *leftward swing,* but by a *rightward swing* of the working class? The answer to this question is all-decisive.

The answer given at the Fifth Congress in 1924 and later on in various articles and speeches was clear and categorical: the strengthening of the revolutionary elements within the labor movement of Europe, the new rising wave, the approaching proletarian revolution—all these brought about the "debacle" of the Opposition.

Now, however, the sharp and prolonged turn of the political conjuncture after 1923 towards the right and not towards the left has already become a well-established, generally recognized, and incontrovertible fact. Consequently, the other fact is equally incontrovertible, to wit, that the inception and intensification of the struggle against the Opposition and the accentuation of this struggle up to the point of expulsions and exile is most closely connected with the political process of bourgeois stabilization in Europe. To be sure, this process was interrupted during the last four years by major revolutionary events. But new mistakes of the leadership, even more grievous than those of 1923 in Germany, gave the victory to the enemy each time under the worst possible conditions for the proletariat and the Communist Party and thereby created new sources of sustenance for bourgeois stabilization. The international revolutionary movement suffered defeats and together with it the left, proletarian, Leninist wing of the CPSU and the Comintern went down in defeat.

This explanation would be incomplete were we to overlook the internal process in the economic and political life of the USSR arising out of this world situation; namely, that the contradictions on the basis of the NEP were growing while the leadership did not correctly understand the problem of the economic *smychka* between the city and the country, underestimated the disproportions and the tasks of industrialization, did not grasp the significance of a planned economy, etc.

The growth of the economic and political pressure of the bureaucratic and petty-bourgeois strata within the country on the basis of defeats of the proletarian revolution in Europe and Asia—that was the historical chain which tightened around the neck of the Opposition during these four years. Whoever fails to understand this will understand nothing at all.

❖

In this analysis we have been compelled at almost every single important stage to oppose the line which was rejected under the name of Trotskyism to the line that was actually carried through. The meaning of this struggle in its generalized aspects is distinctly clear to every Marxist. If the occasional and partial charges of "Trotskyism" corroborated by adducing a mass of actual and imaginary quotations of the last twenty-five years could temporarily confuse, then the cohesive and generalized evaluation of the ideological struggle of the last five years is proof of the fact that two lines were at hand here. One of them was a conscious and consistent line; it was a continuation and development of the theoretical and strategical principles of Lenin in their application to the internal questions of the USSR and the questions of the world revolution; it was the line of the Opposition. The second line was an unconscious, contradictory, and vacillating line, sliding down in zigzags from Leninism under the pressure of hostile class forces in the period of the international political reflux; this was the line of the official leadership. At great turning points men frequently find it easier to abandon their conceptions than the habitual phraseology. That is a general law of all those whose ideological colors fade. While revising Lenin in almost all essential points, the leadership passed off this revisionism as a development of Leninism and at the same time characterized the international revolutionary essence of Leninism as Trotskyism. It did this not only in order to mask itself both outwardly and inwardly but also in order to adapt itself more easily to the process of its own downsliding.

Whoever wants to understand this will not fling at us the cheap reproach that we have connected the criticism of the draft program with an exposure of the legend of Trotskyism. The present draft program is the product of an ideological epoch that was permeated with this legend. The authors of the draft were the ones who fed this legend the most, who always proceeded from it and utilized it as the measuring rod of all things. The whole draft is a reflection of precisely this epoch.

Political history has been enriched by a new and extraordinarily instructive chapter. It might be entitled the chapter on the Power of Mythology, or more simply, Ideological Calumny as a Political Weapon. Experience teaches us that it is impermissible to underestimate this weapon. We have still far from accomplished "the leap from the realm of necessity to the realm of freedom," and we still live in a class society which is unthinkable without obscurantism, prejudices, and superstitions. A myth that corresponds to certain interests or traditional customs can always wield a great power in a class society. But on the basis of a myth alone, even if it is planfully organized and has at its disposal all the resources of state power, no great policy can be carried on, least of all a revolutionary policy, especially in our epoch of abrupt changes. Mythology must inevitably become entangled in the web of its own contradictions. We have already mentioned a small part, though perhaps the most important part of these contradictions. Quite independently of whether external circumstances will permit us to carry out our analysis to the end, we firmly take into consideration that our subjective analysis will be supported by the objective analysis which historical events will provide.

The radicalization of the working masses of Europe which found its expression in the last parliamentary elections is an indisputable fact. But this radicalization is now passing only through its initial stages. Such factors as the recent defeat of the Chinese revolution militate against the radicalization and drive for the most part into social democratic channels. We do not at all intend to predict here the tempo at which this process will proceed in the near future. But in any case it is clear that this radicalization will be the harbinger of a new revolutionary situation only from the moment that the gravitation toward the communist party begins to grow at the expense of the great reserves of the social democracy. Such is not the case as yet. But this must take place with iron necessity.

The present indefinite orientation of the Comintern leadership, with its internally discordant endeavors to turn the helm to the left without changing the whole regime and putting a stop to the organizational struggle against the most tested revolutionary elements—this contradictory orientation has arisen not only under the blows of the internal economic difficulties of the USSR which fully confirmed the prognosis of the Opposition; but it also corresponds fully to the *first* stage of the radicalization of the European working masses. The eclecticism of the policy of the Comintern leadership, the eclecticism of the draft program represent, as it were, a snapshot of the present condition of the international working class, which is driven to the left by the course of development but has not yet fixed its course, giving more than nine million votes to the German social democracy.

The further genuine revolutionary upsurge will signify a colossal regrouping within the working class, in all its organizations, including the Comintern. The tempo of this process is still unclear but the lines along which the crystallization will occur are clearly discernible. The working masses will pass from the social democracy to the communist party, section by section. The axis of communist policy will shift over more from right to left. Concurrently, a demand will increasingly rise for the consistent Bolshevik line of the group that was able to swim against the stream despite the hailstorm of accusations and persecutions since the defeat of the German proletariat at the end of 1923.

The organizational methods by which the ideas of genuine, unfalsified Leninism will triumph in the Comintern and consequently in the whole international proletariat depend very largely upon the present leadership of the Comintern and consequently directly upon the Sixth Congress.

However, whatever be the decisions of this congress—we are prepared for the worst—the general estimate of the present epoch and its inner tendencies and especially the evaluation of the experiences of the last five years indicate to us that the Opposition needs no other channel than that of the Comintern. No one will succeed in tearing us away from it. The ideas we defend will become its ideas. They will find their expression in the program of the Communist International.

III

Summary and perspectives of the Chinese Revolution
Its lessons for the countries of the Orient and for the whole of the Comintern

BOLSHEVISM AND MENSHEVISM and the left wing of the German and international social democracy took definite shape on the analysis of the experiences, mistakes, and tendencies of the 1905 revolution. An analysis of the experiences of the Chinese revolution is today of no less importance for the international proletariat.

This analysis, however, has not even begun—it is prohibited. The official literature is engaged in hastily selecting facts to suit the resolutions of the ECCI, the hollowness of which has been completely revealed. The draft program dulls the sharpest points of the Chinese problem whenever possible, but it sets the seal of approval upon the essential points of the fatal line followed by the ECCI in the Chinese question. The analysis of the great historical process is replaced by a literary defense of bankrupt schemas.

1. ON THE NATURE OF THE COLONIAL BOURGEOISIE

The draft program states: "Temporary agreements [with the national bourgeoisie of colonial countries] are admissible only insofar as the bourgeoisie does not obstruct the revolutionary organization of the workers and peasants and wages a genuine struggle against imperialism."

This formula, although it is deliberately tacked on as an incidental proposition, is one of the central postulates of the draft, for the countries of the Orient, at any rate. The main proposition deals, naturally, with the "emancipation [of the workers and peasants] from the influence of the national bourgeoisie." But we judge not from the standpoint of grammar but politically and, moreover, on the basis of experience, and therefore we say: the main proposition is only an incidental one here, while the incidental proposition contains what is most essential. The formula, taken as a whole, is a classic Menshevik noose for the proletariat of the Orient.

What "temporary agreements" are meant here? In politics, as in nature, all things are "temporary." Perhaps we are discussing here purely practical agreements *from one occasion to the next?* It goes without saying that we cannot renounce in advance such rigidly delimited and rigidly practical agreements as serve each time a quite definite aim. For example, such cases as involve agreements with the student youth of the Kuomintang for the organization of an anti-imperialist demonstration, or of obtaining assistance from the Chinese merchants for strikers in a foreign concession, etc. Such cases are not at all excluded in the future, even in China. But in that case why are *general* political conditions adduced here, namely, "... insofar as the bourgeoisie does not obstruct the revolutionary organization of the workers and peasants and wages a genuine [!] struggle against imperialism"? The sole "condition" for every agreement with the bourgeoisie, for each separate, practical, and expedient agreement adapted to each given case, consists in not allowing either the organizations or the banners to become mixed directly or indirectly for a single day or a single hour; it consists in distinguishing between the red and the blue,[52] and in not believing for an instant in the capacity or readiness of the bourgeoisie either to lead a *genuine* struggle against imperialism or *not to obstruct* the workers and peasants. For practical and expedient agreements we have absolutely no use for such a condition as the one cited above. On the contrary, it could only cause us harm, running counter to the general line of our struggle against capitalism, which is not suspended even during the brief period of an "agreement." As was said long ago, purely practical agreements, such as do not bind us in the least and do not oblige us to anything politically, can be concluded with the devil himself, if that is advantageous at a given moment. But it would be absurd in such a case to demand that the devil should *generally* become converted to Christianity, and that he use his horns not against workers and peasants but exclusively for pious deeds. In presenting such conditions we act in reality as the devil's advocates, and beg him to let us become his godfathers.

By its absurd conditions, which serve to paint the bourgeoisie in bright colors in advance, the draft program states clearly and definitely (despite the diplomatic and incidental character of its thesis) that involved here are precisely long-term political blocs and not agreements for specific occasions concluded for practical reasons and rigidly confined to practical aims. But in such a case, what is meant by demands that the bourgeoisie wage a "genuine" struggle and that it "not obstruct" the workers? Do we present these conditions to the bourgeoisie itself, and demand a public promise from it? It will make you any promises you want! It will even send its delegates to Moscow, enter the Peasants International, adhere as a "sympathizing" party to the Comintern,[53] peek into the Red International of Labor Unions. In short, it will promise anything that will give it the opportunity (with our assistance) to dupe the workers and peasants, more efficiently, more easily, and more completely to throw sand in their eyes—until the first opportunity, such as was offered in Shanghai.[54]

But perhaps it is not a question here of political obligations exacted from the bourgeoisie which, we repeat, it will immediately agree to in order thus to transform us into its guarantors before the working masses? Perhaps it is a question here of an "objective" and "scientific" evaluation of a given national bourgeoisie, an expert *a priori* "sociological" prognosis, as it were, of its capacity to wage a struggle and not to obstruct? Sad to say, as the more recent and freshest experience testifies, such an *a priori* prognosis makes fools out of experts as a rule. And it would not be so bad, if only they alone were involved. . . .

There cannot be the slightest doubt on the matter: the text deals precisely with long-term political blocs. It would be entirely superfluous to include in a program the question of occasional practical agreements. For this purpose, a matter-of-fact tactical resolution "On Our Current Tasks" would suffice. Involved here is a question of justifying and setting a programmatic seal of approval upon yesterday's orientation toward the Kuomintang, which doomed the second Chinese revolution[55] to destruction, and which is capable of destroying revolutions in the future.

According to the idea advanced by Bukharin, the real author of the draft, all stakes are placed precisely upon the general evaluation of the colonial bourgeoisie, whose capacity to struggle and not to obstruct must be proved not by its own oaths but in a rigorous "sociological" manner, that is by a thousand and one scholastic schemas adapted to opportunist purposes.

To bring this out more clearly let us refer back to the Bukharin evaluation of the colonial bourgeoisie. After citing the "anti-imperialist content" of colonial revolutions, and quoting Lenin (without any justification whatever), Bukharin proclaims:

"The liberal bourgeoisie in China played an objectively revolutionary role over a period of a number of years, and not months. Then it exhausted itself. This was not all a political 'twenty-four hour' holiday of the type of the Russian liberal revolution of 1905."

Everything here is wrong from the beginning to end.

Lenin really taught us to differentiate rigidly between an

oppressed and oppressor bourgeois nation. From this follow conclusions of exceptional importance. For instance, our attitude toward a war between an imperialist and a colonial country. For a pacifist, such a war is a war like any other. For a communist, a war of a colonial nation against an imperialist nation is a bourgeois revolutionary war. Lenin thus *raised* the national liberation movements, the colonial insurrections, and wars of the oppressed nations, to the level of the bourgeois-democratic revolutions, in particular, to that of the Russian revolution of 1905. But Lenin did not at all place the wars for national liberation *above* bourgeois-democratic revolutions as is now done by Bukharin, after his 180 degree turn. Lenin insisted on a distinction between an oppressed bourgeois nation and a bourgeois oppressor nation. But Lenin nowhere raised and never could raise the question as if the bourgeoisie of a colonial or a semicolonial country in an epoch of struggle for national liberation must be more progressive and more revolutionary than the bourgeoisie of a noncolonial country in the epoch of the democratic revolution. This does not flow from anything in theory; there is no confirmation of it in history. For example, pitiful as Russian liberalism was, and hybrid as was its left half, the petty-bourgeois democrats, the Social Revolutionists and Mensheviks, it would nevertheless hardly be possible to say that Chinese liberalism and Chinese bourgeois democracy rose to a higher level or were more revolutionary than their Russian prototypes.

To present matters as if there must inevitably flow from the fact of colonial oppression the revolutionary character of a national bourgeoisie is to reproduce inside out the fundamental error of Menshevism, which held that the revolutionary nature of the Russian bourgeoisie must flow from the oppression of feudalism and the autocracy.

The question of the nature and the policy of the bourgeoisie is settled by the entire internal class structure of a nation waging the revolutionary struggle; by the historical epoch in which that struggle develops; by the degree of economic, political, and military dependence of the national bourgeoisie upon world imperialism as a whole or a particular section of it; finally, and this is most important, by the degree of class activity of the native proletariat, and by the state of its connections with the international revolutionary movement.

A democratic or national liberation movement may offer the bourgeoisie an opportunity to deepen and broaden its possibilities for exploitation. Independent intervention of the proletariat on the revolutionary arena threatens to deprive the bourgeoisie of the possibility to exploit altogether.

Let us observe some facts more closely.

The present inspirers of the Comintern have untiringly repeated that Chiang Kai-shek waged a war "against imperialism" whilst Kerensky marched hand in hand with the imperialists. Ergo: whereas a ruthless struggle had to be waged against Kerensky, it was necessary to support Chiang Kai-shek.

The ties between Kerenskyism and imperialism were indisputable. One can go even still further back and point out that the Russian bourgeoisie "dethroned" Nicholas II with the blessings of British and French imperialism. Not only did Milyukov-Kerensky support the war waged by Lloyd George–Poincaré, but Lloyd George and Poincaré also supported Milyukov's and Kerensky's revolution first against the czar, and later against the workers and peasants. This is absolutely beyond dispute.

But how did matters stand in this respect in China? The "February" revolution in China took place in 1911. That revolution was a great and progressive event, although it was accomplished with the direct participation of the imperialists. Sun Yat-sen, in his memoirs, relates how his organization relied in all its work on the "support" of the imperialist states—either Japan, France, or America. If Kerensky in 1917 continued to take part in the imperialist war, then the Chinese bourgeoisie, the one that is so "national," so "revolutionary," etc., supported Wilson's intervention in the war with the hope that the Entente would help to emancipate China. In 1918 Sun Yat-sen addressed to the governments of the Entente his plans for the economic development and political emancipation of China.[56] There is no foundation whatever for the assertion that the Chinese bourgeoisie, in its struggle against the Manchu dynasty, displayed any higher revolutionary qualities than the Russian bourgeoisie in the struggle against czarism; or that there is a principled difference between Chiang Kai-shek's and Kerensky's attitude toward imperialism.

But, says the ECCI, Chiang Kai-shek nevertheless did wage war against imperialism. To present the situation in this manner is to put too crude a face upon reality. Chiang Kai-shek waged war against certain Chinese militarists, the agents of *one* of the imperialist powers. This is not at all the same as to wage a war against imperialism. Even T'an P'ing-shan understood this. In his report to the Seventh Plenum of the ECCI (at the end of 1926) T'an P'ing-shan characterized the policy of the Kuomintang center headed by Chiang Kai-shek as follows:

"In the sphere of international policy it occupies a passive position in the full meaning of that word. . . . It is inclined to fight only against British imperialism; so far as the Japanese imperialists are concerned, however, it is ready under certain conditions to make a compromise with them." (*Minutes of the Seventh Plenum, ECCI*, vol. 1, p. 406.)

The attitude of the Kuomintang toward imperialism was from the very outset not revolutionary but entirely opportunist. It endeavored to smash and isolate the agents of certain imperialist powers so as to make a deal with the selfsame or other imperialist powers on terms more favorable for the Chinese bourgeoisie. That is all. But the gist of the matter lies in the fact that the entire formulation of the question is erroneous.

One must measure not the attitude of every given national bourgeoisie to imperialism "in general," but its attitude to the immediate revolutionary historical tasks of its own nation. The Russian bourgeoisie was the bourgeoisie of an imperialist oppressor state; the Chinese bourgeoisie, a bourgeoisie of an oppressed colonial country. The overthrow of feudal czarism was a progressive task in old Russia. The overthrow of the imperialist yoke is a progressive historical task in China. However, the conduct of the Chinese bourgeoisie in relation to imperialism, the proletariat, and the peasantry, was not more revolutionary than the attitude of the Russian bourgeoisie towards czarism and the revolutionary classes in Russia, but, if anything, viler and more reactionary. That is the only way to pose the question.

The Chinese bourgeoisie is sufficiently realistic and acquainted intimately enough with the nature of world imperialism to understand that a really serious struggle against the latter requires such an upheaval of the revolutionary masses as would primarily become a menace to the bourgeoisie itself. If the struggle against the Manchu dynasty was a task of smaller historical proportions than the overthrow of czarism, then the struggle against world imperialism is a task on a much larger scale; and if we taught the workers of Russia from the very beginning not to believe in the readiness of liberalism and the ability of petty-bourgeois democracy to overthrow czarism and to destroy feudalism, we should no less energetically have imbued the Chinese workers from the outset with the same spirit of distrust. The new and absolutely false theory promulgated by Stalin-Bukharin about the "immanent" revolutionary spirit of the colonial bourgeoisie is, in substance, a translation of Menshevism into the language of Chinese politics. It serves only to convert the oppressed position of China into an internal political premium for the Chinese bourgeoisie, and it throws an additional weight on the scale of the bourgeoisie against the scale of the trebly oppressed Chinese proletariat.

But, we are told by Stalin and Bukharin, the authors of the draft program, Chiang Kai-shek's Northern Expedition[57] roused a powerful movement among the worker and peasant masses. This is incontestable. But did not the fact that Guchkov and Shulgin brought with them to Petrograd the abdication of Nicholas II play a revolutionary role? Did it not arouse the most downtrodden, exhausted, and timid strata of the populace? Did not the fact that Kerensky, who but yesterday was a Trudovik,[58] became the president of the Ministers Council and the commander in chief, rouse the masses of soldiers? Did it not bring them to meetings? Did it not rouse the village to its feet against the landlord? The question could be posed even more widely. Did not the entire activities of capitalism rouse the masses, did it not rescue them, to use the expression of the *Communist Manifesto,* from the idiocy of rural life? Did it not impel the proletarian battalions to the struggle? But does our historical evaluation of the objective role of capitalism as a whole or of certain actions of the bourgeoisie in particular, become a substitute for our active class revolutionary attitude toward capitalism or toward the actions of the bourgeoisie? Opportunist policies have always been based on this kind of nondialectical, conservative, tail-endist "objectivism." Marxism on the contrary invariably taught that the revolutionary consequences of one or another act of the bourgeoisie, to which it is compelled by its position, will be fuller, more decisive, less doubtful, and firmer, the more independent the proletarian vanguard will be in relation to the bourgeoisie, the less it will be inclined to place its fingers between the jaws of the bourgeoisie, to see it in bright colors, to overestimate its revolutionary spirit or its readiness for a "united front" and for a struggle against imperialism.

The Stalinist and Bukharinist appraisal of the colonial bourgeoisie cannot stand criticism, either theoretical, historical, or political. Yet this is precisely the appraisal, as we have seen, that the draft program seeks to canonize.

One unexposed and uncondemned error always leads to another, or prepares the ground for it.

If yesterday the Chinese bourgeoisie was enrolled in the united revolutionary front, then today it is proclaimed to have "definitely gone over to the counterrevolutionary camp." It is not difficult to expose how unfounded are these transfers and enrollments which have been effected in a purely administrative manner without any serious Marxian analysis whatever.

It is absolutely self-evident that the bourgeoisie in joining the camp of the revolution does so not accidentally, not because it is light-minded, but under the pressure of its own class interests. For fear of the masses the bourgeoisie subsequently deserts the revolution or openly displays its concealed hatred of the revolution. But the bourgeoisie can go over "*definitely* to the counterrevolutionary camp," that is, free itself from the necessity of "supporting" the revolution again, or at least of flirting with it, only in the event that its fundamental class aspirations are satisfied either by revolutionary means or in another way (for instance, the Bismarckian way). Let us recall the history of the period of 1848–1871. Let us recall that the Russian bourgeoisie was able to turn its back so bluntly upon the revolution of 1905 only because the revolution gave it the State Duma, that is, it received the means whereby it could bring direct pressure to bear on the bureaucracy and make deals with it. Nevertheless, when the war of 1914–17 revealed the inability of the "modernized" regime to secure the basic interests of the bourgeoisie, the latter again turned towards the revolution, and made its turn more sharply than in 1905.

Can anyone maintain that the revolution of 1925–27 in China has at least partly satisfied the basic interests of Chinese capitalism? No. China is today just as far removed from real national unity and from tariff autonomy as it was prior to 1925.[59] Yet, the creation of a unified domestic market and its protection from cheaper foreign goods is a life-and-death question for the Chinese bourgeoisie, a question second in importance only to that of maintaining the basis of its class domination over the proletariat and the peasant poor. But, for the Japanese and the British bourgeoisie the maintenance of the colonial status of China is likewise a question of no less importance than economic autonomy is for the Chinese bourgeoisie. That is why there will still be not a few leftward zigzags in the policy of the Chinese bourgeoisie. There will be no lack of temptations in the future for the amateurs of the "national united front." To tell the Chinese communists today that their alliance with the bourgeoisie from 1924 to the end of 1927 was correct but that it is worthless now because the bourgeoisie has definitely gone over to the counterrevolutionary camp, is to disarm the Chinese communists once again in face of the coming objective changes in the situation and the inevitable leftward zigzags of the Chinese bourgeoisie. The war now being conducted by Chiang Kai-shek against the north already overthrows completely the mechanical schema of the authors of the draft program.

◆◆

But the principled error of the official formulation of the question will doubtless appear more glaringly, more convincingly, and more incontrovertibly if we recall the fact which is still fresh in our minds, and which is of no little importance, namely, that czarist Russia was a combination of oppressor and oppressed nations, that is of Great Russians and "foreigners," many of whom were in a completely colonial or semicolonial status. Lenin not only demanded that the greatest attention be paid to the national problem of the peoples in czarist Russia but also proclaimed (against Bukharin and others) that it was the elementary duty of the proletariat of the dominant nation to support the struggle of the oppressed nations for their self-determination, up to and including separation. But did the party conclude from this that the bourgeoisie of the nationalities oppressed by czarism (the Poles, Ukrainians, Tartars, Jews, Armenians, and others) were more progressive, more radical, and more revolutionary than the Russian bourgeoisie? Historical experience bears out the fact that the Polish bourgeoisie—notwithstanding the fact that it suffered both from the yoke of the autocracy and from national oppression—was more reactionary than the Russian bourgeoisie and, in the State Dumas, always gravitated not towards the Cadets but towards the Octobrists. The same is true of the Tartar bourgeoisie. The fact that the Jews had absolutely no rights whatever did not prevent the Jewish bourgeoisie from being even more cowardly, more reactionary, and more vile than the Russian bourgeoisie. Or perhaps the Estonian bourgeoisie, the Lettish, the Georgian, or the Armenian bourgeoisie were more revolutionary than the Great Russian bourgeoisie? How could anyone forget such historical lessons!

Or should we perhaps recognize today, after the event, that Bolshevism was wrong when—in contradistinction to the Bund, the Dashnaks, the PPSers,[60] the Georgian and other Mensheviks—it called upon the workers of *all* the oppressed nationalities, of all the colonial peoples in czarist Russia, at the very dawn of the bourgeois-democratic revolution, to dissociate themselves and form their own autonomous class organizations, to break ruthlessly all organizational ties not only with the liberal bourgeois, but also with the revolutionary petty-bourgeois parties, to win over the working class in the struggle against these parties, and through the workers fight against these parties for influence over the peasantry? Did we not commit here a "Trotskyist" mistake? Did we not skip over, in relation to these oppressed, and in many cases very backward nations, the phase of development corresponding to the Kuomintang?

As a matter of fact how easily one could construct a theory that the PPS, Dashnaktsutiun, the Bund, etc., were "peculiar" forms of the necessary collaboration of the various classes in the struggle against the autocracy and against national oppression![61] How can such historical lessons be forgotten?

For a Marxist it was clear even prior to the Chinese events of the last three years—and today it should be clear even to the blind—that foreign imperialism, as a direct factor in the internal life of China, renders the Chinese Milyukovs and Chinese Kerenskys in the final analysis even more vile than their Russian prototypes. It is not for nothing that the very first manifesto issued by our party proclaimed that the further east we go, the lower and viler becomes the bourgeoisie, the greater are the tasks that fall upon the proletariat. This historical "law" fully applies to China as well.

"Our revolution is a bourgeois revolution, the workers must support the bourgeoisie—say the worthless politicians from the camp of the liquidators. Our revolution is a bourgeois revolution, say we who are Marxists. The workers must open the eyes of the people to the fraud of the bourgeois politicians, teach them not to place trust in promises and to rely on *their OWN* forces, on *their OWN* organization, on *their OWN* unity, and on *their OWN* weapons alone." (Lenin, *Works*, vol. 14, part 1, p. 11.)*

This Leninist thesis is compulsory for the Orient as a whole. It must by all means find a place in the program of the Comintern.

2. THE STAGES OF THE CHINESE REVOLUTION

The first stage of the Kuomintang was the period of domination of the national bourgeoisie under the apologetic label of a "bloc of four classes." The second period, after Chiang Kai-shek's coup d'état, was an experiment of parallel and "independent" domination of Chinese Kerenskyism, in the shape of the Hankow government[62] of the "left" Wang Ching-wei. While the Russian Narodniks,[63] together with the Mensheviks, lent to their short-lived "dictatorship" the form of an open dual power, the Chinese "revolutionary democracy" did not even reach that stage. And inasmuch as history in general does not work to order, there only remains for us to understand that *there is not* and *will not be* any other "democratic

---

* "Letters from Afar" (March-April 1917) in *LCW*, vol. 23 p. 306.

dictatorship" except the dictatorship exercised by the Kuomintang since 1925. This remains equally true regardless of whether the semi-unification of China accomplished by the Kuomintang is maintained in the immediate future or the country is again dismembered. But precisely at a time when the class dialectics of the revolution, having spent all its other resources, clearly and conclusively put on the order of the day the *dictatorship of the proletariat,* leading the countless millions of oppressed and disinherited in city and village, the ECCI advanced the slogan of a *democratic* (i.e., bourgeois democratic) dictatorship of the workers and peasants. The reply to this formula was the Canton insurrection[64] which, with all its prematurity, with all the adventurism of its leadership, raised the curtain of a new stage, or, more correctly, of the coming *third* Chinese revolution. It is necessary to dwell on this point in some detail.

Seeking to insure themselves against their past sins, the leadership monstrously forced the course of events at the end of last year and brought about the Canton miscarriage. However, even a miscarriage can teach us a good deal concerning the organism of the mother and the process of gestation. The tremendous and, from the standpoint of theory, truly decisive significance of the Canton events for the fundamental problems of the Chinese revolution is conditioned precisely upon the fact that we have here a phenomenon rare in history and politics, a virtual *laboratory experiment on a colossal scale.* We have paid for it dearly, but this obliges us all the more to assimilate its lessons.

One of the fighting slogans of the Canton insurrection, according to the account in *Pravda* (no. 31), was the cry "Down with the Kuomintang!" The Kuomintang banners and insignia were torn down and trampled underfoot. But even after the "betrayal" of Chiang Kai-shek, and the subsequent "betrayal" of Wang Ching-wei (betrayals not of their own class, but of our ... illusions), the ECCI had issued the solemn vow that: "We will not surrender the banner of the Kuomintang!"[65]

The workers of Canton outlawed the Kuomintang Party, *declaring all of its tendencies illegal.* This means that for the solution of the basic national tasks, not only the big bourgeoisie but also the petty bourgeoisie was incapable of producing a political force, a party, or a faction, in conjunction with which the party of the proletariat might be able to solve the tasks of the bourgeois-democratic revolution. The key to the situation lies precisely in the fact that *the task of winning the movement of the poor peasants already fell entirely upon the shoulders of the proletariat,* and directly upon the Communist Party; and that the approach to a genuine solution of the bourgeois-democratic tasks of the revolution necessitated the concentration of all power in the hands of the proletariat.

Pravda carried the following report about the policies of the short-lived Canton soviet government:

"In the interests of the workers, the Canton soviet issued decrees establishing . . . workers control of industry through the factory committees . . . the nationalization of big industry, transportation, and banks."

Further on such measures are mentioned as: "The confiscation of all dwellings of the big bourgeoisie for the benefit of the toilers. . . ."

Thus it was the Canton workers who were in power and moreover, the government was actually in the hands of the Communist Party. The program of the new state power consisted not only in the confiscation of whatever feudal estates there may be in Kwangtung in general; not only in the establishment of the workers control of production; but also in the nationalization of big industry, banks, and transportation, and even the confiscation of bourgeois dwellings and all bourgeois property for the benefit of the toilers. The question arises: if these are the methods of a bourgeois revolution then what should the proletarian revolution in China look like?

Notwithstanding the fact that the directives of the ECCI had nothing to say on the subject of the proletarian dictatorship and socialist measures; notwithstanding the fact that Canton is more petty bourgeois in character than Shanghai, Hankow, and other industrial centers of the country, the revolutionary overturn effected *against the Kuomintang* led automatically to the dictatorship of the proletariat which, at its very first steps, found itself compelled by the entire situation to resort to more radical measures than those with which the October Revolution began. And this fact, despite its paradoxical appearance, flows quite lawfully from the social relations of China as well as from the entire development of the revolution.

Large and middle-scale landed estates (such as obtain in China) are most closely interlinked with city capital, including foreign capital. There is no caste of feudal landlords in China in opposition to the bourgeoisie. The most widespread, common, and hated exploiter in the village is the kulak-usurer, the agent of finance capital in the cities. The agrarian revolution is therefore just as much antifeudal as it is antibourgeois in character. In China, there will be practically no such stage as the first stage of our October Revolution in which the kulak marched with the middle and poor peasant, frequently at their head, against the landlord. The agrarian revolution in China signifies from the outset, as it will signify subsequently, an uprising not only against the few genuine feudal landlords and the bureaucracy, but also against the kulaks and usurers. If in our country the poor peasant committees appeared on the scene only during the second stage of the October Revolution, in the middle of 1918, in China, on the contrary, they will, in one form or another, appear on the scene as soon as the agrarian movement revives. The drive on the rich peasant will be the first and not the second step of the Chinese October.

The agrarian revolution, however, is not the sole content of the present historical struggle in China. The most extreme agrarian revolution, the general division of land (which will naturally be supported by the Communist Party to the very end), will not by itself provide a way out of the economic blind alley. China requires just as urgently national unity and economic sovereignty, that is, customs autonomy, or more correctly, a monopoly of foreign trade. And this means *emancipation from world imperialism*—imperialism for which China remains the most important prospective source not only of enrichment but also of actual existence, constituting a safety valve against the internal explosions of European capitalism today and American capitalism tomorrow. This is what predetermines the gigantic scope and monstrous sharpness of the struggle that faces the masses of China, all the more so now when the depth of the stream of the struggle has already been plumbed and felt by all of its participants.

The enormous role of foreign capital in Chinese industry and its way of relying directly in defense of its plunder on its own "national" bayonets,[66] render the program of workers control in China even less realizable than it was in our country. The direct expropriation first of the foreign capitalist and then of the Chinese capitalist enterprises will most likely be made imperative by the course of the struggle, on the day after the victorious insurrection.

Those objective sociohistorical causes which predetermined the "October" outcome of the Russian revolution rise before us in China in a still more accentuated form. The bourgeois and proletarian poles of the Chinese nation stand opposed to each other even more irreconcilably, if this is at all possible, than they did in Russia, since, on the one hand the Chinese bourgeoisie is directly bound up with foreign imperialism and the latter's military machine, and since, on the other hand, the Chinese proletariat has from the very beginning established a close bond with the Comintern and the Soviet Union. Numerically the Chinese peasantry constitutes an even more overwhelming mass than the Russia peasantry.[67] But being crushed in the vise of world contradictions, upon the solution of which in one way or another its fate depends, the Chinese peasantry is even less capable of playing a *leading* role than the Russian. At present this is no longer a matter of theoretical forecast, but a fact verified completely in all its aspects.

These fundamental and, at the same time, incontrovertible

social and political prerequisites of the third Chinese revolution demonstrate not only that the formula of the democratic dictatorship has *hopelessly outlived its usefulness,* but also that the third Chinese revolution, despite the great backwardness of China, or more correctly, because of this great backwardness as compared with Russia, will not have a "democratic" period, not even such a six-month period as the October Revolution had[68] (November 1917 to July 1918); but it will be compelled from the very outset to effect the most decisive shakeup and abolition of bourgeois property in city and village.

To be sure, this perspective does not harmonize with the pedantic and schematic conceptions concerning the interrelations between economics and politics. But the responsibility for this disharmony so disturbing to the prejudices which have newly taken root and which were already dealt a not inconsiderable blow by the October Revolution must be placed not on "Trotskyism" but on the *law of uneven development.* In this particular case this law is especially applicable.

It would be unwise pedantry to maintain that, had a Bolshevik policy been applied in the revolution of 1925–27, the Chinese Communist Party would *unfailingly* have come to power. But it is contemptible philistinism to assert that such a possibility was entirely out of the question. The mass movement of workers and peasants was on a scale entirely adequate for this,[69] as was also the disintegration of the ruling classes. The national bourgeoisie sent its Chiang Kai-sheks and Wang Ching-weis as envoys to Moscow, and through its Hu Hanmins knocked at the door of the Comintern, precisely because it was hopelessly weak in face of the revolutionary masses; it realized its weakness and sought to insure itself. Neither the workers nor the peasants would have followed the national bourgeoisie if we ourselves had not dragged them by a rope. Had the Comintern pursued any sort of correct policy, the outcome of the struggle of the Communist Party for the masses would have been predetermined—the Chinese proletariat would have supported the communists, while the peasant war would have supported the revolutionary proletariat.

If, at the beginning of the Northern Expedition we had begun to organize soviets in the "liberated" districts (and the masses were instinctively aspiring for that with all their might and main) we would have secured the necessary basis and a revolutionary running start, we would have rallied around us the agrarian uprisings, we would have built *our own* army, we would have disintegrated the enemy armies and despite the youthfulness of the Communist Party of China, the latter would have been able, thanks to proper guidance from the Comintern, to mature in these exceptional years and to assume power, if not in the whole of China at once, then at least in a considerable part of China. And, above all, we would have had a *party*.

But something absolutely monstrous occurred precisely in the sphere of leadership—a veritable historical catastrophe. The authority of the Soviet Union, of the Bolshevik Party, and of the Comintern served entirely, first, to support Chiang Kai-shek against an independent policy of the Communist Party, and then to support Wang Ching-wei as the leader of the agrarian revolution. Having trampled underfoot the very basis of Leninist policy and after breaking the spine of the young Communist Party of China, the ECCI predetermined the victory of Chinese Kerenskyism over Bolshevism, of the Chinese Milyukovs over the Kerenskys, and of British and Japanese imperialism over the Chinese Milyukovs.

In this and in this alone lies the meaning of what took place in China in the course of 1925–27.

3. DEMOCRATIC DICTATORSHIP OR A DICTATORSHIP OF THE PROLETARIAT?

But how did the last plenum of the ECCI evaluate the experiences of the Chinese revolution, including the experience of the Canton insurrection? What further perspectives did it outline? The resolution of the February (1928) plenum, which is the key to the corresponding sections of the draft program on this subject, says concerning the Chinese revolution:

"It is incorrect to characterize it as a 'permanent' revolution [the position of the representative of the ECCI]. The tendency to skip [?] over the bourgeois-democratic stage of the revolution while simultaneously [?] appraising the revolution as a 'permanent' revolution is a mistake analogous to that committed by Trotsky in 1905 [?]."

The ideological life of the Comintern since Lenin's departure from its leadership, that is, since 1923, consisted primarily in a struggle against so-called Trotskyism and particularly against the "permanent revolution." How is it, then, that in the fundamental question of the Chinese revolution not only the Central Committee of the Communist Party of China, but also the official delegate of the Comintern, i.e., a leader who was sent with special instructions, happen to commit the very same "mistake" for which hundreds of men are now exiled to Siberia and put in prison? The struggle around the Chinese question has been raging for some two and a half years. When the Opposition declared that the old Central Committee of the Communist Party of China (Ch'en Tu-hsiu), under the influence of the false directives from the Comintern, conducted an opportunist policy, this evaluation was declared to be "slander." The leadership of the Communist Party of China was pronounced irreproachable. The celebrated T'an P'ing-shan declared amid the general approval of the Seventh Plenum of the ECCI that "At the very first manifestations of Trotskyism, the Communist Party of China and the Young Communist League immediately adopted a unanimous resolution against Trotskyism." (*Minutes,* p. 205.)

But when, not withstanding these "achievements," events unfolded their tragic logic which led to the first and then to the second and even more frightful debacle of the revolution, the leadership of the Communist Party of China, formerly flawless, was rebaptized as Menshevik and deposed in the space of twenty-four hours. At the same time a decree was promulgated that the new leadership fully reflected the line of the Comintern.[70] But no sooner did a new and a serious test arise than it was discovered that the new Central Committee of the Communist Party of China was guilty (as we have already seen, not in words, but in actions) of swerving to the position of the so-called permanent revolution. The delegate of the Comintern took the very same path. This astonishing and truly incomprehensible fact can be explained only by the yawning "scissors" between the instructions of the ECCI and the real dynamics of the revolution.

We shall not dwell here upon the myth of the "permanent revolution" of 1905 which was placed in circulation in 1924 in order to sow confusion and bewilderment. We shall confine ourselves to an examination of how this myth broke down on the question of the Chinese revolution.

The first paragraph of the February resolution, from which the above-quoted passage was taken, gives the following motives for its negative attitude toward the so-called permanent revolution:

"The current period of the Chinese revolution is a period of a bourgeois-democratic revolution which has not been completed either from the economic standpoint (the agrarian revolution and the abolition of feudal relations), or from the standpoint of the national struggle against imperialism (the unification of China and the establishment of national independence), or from the standpoint of the class nature of the state (the dictatorship of the proletariat and the peasantry). . . ."

This presentation of motives is an unbroken chain of mistakes and contradictions.

The ECCI taught that the Chinese revolution must secure for China the opportunity to develop along the road to socialism. This goal could be achieved only if the revolution did not halt merely at the solution of the bourgeois-democratic tasks but continued to unfold, passing from one stage to the next, i.e., continued to develop uninterruptedly (*or permanently*) and thus lead China toward a socialist development. This is precisely what Marx understood by the term "permanent revolution." How then can we, on the one hand, speak of a noncapitalist path of development for China and, on the other, deny the permanent character of the revolution in general?

But—insists the resolution of the ECCI—the revolution has not been completed, either from the standpoint of the agrarian revolution or from the standpoint of the national struggle against imperialism. Hence it draws the conclusion about the bourgeois-democratic character of the "present period of the Chinese revolution." As a matter of fact the "present period" is a period of counterrevolution. The ECCI doubtlessly intends to say that the new resurgence of the Chinese revolution, or *the third Chinese revolution,* will bear a bourgeois-democratic character because the second Chinese revolution of 1925–27 solved neither the agrarian question nor the national question. However, even thus amended, this reasoning is based upon a total failure to understand the experiences and lessons of both the Chinese and the Russian revolutions.

The February 1917 revolution in Russia left unsolved all the internal and international problems which had led to the revolution—serfdom in the villages, the old bureaucracy, the war, and economic debacle. Taking this as a starting point, not only the SRs and the Mensheviks, but also a considerable section of the leadership of our own party tried to prove to Lenin that the "present period of the revolution is a period of the bourgeois-democratic revolution." In this, its basic consideration, the resolution of the ECCI merely copies the objections which the opportunists raised against the struggle for the dictatorship of the proletariat waged by Lenin in 1917.

Furthermore, it appears that the bourgeois-democratic revolution remains unaccomplished not only from the economic and national standpoint, but also from the "standpoint of the class nature of the state (the dictatorship of the proletariat and the peasantry)." This can mean only one thing: that the Chinese proletariat is forbidden to struggle for the conquest of power so long as no "genuine" democratic government stands at the helm in China. Unfortunately, no instructions are forthcoming as to where we can get it.

The confusion is further increased by the fact that the slogan of soviets was rejected for China in the course of these two years on the ground that the creation of soviets is permissible presumably only during the transition to the proletarian revolution (Stalin's "theory")[71]. But when the soviet revolution broke out in Canton and when its participants drew the conclusion that this was precisely the transition to the proletarian revolution, they were accused of "Trotskyism." Is the party to be educated by such methods? Is this the way to assist it in the solution of supreme tasks?

To save a hopeless position, the resolution of the ECCI (without any connection whatever with the entire trend of its thought) rushes in posthaste to its last argument—taken from imperialism. It appears that the tendency to skip over the bourgeois-democratic stage ". . . is all the more [!] harmful because such a formulation of the question eliminates [?] the most important national peculiarity of the Chinese revolution, which is a semicolonial revolution."

The only meaning that these senseless words can have is that the imperialist yoke will be overthrown by some sort of nonproletarian dictatorship. But this means that the "most important national peculiarity" has been dragged in at the last moment in order to paint the Chinese national bourgeoisie or the Chinese petty-bourgeois "democracy" in bright colors. This argument can have no other meaning. But this only "meaning" has been adequately examined by us in our chapter "On the Nature of the Colonial Bourgeoisie." There is no need to return to this subject.

China is still confronted with a vast, bitter, bloody, and prolonged struggle for such elementary things as the liquidation of the most "Asiatic" forms of slavery, national emancipation, and unification of the country. But as the course of events has shown, it is precisely this that makes impossible in the future any petty-bourgeois leadership or even semileadership in the revolution. The unification and emancipation of

China today is an international task, no less so than the existence of the USSR. This task can be solved only by means of a desperate struggle on the part of the downtrodden, hungry, and persecuted masses under the direct leadership of the proletarian vanguard—a struggle not only against world imperialism, but also against its economic and political agency in China, against the bourgeoisie, including the "national" bourgeoisie and all its democratic flunkeys. And this is nothing else than the road toward the dictatorship of the proletariat.

Beginning with April, 1917, Lenin explained to his opponents, who accused him of having adopted the position of the "permanent revolution," that the dictatorship of the proletariat and the peasantry was realized partially in the epoch of dual power. He explained later that this dictatorship met with its further extension during the first period of Soviet power from November 1917 until July 1918, when the entire peasantry, together with the workers, effected the agrarian revolution while the working class did not as yet proceed with the confiscation of the mills and factories, but experimented with workers control. So far as the "class nature of the state" was concerned, the democratic-SR-Menshevik "dictatorship" gave all that it could give— the miscarriage of dual power. As to the agrarian overturn, the revolution gave birth to a perfectly healthy and strong baby, but it was the proletarian dictatorship that functioned as the midwife. In other words, what the theoretical formula of the dictatorship of the proletariat and the peasantry had combined, was dissociated in the course of the actual class struggle. The hollow shell of semipower was provisionally entrusted to Kerensky-Tseretelli, while the real kernel of the agrarian-democratic revolution fell to the share of the victorious working class. This dialectical dissociation of the democratic dictatorship, the leaders of the ECCI failed to understand. They drove themselves into a political blind alley by condemning mechanically any "skipping over the bourgeois-democratic stage" and by endeavoring to guide the historical process in accordance with circular letters. *If we are to understand by the bourgeois-democratic stage, the accomplishment of the agrarian revolution by means of a "democratic dictatorship," then it was the October Revolution itself that audaciously "skipped" over the bourgeois-democratic stage.* Should it not be condemned for it?

Why is it then that the historically inevitable course of events which was the highest expression of Bolshevism in Russia must prove to be "Trotskyism" in China? No doubt owing to the very same logic which declares to be suitable for China the theory of the Martynovs, a theory fought by Bolshevism for two decades in Russia.

But is it at all permissible to draw here an analogy with Russia? Our answer is that the slogan of a democratic dictatorship of the proletariat and the peasantry was constructed by the leaders of the ECCI exclusively and entirely in accordance with the method of analogy, but a formal and literary analogy and not a materialist and historical analogy. An analogy between China and Russia is entirely admissible if we find the proper approach to it, and Lenin made excellent use of such an analogy. Moreover he did so not *after* but before the events, as if he had foreseen the future blunders of the epigones. Hundreds of times Lenin had to defend the October Revolution of the proletariat that had the audacity to conquer power *notwithstanding the fact* that the bourgeois-democratic tasks had not been solved. Precisely *because of that, and precisely in order to do that,* replied Lenin. Addressing himself to the pedants, who in their arguments against the conquest of power referred to the economic immaturity of Russia for socialism, which was "incontestable" for him (*Works,* vol. 18, part 2, p. 119), Lenin wrote on January 16, 1923:

"It does not even occur to them, for instance, that Russia standing on the border between civilized countries and countries which were for the first time definitely drawn by this war into the vortex of civilization, all Eastern countries and non-European countries—that Russia therefore could and should have manifested certain peculiarities which fall, of course, along the general lines of world development but which make its revolution different from all preceding revolutions of the

Western European countries and which introduce certain partial innovations in approaching the countries of the Orient." (*Ibid.*, p. 118.)*

The "peculiarity" which brings Russia *closer* to the countries of the Orient was seen by Lenin precisely in the fact that the young proletariat, at an early stage, had to grasp the broom and sweep feudal barbarism and all sort of rubbish from its path toward socialism.

If, consequently, we are to take as our starting point the Leninist analogy between China and Russia, then we must say: from the standpoint of the *"political nature of the state,"* all that could have been obtained through the democratic dictatorship in China has been put to the test, first in Sun Yat-sen's Canton, then on the road from Canton to Shanghai, which culminated in the Shanghai coup d'état and then in Wuhan where the Left Kuomintang appeared in its chemically pure form, i.e., according to the directive of the ECCI, as the organizer of the agrarian revolution, but in reality as its hangman. But the social *content* of the bourgeois-democratic revolution will fill the initial period of the coming dictatorship of the Chinese proletariat and the peasant poor. To advance now the slogan of democratic dictatorship of the proletariat and the peasantry after the role not only of the Chinese bourgeoisie, but also of Chinese "democracy" has been put to a thorough test, after it has become absolutely incontestable that "democracy" will play even a greater hangman's role in the coming battles than in the past—to advance this slogan now is simply to create the means of covering up the new varieties of Kuomintangism and to prepare a noose for the proletariat.

Let us recall for the sake of completeness what Lenin tersely said about those Bolsheviks who insisted upon counterposing to the SR-Menshevik experience the slogan of a "genuine" democratic dictatorship:

"Whoever now talks only about the 'revolutionary-demo-

---

* "Our Revolution," in *LCW*, vol. 33, p. 477. Also in *Lenin's Final Fight*, p. 221.

cratic dictatorship of the proletariat and peasantry' has lost touch with life, has, in virtue of this circumstance, *gone over,* in practice, to the petty bourgeoisie against the proletarian *class* struggle; and he ought to be relegated to the museum of 'Bolshevik' prerevolutionary antiquities (or, as one might call it, the museum of 'old Bolsheviks')." (*Works*, vol. 14, part 1, p. 29.)*

These words ring as if they were actually spoken today.

Of course it is not at all a question of calling the Communist Party of China to an immediate insurrection for the seizure of power. The pace depends entirely upon the circumstances. The consequences of defeat cannot be removed merely by revising the tactic. The revolution is now subsiding. The half-concealing resolution of the ECCI, the bombast about imminent revolutionary onslaughts, while countless people are being executed and a terrific commercial and industrial crisis rages in China, are criminal light-mindedness and nothing else. After three major defeats an economic crisis does not rouse but, on the contrary, depresses the proletariat which, as it is, has already been bled white, while the executions only destroy the politically weakened party.[72] We are entering in China into a period of reflux, and consequently into a period in which the party deepens its theoretical roots, educates itself critically, creates and strengthens firm organizational links in all spheres of the working-class movement, organizes rural nuclei, leads and unites partial, at first defensive and later offensive, battles of the workers and the peasant poor.

What will turn the tide in the mass movement? What circumstances will give the necessary revolutionary impulsion to the proletarian vanguard at the head of the many-millioned masses? This cannot be predicted. The future will show whether internal processes alone will be sufficient or an added impulsion will have to come from without.

---

* "Letters on Tactics" (April 21–26, 1917) in *LCW,* vol. 24, p. 45.

There are sufficient grounds for assuming that the smashing of the Chinese revolution, directly due to the false leadership, will permit the Chinese and foreign bourgeoisie to overcome to a lesser or greater degree the frightful economic crisis now raging in the country. Naturally, this will be done on the backs and bones of the workers and peasants. This phase of "stabilization" will once again group and fuse together the workers, restore their class self-confidence in order subsequently to bring them into still sharper conflict with the enemy, but on a higher historical stage. It will be possible to speak seriously about the perspective of an agrarian revolution only on the condition that there will be a new mounting wave of the proletarian movement on the offensive.

It is not excluded that the first stage of the coming third revolution may reproduce in a very abridged and modified form the stages which have already been passed, presenting, for instance, some new parody of the "national united front." But this first stage will be sufficient only to give the Communist Party a chance to put forward and announce its "April" thesis, that is, its program and tactics of the seizure of power, before the popular masses.

But what does the draft program say on this?

"The transition to the proletarian dictatorship is possible here [in China] only after a series of preparatory stages [?] only as a result of a whole period of the growing over [??] of the bourgeois-democratic revolution into the socialist revolution."

In other words, all the "stages" that have already been gone through are not to be taken into account. The draft program still sees ahead what has already been left behind. This is precisely what is meant by a tail-endist formulation. It opens wide the gates for new experiments in the spirit of the Kuomintang course. Thus the concealment of the old mistakes inevitably prepares the road for new errors.

If we enter the new upsurge, which will develop at an incomparably more rapid tempo than the last one, with a blueprint of "democratic dictatorship" that has already outlived its usefulness, there can be no doubt that the third Chinese revolution, like the second, will be led to its doom.[73]

4. ADVENTURISM AS THE PRODUCT OF OPPORTUNISM

The second paragraph of the same resolution of the February plenum of the ECCI says:

"The first wave of the broad revolutionary movement of workers and peasants which in the main proceeded under the slogans, and to a considerable extent *under the leadership of the Communist Party,* is over. It ended in several centers of the revolutionary movement with *heaviest defeats* for the workers and peasants, the physical extermination of the communists and revolutionary cadres of the labor and peasant movement in general." (Our emphasis.)

When the "wave" was surging high, the ECCI said that the whole movement was entirely under the blue banner and leadership of the Kuomintang which even took the place of soviets. It is precisely on that ground that the Communist Party was subordinated to the Kuomintang. But that is exactly why the revolutionary movement ended with "heaviest defeats." Now when these defeats have been recognized, an attempt is being made to erase the Kuomintang from the past as if it had never existed, as if the ECCI had not declared the blue banner its own.

There have been no defeats either in Shanghai or in Wuhan in the past; there were merely transitions of the revolution "into a higher phase"—that is what we have been taught.[74] Now the sum total of these transitions is suddenly declared to be "heaviest defeats for the workers and peasants." However, in order to mask to some extent this unprecedented political bankruptcy of forecasts and evaluations, the concluding paragraph of the resolution declares:

"The ECCI makes it the duty of all sections of the CI to fight against the social democratic and Trotskyist slanders to the effect that the Chinese revolution has been liquidated [?]."

In the first paragraph of the resolution we were told that "Trotskyism" was the idea of the *permanent* Chinese revolution, that is, a revolution which is precisely at this time growing over from the bourgeois to the socialist phase; from the last paragraph we learn that according to the "Trotskyists," "the Chinese revolution has been liquidated." How can a *"liquidated"* revolution be a *permanent* revolution? Here we have Bukharin in all his glory.

Only complete and reckless irresponsibility permits of such contradictions which corrode all revolutionary thought at its roots.

If we are to understand by "liquidation" of the revolution the fact that the labor and peasant offensive has been beaten back and drowned in blood, that the masses are in a state of retreat and decline, that before another onslaught there must be, apart from many other circumstances, a molecular process at work among the masses which requires a certain period of time, the duration of which cannot be determined beforehand; if "liquidation" is to be understood in this way, it does not in any manner differ from the "heaviest defeats" which the ECCI has finally been compelled to recognize. Or are we to understand liquidation literally, as the actual elimination of the Chinese revolution, that is, of the very possibility and inevitability of its rebirth on a new plane? One can speak of such a perspective seriously and so as not to create confusion only in two cases—if China were doomed to dismemberment and complete extirpation, an assumption for which there is no basis whatever, or if the Chinese bourgeoisie would prove capable of solving the basic problems of Chinese life in its own nonrevolutionary way. Is it not this last variant which the theoreticians of the "bloc of four classes," who directly drove the Communist Party under the yoke of the bourgeoisie, seek to ascribe to us now?

History repeats itself. The blind men who did not understand the scope of the defeat of 1923, for a year and a half accused us of "liquidationism" towards the German revolution. But even this lesson, which cost the International so dearly, taught them nothing. At present they use their old rubber stamps, only this time substituting China for Germany. To be sure, their need to find "liquidators" is more acute today than it was four years ago, for this time it is much too obviously apparent that if anybody did "liquidate" the second Chinese revolution it was the authors of the "Kuomintang" course.

The strength of Marxism lies in its ability to foretell. In this sense the Opposition can point to an absolute confirmation in experience of its prognosis. At first concerning the Kuomintang as a whole, then concerning the "Left" Kuomintang and the Wuhan government, and, finally, concerning the "deposit" on the third revolution, that is the Canton insurrection. What further confirmation could there be of one's theoretical correctness?

The very same opportunist line, which through the policy of capitulation to the bourgeoisie has already brought heaviest defeats to the revolution during its first two stages, "grew over" in the third stage into a policy of adventurous raids on the bourgeoisie[75] and thus made the defeat final.

Had the leadership not hurried yesterday to leap over the defeats which it had itself brought about, it would first of all have explained to the Communist Party of China that victory is not gained in one sweep, that on the road to the armed insurrection there still remains a period of intense, incessant, and savage struggle for political influence on the workers and peasants.

On September 27, 1927, we said to the Presidium of the ECCI:

"Today's papers report that the revolutionary army has occupied Swatow. It is already several weeks that the armies of Ho Lung and Yeh T'ing have been advancing. *Pravda* calls these armies revolutionary armies.... But I ask you: what prospects does the movement of the revolutionary army which captured Swatow raise before the Chinese revolution? What are the slogans of the movement? What is its program? What should be its organizational forms?[76] What has become of the slogan of Chinese soviets, which *Pravda* suddenly advanced for a single day in July?"*

Without first counterposing the Communist Party to the Kuomintang as a whole, without the party's agitation among the masses for soviets and a soviet government, without an independent mobilization of the masses under the slogans of the agrarian revolution and of national emancipation, without the creation, broadening, and strengthening of the local soviets of workers, soldiers, and peasants deputies, the insurrection of Ho Lung and Yeh T'ing, even apart from their opportunist policy, could not fail to be only an isolated adventure, a pseudo-communist Makhno[77] feat; it could not fail to crash against its own isolation. And it has crashed.

The Canton insurrection was a broader and deeper repetition of the Ho Lung–Yeh T'ing adventure, only with infinitely more tragic consequences.

The February resolution of the ECCI combats putschistic moods in the Communist Party of China, that is, tendencies toward armed uprisings. It does not say, however, that these tendencies are a reaction to the entire opportunist policy of 1925–27, and an inevitable consequence of the purely military command issued from above to "change the step," without an evaluation of all that had been done, without an open revaluation of the basis of the tactic, and without a clear perspective. Ho Lung's campaign and the Canton insurrection were—and under the circumstances could not fail to be—breeders of putschism.

A real antidote to putschism as well as to opportunism can be only a clear understanding of the truth that the leadership of the armed insurrection of the workers and poor peasants, the seizure of power, and the institution of a revolutionary dictatorship fall henceforth entirely upon the shoulders of the Communist Party

---

* "Speech to the Presidium of the ECCI," in *Leon Trotsky on China* (New York: Pathfinder, 1976), p. 270.

of China. If the latter is permeated thoroughly with the understanding of this perspective, it will be as little inclined to improvize military raids on towns or armed insurrections in traps as to chase humbly after the enemy's banner.

The resolution of the ECCI condemns itself to utter impotence by the fact alone that in arguing most abstractly concerning the inadmissibility of leaping over stages and the harmfulness of putschism, it entirely ignores the class content of the Canton insurrection and the short-lived soviet regime which it brought into existence. We Oppositionists hold that this insurrection was an adventure of the leaders in an effort to save their "prestige." But it is clear to us that even an adventure develops according to laws which are determined by the structure of the social milieu. That is why we look to the Canton insurrection for the features of the future phase of the Chinese revolution. These features fully correspond with our theoretical analysis made prior to the Canton uprising. But how much more imperative it is for the ECCI, which holds that the Canton uprising was a correct and normal link in the chain of struggle, to give a clear class characterization of the Canton insurrection. However, there is not a word about this in the resolution of the ECCI, although the plenum met immediately after the Canton events. Is this not the most convincing proof that the present leadership of the Comintern, because it stubbornly pursues a false policy, is compelled to occupy itself with the fictitious errors of 1905 and other years without daring to approach the Canton insurrection of 1927, the meaning of which completely upsets the blueprint for revolutions in the East which is set down in the draft program?

5. SOVIETS AND REVOLUTION

In the February resolution of the ECCI the representatives of the Comintern, "Comrade N.[78] and others," are made responsible for the "absence of an *elected* soviet in Canton as an organ of insurrection." (Emphasis in the original.) Behind this charge in reality lies an astounding admission.

In the report of *Pravda* (no. 31), written on the basis of first-hand documents, it was stated that a soviet government had been established in Canton. But not a word was mentioned to indicate that the Canton soviet was *not* an elected organ, i.e., that it was not a *soviet*—for how can there be a soviet which was not elected? We learn this from the resolution.[79] Let us reflect for a moment on the significance of this fact. The ECCI tells us now that a soviet is necessary to effect an armed insurrection, but by no means prior to that time. But lo and behold! When the date for the insurrection is set, there is no soviet. To create an elected soviet is not an easy matter. It is necessary that the masses know from experience what a soviet is, that they understand its form, that they have learned something in the past to accustom them to an elected soviet organization. There was not even a sign of this in China, for the slogan of soviets was declared to be a Trotskyist slogan precisely in the period when it should have become the nerve center of the entire movement. When, however, helter-skelter, a date was set for an insurrection so as to skip over their own defeats, they simultaneously had to *appoint* a soviet as well. If this error is not laid bare to the core, the slogan of soviets can be transformed into a strangling noose of the revolution.

Lenin in his time explained to the Mensheviks that the fundamental historical task of the soviets is to organize, or help organize, the conquest of power so that on the day after the victory they become the organ of that power. The epigones—and not the disciples—draw from this the conclusion that soviets can be organized only when the twelfth hour of the insurrection has struck. Lenin's broad generalization they transform *post factum* into a little recipe which does not serve the interests of the revolution but imperils it.

Before the Bolshevik soviets in October 1917 captured power, the SR and Menshevik soviets had existed for nine months. Twelve years before, the first revolutionary soviets existed in Petersburg, Moscow, and scores of other cities. Before the soviet of 1905 was extended to embrace the mills and factories of the capital, there was created in Moscow during the strike, a soviet of printers' deputies. Several months before this, in May 1905, a mass strike in Ivanovo-Voznesensk set up a leading organ which already contain all the essential features of a soviet of workers deputies. Between the first experiment of setting up a soviet of workers deputies and the gigantic experiment of setting up a soviet government, more than twelve years rolled by. Of course, such a period is not at all required for all other countries, including China. But to think that the Chinese workers are capable of building soviets on the basis of the little recipe that has been substituted for Lenin's broad generalization is to substitute impotent and importunate pedantry for the dialectic of revolutionary action. Soviets must be set up not on the eve of the insurrection, not under the slogan of immediate seizure of power—for if the matter has reached the point of the seizure of power, if the masses are prepared for an armed insurrection *without a soviet,* it means that there have been other organizational forms and methods which made possible the performance of the preparatory work to insure the success of the uprising. Then the question of soviets becomes of secondary importance and is reduced to a question of organizational technique or merely to a question of denomination. The task of the soviets is not merely to issue the call for the insurrection or to carry it out, but *to lead the masses toward the insurrection through the necessary stages.* At first the soviet rallies the masses not to the slogan of armed insurrection, but to partial slogans, so that only later, step by step, the masses are brought towards the slogan of insurrection without scattering them on the road and without allowing the vanguard to become isolated from the class. The soviet appears most often and primarily in connection with strike struggles which have the perspectives of revolutionary development, but are in the given moment limited merely to economic demands. The masses must sense and understand while in action that the soviet is *their* organization, that it marshals the forces for a struggle, for resistance, for self-defense, and for an offensive. They can sense and understand this not from an action of a single day nor in general from any single act, but from the experience of several weeks, months, and perhaps years, with or without interruptions. That is why only an epigonic and bureaucratic leadership can restrain the awakening and rising masses from creating soviets in conditions when the country is passing through an epoch of revolutionary upheavals and when the working class and the poor peasants have before them the prospect of capturing power, even though this is a perspective of one of the subsequent stages and even if this perspective can be envisaged in the given phase only by a small minority. Such was always our conception of the soviets. We evaluated the soviets as that broad and flexible organizational form which is accessible to the masses who have just awakened at the very first stages of their revolutionary upsurge; and which is capable of uniting the working class in its entirety, independent of the size of that section which, in the given phase, has already matured to the point of understanding the task of the seizure of power.

Is any documentary evidence really necessary? Here, for instance, is what Lenin wrote about the soviets in the epoch of the first revolution:

"The Social Democratic Labor Party of Russia [the name of the party at that time] has never refused to utilize at *moments of greater or smaller revolutionary upsurge* certain nonparty organizations of the type of soviets of workers deputies in order to strengthen the influence of the social democrats on the working class and to consolidate the social democratic labor movement." (*Works,* vol. 8, p. 215.)*

One could cite voluminous literary and historic evidence

---

* "Draft Resolutions for the Fifth Congress of the RSDLP: Nonparty Workers' Organizations and the Anarcho-Syndicalist Trend among the Proletariat" (February-March 1907) in *LCW,* vol. 12, p. 143.

of this type. But one would imagine that the question is sufficiently clear without them.

In contradistinction to this the epigones have converted the soviets into an organizational parade uniform with which the party simply dresses up the proletariat on the eve of the capture of power. But this is precisely the time when we find that the soviets cannot be improvised in twenty-four hours, by order, for the direct purpose of an armed insurrection. Such experiments must inevitably assume a fictitious character and the absence of the most necessary conditions for the capture of power is masked by the external ritual of a soviet system. That is what happened in Canton where the soviet was simply appointed to observe the ritual. That is where the epigone formulation of the question leads.

※

During the polemics on the Chinese events the Opposition was accused of the following alleged flagrant contradiction: whereas from 1926 on the Opposition advanced the slogan of soviets for China, its representatives spoke against the slogan of soviets for Germany in the autumn of 1923. On no other point perhaps has scholastic political thought expressed itself so glaringly as in this accusation. Yes, we demanded for China a *timely* start for the creation of soviets as *independent* organizations of workers and peasants, *when the wave of revolutionary upsurge was mounting*.

The chief significance of the soviets was to be that of *opposing the workers and peasants to the Kuomintang bourgeoisie* and its Left Kuomintang agency. The slogan of soviets in China meant above all the break with the suicidal and infamous "bloc of four classes" and the withdrawal of the Communist Party from the Kuomintang. The center of gravity consequently lay not in bare organizational forms, but in the class line.

In the autumn of 1923 in Germany it was a question of organizational form only. As a result of the extreme passivity, backwardness, and tardiness of the leadership of the Comintern and the Communist Party of Germany, the moment for a timely call for the organization of soviets was missed. The factory committees, due to pressure from below and of their own accord, had occupied in the labor movement of Germany by the autumn of 1923 the place which would no doubt have been much more successfully occupied by soviets had there been a correct and daring policy on the part of the Communist Party. The acuteness of the situation had in the meantime reached its sharpest point. To lose any more time would have meant definitely to miss the revolutionary situation. The insurrection was finally placed on the order of the day, with very little time left. To advance the slogan of soviets under such conditions would have been the greatest pedantic stupidity conceivable. The soviet is not a talisman with omnipotent powers of salvation. In a situation such as had then developed, the hurried creation of soviets would only have duplicated the factory committees. It would have become necessary to deprive the latter of their revolutionary functions and to transfer them to the newly created and still utterly unauthoritative soviets. And when was this to be done? Under conditions in which each day counted. This would have meant to substitute for revolutionary action a most pernicious game in organizational gewgaws.

It is incontestable that the organizational form of a soviet can be of enormous importance; but only at a time when it furnishes a timely reflection of the correct political line. And conversely, it can acquire a no less negative meaning if it is converted into a fiction, a fetish, a bagatelle. The German soviets created at the very last moment in the autumn of 1923 would have added nothing politically; they would only have caused organizational confusion. What happened in Canton was even worse yet. The soviet which was created in a hurry to observe the ritual was only a masquerade for the adventurist putsch. That is why we discovered, after it was all over, that the Canton soviet resembled an ancient Chinese dragon simply drawn on paper. The policy of pulling rotten strings and paper dragons is not our policy. We were against improvizing soviets by telegraph in Germany in September 1923. We were for the creation of soviets in China in 1926. We were against the masquerade soviet in Canton in 1927. There are no contradictions here. We have here instead the profound unity of the conception of the dynamics of the revolutionary movement and its organizational forms.

The question of the role and significance of the soviets, which had been distorted and confused and obscured by the theory and practice of recent years, has not been illuminated in the least in the draft program.

6. THE QUESTION OF THE CHARACTER OF THE COMING CHINESE REVOLUTION

The slogan of the dictatorship of the proletariat, which leads behind it the peasant poor, is inseparably bound up with the question of the socialist character of the coming, third revolution in China. And inasmuch as not only history repeats itself but also the mistakes which people counterpose to its requirements, we can already hear the objection that China has not yet matured for a socialist revolution. But this is an abstract and lifeless formulation of the question. For has Russia, taken by itself, matured for socialism? According to Lenin— No! It has matured for the dictatorship of the proletariat as the only method for solving unpostponable national tasks. But the destiny of the dictatorship as a whole is determined in the last analysis by the trend of *world* development, which, of course, does not exclude but rather presupposes a correct policy on the part of the proletarian dictatorship, the consolidation and development of the workers and peasants alliance, an all-sided adaptation to national conditions on the one hand, and to the trend of world development on the other. This fully holds true for China as well.

In the same article entitled "On Our Revolution" (January 16, 1923), in which Lenin establishes that the peculiarity of Russia proceeds along the lines of the peculiar development of the Eastern countries, he brands as "infinitely hackneyed" the argument of European social democracy to the effect "that we have not matured for socialism, that we lack, as some of these 'erudite' gentlemen say, the objective economic prerequisites for socialism." But Lenin ridicules the "erudite" gentlemen not because he himself recognized the *existence* of the economic prerequisites for socialism in Russia but because he holds that the rejection of the seizure of power does not at all follow, as pedants and philistines think, from the absence of these prerequisites necessary for an *independent* construction of socialism. In this article of his, Lenin for the hundred and first time, or, rather, for the thousand and first time replies to the sophisms of the heroes of the Second International: "This *incontrovertible consideration* [the immaturity of Russia for socialism]... is not decisive for the evaluation of our revolution." (*Works,* vol. 18, part 21, pp. 118*f.*)* That is what the authors of the draft program refuse and are unable to understand. In itself the thesis of the economic and cultural immaturity of China as well as Russia—China, of course, more so than Russia—is incontrovertible. But hence it does not at all follow that the proletariat has to renounce the conquest of power, when this conquest is dictated by the entire historical context and the revolutionary situation in the country.

The concrete, historical, political, and actual question is reducible not to whether China has economically matured for "its own" socialism, but whether China has ripened politically for the proletarian dictatorship. These two questions are not at all identical. They might be regarded as identical were it not for the law of uneven development. This is where this law is in place and fully applies to the interrelationship between economics and politics. Then China has matured for the dicta-

★ "Our Revolution," in *LCW,* vol. 33, pp. 477–78.

torship of the proletariat? Only the experience of the struggle can provide a categorical answer to this question. By the same token, only the struggle can settle the question as to when and under what conditions the real unification, emancipation, and regeneration of China will take place. Anyone who says that China has not matured for the dictatorship of the proletariat declares thereby that the third Chinese revolution is postponed for many years to come.

Of course, matters would be quite hopeless if feudal survivals did really *dominate* in Chinese economic life, as the resolutions of the ECCI asserted. But fortunately, *survivals* in general cannot dominate. The draft program on this point, too, does not rectify the errors committed, but reaffirms them in a roundabout and nebulous fashion. The draft speaks of the "predominance of medieval feudal relations both in the economics of the country and in the political superstructure. . . ." This is false to the core. What does *predominance* mean? Is it a question of the number of people involved? Or the dominant and leading role in the economics of the country? The extraordinarily rapid growth of home industry on the basis of the all-embracing role of mercantile and bank capital; the complete dependence of the most important agrarian districts on the market; the enormous and ever-growing role of foreign trade; the all-sided subordination of the Chinese village to the city—all these bespeak the unconditional predominance, the direct domination of capitalist relations in China. The social relations of serfdom and semiserfdom are undeniably very strong. They stem in part from the days of feudalism; and in part they constitute a new formation, that is, the regeneration of the past on the basis of the retarded development of the productive forces, the surplus agrarian population, the activities of merchants' and usurers' capital, etc. However, it is capitalist relations that *dominate* and not "feudal" (more correctly, serf and, generally, precapitalist) relations. Only thanks to this dominant role of capitalist relations can we speak seriously of the prospects of proletarian hegemony in the national revolution. Otherwise, there is no making the ends meet.

"The strength of the proletariat in any capitalist country is infinitely greater than the proportion of the proletariat in the total population. This is due to the fact that the proletariat is in economic command of the central points and nerve centers of the entire capitalist system of economy, and also because the proletariat expresses economically and politically the *real* interests of the vast majority of the toilers under capitalism.

"For this reason the proletariat, even if it constitutes the minority of the population (or in cases where the conscious and truly revolutionary vanguard of the proletariat comprises the minority of the population), is capable both of overthrowing the bourgeoisie and of attracting subsequently to its side many allies from among the masses of semiproletarians and petty bourgeois, who will never come out beforehand for the domination of the proletariat, who will not understand the conditions and tasks of this domination, but who will convince themselves solely from their subsequent experiences of the inevitability, justice, and legitimacy of the proletarian dictatorship." (Lenin, *Works,* "The Year 1919," vol. 16, p. 458.)*

The role of the Chinese proletariat in production is already very great. In the next few years it will only increase still further. Its political role, as events have shown, could have been gigantic. But the whole line of the leadership was directed entirely against permitting the proletariat to conquer the leading role.

The draft program says that successful socialist construction is possible in China "only on the condition that it is directly supported by countries under the proletarian dictatorship." Thus, here, in relation to China, the same principle is recognized which the party has always recognized in regard to Russia. But if China lacks sufficient inner forces for an *independent* construction of socialist society, then according to the theory

---

* "The Constituent Assembly Elections and the Dictatorship of the Proletariat," in *LCW,* vol. 30, p. 274.

of Stalin-Bukharin, the Chinese proletariat should not seize power at any stage of the revolution. Or it may be that the existence of the USSR settles the question in just the opposite sense. Then it follows that our technology is sufficient to build socialist society not only in the USSR but also in China, i.e., in the two economically most backward countries with a combined population of six hundred million. Or perhaps the *inevitable* dictatorship of the proletariat in China is "inadmissible" because that dictatorship will be included in the chain of the worldwide socialist revolution, thus becoming not only its link, but its driving force? But this is precisely Lenin's basic formulation of the October Revolution, the "peculiarity" of which follows precisely along the lines of development of the Eastern countries. We see thus how the revisionist theory of socialism in one country, evolved in 1925 in order to wage a struggle against Trotskyism, distorts and confuses matters each time a new major revolutionary problem is approached.

The draft program goes still further along this same road. It counterposes China and India to "Russia before 1917" and Poland ("etc,"?) as countries with "a certain *minimum* of industry sufficient for the triumphant construction of socialism," or (as is more definitely and therefore more erroneously stated elsewhere) as countries possessing the "necessary and sufficient material prerequisites . . . for the complete construction of socialism." This, as we already know, is a mere play upon Lenin's expression "necessary and sufficient" prerequisites; a fraudulent and an impermissible jugglery because Lenin definitely enumerates the *political and organizational prerequisites,* including the *technical, cultural, and international* prerequisites. But the chief point that remains is: how can one determine a priori the "minimum of industry" sufficient for the complete building of socialism once it is a question of an uninterrupted world struggle between two economic systems, two social orders, and a struggle, moreover, in which our *economic* base is infinitely the weaker?

If we take into consideration only the economic lever, it is clear that we in the USSR, and all the more so in China and India, have a far shorter arm of the lever than world capitalism. But the entire question is resolved by the *revolutionary struggle* of the two systems on a world scale. In the political struggle, the long arm of the lever is *on our side,* or, to put it more correctly, it can and must prove so in our hands, if our policy is correct.

Again, in the same article "On Our Revolution," after stating that "a certain cultural level is necessary for the creation of "socialism," Lenin adds: "although no one can tell what this certain cultural level is."* Why can no one tell? Because the question is settled by the struggle, by the rivalry between the two social systems and the two cultures, *on an international scale.* Breaking completely with this idea of Lenin's, which flows from the very essence of the question, the draft program asserts that in 1917 Russia had precisely the "minimum technology" and consequently also the culture necessary for the building of socialism in one country. The authors of the draft attempt to tell in the program that which "no one can tell" a priori.

It is impermissible, impossible, and absurd to seek a criterion for the "sufficient minimum" within national states ("Russia prior to 1917") when the whole question is settled by international dynamics. In this false, arbitrary, isolated national criterion rests the theoretical basis of national narrowness in politics, the precondition for inevitable national-reformist and social-patriotic blunders in the future.

7. ON THE REACTIONARY IDEA OF 'TWO-CLASS WORKERS AND PEASANTS PARTIES' FOR THE ORIENT

The lessons of the second Chinese revolution are lessons for the entire Comintern, but primarily for all the countries of the Orient.

---

* "Our Revolution," in *LCW,* vol. 33, p. 478.

All the arguments presented in defense of the Menshevik line in the Chinese revolution must, if we take them seriously, hold trebly good for India. The imperialist yoke assumes in India, the classic colony, infinitely more direct and palpable forms than in China. The survivals of feudal and serf relations in India are immeasurably deeper and greater. Nevertheless, or rather precisely for this reason, the methods which, applied in China, undermined the revolution, must result in India in even more fatal consequences. The overthrow of Hindu feudalism and of the Anglo-Hindu bureaucracy and British militarism can be accomplished only by a gigantic and an indomitable movement of the popular masses which precisely because of its powerful sweep and irresistibility, its international aims and ties, cannot tolerate any halfway and compromising opportunist measures on the part of the leadership.

The Comintern leadership has already committed not a few mistakes in India. The conditions have not yet allowed these errors to reveal themselves on such a scale as in China. One can, therefore, hope that the lessons of the Chinese events will permit of a more timely rectification of the line of the leading policy in India and in other countries of the Orient.

The cardinal question for us here, as everywhere and always, is the question of the Communist Party, its complete independence, its irreconcilable class character. The greatest danger on this path is the organization of so-called workers and peasants parties in the countries of the Orient.

Beginning with 1924, a year which will go down as the year of open revision of a number of fundamental theses of Marx and Lenin, Stalin advanced the formula of the "two-class workers and peasants parties for the Eastern countries." It was based on the selfsame national oppression which served in the Orient to camouflage opportunism, as did "stabilization" in the Occident. Cables from India, as well as from Japan, where there is no national oppression, have of late frequently mentioned the activities of provincial "workers and peasants parties," referring to them as organizations which are close and friendly to the Comintern, as if they were almost our "own" organizations, without, however, giving any sort of concrete definition of their political physiognomy; in a word, writing and speaking about them in the same way as was done only a short while ago about the Kuomintang.

Back in 1924, *Pravda* reported that: "There are indications that the movement of national liberation in Korea is gradually taking shape in the form of the creation of a workers and peasants party." (*Pravda*, March 2, 1924.)

And in the meantime Stalin lectured to the communists of the Orient that "The communists must pass from the policy of a united national front . . . to the policy of a revolutionary bloc between the workers and petty bourgeoisie. In such countries this bloc can assume the form of a single party, a workers and peasants party, akin to the Kuomintang. . . ." (Stalin, *Problems of Leninism*, p. 264.)

The ensuing tiny "reservations" on the subject of independence of the communist parties (obviously, "independence" like that of the prophet Jonah inside the whale's belly) served only for the purpose of camouflage. We are profoundly convinced that the Sixth Congress must state that the slightest equivocation in this sphere is fatal and will be rejected.

It is a question here of an absolutely new, entirely false, and thoroughly anti-Marxian formulation of the fundamental question of the party and of its relation to its own class and other classes.

The necessity for the Communist Party of China to enter the Kuomintang was defended on the ground that in its social composition the Kuomintang is a party of workers and peasants, that nine-tenths of the Kuomintang—this proportion was repeated hundreds of times—belonged to the revolutionary tendency and were ready to march hand in hand with the Communist Party. However, during and since the coups d'état in Shanghai and Wuhan, these revolutionary nine-tenths of the Kuomintang disappeared as if by magic. No one has found a trace of them. And the theoreticians of class collaboration in China, Stalin, Bukharin, and others, did not even take the trouble to explain what has become of the nine-tenths of the members of the Kuomintang—the nine-tenths workers and peasants, revolutionists, sympathizers, and entirely our "own." Yet, an answer to this question is of decisive importance if we are to understand the destiny of all these "two-class" parties preached by Stalin; and if we are to be clarified upon the very conception itself, which throws us far behind not only the program of the CPSU of 1919, but also the *Communist Manifesto* of 1847.

The question of where the celebrated nine-tenths vanished can become clear to us only if we understand, first, the impossibility of a bi-composite, that is a two-class party, expressing simultaneously two mutually exclusive historical lines—the proletarian and petty-bourgeois lines; secondly, the impossibility of realizing in capitalist society an independent peasant party, that is, a party expressing the interests of the peasantry, which is at the same time independent of the proletariat and the bourgeoisie.

Marxism has always taught, and Bolshevism too accepted, and taught, that the peasantry and proletariat are two different classes, that it is false to identify their interests in capitalist society in any way, and that a peasant can join the Communist Party only if, from the property viewpoint, he adopts the views of the proletariat. The alliance of the workers and peasants under the dictatorship of the proletariat does not invalidate this thesis, but confirms it, in a different way, under different circumstances. If there were no *different* classes with *different* interests, there would be no talk even of an *alliance*. Such an alliance is compatible with the socialist revolution only to the extent that it enters into the iron framework of the dictatorship of the proletariat. In our country the dictatorship is incompatible with the existence of a so-called Peasants League precisely because every "independent" peasant organization aspiring to solve all national political problems would inevitably turn out to be an instrument in the hands of the bourgeoisie.

Those organizations which in capitalist countries label

themselves peasant parties are in reality one of the varieties of bourgeois parties. Every peasant who has not adopted the proletarian position, abandoning his proprietor psychology, will inevitably follow the bourgeoisie when it comes to fundamental political issues. Of course, every bourgeois party that relies or seeks to rely on the peasantry and, if possible, on the workers, is compelled to camouflage itself, that is, to assume two or three appropriate colorations. The celebrated idea of "workers and peasants parties" seems to have been specially created to camouflage bourgeois parties which are compelled to seek support from the peasantry but who are also ready to absorb workers into their ranks. The Kuomintang has entered the annals of history for all time as a classic type of such party.

Bourgeois society, as is known, is so constructed that the propertyless, discontented, and deceived masses are at the bottom and the contented fakers remain on top. Every bourgeois party, if it is a real party, that is, if it embraces considerable masses, is built on the selfsame principle. The exploiters, fakers, and despots compose the minority in class society. Every capitalist party is therefore compelled in its internal relations, in one way or another, to reproduce and reflect the relations in bourgeois society as a whole. In every mass bourgeois party the lower ranks are therefore more democratic and further to the "left" than the tops. This holds true of the German Center, the French Radicals, and particularly the social democracy. That is why the constant complaints voiced by Stalin, Bukharin, and others that the tops do not reflect the sentiments of the "Left" Kuomintang rank and file, the "overwhelming majority," the "nine-tenths," etc., etc., are so naive, so unpardonable. That which they represented in their bizarre complaints to be a temporary, disagreeable misunderstanding which was to be eliminated by means of organizational measures, instructions, and circular letters, is in reality a cardinal and basic feature of a bourgeois party, particularly in a revolutionary epoch.

It is from this angle that the basic arguments of the authors of the draft program in defense of all kinds of opportunist blocs in general—both in England and China—must be judged. According to them, fraternization with the tops is done exclusively in the interests of the rank and file. The Opposition, as is known, insisted on the withdrawal of the party from the Kuomintang:

"The question arises," says Bukharin, "why? Is it because the leaders of the Kuomintang are vacillating? And what about the Kuomintang masses, are they mere 'cattle'? Since when is the attitude to a mass organization determined by what takes place at the 'high' summit!" (*The Present Situation in the Chinese Revolution.*)

The very possibility of such an argument seems impossible in a revolutionary party. Bukharin asks, "And what about the Kuomintang masses, are they mere cattle?" Of course they are cattle. The masses of any bourgeois party are always cattle, although in different degrees. But for us, the masses are not cattle, are they? No, that is precisely why we are forbidden to drive them into the arms of the bourgeoisie, *camouflaging the latter under the label of a workers and peasants party.* That is precisely why we are forbidden to subordinate the proletarian party to a bourgeois party, but on the contrary, must at every step, oppose the former to the latter. The "high" summit of the Kuomintang of whom Bukharin speaks so ironically, as of something secondary, accidental, and temporary is in reality the soul of the Kuomintang, its social essence. Of course, the bourgeoisie constitutes only the "summit" in the party as well as in society. But this summit is powerful in its capital, knowledge, and connections: it can always fall back on the imperialists for support, and what is most important, it can always resort to the actual political and military power which is intimately fused with the leadership in the Kuomintang itself. It is precisely this summit that wrote laws against strikes, throttled the uprisings of the peasants, shoved the communists into a dark corner, and, at best, allowed them to be only one-third of the party, exacted an oath from them that petty-bourgeois Sun Yat-senism takes precedence over Marxism.[80] The rank and file were picked and harnessed by this summit, serving it, like Moscow, as a "left" support, just as the generals, compradores, and imperialists served it as a right support. To consider the Kuomintang not as a *bourgeois party, but as a neutral arena of struggle for the masses,* to play with words about nine-tenths of the left rank and file in order to mask the question as to who is the real master, meant to add to the strength and power of the summit, to assist the latter to convert ever broader masses into "cattle," and, under conditions most favorable to it to prepare the Shanghai coup d'état. Basing themselves on the reactionary idea of the two-class party, Stalin and Bukharin imagined that the communists, together with the "Lefts," would secure a majority in the Kuomintang and thereby power in the country, for, in China, power is in the hands of the Kuomintang. In other words, they imagined that *by means of ordinary elections at Kuomintang congresses power would pass from the hands of the bourgeoisie to the proletariat.* Can one conceive of a more touching and idealistic idolization of "party democracy" . . . in a bourgeois party. For indeed, the army, the bureaucracy, the press, the capital are all in the hands of the bourgeoisie. Precisely, because of this and this alone it stands at the helm of the ruling party. The bourgeois "summit" tolerates or tolerated "nine-tenths" of the Lefts (and Lefts of *this sort*), only insofar as they did not venture against the army, the bureaucracy, the press, and against capital. By these powerful means the bourgeois summit kept in subjection not only the so-called nine-tenths of the "left" party members but also the masses as a whole. In this the theory of the bloc of classes, the theory that the Kuomintang is a workers and peasants party, provides the best possible assistance for the bourgeoisie. When the bourgeoisie later comes into hostile conflict with the masses and shoots them down, in this clash between the two real forces, the bourgeoisie and the proletariat, not even the bleating of the celebrated nine-tenths is heard. The pitiful democratic fiction evaporates without a trace in face of the bloody reality of the class struggle.

Such is the genuine and only possible political mechanism

of the "two-class workers and peasants parties for the Orient." There is no other and there will be none.

❖

Although the idea of the two-class parties is motivated on national oppression, which allegedly abrogates Marx's class doctrine, we have already heard about "workers and peasants" mongrels in Japan, where there is no national oppression at all. But that isn't all, the matter is not limited merely to the Orient. The "two-class" idea seeks to attain universality. In this domain, the most grotesque features were assumed by the above-mentioned Communist Party of America in its effort to support the presidential candidacy of the bourgeois, "antitrust" Senator La Follette, so as to yoke the American farmers by this means to the chariot of the social revolution. Pepper, the theoretician of this maneuver, one of those who ruined the Hungarian revolution because he overlooked the Hungarian peasantry,[81] made a great effort (by way of compensation, no doubt) to ruin the Communist Party of America by dissolving it among the farmers. Pepper's theory was that the superprofit of American capitalism converts the American proletariat into a world labor aristocracy, while the agrarian crisis ruins the farmers and drives them onto the path of social revolution. According to Pepper's conception, a party of a few thousand members, consisting chiefly of immigrants, had to fuse with the farmers through the medium of a bourgeois party and by thus founding a "two-class" party, insure the socialist revolution in the face of the passivity or neutrality of the proletariat corrupted by superprofits. This insane idea found supporters and half-supporters among the upper leadership of the Comintern. For several weeks the issue swayed in the balance until finally a concession was made to the ABC of Marxism (the comment behind the scenes was: Trotskyist prejudices). It was necessary to lasso the American Communist Party in order to tear it away from the La Follette party[82] which died even before its founder.

Everything invented by modern revisionism for the Orient is carried over later to the West. If Pepper on one side of the Atlantic Ocean tried to spur history by means of a two-class party then the latest dispatches in the press inform us that the Kuomintang experience finds its imitators in Italy where, apparently, an attempt is being made to foist on our party the monstrous slogan of a "republican assembly on the basis [?!] of workers and peasants committees." In this slogan the spirit of Chiang Kai-shek embraces the spirit of Hilferding. Will we really come to that?[83]

❧

In conclusion there remains for us only to recall that the idea of a workers and peasants party sweeps from the history of Bolshevism the entire struggle against the Populists (Narodniks), without which there would have been no Bolshevik Party. What was the significance of this historical struggle? In 1909, Lenin wrote the following about the Social-Revolutionists:

"The fundamental idea of their program was not at all that 'an alliance of the forces' of the proletariat and the peasantry is necessary, but that there is no *class abyss* between the former and the latter and that there is no need to draw a line of class demarcation between them, and that the social democratic idea of the petty-bourgeois nature of the peasantry that distinguishes it from the proletariat is fundamentally false." (*Works*, vol. 11, part 1, p. 198.)*

In other words, the two-class workers and peasants party is the central idea of the Russian Narodniks. Only in the struggle against this idea could the party of the proletarian van-

---

* "How the Socialist Revolutionaries Sum Up the Revolution and How the Revolution Has Summed Them Up," in *LCW*, vol. 15, p. 331.

guard in peasant Russia develop.

Lenin persistently and untiringly repeated in the epoch of the 1905 revolution that

"Our attitude towards the peasantry must be distrustful, we must *organize separately from it,* be ready for a struggle against it, to the extent that the peasantry comes forward as a reactionary or antiproletarian force." (*Works,* vol. 6, p. 113. Our emphasis.)*

In 1906 Lenin wrote:

"Our last advice: proletarians and semiproletarians of city and country, organize yourselves separately! Place no trust in any small proprietors, even the petty ones, even those who 'toil'.... We support the peasant movement to the end, but we must remember that it is a movement of another class, *not the one* that can or will accomplish the socialist revolution." (*Works,* vol. 9, p. 410.)†

This idea reappears in hundreds of Lenin's major and minor works. In 1908, he explained:

"The alliance between the proletariat and the peasantry must in no case be interpreted to mean a *fusion of the different classes or parties* of the proletariat and the peasantry. Not only fusion, but even *any sort of lasting concord* would be fatal for the socialist party of the working class and *weaken* the revolutionary democratic struggle." (*Works,* vol. 11, part 1, p. 79. Our emphasis.)‡

Could one condemn the very idea of a workers and peasants party more harshly, more ruthlessly, and more devastatingly?

Stalin, on the other hand, teaches that "The revolutionary anti-imperialist bloc ... must, though not always [!] necessarily [!], assume the form of a single workers and peasants party, bound formally [?] by a single platform." (*Problems of Leninism,* p. 265.)

---

* "The Proletariat and the Peasantry," in *LCW,* vol. 8, p. 234.
† "Revision of the Agrarian Program of the Workers Party," in *LCW,* vol. 10, p. 191.
‡ "The Assessment of the Russian Revolution," in *LCW,* vol. 15, p. 57.

Lenin taught us that an alliance between workers and peasants must in no case and never lead to merger of the parties. But Stalin makes only one concession to Lenin: although, according to Stalin, the bloc of classes must assume "the form of a single party," a workers and peasants party like the Kuomintang—*is not always obligatory*. We should thank him for at least this concession.

Lenin put this question in the same irreconcilable spirit during the epoch of the October Revolution. In generalizing the experience of the three Russian revolutions, Lenin, beginning with 1918, did not miss a single opportunity to repeat that there are two decisive forces in a society where capitalist relations predominate—the bourgeoisie and the proletariat.

"If the peasant does not follow the workers, he marches behind the bourgeoisie. There is and there can be no middle course." (*Works,* vol. 16, "The Year 1919," p. 219.)*

Yet a "workers and peasants party" is precisely an attempt to create a middle course.

Had the vanguard of the Russian proletariat failed to oppose itself to the peasantry, had it failed to wage a ruthless struggle against the all-devouring petty-bourgeois amorphousness of the latter, it would inevitably have dissolved itself among the petty-bourgeois elements through the medium of the Social Revolutionary Party or some other "two-class party" which, in turn, would inevitably have subjected the vanguard to bourgeois leadership. In order to arrive at a revolutionary alliance with the peasantry—this does not come gratuitously—it is first of all necessary to separate the proletarian vanguard, and thereby the working class as a whole, from the petty-bourgeois masses. This can be achieved only by training the proletarian party in the spirit of unshakable class irreconcilability.

The younger the proletariat, the fresher and more direct its

---

* "First All-Russia Congress on Adult Education: Deception of the People with Slogans of Freedom and Equality," in *LCW,* vol. 29, p. 370.

"blood ties" with the peasantry, the greater the proportion of the peasantry to the population as a whole, the greater becomes the importance of the struggle against any form of "two-class" political alchemy. In the West the idea of a workers and peasants party is simply ridiculous. In the East it is fatal. In China, India, and Japan this idea is mortally hostile not only to the hegemony of the proletariat in the revolution but also to the most elementary independence of the proletarian vanguard. The workers and peasants party can only serve as a base, a screen, and a springboard for the bourgeoisie.

It is fatal that in this question, fundamental for the entire East, modern revisionism only repeats the errors of old social democratic opportunism of prerevolutionary days. Most of the leaders of European social democracy considered the struggle of our party against SRs to be mistaken and insistently advocated the fusion of the two parties, holding that for the Russian "East" a two-class workers and peasants party was exactly in order. Had we heeded their counsel, we should never have achieved either the alliance of the workers and the peasants or the dictatorship of the proletariat. The "two-class" workers and peasants party of the SRs became, and could not help becoming in our country, the agency of the imperialist bourgeoisie, i.e., it tried unsuccessfully to fulfill the same historic role which was successfully played in China by the Kuomintang in a different and "peculiar" Chinese way, thanks to the revisionists of Bolshevism. Without a relentless condemnation of the very idea of workers and peasants parties for the East, there is not and there cannot be a program of the Comintern.

8. THE ADVANTAGES SECURED FROM THE PEASANTS INTERNATIONAL MUST BE PROBED

One of the principal, if not *the* principal, accusations hurled against the Opposition, was its "underestimation" of the peasantry. On this point, too, life has made its tests and rendered its verdict along national and international lines. In every case the official leaders proved guilty of *underestimating the role and significance of the proletariat in relation to the peasantry*. In this the greatest shifts and errors took place, in the economic and political fields and internationally. At the root of the internal errors since 1923 lies an underestimation of the significance, for the whole of national economy and for the alliance with the peasantry, of state industry under the management of the proletariat. In China, the revolution was doomed by the inability to understand the leading and decisive role of the proletariat in the agrarian revolution.

From the same standpoint, it is necessary to examine and evaluate the entire work of the Krestintern,[84] which from the beginning was merely an experiment—an experiment, moreover, which called for the utmost care and rigid adherence to principles. It is not difficult to understand the reason for this.

The peasantry, by virtue of its entire history and the conditions of its existence, is the least international of all classes. What are commonly called national traits have their chief source precisely in the peasantry. From among the peasantry, it is only the semiproletarian masses of the peasant poor who can be guided along the road of internationalism, and only the proletariat can guide them. Any attempt at a shortcut is merely playing with the classes, which always means playing to the detriment of the proletariat. The peasantry can be attracted to internationalist politics only if it is torn away from the influence of the bourgeoisie by the proletariat and if it recognizes in the proletariat not only its ally, but its leader. Conversely, attempts to organize the peasants of the various countries into an independent international organization, over the head of the proletariat and without regard to the national communist parties, are doomed in advance to failure. In the final analysis such attempts can only harm the struggle of the proletariat in each country for hegemony over the agricultural laborers and poor peasants.

In all bourgeois revolutions as well as counterrevolutions, beginning with the peasant wars of the sixteenth century and even before that time, the various strata of the peasantry played an enormous and at times even decisive role. But it never played an *independent* role. Directly or indirectly, the peasantry always supported one political force against another. By itself it never constituted an independent force capable of solving national political tasks. In the epoch of finance capital the process of the polarization of capitalist society has enormously accelerated in comparison to earlier phases of capitalist development. This means that the specific gravity of the peasantry has diminished and not increased. In any case, the peasant is less capable in the imperialist epoch of *independent* political action on a national, let alone international scale, than he was in the epoch of industrial capitalism. The farmers of the United States today are incomparably less able to play an independent political role than they were forty or fifty years ago when, as the experience of the Populist movement shows, they could not and did not organize an independent national political party.

The temporary but sharp filip to agriculture in Europe resulting from the economic decline caused by the war gave rise to illusions concerning the possible role of the "peasant," i.e., of bourgeois pseudopeasant parties demagogically counterposing themselves to the bourgeois parties. If in the period of stormy peasant unrest during the postwar years one could still risk the experiment of organizing a Peasants International, in order to test the new relations between the proletariat and the peasantry and between the peasantry and the bourgeoisie, then it is high time now to draw the theoretical and political balance of the five years' experience with the Peasants International, to lay bare its vicious shortcomings and make an effort to indicate its positive aspects.

One conclusion, at any rate, is indisputable. The experience of the "peasant" parties of Bulgaria, Poland, Romania, and Yugoslavia (i.e., of all the backward countries); the old experience of our Social Revolutionists, and the fresh experience (the blood is still warm) of the Kuomintang; the episodic experiments in advanced capitalist countries, particularly the La Follette–Pepper experiment in the United States—have all shown beyond question that in the epoch of capitalist decline there is even less reason than in the epoch of rising capitalism to look for *independent, revolutionary, antibourgeois peasant parties.*

"The city cannot be equated to the village, the village cannot be equated to the city in the historical conditions of the present epoch. The city inevitably *leads the village,* the village inevitably *follows the city.* The only question is *which* of the urban classes will lead the village." (Lenin *Works,* vol. 16, "The Year 1919," p. 442.)*

In the revolutions of the East the peasantry will still play a decisive role, but once again, this role will be neither leading nor independent. The poor peasants of Hupeh, Kwangtung, or Bengal can play a role not only on a national but on an international scale, but only if they support the workers of Shanghai, Canton, Hankow, and Calcutta. This is the only way out for the revolutionary peasant on an *international* road. It is hopeless to attempt to forge a direct link between the peasant of Hupeh and the peasant of Galicia or Dobrudja, the Egyptian fellah and the American farmer.

It is in the nature of politics that anything which does not serve a direct aim inevitably becomes the instrument of other aims, frequently the opposite of the one sought. Have we not had examples of a bourgeois party, relying on the peasantry or seeking to rely upon it, deeming it necessary to seek insurance for itself in the Peasants International, for a longer or shorter period, if it could not do so in the Comintern, in order to secure protection from the blows of the Communist Party in its own country? Like Purcell, in the trade union field, protected himself through the Anglo-Russian Committee? If La

---

* "The Constituent Assembly Elections and the Dictatorship of the Proletariat," in *LCW,* vol. 30, p. 257.

Follette did not try to register in the Peasants International, that was only because the American Communist Party was so extremely weak. He did not have to. Pepper, uninvited and unsolicited, embraced La Follette without that. But Radić, the banker-leader of the Croatian rich peasants, found it necessary to leave his visiting card with the Peasants International on his way to the cabinet. The Kuomintang went infinitely further and secured a place for itself not only in the Peasants International and the League Against Imperialism, but even knocked at the doors of the Comintern and was welcomed there with the blessing of the Politbureau of the CPSU, marred by only one dissenting vote.

It is highly characteristic of the leading political currents of recent years that at a time when tendencies in favor of liquidating the Profintern [Red International of Labor Unions] were very strong (its very name was deleted from the statutes of the Soviet trade unions), nowhere, so far as we recall, has the question ever been raised in the official press as to the precise conquests of the Krestintern, the Peasants International.

The Sixth Congress must seriously review the work of the Peasants "International" from the standpoint of proletarian internationalism. It is high time to draw a Marxian balance to this long drawn-out experiment. In one form or another the balance must be included in the program of the Comintern. The present draft does not breathe a single syllable either about the "millions" in the Peasants International, or for that matter, about its very existence.

CONCLUSION

We have presented a criticism of certain fundamental theses in the draft program; extreme pressure of time prevented us from dealing with all of them. There were only two weeks at our disposal for this work. We were therefore compelled to limit ourselves to the most pressing questions, those most closely bound up with the revolutionary and internal party struggles during the recent period.

Thanks to our previous experience with so-called "discussions," we are aware beforehand that phrases torn out of their context and slips of the pen can be turned into a seething source of new theories annihilating "Trotskyism." An entire period has been filled with triumphant crowing of this type. But we view with utmost calm the prospect of the cheap theoretical scorpions that this time, too, may descend upon us.

Incidentally, it is quite likely that the authors of the draft program, instead of putting into circulation new critical and expository articles, will prefer to resort to further elaboration of the old Article 58. Needless to say, this kind of argument is even less valid for us.

The Sixth World Congress is faced with the task of adopting a program. We have sought to prove throughout this entire work that there is not the slightest possibility of taking the draft elaborated by Bukharin and Stalin as the basis of the program.

The present moment is the turning point in the life of the CPSU and the entire Comintern. This is evidenced by all the recent decisions and measures of the CEC of our party and the February plenum[85] of the ECCI. These measures are entirely inadequate, the resolutions are contradictory, and certain among them, like the February resolution of the ECCI on the Chinese revolution, are false to the core. Nevertheless throughout all these resolutions there is a tendency to take a turn to the left. We have no ground whatever for overestimating it, all the more so since it proceeds hand in hand with a campaign of extermination against the revolutionary wing, while the right wing is being protected. Notwithstanding all this, we do not for a moment entertain the notion of ignoring this leftward tendency, forced by the impasse created by the old course. Every genuine revolutionist at his post will do everything in his power to facilitate the development of these symptoms of a left zigzag into a revolutionary Leninist course, with the least difficulties and convulsions in the party. But we are still far removed from this today. At present the Comintern is perhaps passing through its most acute period of development, a period in which the old course is far from having been liquidated, while the new course brings in eruptions of alien elements. The draft program reflects in whole and in part this transitional condition. Yet, such periods, by their very nature, are least favorable for the elaboration of documents that must determine the activity of our international party for a number of years ahead. Difficult as it may be, we must bide our time—after so much time has been lost already. We must permit the muddled waters to settle. The confusion must pass, the contradictions must be eliminated, and the new course take definite shape.

The congress has not convened for four years. For nine years the Comintern has existed without a definitive program. The only way out at the present moment is this: that the Seventh World Congress be convened a year from today, putting an end once and for all to the attempts at usurping the supreme powers of the Comintern as a whole, a normal regime be reestablished, such a regime as would allow of a genuine discussion of the draft program and permit us to oppose to the eclectic draft, another, a Marxist-Leninist draft. There must be no forbidden questions for the Comintern, for the meetings and conferences of its sections, and for its press. During this year the entire soil must be deeply plowed by the plow of Marxism. Only as a result of such labor can the international party of the proletariat secure a program, a beacon which will illuminate with its penetrating rays, and throw reliable beams far into the future.

ALMA ATA
JUNE 1928

What Now?

1. THE AIM OF THIS LETTER

The purpose of this letter is to achieve clarity without suppressing or exaggerating anything. Clarity is the indispensable condition for revolutionary policy.

This attempt to arrive at an understanding can have meaning only if it is free from all traces of reticence, duplicity, and diplomacy. This requires that all things be called by their names, including those which are most unpleasant and grievous for the party. It has been the custom in such cases to raise a hue and cry that the enemy will seize upon the criticism and use it. At the present moment, it would be maladroit to pose the question of whether the class enemy can glean the greatest profit from the policy of the leadership that has led the Chinese revolution to its cruelest defeats, or from the stifle warnings of the Opposition that have disturbed the false prestige of infallibility.

The same thing might be said on the question of the Anglo-Russian Committee, the grain collections, the kulak in general, and the line followed by the leadership of any communist party. No, it is not the criticism of the Opposition that has retarded the growth of the Comintern during the last five years. The social democracy has no doubt attempted in a number of instances to glean a little profit from the criticisms of the Opposition. It still has enough sense and cunning for that. It would have been strange had it failed to do so. The social democracy at present is a parasitic party, in the broad historical sense of the term. Fulfilling the work of guaranteeing bourgeois society from below, that is to say, protecting it on the essential side, the social democracy during the postwar years, particularly after the year 1923, when it was obviously being reduced to a cipher, has thrived upon the mistakes and oversights of the communist parties, their capitulations at the decisive moments, or, on the other hand, their adventuristic attempts to resuscitate a revolutionary situation which has already passed. The capitulation of the Comintern in the autumn of 1923, the subsequent stubborn failure of the leadership to understand the import of this colossal defeat, the adventuristic ultraleft line of 1924 to 1925, the gross opportunist policy of 1926 to 1927—these are what caused the regeneration of the social democracy and enabled it to poll more than nine million votes in the last German elections. To argue, under these conditions, that the social democracy now and then pulls out of its context some critical remark or other of the Opposition, and after slobbering over it offers it to the workers, is really to waste time with bagatelles. The social democracy would not be what it is if it did not go even further, if in the guise of its left wing—which is as necessary a safety valve in a social democratic party as the party itself is in bourgeois society—it did not express from time to time spurious "sympathies" for the Opposition, insofar as the latter remains a small and suppressed minority and inasmuch as such "sympathies" cost the social democrats nothing and at the same time arouse the responsive sympathies of the workers.

The present social democracy has not and cannot have a line of its own on the fundamental questions. In this domain, its line is dictated by the bourgeoisie. But if the social democracy simply repeated everything said by the bourgeois parties, it would cease to be useful to the bourgeoisie. Upon secondary, intangible, or remote questions, the social democracy not only may but must play with all the colors of the rainbow, including bright red. Moreover, by seizing upon this or that judgment of the Opposition, the social democracy hopes to provoke a split in the Communist Party. In the eyes of anyone who understands the workings of such a mechanism, the attempts to discredit the Opposition by referring to the fact that some right-wing grafter or left-wing stripling of the social democracy quotes approvingly a sentence from our criticism, must appear in a pitiable ideological light. Basically, however, in all questions of *politics* that are in the least serious, above all in the questions of China and of the Anglo-Russian Committee, the sympathies of the international social democracy have been on the side of the "realistic" policy of the leadership, and in no wise on ours.

But much more important is the general judgment which the bourgeoisie itself passes on the tendencies struggling within the framework of the Soviet Union and of the Comintern. The bourgeoisie has no reason to dodge or dissemble on this question, and here it must be said that all—even the least—serious, important, and authoritative organs of world imperialism, on both sides of the ocean, consider the Opposition their mortal enemy. Throughout the entire recent period, they have either directly expressed their qualified and prudent sympathy for a number of measures taken by the official leadership, or they have expressed themselves to the effect that the total liquidation of the Opposition, its complete physical annihilation (Austen Chamberlain even demanded the firing squad), is the necessary premise for the "normal evolution" of the Soviet power towards a bourgeois regime. Even from memory, without having any sources for reference at our disposal, we can point to numerous declarations of this type: the *Information Bulletin* of French heavy industry (January 1927), the pronouncements of the London and New York *Times*, the declaration of Austen Chamberlain, which was reprinted by many publications, including the American weekly, the *Nation,* etc. The fact alone has been sufficient to compel our official party press, after its initial and not entirely successful attempts, to stop entirely reprinting the judgments passed by our class enemies upon the crisis which our party has undergone during the last months and is still undergoing. These declarations have emphasized much too sharply the revolutionary class nature of the Opposition.

We believe, therefore, that a great deal would be gained for the cause of clarity, if by the time the Sixth Congress convened two conscientiously collated books were published: a *White Book* containing the judgments of the serious capitalist press with regard to the controversies in the Comintern, and a *Yellow Book* with parallel judgments of the social democracy.

In any case, the fake bogey of the possible attempts on the part of the social democrats to involve themselves in our disputes will not keep us for a moment from pointing out clearly and precisely what we consider to be fatal for the policy of the Comintern, and what, in our opinion, is salutary. We will be able to crush it, not by resorting to diplomacy, not by playing hide-and-seek, but by means of that correct revolutionary policy which is still to be elaborated.

◆◆

At this time, with the publication of the draft program, all the fundamental theoretical and practical problems of the international proletarian revolution must naturally be examined in the light of the new draft. In fact, the task of the latter consists in furnishing, along with a theoretic method of handling the problems to be considered, a generalized verification and appraisal of all the experience already acquired by the Comintern. It is only by viewing the problem in this way that we can succeed in checking up and in arriving at a healthy judgment of the draft itself, in establishing the extent of its accuracy with regard to principles and the degree of its completeness and viability. We have formulated this criticism, insofar as it could be done in the very limited amount of time at our disposal, in a special document devoted to the draft program. The fundamental problems which it seemed to us most essential to illumine in our criticism, we grouped into the three following chapters: (1) The Program of International Revolution or a Program of Socialism in One Country? (2) Strategy and Tactics in the Imperialist Epoch (3) Summary and Perspectives of the Chinese Revolution: Its Lessons for the Countries of the Orient and for the Whole of the Comintern.

We have endeavored to analyze these problems by examining the living experience of the international workers movement and more particularly that of the Comintern during the last five years. From it we drew the conclusion that the new draft is completely inconsistent, shot through with eclecticism in its principled theses, lacking in system, incomplete, and patchy in its exposition. The section dealing with strategy is primarily characterized by its tendency to avoid the profound and tragic questions of revolutionary experience in the last few years.

We shall not here return to the questions examined in the document already sent to the congress. The aim of the present letter is altogether different, as can readily be seen from what has been said above. It has to do, let us say, with conjuncture and policy: in the general perspective, we must find what is the exact place occupied by the leftward turn now officially effected, in order to make it a point of departure for the rapprochement of tendencies existing in the Communist Party of the USSR and in the Comintern, which up to yesterday were drawing further and further apart. Obviously, there can be no question of a rapprochement save on the basis of perfect clarity in ideas and not at all on that of flattery or of bureaucratic Byzantinism.

This turn has manifested itself most crassly by far in the internal problems of the USSR, whence came the impulsion which produced it. We therefore intend to devote this letter mainly to problems of the crisis in the CPSU, which is a result of the crisis in the Soviet revolution. But since, while examining the cardinal questions of the evolution of the workers state we cannot in any way "abstract ourselves from the international factor," which is of *decisive* importance in all our internal developments and problems, we are compelled, in this letter also, to characterize briefly the conditions and methods of work of the Comintern, by repeating certain of our theses devoted to the draft program.

As a conclusion to these introductory observations, I wish to express my firm conviction that the criticism of the draft program, as well as the present letter to the congress, will be brought to the attention of all the members of the congress.[86] I have an indefeasible right to that, if only because the Fifth Congress elected me an alternate on the Executive Committee. This letter, considered formally, is a statement of the reasons for my appeal against the unjust decisions that have deprived me of the rights and duties with which I was charged at the supreme order of the Comintern.

2. WHY HAS NO CONGRESS OF THE COMINTERN BEEN CONVOKED FOR MORE THAN FOUR YEARS?

More than four years have elapsed since the Fifth World Congress. During this period, the line of the leadership has been radically altered, together with the composition of the leadership of different sections, as well as of the Comintern as a whole. The chairman elected by the Fifth Congress has been not only deposed but even expelled from the party, and readmitted only on the eve of the Sixth Congress.[87] All this was effected without the participation of a congress, although there were no objective obstacles to prevent its being convoked. In the most vital questions of the world working-class movement and of the Soviet republic, the congress of the Comintern proved to be superfluous; it was adjourned from year to year as an obstacle and a dead weight. It was convoked only at a time when the conclusion was reached that the congress would be confronted with entirely accomplished facts.

According to the letter and spirit of democratic centralism, the congress should occupy a decisive place in the life of the party. This life has always found its supreme expression in the congresses, their preparation, and their work. At the present time, the congresses have become a dead weight and an onerous formality. The Fifteenth Congress of the CPSU was arbitrarily postponed for more than a year. The congress of the Comintern has convened after a lapse of four years. And what years! In the course of these four years, filled with the greatest historical events and most profound differences in views, plenty of time was found for countless bureaucratic congresses and conferences, for the utterly rotten conferences of the Anglo-Russian Committee, for the congresses of the decorative League of Struggle Against Imperialism, for the jubilee theatrical congress of the Friends of the Soviet Union—the only time and place that could not be found was for the three regular congresses of the Communist International.[88]

During the civil war and the blockade, when the foreign delegates had to overcome unprecedented difficulties, and when some of them lost their lives en route, the congresses of the CPSU and of the Comintern convened regularly in conformance with the statutes and the spirit of the proletarian party. Why is this not being done now? To pretend that we are now too busy with "practical" work is simply to recognize that the mind and the will of the party hinder the work of the leadership and that the congresses are a fetter in the most serious and important affairs. This is the road of the bureaucratic liquidation of the party.

Formally, during these last four years and more, all questions have been decided by the ECCI or by the Presidium; as a matter of fact, however, they were decided by the Political Bureau of the Communist Party of the Soviet Union, or rather, to be more precise, by the Secretariat, basing itself upon the party apparatus that depends upon it. In question here is not, of course, the ideological influence of the CPSU. This influence was infinitely greater under Lenin than it is today, and it had a mighty creative importance. No, what is in question here is the almighty Secretariat of the CEC of the CPSU, functioning purely behind the scenes—a phenomenon of which there was not even a sign under Lenin and against which Lenin strictly warned in the last advice he gave to the party.[89]

The Comintern has been proclaimed the only international party to which all national sections are completely subordinated. In this question Lenin played the role of moderator to the end of his days. On more than one occasion he warned against centralist predilections on the part of the leadership, fearing that, if the political preconditions were lacking, centralism would degenerate into bureaucratism. The development of the political and ideological maturity of the communist parties has its own internal rhythm, based on their own experiences. The existence of the Comintern and the decisive role played in it by the CPSU can accelerate this rhythm. But this acceleration can be conceived only within certain imperative limits. When they are overstepped by attempts to substitute strictly administrative measures for independent activity, for self-criticism, for the capacity of self-orientation, directly opposite results may be attained, and in a whole series of cases such directly opposite results have been reached. Nevertheless, when Lenin ceased working, the ultracentralist manner of handling questions was the one which triumphed. The Executive Committee was proclaimed as the central committee with full powers in the united world party, responsible only to the congresses of the world party. But what do we see in reality? The congresses were not called precisely when they were most needed: the Chinese revolution by itself would have justified the calling of two congresses. Theoretically, the Executive Committee is a powerful center of the world workers movement; in reality, during the past few years it has been repeatedly revamped in a ruthless fashion. Certain of its members, elected by the Fifth Congress, who played a leading role within it, were deposed. The same thing took place in all the sections of the Comintern, or at least in the most important ones. Who was it, then, that revamped the Executive Committee, which is responsible only to the congress, if the latter was not convoked? The answer is quite clear. The directing nucleus of the CPSU, whose personnel was changing, selected each time anew the members of the Executive Committee, in complete disregard of the statutes of the Comintern and the decisions of the Fifth Congress.

The changes effected in the directing nucleus of the CPSU itself were likewise always introduced in some unexpected fashion, behind the back not only of the Comintern, but of the CPSU itself, in the interval between congresses and independent of the latter, by means of physical force on the part of the apparatus.

The "art" of leadership consisted of confronting the party with a fait accompli. Then the congress, postponed in conformity with the workings of the mechanism operating behind the scenes, was selected in a manner corresponding rigorously with the new composition of the leadership. At the same time the directing nucleus of the preceding day, elected by the previous congress, was simply labeled as an "antiparty summit."

It would take too long to enumerate all the most important stages of this process. I shall limit myself to citing a single fact, but one which is worth a dozen. The Fifth Congress, not only from the formal point of view, but in fact as well, was headed by the Zinoviev group. It is precisely this group that gave the fundamental tone to this congress, by its struggle against so-called Trotskyism. The needs engendered behind the scenes and the machinations of this struggle contributed in great measure to creating the deviation in the entire orientation of the congress. This became the source of the greatest errors during the years that followed. They are discussed in detail elsewhere. Here we need only single out the fact that the leading faction of the Fifth Congress was unable to maintain itself until the Sixth Congress in any party of the Comintern. As for the central group of this faction, it affirmed, in the person of Zinoviev, Kamenev, Sokolnikov, and others, in the declaration of July 1926, that "at the present time *there can no longer be any doubt* that the principal nucleus of the Opposition of 1923 correctly warned against the dangers of deviating from the proletarian line and against the menacing growth of the apparatus regime."

But that is not all. At the time of the joint plenum of the Central Committee and of the Central Control Commission (July 14–23, 1926), Zinoviev, the director and inspirer of the Fifth Congress, declared—and this stenographic declaration was published again by the Central Committee before the fifteenth party congress—that he, Zinoviev, considered as "the principal errors committed during his life," the following two: his mistake of 1917[90] and his struggle against the Opposition of 1923.

"I consider," said Zinoviev, "the second error as being more dangerous, for the mistake of 1917, committed during Lenin's life, was rectified by Lenin . . . whereas my error of 1923 consisted in the fact that . . ."

Ordzhonikidze: "Then why did you stuff the heads of everyone in the party? . . ."

Zinoviev: "Yes, in the question of the deviation and in the question of bureaucratic oppression by the apparatus, Trotsky proved to be correct as against you."

But the question of backsliding, that is to say of the *political line,* and that of *the party regime,* completely comprise the sum total of the divergences. Zinoviev, in 1926, concluded that the Opposition of 1923 was right on these questions, and that the greatest error of his life, greater even than his resistance to the October overturn, was the struggle he conducted in 1923–25 against "Trotskyism." Nevertheless, in the course of the last few days, the newspapers have published a decision of the Central Control Commission readmitting Zinoviev and Co. into the party, as they had "renounced their Trotskyist follies." This whole, absolutely incredible episode, which will seem like the work of some satirist to our grandchildren and great-grandchildren—although it is completely attested by documents—would perhaps not warrant mention in this letter if it concerned only a person or a group, if the affair were not intimately bound up with the ideological struggle that has been waged in the Comintern for the past few years, if it had not grown organically from the same conditions that permitted dispensing with the congress for four years, that is to say, by virtue of the unrestricted power of bureaucratic methods.

At the present time, the ideology of the Comintern is not guided but manufactured to order. Theory, ceasing to be an instrument of knowledge and foresight, has become an administrative technical tool. Certain views are attributed to the Opposition and on the basis of these "views" the Opposition is judged. Certain individuals are associated with "Trotskyism" and are subsequently recalled as if it were a matter of functionaries constituting the personnel of a chancellery. The case of Zinoviev is not at all exceptional. It is simply more outstanding than the others, for after all no less a person than the ex-chairman of the Comintern is involved, the director and inspirer of the Fifth Congress.

Ideological upheavals of this type inevitably accompany organizational upheavals, which always come from above and which have already been constituted into a system, forming in a way the normal regime not only of the CPSU but also of other parties in the Comintern. The official reasons for deposing an undesirable leadership rarely coincide with the true motives. Duplicity in the domain of ideas is an inevitable consequence of the complete bureaucratization of the regime. More than once in the course of these years have the leading elements of the communist parties in Germany, France, England, America, Poland, etc., resorted to monstrous opportunist measures. But they went completely unpunished, for they were protected by the position they took on the internal questions of the CPSU. To vote, and even more, to howl against the Opposition, is to insure oneself against any blows from above. As for the blows which might come from below, a guarantee against them is furnished by the fact that the apparatus is free from any control.

The latest instances are still very fresh in everybody's mind. Up to very recently, the Chinese leadership of Ch'en Tu-hsiu, of T'an P'ing-shan, and Co., completely Menshevik, enjoyed the full support of the Executive Committee of the Comintern, as against the criticism of the Opposition. There is nothing astonishing in that: at the time of the Seventh Plenum of the ECCI, T'an P'ing-shan swore that:

". . . At the very first appearance of Trotskyism, the Chinese Communist Party and the Chinese Communist Youth unanimously adopted a resolution against Trotskyism." (*Minutes,* p. 805.)

An enormous role is played in the ECCI itself and within its apparatus by elements which resisted and hindered, insofar as they were able, the proletarian revolution in Russia, Finland, Germany, Bulgaria, Hungary, Poland, and other countries, but who, in good time, made up for this by presenting their credentials in the struggle against "Trotskyism." T'an P'ing-shan is only the disciple of these elements; if abuse is heaped on him, while his masters are able to evade it, it is because the irresponsible regime requires an occasional scapegoat.

It is unfortunately impossible not alone to dispute, but even to endeavor to soften the formal assertion that the most outstanding, the most general, and at the same time, the most perilous characteristic trait of the last five years has been the gradual and increasingly accelerated *growth of bureaucratism* and of the arbitrariness which is linked with it, not only in the CPSU but in the Comintern as a whole.

The ignoring of and trampling upon statutes, the continual creation of upheavals in the organization and in the domain of ideas, the postponement of congresses, and conferences which are each time confronted with accomplished facts, the growth of arbitrariness—all this can not be accidental, all this must have profound causes.

It would be unworthy of Marxism to explain these phenomena solely or principally on personal grounds, as the struggle of cliques for power, etc. It goes without saying that all factors of this kind play an important role (see the Testament of Lenin). But involved here is so profound and so prolonged a process that its causes must be not only psychological but political as well, and so indeed they are.

The principal source of the bureaucratization of the whole regime of the CPSU and the Comintern, lies in the ever increasing gap between the political line of the leadership and the historical line of the proletariat. The less these two lines have coincided, the more the line of the leadership has revealed itself refuted by events, the harder it has been to apply the line by resorting to party measures, by exposing it to criticism, and the more it has had to be imposed on the party from above, by measures of the apparatus and even of the state.

But the growth of the gap between the line of the leadership and the historical line of the proletariat, that is to say, the Bolshevik line, can occur only under the pressure of nonproletarian classes. This pressure, considered generally, has grown to extraordinary proportions in the course of the last five years, cutting across violent oscillations in both directions, throughout the world as well as inside the USSR. The more the apparatus freed itself from the criticism and control of its own party, so much the more did the leadership become susceptible and conciliatory to the aspirations and suggestions of nonproletarian classes, transmitted through the medium of the apparatus. This operated to shift the political line still further to the right and consequently required even harsher bureaucratic measures in order to impose it on the proletarian vanguard.

The process of political backsliding was thus inevitably completed by organizational repressive measures. Under these conditions the leadership refused absolutely to tolerate Marxian criticism any longer. The bureaucratic regime is "formalistic"; scholasticism is the ideology most suitable to it. The last five years constitute in their entirety a period devoted to the scholastic distortion of Marxism and Leninism, to their slavish adaptation to the requirements of political backsliding and the spirit of bureaucratic usurpation. "Allow the kulak to grow into socialism," "enrich yourselves!" the recommendations "not to leap over stages," the "bloc of four classes," the "two-class parties," "socialism in one country"—all these ideas and slogans of centrism sliding to the right have inevitably engendered the application of articles of the Penal Code against the real disciples of Marx and of Lenin.

It goes without saying that the Marxian interpretation of the causes of scholastic impoverishment, of the progress of bureaucratism and arbitrariness, does not in the least absolve the leadership from personal responsibility, but on the contrary makes that responsibility even greater.

3. THE POLICY OF 1923–27

Unquestionably, one of the prime motives behind the repeated postponements of the call for the Sixth Congress was the desire to await some great international victory. In such cases, men are apt more easily to forget recent defeats. But no victories were forthcoming, nor is this accidental.

During this period, European and world capitalism found themselves granted a new and serious reprieve. The social democracy strengthened itself considerably after 1923. The communist parties grew insignificantly—in any case, infinitely less than was presaged in the prophecies which inspired the Fifth Congress. We must note that this applies both to the organizations of the Comintern and to their influence among the masses. Taken together, the latter followed a declining curve from the autumn of 1923 and during the whole period under consideration. It is doubtful if anyone can be found bold enough to assert that the communist parties were able in these four or five years to maintain the continuity and stability of their leadership. On the contrary, these qualities were found to be completely impaired even in the party where they were formerly most guaranteed: in the Communist Party of the USSR.

The Soviet republic made serious progress from the standpoint of economy and culture in the course of the elapsed period, demonstrating to the world for the first time the power and importance of socialist methods of management and especially the great possibilities lodged in them. But these successes developed on the basis of the so-called stabilization of capitalism, which itself was the result of a whole series of defeats of the world revolution. Not only did that considerably worsen the external situation of the Soviet republic, but it exercised a great influence upon the internal relation of forces in a direction hostile to the proletariat.

The fact that the USSR continues to exist, according to Lenin's expression, as an "isolated frontier in a completely capitalist world," has led, by virtue of an erroneous leadership, to forms of development of the national economy in which capitalist forces and tendencies have acquired a serious, or, more exactly, an alarming scope. Contrary to optimistic assertions, the internal relation of forces in economy and politics has changed to the disadvantage of the proletariat. Hence, a series of painful crises from which the CPSU has failed to emerge.

The *fundamental* cause of the crisis of the October Revolution is the retardation of the world revolution, caused by a whole series of cruel defeats of the proletariat. Up to 1923, these were the defeats of postwar movements and insurrections confronted with the nonexistence of the communist parties at the beginning, and their youth and weakness subsequently. From 1923 on, the situation changed sharply. We no longer have before us simply defeats of the proletariat, but routs of the policy of the Comintern. The blunders committed by this policy in Germany, England, China, and those of smaller scope which were perpetrated in a whole series of other countries, are of such a nature as cannot be duplicated in the history of the Bolshevik Party; to duplicate them, one is forced to examine the history of Menshevism during the years 1905–17, or the decades preceding.

The retardation in growth of the Comintern is the immediate result of its erroneous policy during the last five years. There is no holding that the "stabilization" is responsible for it, save by conceiving the nature of the latter in a purely scholastic way, and particularly by trying to dodge the responsibility. The stabilization did not fall from the sky; it is not the fruit of an automatic change in the living conditions of world capitalist economy. It is the result of an unfavorable change in the political relation of class forces. The proletariat saw its forces drained by the capitulation of the leadership in Germany in 1923; it was tricked and betrayed in England by a leadership with which the Comintern continued to maintain a bloc in 1926; in China, the policy of the Executive Committee of the Comintern drove the proletariat into the noose of the Kuomintang in 1925-27. These are the immediate and indisputable causes of the defeats, and what is no less important, these are the reasons for the *demoralizing character* of these failures. To try to prove that the defeats were inevitable even if the policy followed had been correct, is to fall into depraved fatalism and to renounce the Bolshevik conception of the role and importance of a revolutionary leadership.

The rout of the proletariat, conditioned by a false policy, provided the bourgeoisie with a respite from the political point of view. The bourgeoisie utilized the respite to consolidate its economic positions. These are the causes which furnished the point of departure for the period of stabilization that began on the day in October 1923 when the German Communist Party capitulated. To be sure, the consolidation of its economic positions obtained by the bourgeoisie acts in its turn as a "stabilizing" factor upon the political environment. But the fundamental cause of the ascendancy of capitalism during the period of stabilization of the last five years lies in the fact that the leadership of the Comintern did not measure up to the events from any point of view. Revolutionary situations were not lacking. But the leaders were chronically incapable of taking advantage of them. This defect is not of a personal or accidental character; it is the inevitable consequence of the centrist course, which may camouflage its inconsistency during a period of lull but ineluctably brings about catastrophes during the abrupt changes of a revolutionary period.

The internal evolution of the USSR and of the leading party reflected completely the shifts in the international situation, thus refuting by example the new reactionary theories of isolated development and of socialism in one country.

Naturally, the course of the leadership within the USSR was the same as that of the ECCI: centrism sliding to the right. In the internal policy, as well as on the international arena, it caused the same profound harm, weakening the economic and political positions of the proletariat.

In order to understand the significance of the turn to the left now being effected, it is necessary to become completely and clearly cognizant not only of the general line of conduct swerving into right centrism, which was completely unmasked in 1926–27, but also the course during the preceding period of ultraleftism of 1923–25 which prepared the backsliding. It is thus a matter of passing judgment on the five years after Lenin's death, during which, under the pressure of hostile class forces and because of the instability and shortsightedness of the leadership, there ensued a correction, a modification, and an actual revision of Leninism in the matter both of internal and international problems.

As early as the Twelfth Congress of the CPSU, in the spring of 1923, two positions stood out clearly on the issue of the economic problems of the Soviet Union; they developed during the five following years and may be checked in the light of the crisis in grain collections during the past winter. The Central Committee held that the principal danger threatening the alliance with the peasantry arose from a premature development of industry; it found confirmation of this point of view in the supposed "selling crisis" of the autumn of 1923. Despite the episodic character of this crisis, it left a deep impression on the economic policy of the official leadership. The point of view which I had developed at the Twelfth Congress (spring of 1923) advanced the contrary estimate, that the essential danger threatening the *smychka* and the dictatorship of the proletariat lay in the "scissors" symbolizing the divergence between the prices of agricultural and industrial products, reflecting the *backwardness* of industry; the continuation, and even more so the accentuation, of this disproportion, would inevitably bring about a differentiation in agriculture and handicrafts and a general growth of capitalist forces.[91] I had already developed this point of view very clearly as early as the Twelfth Congress. At that time I also formulated the idea, among others, that *if industry remained backward,* good harvests would become a mainspring for capitalist and not socialist tendencies; they would deliver into the hands of capitalist elements an instrument for disorganizing socialist economy.

These fundamental formulas presented by the two sides subsequently cut across the struggle of the succeeding five years. During these years, accusations, absurd and reactionary in their essence, continually resounded against the Opposition, declaring that "it is afraid of the muzhik," that "it fears a good crop," that "it fears the enrichment of the village," or better yet, that "it wishes to plunder the peasant." Thus, as early as the Twelfth Congress, and especially during the discussion of autumn 1923, the official faction rejected class criteria and operated with notions like "peasantry" in general, "good crop" in general, "enrichment" in general. In this manner of treating the question, there was already making itself felt the pressure of new bourgeois layers, which were forming on the base of the NEP, which were connecting themselves with the state apparatus, which resisted repression and sought to evade the rays of the Leninist searchlight.

Events of an international order acquired a decisive importance in this process. The second half of 1923 was a period of tense expectation of the proletarian revolution in Germany.

The situation was evaluated at too late a date and in a hesitant way. Great friction was generated within the official Stalin-Zinoviev leadership; true, it remained within the framework of the common centrist line. Despite all warnings, a change in tempo was undertaken only at the last moment; everything ended in a frightful capitulation by the leadership of the German Communist Party, which surrendered the decisive positions to the enemy without a struggle.

This defeat was of an alarming character in itself. But it acquired even more painful significance because the leadership of the ECCI, which in a very large measure caused this defeat by its policy of lagging at the tail of events, did not understand the extent of the rout, did not comprehend its great depth, simply failed to recognize it.

The leadership obstinately insisted that the revolutionary situation was continuing to develop and that decisive battles were going to be waged shortly. *It is on the basis of this radically false evaluation that the Fifth Congress established its orientation towards the middle of 1924.*

As against this, the Opposition, during the second half of 1923, sounded the alarm on the political denouement which was approaching, demanded a course truly directed towards armed insurrection, and insistently warned that in such historic moments, a few weeks, and sometimes a few days, decide the fate of the revolution for many years to come. On the other hand, during the following six months which preceded the Fifth Congress, the Opposition persistently repeated that the revolutionary situation was already missed; that sail had to be taken in, in expectation of contrary and unfavorable winds, that it was not the insurrection that was on the agenda, but defensive battles against an enemy which has assumed the offensive—uniting the masses for partial demands, creating points of support in the trade unions, etc.

But the clear understanding of what had taken place and what was imminent was branded as "Trotskyism," and condemned as "liquidationism." The Fifth Congress demonstratively oriented towards insurrection in the presence of a political ebb tide. With a single stroke it disoriented all the communist parties by sowing confusion among them.

The year 1924, the year of the abrupt and clear swing towards stabilization, became the year of adventures in Bulgaria and in Estonia, of the ultraleft course in general, which ran counter to the march of events with increasingly greater force. From this time dates the beginning of the quest for ready-made revolutionary forces outside the proletariat, whence the idealization of pseudopeasant parties in various countries, the flirtation with Radić and La Follette, the exaggeration of the role of the Peasant International to the detriment of the Red International of Labor Unions, the false evaluation of the English trade union leadership, a friendship above classes with the Kuomintang, etc. All of these crutches upon which the ultraleft course adventurously sought to support itself, subsequently became the principal pillars of the obviously rightward course, which replaced the former after the ultraleftists no longer found themselves faced with the situations that crashed against the process of stabilization of 1924–25.

The defeat of the German proletariat was the shock which precipitated a discussion in the autumn of 1923 that had as its task, according to the conception of the official leadership of the CPSU, to approve as an internal policy the course of passive adaptation to spontaneous economic developments (struggle against "superindustrialization," ridicule of the planning principle, etc.). So far as international problems were concerned, the most important thing was to conceal the fact that the most assured of revolutionary situations had been missed.

Nevertheless, the fact of the rout of the German proletariat had penetrated the consciousness of the masses, which had been brought to high tension by the anxious waiting of 1923. The capitulation of the German leadership introduced into the ranks of the workers, not only in Germany but in the USSR as well, and also in other countries, elements of bitter skepticism towards the world revolution in general. The defeats in Bulgaria and Estonia then came to add to this. Towards the middle of 1925, it finally became necessary to admit officially the existence of the stabilization (a year and a half after it visibly began); that was done at a time when profound fissures were already being produced in it (in England, in China). A certain disappointment in the world revolution, which likewise partly seized the masses, pushed the centrist leadership towards strictly national perspectives, which were soon wretchedly crowned by the theory of socialism in one country.

The ultraleftism of 1924–25, incapable of understanding the situation, was all the more brutally supplanted by a shift to the right, which under the star of the theory of "not leaping over stages," brought the policy of adaptation to the colonial bourgeoisie, to the petty-bourgeois democracy and the trade union bureaucracy, to the kulaks, baptized as "powerful middle peasants," and to the functionaries, in the name of "order" and of "discipline."

The right-centrist policy which kept up appearances of Bolshevism in secondary questions was carried away by the flood tide of great events and found its strictly Menshevik and devastating coronation in the question of the Chinese revolution and the Anglo-Russian Committee. Never in the course of all revolutionary history had centrism until then described the rising and declining curve to such perfection; it is to be doubted that it will ever again be able to describe a similar one, for in this case it had at its disposal the powerful resources of the Comintern in the material domain and in that of ideas; it could arm itself in advance against any resistance, and against all criticism, too, by means of all the resources which the proletarian state had at its disposal.

The objective consequences of the policy of the ECCI provided new mainsprings which fed the stabilization, still further postponed the revolution, and tremendously aggravated the international position of the USSR.

❖

It was in the course of the struggle of the two tendencies which began in 1923 that the question of the tempo of socialist construction which, from the standpoint of theory, bound into a solid knot the divergences of views in internal and international questions.

The official leadership, deceived by the illusions of the period of reconstruction (1923–27) which was effected on the basis of capital ready at hand, taken from the bourgeoisie, slid further and further towards the position of isolated economic development as a goal in itself. And it is precisely upon this grossest of errors that, thanks to the blows dealt by the international defeats, there subsequently grew up the theory of socialism in a single country. Rupture with world economy was preached precisely at the moment when the conclusion of the period of reconstruction made the need of connection with world economy increasingly imperative.

The question of the tempo of our economic development was not posed at all by the official leadership. This leadership did not in the slightest understand that Soviet economy was regulated all the more rigidly by the world market in proportion as it was obliged to link up with this market through export and import trade.

When we insistently pointed out that the tempo of Soviet construction is conditioned by world economy and world politics, the directors and inspirers of the official line replied to us: "There is no need to inject the international factor into our socialist development" (Stalin), or on the other hand: "We will construct socialism if it be only at a snail's pace" (Bukharin). If one is not afraid to follow this idea logically to its conclusion, that is to say, that there is "no need to inject the international factor" into the question of the tempo of our economic development, one will see that it means simply that there is no need to "inject" the Comintern into the fate of the October Revolution, for the Comintern is nothing else than the revolutionary expression of the "international factor." But the point is that centrism never pursues its ideas to their end.

The question of tempo is obviously of decisive importance not only in economics but especially in politics, which is "concentrated economics."

If in internal affairs we were being retarded because of the wrong way of approaching economy, retarding it to an ever greater degree from fear of too great an advance, then, on the contrary, in the face of the problems of the international revolution, the systematic loss of tempo was due to centrist incapacity to estimate in full the revolutionary situation and to take advantage of it at the critical moments. To be sure, it would be vain pedantry to state that the German proletariat, guided by a correct leadership, would *certainly* have conquered and held power; or that the English proletariat, if the leadership had seen correctly, would *certainly* have overthrown the General Council and thus considerably hastened the hour of proletarian victory; or that the Chinese proletariat, had it not been deceived by being forced under the banner of the Kuomintang, would have brought the agrarian revolution to a victorious conclusion and would *certainly* have seized the power by leading the poor peasants after it. But *the door was open to these three eventualities,* and in Germany—wide open. As against this, the leadership acted counter to the class struggle, strengthened the enemy at the expense of its own class and thus did everything to guarantee defeat.

The question of tempo is decisive in every struggle and all the more so in a struggle on a world scale. The fate of the Soviet republic cannot be separated from that of the world revolution. No one has placed centuries or even many decades at our disposal so that we may use them as we please. The question is settled by the dynamics of the struggle, in which the enemy profits by each blunder, each oversight, and occupies every inch of undefended territory. Without a correct economic policy, the proletarian dictatorship in the USSR will crumble, will be unable to endure long enough to be saved from without, and will thereby inflict infinite damage upon the international proletariat. Without a correct policy of the Comintern, the world revolution will be delayed for an indefinite historical period; but it is time that decides. What is lost by the international revolution is gained by the bourgeoisie. The construction of socialism is a contest between the Soviet state and not only the internal bourgeoisie, but also the world bourgeoisie, a contest waged on the basis of the worldwide class struggle. If the bourgeoisie is able to wrest a new large historic period from the world proletariat, it will, by basing itself on the powerful preponderance of its technology, of its wealth, of its army and its navy, overthrow the Soviet dictatorship; the question whether it will attain this by economic, political, or military means, or a combination of the three, is of secondary importance.

Time is a decisive factor, not merely an important one. It is not true that we will be able to build "complete socialism," if the Comintern continues the policy which found its expression in the capitulation of the German party in 1923, in the Estonian putsch in 1924, in the ultraleft errors of 1924–25, in the infamous comedy of the Anglo-Russian Committee of 1926, in the uninterrupted series of blunders which doomed the Chinese revolution of 1925–27. The theory of socialism in one country accustoms us to regard these errors with indulgence, as if we had all the time we want at our disposal. A profound error! Time is a decisive factor in politics, especially in periods of sharp historic turns, when a life-and-death struggle between two systems is unfolding. We must dispose of time with the greatest economy: the Comintern will not survive five years of mistakes like those which have been committed by its leadership since 1923. It holds, thanks to the attraction that the October Revolution exercises over the masses, the banner of Marx and Lenin; but it has been living during the course of the last period on its basic capital. *The Communist International will not survive five more years of similar mistakes.* But, if the Comintern crumbles, neither will the USSR long endure. The bureaucratic psalms announcing that socialism has been nine-tenths realized in our country (Stalin) will then appear as stupid verbiage. Certainly, even in this case the proletarian revolution would be able in the end to pioneer new roads to victory. But when? And at the price of what sacrifices and countless victims? The new generation of international revolutionists would have to tie up anew the broken threads of continuity and conquer anew the confidence of the masses in the greatest banner in history, which may be compromised by an uninterrupted chain of mistakes, upheavals, and falsifications in the domain of ideas.

These words must be said clearly and distinctly to the international proletarian vanguard, without in the least fearing the inevitable howlings, screechings, and persecutions on the part of those whose optimism survives only because they shut their eyes out of cowardice so as not to see the reality.

That is why, for us, the policy of the Comintern dominates all other questions. Without a correct international policy, all the possible economic successes in the USSR will not save the October Revolution and will not lead to socialism. To speak more exactly: without a correct international policy, there can be no correct policy in internal affairs either, for the line is one. The false way in which the chairman of a Soviet district committee approaches the kulak is only a small link in the chain whose largest links are constituted by the attitude of the Red trade unions towards the General Council, or of the Central Committee of the CPSU towards Chiang Kai-shek and Purcell.

The stabilization of the European bourgeoisie, the strengthening of the social democracy, the retardation in the growth of the communist parties, the strengthening of capitalist tendencies in the USSR, the shift to the right of the policy of the leadership of the CPSU and of the Comintern, the bureaucratization of the entire regime, the rabid campaign against the left wing, driven into the Opposition—all these processes are indissolubly bound together, characterizing a period of weakening, certainly provisional, but deep-going, of the positions of the proletarian revolution, a period of pressure exerted by enemy forces upon the proletarian vanguard.

4. RADICALIZATION OF THE MASSES AND QUESTIONS OF LEADERSHIP

The February plenum of the ECCI (1928) made an undeniable attempt at a leftward turn, that is to say, towards the opinions defended by the Opposition, on two questions of paramount importance: the policy of the English and French communist parties. One might attribute a decisive importance, and not merely a symptomatic one, to this turn, despite all its incoherence, if it had been accompanied by the application of the fundamental rule of Lenin's strategy: condemn *a false policy in order to pave the way for a correct policy.* The united front in France, in Germany, and in other countries was directed along the lines of the Anglo-Russian Committee. The course of the latter was almost as disastrous for the English Communist Party as was the course of the Kuomintang for the Chinese Communist Party.

As far as the resolution on the Chinese question is concerned, not only does it sanctify all the errors committed but it prepares for new ones which are no less cruel.

The resolution of the February plenum on the Russian question is a far better mirror of the regime of the Comintern than any one political line. It will suffice to state that this resolution contains the following assertion:

"The Trotskyists, together with the social democracy, are banking on the overthrow of the power of the Soviets." (*Pravda,* February 19, 1928.)

Men who out of docility raise their hands to vote for such affirmations without believing a single word (for only a complete idiot can *believe* that the Opposition is banking on the overthrow of the power of the Soviets), such men do not always find the courage, as experience testifies, to raise their hands in a determined struggle against the class enemy.

Taken altogether, the February plenum symbolizes a contradictory attempt at a left turn. From the political point of view this attempt is conditioned upon an undeniable shift that is taking place in the mood of the great working-class masses, principally in Europe and especially in Germany. There can be no talk of a correct leadership without a clear understanding of the character of this shift and the perspectives that it opens.

In his speech, or rather in the broadside of insults which he flung at the Opposition, Thälmann stated at the February plenum of the ECCI:

"The Trotskyists fail to perceive the radicalization of the international working class and do not notice that the situation is becoming more and more revolutionary." (*Pravda,* February 17, 1928.)

Then he passes, as is customary, to the ritualistic demonstration which seeks to prove that together with Hilferding we are burying the world revolution. One might ignore these puerile tales, if what were involved here were not the second largest party of the Comintern, represented in the ECCI by Thälmann. What is this radicalization of the working class which the Opposition fails to perceive? It is what Thälmann and many others with him had likewise termed as "radicalization" in 1921, in 1925, in 1926, and in 1927. The decline in influence of the Communist Party after its capitulation in 1923 and the growth of the social democracy did not exist for them. They did not even ask themselves what were the causes of these phenomena. It is difficult to speak to a man who does not want to learn the first letters of the political alphabet. Unfortunately it is not solely a question of Thälmann; he is not even of any importance by himself. Nor is Semard. The Third Congress was a real school of revolutionary strategy. It taught how to *differentiate.* That is the first condition, no matter what the job. There are periods of high tide and periods of ebb tide. But the former and the latter pass in turn through various phases of development. It is necessary from the point of view of tactic, to adapt the policy of each of these stages being experienced, while maintaining at the same time the general line of conduct in its orientation towards the conquest of power and being always prepared, so as not to be taken unawares by a sharp change in the situation. The Fifth Congress turned topsy-turvy the lessons of the Third. It turned its back to the objective situation; it substituted for analysis of events an agitational rubber stamp: "The working class is becoming more and more radical, the situation is becoming more and more revolutionary."

In reality, it is only during the past year that the German

working class has begun to recover from the consequences of the 1923 defeat. The Opposition was the first to notice it. In a document published by us, from which Thälmann quoted, we state the following:

"An undeniable shift to the left is occurring in the European working class. It is manifesting itself in a sharpening of the strike struggles and a growth in the number of communist votes. But this is only the first stage in the shift. The number of social democratic voters is increasing, parallel with the growth of the communist votes, and in part outstripping the latter. If this process develops and deepens, we will enter the following phase, when the shift will begin, from the social democracy to communism." (Trotsky, *On the New Stage*.)*

Insofar as the data relating to the latest elections in Germany and in France permit us to judge, the above evaluation of the condition of the European working class, especially the German, can be regarded almost as beyond dispute. Unfortunately the press of the Comintern, including that of the CPSU, furnishes absolutely no analyses which are serious, thorough, documented, illustrated by figures, of the moods and tendencies existing in the proletariat. Statistics, insofar as they are presented, are simply adjusted to a particular tendency having as its aim the preservation of the leadership's "prestige." They continually pass in silence over the factual data of exceptional importance which determine the curve of the workers movement during the 1923–28 period if these data refute false judgments and instructions. All this makes it extremely difficult to judge the dynamics of the radicalization of the masses, its tempo, its scope, its possibilities.

Thälmann did not have the slightest right to say to the February plenum of the ECCI that ". . . The Trotskyists fail to perceive the radicalization of the international working class." Not only had we perceived the radicalization of the *European* proletariat, but in that connection we had estab-

---

* "At a New Stage," in *Challenge of the Left Opposition (1926–27)*, p. 502.

lished, as early as last year, our evaluation of the conjuncture. The latter was completely confirmed by the May (1928) elections to the Reichstag. The radicalization is passing through its first phase, still directing the masses into the social democratic channels. In February, Thälmann refused to see this; he insisted: "The situation is becoming more and more revolutionary." In such a general form, this statement is only a hollow phrase. Can one say that "the situation is becoming more and more [?] revolutionary" if the social democracy, the main prop of the bourgeois regime, is growing?

In order to approach a revolutionary situation the "radicalization" of the masses must in any case still pass through a preliminary phase in which the workers will flock from the social democracy to the communist party. Assuredly, as a partial phenomenon, this is already taking place now. But the principal direction of the flow is not yet that at all. To confound an initial stage of radicalization, which is still half-pacifist, half-collaborationist, with a revolutionary stage, is to head towards cruel blunders. It is necessary to learn how to differentiate. Anyone who merely repeats from year to year that "the masses are becoming radicalized, the situation is revolutionary," is not a Bolshevik leader, but a tub-thumping agitator; it is certain that he will not recognize the revolution when it really approaches.

The social democracy is the chief prop of the bourgeois regime. But this prop contains contradictions within itself. If the workers were passing from the Communist Party to the social democracy, one could speak with perfect certainty of the consolidation of the bourgeois regime. It was so in 1924. At that time Thälmann and the other leaders of the Fifth Congress were unable to understand it; that is why they replied with insults to our arguments and advice. At present the situation is different. The Communist Party is growing *alongside* of the social democracy, but not yet directly *at the expense* of the latter. The masses are streaming in parallel lines to the two parties; up to now the flow towards the social democracy is the larger. The abandonment of the bourgeois parties by the workers and their awakening from political apathy, which lie at bottom of these processes, obviously do not constitute a strengthening of the bourgeoisie. But neither does the growth of the social democracy constitute a revolutionary situation. It is necessary to learn how to differentiate. How should the present situation be qualified then? It is a transitional situation, containing contradictions, not yet differentiated, still disclosing various possibilities. The subsequent development of this process must be vigilantly watched, without one's getting drunk on cut-and-dried phrases, and holding oneself always ready for sharp turns in the situation.

The social democracy is not merely gratified by the growth of the number of its voters; it is following the flood of workers with great anxiety for it creates great difficulties for it. Before the workers begin to pass *en masse* from the social democracy to the Communist Party (and the arrival of such a moment is inevitable), we must expect new and great friction inside the social democracy itself, the formation of more deep-going groupings and splits, etc. That will very probably open up the field to active, offensive, tactical operations on the part of the Communist Party along the line of the "united front" in order to hasten the process of revolutionary differentiation of the masses, that is to say, primarily the pulling away of workers from the social democracy. But woe unto us if the "maneuvers" reduce themselves to the fact that the Communist Party will again look into the mouth of the "left" social democrats (and they may still go far to the left), while waiting for their wisdom teeth to grow. We saw "maneuvers" of this kind practiced on a small scale in Saxony in 1923, and on a large scale in England and China in 1925-27. In all these cases they led to the missing of the revolutionary situation and to great defeats.

The judgment of Thälmann is not his own; this can be seen from the draft program which states:

"The process of radicalization of the masses which is sharpening, the growth of the influence and of the authority of the communist parties . . . all this clearly shows that a new revolutionary wave is mounting in the imperialist centers."

To the extent that this is a programmatic generalization, it is radically false. The epoch of imperialism and of proletarian revolutions has already known and will again know in the future not only a "process of radicalization which is sharpening," but also periods when the masses move to the right; not only of growth of the influence of the communist parties, but also of a temporary decline of that influence, especially in the event of errors, blunders, capitulations. If it is a question of judging from the standpoint of *conjuncture,* more or less true for certain countries, in the given period, but not at all for the entire world, then the place for this judgment is in a resolution and not in a program. The program is written for the entire epoch of proletarian revolutions. Unfortunately, in the course of these five years, the leadership of the Comintern has given no proof of comprehension in matters of dialectic regarding the growth and the disappearance of revolutionary situations. On these subjects it has remained in a permanent scholasticism, treating of "radicalization" without studying in a fundamental way the living stages of the struggle of the world proletariat.

By reason of the defeat experienced by Germany in the course of the great war, the political life of the country was distinguished by the special character of its crises; this placed the German proletarian vanguard in the presence of situations fraught with responsibilities. The defeats of the German proletariat during the five postwar years were immediately due to the extraordinary weakness of the revolutionary party; in the course of the subsequent five years they were due to the errors of the leadership.

In 1918–19, the revolutionary situation still completely lacked a revolutionary proletarian party. In 1921 when the ebb set in, the Communist Party which was already fairly strong, attempted to provoke a revolution despite the fact that the immediate premises for it were lacking. The preparatory work ("the struggle for the masses") which then followed resulted in a right deviation in the party. The leadership, deprived of revolutionary scope and initiative, suffered shipwreck in the sharp leftward shift in the whole situation (autumn of 1923). The right wing was supplanted by the left wing, whose domination nevertheless already coincided with the revolutionary ebb. But the Lefts refused to understand it and obstinately maintained "the course towards insurrection." From that, new errors were born which weakened the party and brought about the overthrow of the left leadership. The present Central Committee, leaning secretly upon a section of the "Rights," mercilessly struggled all the time against the left, repeating all the while mechanically that the masses were becoming radicalized, that the revolution was near.

The history of the evolution of the German Communist Party presents a picture of abrupt alternation of factions assuming power, depending upon the oscillations of the political curve: each directing group, at the time of each abrupt upward or downward turn of the political curve, that is, either towards a provisional "stabilization" or, on the contrary, towards a revolutionary crisis, suffers shipwreck and yields place to the competing group. It so happened that the right group had as its weakness an incapacity for knowing how, in case of a change in the situation, to switch all activity onto the rails of the revolutionary struggle for the conquest of power. As against this, the weakness of the left group was due to the fact that it could neither recognize nor understand the necessity of mobilizing the masses for transitional demands, springing from the objective situation during the preparatory period. The weak side of one group was supplemented by the weaknesses of the other. Since the leadership was replaced at the time of each break in the situation, the leading cadres of the party were unable to acquire a wider experience, extending through advance and decline, through flood and ebb, through retreat and attack. A truly revolutionary leadership cannot be educated unless it understands our epoch as an epoch of sudden shifts and sharp turns. The selection of leaders in random fashion, chosen by appointment, inevitably contains within itself the latent danger of a new bankruptcy of the leadership at the very first major social crisis.

To lead means to foresee. It is necessary, in a reasonable interval, to stop flattering Thälmann solely because he grubs in the gutter for the vilest epithets to fling at the Opposition, just as T'an P'ing-shan was petted at the Seventh Plenum simply because he translated Thälmann's insults into Chinese. The German party must be told that the judgment passed by Thälmann in February on the political situation is vulgar, arbitrary, and false. It is necessary to recognize openly the strategic and tactical blunders committed during the last five years and to study them conscientiously before the wounds they caused have had time to heal: strategic lessons can take root only when they follow events step by step. It is necessary to stop replacing party leaders in order to punish them for mistakes committed by the ECCI or because they do not approve of the GPU when it punishes proletarian revolutionists (Belgium).[92] It is necessary to allow the young cadres to stand on their own feet, helping them, but not ordering them about. It is necessary to stop "appointing" heads simply on the basis of their certificates of good behavior (that is to say, if they are against the Opposition). It is necessary once and for all to give up the system of the Central Committees of protection.

5. HOW THE CURRENT SWING TOWARD THE LEFT IN THE CPSU WAS PREPARED

It is indispensable that we sketch in this summary the policy and regime of the Comintern in order to find the correct place which corresponds to the swing of the leadership to the left. Since this swing issued *directly* from conditions which caused the economic crisis in the USSR, and since it is developing according to a line which particularly touches internal questions, it is indispensable that we examine more closely, and in greater detail, how these questions were presented in the past, up to recently, and what is new in the latest resolutions and measures of the Central Committee of the CPSU. It is only in this way that the correct line of the policy to follow subsequently will be outlined before us.

◆◆

The altogether exceptional difficulties experienced this year (1928) in the grain collections have an enormous importance not only in the economic domain but likewise in that of politics and of the party. It is not accidental that these difficulties have unleashed the turn to the left. On the other hand, by themselves these difficulties establish the balance sheet of a vast period of economic and general policy.

The transition from war communism to socialist economy could have been realized without being accompanied by *great* retreats only if the proletarian revolution had been immediately extended to the *advanced* countries. The fact that this extension was delayed for years led us to the great retreat of the NEP, a deep and lasting retreat, in the spring of 1921. The proportions of the indispensable retreat were established not only theoretically but also by feeling out the ground in practice. In the autumn of 1921 it was already necessary further to deepen the retreat.

On October 29, 1921, that is, seven months after the transition to the NEP, Lenin stated at the Moscow District Conference:

"This transition to the New Economic Policy which was effected in the spring, this retreat on our part . . . has it proved adequate so that we can stop retreating, so that we can prepare to take the offensive? No, it has still proved inadequate. . . . And we are now obliged to admit it, if we do not want to hide our heads in ostrich fashion, if we don't want to appear like fellows who do not see their own defeat, if we are not afraid of seeing the danger that confronts us. We must recognize that the retreat has proved to be inadequate, that it is necessary to execute a supplementary retreat, a further retreat in the course of which we will pass from state capitalism to the creation of purchases, of sales, and of monetary circulation regulated by the state.... That is why we are in the situation of men who still continue to be forced to retreat in order finally to pass to the offensive at a further stage." (*Works,* vol. 18, pp. 397f.)

And later, in the same speech:

"To conceal from oneself, from the working class, from the masses, that in the economic domain, in the spring of 1921 and at present, too, in the autumn-winter of 1921–22, we are still continuing to retreat, is to condemn ourselves to complete unconsciousness, is to be devoid of the courage to face the situation squarely. Under such conditions, work and struggle would be impossible." (*Ibid.,* pp. 399f.)★

It was only in the spring of the following year, in 1922, that Lenin decided to give the signal to halt the retreat. He spoke of it for the first time on March 6, 1922, at a session of the fraction of the metal workers congress:

"We can now say that this retreat, in the sense of concessions which we made to capitalists, is completed.... And I hope, and I am certain, that the party congress will also state so officially in the name of the leading party of Russia." (*Works,* vol. 18, part 2, p. 13.)

And immediately he added an explanation, frank and honest as always, truly Leninist:

"All talk of the cessation of the retreat must not be understood in the sense that we have already created the foundation of the new economy and that we can proceed tranquilly. No, the foundation has not yet been created." (*Works,* vol. 18, part 2, p. 13.)†

★ "Seventh Moscow Gubernia Conference of the RCP: Report on the New Economic Policy," in *LCW,* vol. 33, pp. 95–97.

† "The International and Domestic Situation of the Soviet Republic," in *LCW,* vol. 33, pp. 220–21.

The Eleventh Congress, on the basis of Lenin's report, adopted the following resolution on this question:

"The congress takes note that the sum total of the measures applied and decided upon during the course of the past year exhausts the necessary concessions made by the party to private capitalism and considers that in this sense the retreat is completed." (*Minutes,* p. 143.)

This resolution, deeply pondered, and, as we have seen, carefully prepared, presupposed consequently that the new points of departure occupied by the party would furnish the possibility of inaugurating the socialist offensive, slowly, but *without new movements of retreat.*

Nevertheless, the hopes of the last congress which Lenin led did not prove accurate on this point. In the spring of 1925 there came the necessity of executing a new retreat: granting to the rich classes of the village the right to exploit lower strata by hiring labor and renting land.

The necessity for this new retreat, immense in its consequences, which had not been foreseen by the strategic plan of Lenin in 1922, was due not only to the fact that the limits of the retreat had been drawn "too short" (the most elementary prudence made that imperative) but also because during 1923–24, the leadership understood neither the situation nor the tasks which devolved upon it, and lost time while under the delusion that it was "gaining" time.

But that is not all. The new painful retreat in April 1925 was not called, as Lenin would have called it, a profound defeat and retreat; it was presented as a victorious step of the *smychka,* as a mere link in the general mechanism of building socialism. It is precisely against such proceedings that Lenin had warned all his life, and especially in the autumn of 1921 when it became necessary to continue and deepen the retreat begun in the spring.

"It is not the defeat which is so dangerous," said Lenin in the above quoted speech at the Moscow District Conference, "as the fear of admitting one's defeat, the fear of drawing from it all the conclusions. . . . We must not be afraid of admitting defeats. We must learn from the experience of the defeats. If we adopt the opinion that by admitting defeats we induce despondency and a weakening of energy for the struggle, similar to a surrender of positions, we would have to say that such revolutionists are absolutely not worth a damn. . . . Our strength in the past was, as it will remain in the future, that we can take the heaviest defeats into account with perfect coolness, learning from their experience what must be modified in our activity. That is why it is necessary to speak candidly. This is vital and important not alone for the purpose of theoretical correctness, but also from the practical point of view. *We cannot learn to solve the problems of today by new methods if yesterday's experience has not made us open our eyes in order to see wherein the old methods were at fault.*" (*Works*, vol. 18, part 1, p. 396.)*

But this remarkable warning was completely forgotten the day after Lenin departed from leadership; it has not been really remembered a single time up to now.

Inasmuch as the decisions of April 1925 legalized the developing differentiation in the village and opened the floodgates to it, the *smychka* signified in the future an ever-growing commodity exchange between the workers state and the kulak. Instead of recognizing this terrible danger, the servile theory of integrating the kulak into socialism was immediately created. For the first time, this process in its entirety was presented to the party conference, in the name of the party, as the "building of socialism in one country" independent of world economy and world revolution. Thus the very appearance of this petty-bourgeois, reactionary theory is due not to the real successes of socialist construction, which are indisputable, but precisely to the setbacks of the latter and to the need thereby engendered among the leaders to provide

---

* "Seventh Moscow Gubernia Conference of the RCP: Report on the New Economic Policy," in *LCW*, vol. 33, pp. 93–94.

the proletariat a "moral" solace as a counterbalance to the new material concessions granted to capitalism.

The resolution of the Fourteenth Congress (January 1926) on industrialization voiced a whole series of correct theses, repeating almost word for word certain ideas that the Opposition had developed on this subject during 1923–25. But alongside of this resolution a campaign was waged against the left wing, labeled as "superindustrialists," that is to say, against those who did not want the adopted decisions simply to remain on paper; our warnings about the kulak danger were presented under the absurd designation of "panic"; the positing of the fact that the differentiation of classes was taking place in the village was punished as anti-Soviet propaganda; the demand for the exercise of stronger pressure upon the kulak to the advantage of industry was labeled as a tendency to "plunder the peasants" (Stalin-Rykov-Kuibyshev manifesto[93]); after all this the resolution on industrialization had as little influence on the real economic process as had been the case with certain other resolutions of the Fourteenth Congress on party democracy and on collective leadership in the Comintern.

In 1926 the Opposition formulated the discussion on the *smychka*, which began as far back as the spring of 1923, in the following way:

"*Question:* Is it true that the policy of the Opposition threatens to disrupt the *smychka* between the proletariat and the peasantry?

"*Answer:* This accusation is false to the core. The *smychka* is threatened at this moment by the lag in industry, on the one hand, and by the growth of the kulak, on the other. The lack of industrial products is driving a wedge between country and city. In the political and economic domains, the kulak is beginning to dominate the middle and poor peasants, opposing them to the proletariat. *This development is still in its very first stages*. It is precisely this that threatens the *smychka*. The underestimation of the lag in industry and of the growth of the kulak disrupts the correct, Leninist leadership of the alliance between the two classes, this basis of the dictatorship under the conditions in our country." (*Questions and Answers*.)*

Let us stress here that in this question also the Opposition exaggerated nothing, despite the bitterness of the struggle, when, rising in opposition to the renegade theory of integrating the kulak into socialism, good only for paving the way to our integration into capitalism, we stated in 1926 that the kulak danger was "still in its very first stages." We had pointed out, from 1923 on, the direction from which the danger was coming. We had pictured its growth at each new stage. In what else does the art of leadership consist if not in being able to grasp a danger in time, that is to say, when it is still "in its first stages," and to prevent the possibility of its further development? *To lead is to foresee*—not to persecute those who are able to foresee.

To the greatest misfortune of the party, it was impossible even to make public the above-quoted lines. For having propagated them, the best militants were expelled from the party by functionaries without an idea in their heads, who did not want to think of tomorrow, and who were, moreover, incapable of doing so.

On December 9, 1926, at the Seventh Plenum of the ECCI, Bukharin denounced the Opposition in the following terms, on the subject of the *smychka* and of the grain collections:

"What was the most powerful argument that our Opposition used against the Central Committee of the party (I have in mind here the autumn of 1925)? They said then: the contradictions are growing monstrously, and the CC of the party fails to understand this. They said: the kulaks, in whose hands almost the entire grain surplus is concentrated, have organized 'the grain strike' against us. That is why the grains are coming in so poorly. We all heard this. . . . The Opposition estimated that all the rest was only the political expression of this fundamental phenomenon. Subsequently the same comrades intervened to state: the kulak has entrenched himself still further, the danger has still further

---

* "Questions and Answers about the Opposition" in Trotsky, *Challenge of the Left Opposition (1926–27),* p. 104.

increased. Comrades, if the first and second affirmations had been correct, we would have even a stronger 'kulaks' strike' against the proletariat this year.... The Opposition slanders us by stating that we are contributing to the growth of the kulaks, that we are continually making concessions, that we are helping the kulaks to organize the grain strike; the real results are proof of just the contrary...."(*Minutes,* vol. 2, p. 118.)

Does not this single quotation from Bukharin demonstrate by itself the complete blindness of the leadership on the key question of our economic policy?

Bukharin, however, was no exception. He only "generalized" theoretically the blindness of the leadership. The most responsible leaders of the party and of economy vied with each other in declaring that we had overcome crises (Rykov), that we were dominating the peasant market, and that the question of grain collections had become strictly a purely organizational question of the Soviet apparatus (Mikoyan). The resolution of the July plenum of the Central Committee in 1927 announced that the development of economic activity during the course of that year had been, taken together, without any crises. At the same time, the official press affirmed in unison that the scarcity of goods in the country had, if not completely disappeared, at least been considerably ameliorated.

To counterbalance all this the Opposition wrote anew in its theses for the Fifteenth Congress:

"The decrease in the total amount of grains collected is, on the one hand, direct evidence of the profound disturbance existing in the relations between the city and the country and, on the other hand, it is a source of new difficulties which threaten us."

Where is the root of our difficulties? The Opposition replied:

"In the course of recent years industry developed too slowly, lagging behind the development of national economy as a whole.... Owing to this, the dependence of state economy on kulak and capitalist elements is growing in the domain of raw materials, in export, and in foodstuffs."*

Let us recall also that the sharpest intervention of the Opposition was the one during the anniversary demonstration on November 7, 1927; the sharpest slogan formulated in this intervention was: "Let us turn our fire against the right: against the kulak, the jobber, and the bureaucrat; against the kulak and the jobber sabotaging the grain collections; against the bureaucrat organizing or sleeping during the Donetz trial." The controversy, which was no minor one, and wherein the head of the revolution was at stake, ended in the winter of 1927–28 accompanied by threats of GPU agents, while decisions were hurriedly signed punishing by exile, in conformity with Article 58, the "deviations" which varied from the general centrist blindness, from that of Bukharin in particular.

Had it not been for the whole preceding work of the Opposition beginning with the theses of 1923 and ending with the placards of November 7, 1927; had not the Opposition established a correct prognosis in advance, and had it not raised a justified alarm in the party and working-class ranks, the crisis in the grain collections would have only hastened the development of the right-wing course towards the further unleashing of capitalist forces.

More than once before in history has the proletarian vanguard, or even the vanguard of the vanguard, paid with its own destruction for a new step forward by its class or for checking an offensive by its enemies.

6. ONE STEP FORWARD, HALF A STEP BACKWARD

It was the crisis in grain collections, unlike the Chinese, Anglo-Russian, and other crises, which could not be passed over in

---

* "Countertheses on the Five-Year Plan," in Trotsky, *Challenge of the Left Opposition (1926–27)*, p. 457.

silence, that provided an impulse towards a new phase in policy. It had its immediate repercussions not only in the entire economy but also in the daily life of each worker. That is why the new political period dates from the grain collections.

Without any connection at all with the past, the party was treated on February 15, 1928, in *Pravda,* to a leading article which might have been taken for a restatement, and in part for an almost literal reproduction, of the *Platform of the Opposition* presented at the Fifteenth Congress.

This unexpected article, written under the direct pressure of the crisis in grain collections, announced:

"Among a whole number of causes which have determined the difficulties experienced in grain collections, it is necessary to single out the following. The village has expanded and enriched itself. Above all it is the kulak who has expanded and enriched himself. Three years of good crops have not passed without leaving their mark."

Thus, the refusal of the village to give the city grain is due to the fact that the "village has enriched itself," that is to say, that it has realized as best it could Bukharin's slogan: "Enrich yourselves!" But why then does the enrichment of the village undermine the *smychka* instead of consolidating it? Because, the article replies, *"Above all it is the kulak who has expanded and enriched himself."* Thus the theory affirming that the middle peasant had expanded during these years at the expense of the kulak and the poor peasant, was abruptly rejected as so much useless rubbish. *"Above all* it is the kulak who has expanded and enriched himself."

However, even the enrichment of the kulaks in the villages does not by itself explain the disorganization of the exchange between the city and the country. The alliance with the kulak is not a socialist alliance. But the grain crisis consists in the fact that even this *smychka* is nonexistent. Ergo, not only has the kulak expanded and enriched himself, but he does not even find it necessary to exchange his hoarded natural produce for the *chervonetz;*[94] as for the goods that he wants and is able to get in town, he pays for them with a quantity of grain, which is absolutely inadequate for the city. *Pravda* also formulates the second cause, which is at bottom the fundamental reason of the grain crisis.

"The increase in the income of the peasantry ... in the presence of a relative backwardness in the supply of industrial products permits the peasants in general and the kulak in particular to hoard grain."

Now the picture is clear. The fundamental cause is the lag in industry and the scarcity of industrial goods. Under these conditions, not only was there no socialist *smychka* established with the poor and middle peasants belonging to the cooperative, but there is not even a capitalist *smychka* with the kulak. If the two quotations from *Pravda* to which we have just referred are compared with those of the Opposition documents presented in the preceding chapter, then it must be admitted that *Pravda* repeats practically verbatim the expressions and ideas of my "Questions and Answers," the penalty for typing which was expulsion from the party.

However, the *Pravda* article does not stop here. While still making the reservation that the kulak is not "the principal hoarder of grains" the article admits that he is the economic authority in the village, that "he has established a *smychka* with the city speculator who pays higher prices for grain," that "he [the kulak] has the possibility of drawing the middle peasant behind him." This description, which characterizes with precision the relations existing in the village, has nothing in common with the official legends of recent years on the dominant and continually increasing economic role of the middle peasant; but for that it coincides entirely with our platform, which was considered an antiparty document. After eleven years of proletarian dictatorship it appears that the kulak is the "economic authority of the village," that "he has the possibility of drawing the middle peasant behind him"—the middle peasant who, while continuing to be the central village figure from the numerical standpoint, finds himself held on the economic leash of the kulak. The reservation to the effect that the kulak is not "the principal hoarder of grain," does not at all soften the picture but makes it more somber. If we accept the rather dubious figure of 20 percent as the share of the grain trade which is currently attributed to the kulak, the fact that the latter can "draw behind him" the middle peasant in the market, that is to say, lead him to sabotage the state grain collections, is made to stand out all the more sharply. The New York banks do not own the totality of goods in circulation either; yet they are the ones who dominate it. Whoever attempts to place this "modest" 20 percent in evidence, only emphasizes thereby that it is enough for the kulak to have a fifth of the grain in his hands for him to seize the dominant role on the grain market. That is how weak an influence the state exerts on the rural economy under conditions of a lagging industry.

Another inevitable reservation, to the effect that the "leading" role of the kulak has been recorded only in several regions and not in all of them, is no palliative either; on the contrary, it even sharpens the alarming meaning of what is happening. These "several" regions were already sufficient to shake the *smychka* between the city and the country to its very foundations. What would have happened had this process been extended in the same degree to all regions?

We are dealing here with a living economic process and not with a stable statistical mean. It is not at all a question of measuring, quantitatively and with precision, this most complex and extensive process as we march along, but it is necessary to determine its quality, that is to say, to show in *what direction the phenomena are growing*. Today, we have 20 percent; tomorrow there may be a great deal more. Certain regions have gone ahead; others lag behind. In point of fact, the authority of the kulak in the village and the possibility he has of drawing the middle peasant behind him are not directly survivals from the past; no, in the latter we have new facts which have arisen on the groundwork of the NEP, following upon the kulak suppression; in this sense, the regions where the phenomenon is more sharply apparent are only pointing the way to the more "backward" ones, providing, naturally, that the course of the economic policy, which has ruled for five years, especially since April 1925, will be continued.

At whose expense has the new "Soviet" kulak gained in authority in the village? At the expense of the dominating workers state and its instruments, state industry and cooperation. If the kulak has obtained the possibility of drawing the middle peasant behind him, against whom will he lead him? Against the workers state! Therein lies the serious and profound *break* in the *economic smychka,* a premise of another, far greater danger, namely, *the break in the political alliance.*

It is no longer a question today, as was the case in the spring of 1923, of anticipating events, nor one of theoretical considerations, but of rigorously verified facts. Despite the dictatorship of the proletariat, despite the nationalization of the land, despite state-protected cooperation, the retardation experienced by industry has in a few years placed the reins in the village in the hands of the mortal enemies of socialist construction. This was certified by *Pravda* for the first time on February 15, 1928.

From all this, despairing conclusions need not at all be drawn. But before everything else, the clear and complete truth must be presented to the party. Nothing must be underrated or embellished. That is why the article of *Pravda,* in spite of its petty, equivocal reservations, constitutes a serious step forward. By that alone, it considerably reduces the distance, on this question, separating the line of the Opposition from that followed by the leadership in the course of the past five years. All Oppositionists can only welcome this. But after this step forward there ensued at least half a step backward. As soon as the situation became less acute, from the standpoint of the grain collections, thanks to emergency administrative measures, the machine of official optimism was set into motion again.

The last programmatic manifesto of the Central Committee of June 3, 1928, states:

"The resistance of the kulaks grew on the basis of a general increase in the productive forces of the country, *despite a still greater growth of the socialist sector of the economy.*"

If that is the case, if that is true, there is no room for alarm. Then there remains only to keep calmly building "socialism in one country" without disrupting the line of activity. If the specific weight of capitalist elements, that is to say, the kulak especially, is annually declining within the economy, then what is the occasion for so sudden a "panic" before the kulak? The question is resolved by the dynamic relationship between two struggling forces: socialism and capitalism—who will vanquish whom? The kulak is either "terrifying" or "harmless" depending solely upon the direction in which this relationship shifts. The manifesto of the CC vainly seeks to salvage, in this section, the resolution of the Fifteenth Congress, which proceeded from the alleged constantly growing preponderance of socialist elements in the economy over the capitalist elements. But indeed the article in the February 15 issue of *Pravda* is a public refutation of this incorrect thesis which has been disproved in practice by the entire course of operations necessitated during the grain collections. How does this jibe logically?

Had the socialist sector grown more rapidly than the nonsocialist during these three years of good harvests, we might perhaps have still had a commercial and industrial crisis, manifesting itself in a surplus of products of state industry that could not find agricultural equivalents. Instead, we have had a crisis in grain collections, which the February 15 issue of *Pravda* correctly explains as the result of the accumulation of the agricultural products on the part of the peasantry and especially the kulaks, products for which there were lacking equivalents in industrial goods. The aggravation of the crisis in grain collections, i.e., the crisis of the *smychka,* as a result of three good crops, can only imply that in the general dynamics of the economic process the socialist sector has become *weaker* as compared with the capitalist and private commodity sector in general.

The correction which has been introduced into this relationship by administrative pressure, absolutely inevitable once the leadership had proved blind, does not in any way change the fundamental conclusion. We are here dealing with a political force in which the kulak is already taking part, even if only partially. However, the very necessity of resorting to emergency methods from the arsenal of war communism is evidence precisely of an unfavorable change in the relationship of forces within the sphere of economic life.

But there is still another criterion which is equally decisive and even more important: the material condition of the working class. If it is true that the national economy is growing (and this is true); if it is true that socialist accumulation is growing more rapidly than private accumulation (as the CC declares, contrary to reality), then it is entirely incomprehensible why the condition of the working class has grown worse during the recent period, and why the recent collective contracts were the source of grave friction and bitter struggle. Not a single worker can posit a "predominance" of this sort of socialist elements over those of growing capitalism, when the standard of living of the nonproletarian elements is rising while that of the proletarian elements is on the decline. This practical criterion, which affects the worker vitally, is completely in harmony with the theoretical criterion and is a refutation of the superficial and formal optimism of the CC.

In face of this objective verification, given by economy and life itself, all attempts to prove "statistically" the predominance of the growth of the socialist sector are rendered absurd. This would be tantamount to an attempt on the part of the head of an army, forced to retreat with losses after a battle, after surrendering important positions, to prove with cunning statistical coefficients that the preponderance lay on his side. No, the kulak has proved (and his arguments are more convincing than statistical combinations, made to comply with optimism) that in this very important battle, to the extent that it was waged with *economic* weapons, the preponderance proved to be on the side of the kulak. The household budget of the working woman also bears witness to this. The question of who will vanquish whom is resolved by the living dynamics of economy. If figures contradict the incontrovertible results of the struggle, and the testimony of life itself, then the figures lie, or, at best, the answer they give refers to a totally different question.

Indeed, we have already had in 1927 instances not only of the entirely admissible administrative intervention into grain collections, but also entirely inadmissible intervention into statistics. On the eve of the Fourteenth Congress, the statistical data refurbished by the secretariat of the CC "absorbed" the kulak almost completely. Merely a few days were required for this socialist victory.

But even if we were to set aside the accommodating nature of statistics, which like all other things suffer from the arbitrariness of the apparatus, there still remains the fact that statistics, especially among us, given the extreme atomization of the most important processes, are always belated. Statistics provide a momentary cross-section of the processes, without catching their tendencies. Herein theory must come to our assistance. Our correct theoretical evaluation of the dynamics of the process predicted beforehand that the lag in industry will turn even the good crops against socialist construction and engender the growth of the kulak in the village and breadlines in the cities. The facts came and they gave their incontrovertible verification.

In the lessons of the crisis in grain collections, summarized in the February article of *Pravda,* we have a compulsory and therefore all the more indisputable confirmation of the increasing disproportion, with the deficit on the side of state economy, i.e., with the decrease of the specific weight of the economic foundations of the proletarian dictatorship. Along with this we have a confirmation of a differentiation in the peasantry already so profound as to place the fate of the grain collections, in other words, the fate of the *smychka,* under the immediate and direct control of the kulak, leading behind him the middle peasant.

If the disproportion between the city and the country has been inherited from the past; if a certain growth of capitalist forces flows inevitably from the very nature of our present economy, then the *aggravation* of the disproportion during the last year and the *shift* in the relation of forces to the side of the kulak is entirely the result of the false class policy of the leadership, which failed to regulate methodically the distribution of the national income, either permitting the reins to slip completely free or hysterically checking them.

In contradistinction to this, the Opposition, since 1923, has been insisting that only a firm planned course based upon a systematic year-to-year overcoming of the disproportion would enable us to endow state industry with a real leading role in relation to the village; and that, on the contrary, the lag of industry would inevitably engender the deepening of class contradictions in the country and the lowering of the specific weight of the economic summits of the proletarian dictatorship.

Consequently we approached the kulak, not as an isolated phenomenon, as Zinoviev and Kamenev attempted to do during the Fourteenth Congress, but on the basis of the decisive relationship between state industry and the private commodity form of rural economy as a whole. Within the confines of village economy we took the kulak, once again not as an isolated phenomenon, but in connection with his economic influence upon the more prosperous layers of the middle peasants and the village as a whole. Finally we took these two fundamental internal processes, not as isolated, but in their relation with the world market, which through export and import exerts an ever more determining influence upon the tempo of our economic development.

Taking all this as our starting point, we wrote in our theses submitted to the Fifteenth Congress:

"Inasmuch as we obtain the grain and the raw material surpluses for export trade primarily from the well-to-do layers of the village, and inasmuch as it is precisely these layers that are hoarding grain the most, it turns out that we are 'regulated' through export trade primarily by the kulak and the well-to-do peasant."*

But an objection may be raised that the Opposition was "premature" in posing questions for which the leadership had already set a date for some time in the future. After all that has been said, it is hardly necessary to dwell upon this puerile Stalinist argument which is fed to the party each time it becomes essential to make up for lost time. Let us present a single piece of telling evidence. On March 9, 1928, at a session of the Moscow Soviet, Rykov said the following on the subject of grain collections:

"This campaign indubitably bears all the distinctive traits of shock-brigade work. If I were asked whether it would not have been better to manage in a more normal way, that is to say, without resorting to such a shock-brigade campaign, in order to overcome the crisis in grain collections, I would give the candid reply that it would have been better. We must recognize that *we have lost time, we were asleep at the beginning* of the difficulties in grain collection, *we failed to take a whole series of measures in time* which were necessary for a successful development of the grain collections campaign." (*Pravda*, March 11, 1928.)

If the delay is recognized in these words primarily from the administrative standpoint, then it is not difficult to supplement them politically. In order to have applied the indispensable administrative measures in time, the party, inspiring and directing the state apparatus, should have been supplied in due time with at least the rough data for a general orientation, such as was given in the leading article of *Pravda* of February 15. The delay consequently bears not an administrative but a party-political character. The principled warnings of the Opposition should have been attentively listened to in time and the practical measures we proposed should have been dis-

---

* "Countertheses on the Five-Year Plan," in *Challenge of the Left Opposition (1926–27)*, pp. 460–61.

cussed in a businesslike manner.

Last year the Opposition proposed, in part, to enforce a compulsory loan to the amount of 150 to 200 million *poods* of grain from 10 percent of the peasant enterprises, i.e., the wealthiest. At that time this proposal was castigated as being a measure of war communism. The party was taught that it is impossible to squeeze the kulak without harming the middle peasant (Stalin at the Fourteenth Congress), or that the kulak does not represent any danger since, you see, he is constrained a priori within the framework of the proletarian dictatorship (Bukharin). But this year recourse had to be taken to Article 107 (i.e., to repressive measures of collecting grain); after which, the CC had to explain that talk about war communism is counterrevolutionary slander, although the committee itself had on the very eve labeled as war communism much more cautious and methodical proposals of the Opposition.

So long as white is called white and black is called black, the correct point of view will be the one which provides the possibility of understanding what is occurring and to foresee the future. The viewpoint of the Opposition comes under this definition, but that of the official leadership never does. In the last analysis, facts stand above the highest institutions. Only in a fit of hierarchic hysteria could anyone demand today, *after* the grain collection campaign of last winter, and the resulting acute crisis in the official policy and ideology, that the Opposition admit its "error." Such a condition has never yet brought anyone any good.

The question here is not *who was right*. This question has a meaning only in connection with the question *which line was correct*. To slur over this last question after the first signs of a turn on the part of the leadership would be the most contemptible and infamous crime against the party. The party has not yet had a chance to find out. All measures, controversies, and steps have real value depending only on whether the party has or has not clarified itself. A principled position has not yet been won. The future has not been secured. For every step forward there follows a half step back.

7. A MANEUVER OR A NEW COURSE?

How should the present turn to the left be evaluated? Are we to see in it a combinationist maneuver or a serious new course, i.e., the resurgence of a proletarian line and international policy? Distrust is entirely in order.

The mere adoption of a decision in order to distract the party's attention—such has become the fundamental method of the present leadership. On the question of industrialization, the poor peasantry, the Chinese revolution, they adopted, one after another, resolutions intended not to clarify, explain, and lead, but, on the contrary, to dissimulate and camouflage what had occurred in reality. Lenin has said that in politics only idiots put faith in words. The post-Leninist period must teach even idiots to rid themselves of this gullibility.

The question whether this is a maneuver or a new course is a question that involves the class interrelations and their reflection in the CPSU, which, as the only party in the country, reacts differently to the pressure of various classes through the various groups within it.

The above-quoted "historical" article of *Pravda* of February 15, contains a remarkable admission relating to this question, that is to say, the reflection of new class groupings within our own party. This is perhaps the most striking section of this article. It reads as follows:

"In our organizations, both in the party and elsewhere, certain elements alien to the party have emerged during the recent period who do not see classes in the village, who do not understand the foundations of our class policy and who attempt to conduct the work in such a way as to offend nobody in the village, to live in peace with the kulak, and generally to maintain popularity among 'all the layers' of the village."

Although reference is made here to members of the party, the above words provide a well-nigh finished portrait of the neobourgeois, Thermidorian[95] politician-realist, in contrast to the communist. *Pravda,* however, doesn't say a single word in explanation of how these elements got into the party. They have "emerged"—and that's all! Whence have they come, through what gates did they enter? Did they penetrate into the party from the outside? And how did they wedge their way in? Or did they sprout inside, and upon what soil? And, mind you, all this has taken place under the conditions of an uninterrupted "Bolshevization" of the party along the line of the peasant question. The article does not go on to explain how the party, despite repeated warnings, could have overlooked the Ustryalovists[96] and Thermidorians up to the very moment when they revealed their *administrative power* in the policy of grain collections, nor how the party allowed itself to lose sight of the kulak up to the very moment when he obtained authority, led the middle peasant behind him, and sabotaged the grain collections. *Pravda* explains none of this. Why bother! In February 1928, we heard for the first time from the central organ what we knew long ago and what we had expressed more than once, namely, that in the party of Lenin there has not only "emerged" but also taken shape a strong right wing which is pulling toward a neo-NEP, i.e., to capitalism by gradations.

Towards the end of 1927, here is what I wrote on this subject:

"The official struggle against the Opposition is being waged under two basic slogans: *Against Two Parties* and *Against 'Trotskyism.'* The fake Stalinist struggle against two parties camouflaged the growth of dual power in the country and the *formation of a bourgeois party at the right wing of the CPSU,* and under the cover of its banner. In a whole series of chancellories and in the cabinets of secretaries, secret conferences were being held between the party retainers of the apparatus and the specialists, Ustryalovist professors, for the purpose of elaborating methods and slogans of the struggle against the Opposition. This is the *genuine* formation of a second party, which seeks by might and main to subordinate to itself, and, in part, does subordinate, the proletarian core of our party and to exterminate its left wing. While screening the formation of this second party, the apparatus accused the Opposition of striving to create a second party—precisely because the Opposition is seeking to tear the proletarian core of the party from under the growing bourgeois influence and pressure, failing which, it is altogether impossible to save the unity of a Bolshevik party. It is sheer illusion to think that the dictatorship of the proletariat can be preserved by spellbinding phrases about an indivisible party. The question of one party or two parties (in the materialistic, class, and not a verbal, agitational sense of the term) is decided precisely by the measure in which it will be possible to arouse and mobilize the forces of resistance inside the party and the proletariat." ("On the New Stage.")*

In June, Stalin gave the following explanation to the students of the highest institutes in Moscow on the subject of a second party:

"There are people who see a way out of the situation in a return to kulak economy, in a development and an unfolding of kulak economy. These people do not dare to speak of a return to landlord economy, since they apparently understand that it is dangerous to babble about such things in our time. But they speak all the more readily about the necessity of an all-sided development of kulak economy . . . in the interest of the Soviet power. These people presuppose that Soviet power could base itself at one and the same time upon two opposite classes: the class of kulaks, whose economic principle is the exploitation of the working class, and the class of workers, whose economic principle is the destruction of all exploitation. This is a hocus-pocus worthy of reactionaries. It is not worthwhile to prove that these reactionary plans have nothing

---

* Trotsky, "At a New Stage," in *Challenge of the Left Opposition (1926–27)*, pp. 502–3.

in common with the interests of the working class, with the principles of Marxism and the tasks of Leninism."

These words represent a somewhat simplified exposition of a section of the introduction of the first chapter of the *Platform of the Opposition*. We do not keep this a secret only because in our opinion Stalin is not threatened with exile for it *as yet*. To be sure, there is no open mention of the formation of a second party in the Stalinist speech. But if, within the proletarian party there are "people" (which people?) who are steering a course toward a kulak capitalist economy and who refrain from speaking about large-scale landlord economy only out of caution; if these "people," whose address is not given, are bound up with each other by this sort of platform, and are guided by it during grain collections, during the elaboration of industrial plans, wage scales, etc., etc., then this is precisely the cadre of a neobourgeois, i.e., Thermidorian party. It is possible to be in a Bolshevik party and *not* steer a course toward Chiang Kai-shek, Purcell, the kulak, and the bureaucrat; or rather, that is the only condition on which one can be in a Bolshevik party. But it is impossible to be in a Bolshevik party and steer a course towards capitalist development. This is the simple idea expressed in our document, "On the New Stage."

Thus, the right wing "emerging" from an unknown cause was for the first time officially noticed during the grain collections. On the day following the Fifteenth Congress, which once again gave proof of 100 percent monolithism, it was discovered that the kulak does not bring his grain to market because, among other things, there are influential groupings in the party desirous of living in peace with all classes, in accordance with the teachings of Tao Tsi-tao, the court philosopher of Chiang Kai-shek. These internal Kuomintangists did not make themselves heard either during the so-called discussion or at the congress. These valiant "party members" were of course the first to vote for the expulsion of the Opposition as a "social-democratic" deviation. They also voted for all the left resolutions, for they have long since learned to understand that resolutions don't count. The Thermidorians in the party are not phrasemongers but men of action. They establish their own special *smychka* with the new proprietors, the petty-bourgeois intellectuals, and the bureaucracy; and they direct the most important branches of economic, cultural, and even party activity from the "national-state" standpoint. But can it be that the Rights are so weak that there is no need to struggle against them?

A clear reply to this question is of decisive importance for the fate of the entire present turn to the left. The first impression is that the Rights are extremely weak. A shout from above proved sufficient to direct immediately along the "left" channel the grain collections and, in part, the general peasant policy. But precisely this extraordinary ease with which results were obtained should serve as a warning against over-hasty conclusions about the weakness of the Rights.

The right wing is a petty-bourgeois, opportunistic, bureaucratic, Menshevik, conciliationist wing that pulls toward the bourgeoisie. It would be an absolutely inconceivable phenomenon, if, in a party containing the revolutionary cadres of Bolshevism and hundreds of thousands of workers, the right wing could become, within a space of a few years, an independent force and openly apply its tendencies, mobilizing the working-class masses. Of course, such a situation does not exist. The right wing is strong as a *transmitting apparatus for the pressure of the nonproletarian classes on the working class*. This implies that the strength of the right wing of the party is located *outside* the party, beyond the confines of the latter. It is the force of the bureaucratic apparatus, of the new proprietors, of the world bourgeoisie. Consequently it is a colossal force. But precisely because the right wing reflects the pressure of other classes within the party, it is incapable as yet of presenting its platform openly and mobilizing the public opinion of the party. It requires a cover; it must lull the vigilance of the proletarian core of the party. The regime of the apparatus provides it with both the former and the latter. Under the inflated monolithism of the party the apparatus conceals the right wing from the view of the revolutionary workers and, at the same time, it terrorizes the workers by dealing blows to the Opposition, which is only the conscious expression of the alarm of the proletariat for the fate of its dictatorship.

The existing breach between the apparatus and the right wing compels the latter to contract its front, strike while retreating, and provisionally bide its time. The Rights well understand that if the apparatus seriously invited the party to analyze the situation, to purge itself by eliminating the Thermidorians, the right wing would find itself completely swept away by the rank and file, who would have no need of resorting to gangs of disrupters and thugs. Thus there would no longer be a lever inside the party upon which the internal bourgeoisie and that of the entire world could lean. To be sure, the onslaught of the bourgeoisie would not disappear immediately or even diminish. But it would have to exert itself directly against the party, which would then see its enemy face to face, and be able to judge coolly the forces and intentions of the latter. The clandestine and underground forms of the pressure of the bourgeoisie, operating through infiltration against the party and the Soviet power, would become impossible. That in itself would be half a victory.

The Rights understand the position they find themselves in. But they also take into account another fact, namely, that it is impossible to invite the party to make a serious purge of its ideas and ranks, that have become considerably encrusted during recent years, by adopting different slogans and pursuing different aims from those presented up to now by the Bolshevik-Leninists (Opposition). But it would then be necessary to change sharply the whole attitude towards the Opposition itself; otherwise the cynical lack of principles of the centrist apparatus would stand crudely in the open. The right wing believes, and not without good cause, that the center will not dare boldly to change its front. The right-wingers retreat, grinding their teeth, and they show thereby that they are not at all desirous of a struggle equally dangerous to themselves and to the center. At the same time they put their demands to the latter: not to change the status quo within the party, that is to say, not to break the bloc between the right and the center against the left; not to incline further to the left than is absolutely required by the present exigency; in other words, to keep in reserve the possibility of returning to the old path and to pass from there onto the road of the neo-NEP.

The right-wingers understand that for the moment they must concede the turn to the left as silently as possible. In any case, *for them* it is *simply a maneuver.* They keep quiet and make their preparations. They expect the left experiment to fail, thanks to the class response from the outside, thanks to internal friction, the secret resistance of the bureaucratic apparatus, and above all, thanks to the innate inclination of centrism to zigzags. The right wing is well acquainted with its allies. Meanwhile, it zealously compromises the center, demonstrating right and left that the latter has invented nothing but is simply repeating what the Opposition said from the very beginning.

So far as the center is concerned, in order not to appear in an awkward position, it continues to clap the Oppositionists into jail. The Rights understand that the more blows the apparatus deals to the left, the more it becomes dependent upon them. They aim to pass from the defensive to the offensive and to take their revenge when the left experiment will be terminated by a defeat (and the Rights, under the present conditions, firmly count on that). Will this happen? Such an eventuality is not at all excluded. It can take place so long as the turn rests upon the status quo in the party. Not only can this happen, *but* it will probably take place, even more, it is inevitable.

Does this imply that the present zigzag excludes the possibility of its developing into a left course? Let us be candid: not only the policy pursued by the leadership during the recent years but also its present conduct must impel us to give a skeptical reply to the above question, insofar as the matter depends upon the foresight and the consistency of the leadership. But the gist of the matter lies precisely in the fact that the initial maneuver has grown over into a profound political zigzag, seizing in its vise ever wider circles of the party and wider class strata. The latter are not interested in the mechanics of the maneuver, in the art of leadership practiced by the leadership for art's sake, but rather in the objective economic and political results arising from the turn. Matters in this sphere have reached a point where the good will, consistency, and, in general, the very intentions of the initiators of the turn find themselves seriously altered by the will and interests of much vaster circles. That is why it would be incorrect to deny the *possibility* of the present zigzag developing in a direction of a consistent proletarian course.

In any case, the Opposition, by virtue of its views and tendencies, must do all in its power to see that the present zigzag is extended into a serious turn onto the Leninist road. Such an outcome would be the healthiest one, that is to say, involving the least convulsions for the party and the dictatorship. This would be the *road of a profound party reform, the indispensable promise of the reform of the Soviet state.*

8. THE SOCIAL BASIS OF THE PRESENT CRISIS

The sounds of the struggle within the party are only an echo of far more profound turmoils. Changes have accumulated within the classes which, if they are not translated in time into the language of Bolshevism, will place the October Revolution in its entirety before a painful crisis.

The haste with which, hardly two months after the Fifteenth Congress, the leadership broke with a course which was considered correct at the time of the congress, is in itself an unfailing symptom of the fact that the process of class shifts taking place in the country, in connection with the whole international situation, has reached a critical stage wherein economic quantities are changing into political qualities. A prognosis in this sense was propounded on several occasions since 1923; it was expressed in the following manner in the theses of the Opposition at the time of the Fifteenth Congress:

"In a country with an overwhelming majority of small and even dwarfish peasants and petty proprietors in general, the most important processes take place up to a certain moment in an atomized and subterranean manner, only in order subsequently to burst into the open in an 'unexpected' manner."*

"Unexpected," obviously, only for those who are incapable of making a Marxist evaluation of processes taking place when these are still only at the beginning of their development.

The grain strike of the kulaks, who drew behind them the middle peasants; the collusion of the Shakhty specialists with capitalists; the protection or semiprotection of the kulak strike by an influential section of the state and party apparatus; the fact that communists were able to shut their eyes to the counterrevolutionary secret maneuvers of technicians and functionaries; the vile license of scoundrels in Smolensk[97] and elsewhere, under the cover of "iron discipline"—all these are already incontrovertible facts of the utmost importance. No communist reasoning in a healthy way would dare affirm that these are casual phenomena which are not characteristic, which have not grown thanks to economic and political processes and thanks to the policy of the party leadership in the course of the last five years. These facts could and should have been foreseen. The theses published by the Opposition at the Fifteenth Congress, which are available to all, state:

"The amalgamation between the kulak, the proprietor, and the bourgeois intellectual, on the one hand, and numerous links of the bureaucracy not only of the state but also of the party, on the other hand, constitutes the most incontrovertible but at the same time most alarming process of our social life. Thence are being born the germs of *dual power* which is

---

* "Platform of the Opposition," in *Challenge of the Left Opposition (1926–27)*, pp. 303–4.

threatening the dictatorship of the proletariat."

The manifesto or circular letter issued by the CC on June 3, 1928, admitted the existence of the "most vicious bureaucratism" in the state apparatus as well as in the party and the trade unions. The circular letter attempts to explain this bureaucratism as follows: (1) survivals from the bureaucratic heritage of the past; (2) product of the backwardness and obscurantism of the masses; (3) their "inadequate knowledge of administration"; (4) failure to draw the masses rapidly enough into the state administration. The above-cited four circumstances do in fact exist. They all serve to explain bureaucratism in some fashion. But none permits of understanding its wild and unrestrained *growth*. The cultural level of the masses should have risen during the past five years. The party apparatus should have learned how to draw the masses into administrative work with greater rapidity. A new generation, raised under Soviet conditions, should have been substituted in considerable proportion for the old functionaries. Bureaucratism should then have declined as a consequence. But the crux of the question lies precisely in the fact that it has grown monstrously; it has become "most vicious bureaucratism"; it has erected into a system such administrative methods as suppression by orders from above, intimidation, repression by economic measures, favoritism, collusion of functionaries through mutual agreement, concessions to the strong, oppression of the weak. The excessively rapid regeneration of these tendencies of the old class apparatus, despite the growth of Soviet economy and the cultural development of the masses, is due to *class* causes, namely, the social consolidation of proprietors, their interlacing with the state apparatus, and their pressure exercised upon the party through the apparatus. Unless one understands the class causes of the growing bureaucratization of the regime, the struggle against the evil resembles too often a windmill flapping its wings but not grinding any grain.

The retarded growth of industry has created an intolerable "scissors" in prices. The bureaucratic struggle to lower prices has only convulsed the market, depriving the worker without giving anything to the peasant. The enormous advantages obtained by the peasantry from the agrarian revolution accomplished by the October are being devoured by the prices of the industrial goods. This corrodes the *smychka,* impelling wide strata in the village to the side of the kulak with his slogan of free trade, internally and externally. Under these conditions the trader in the interior finds favorable soil and cover, while the bourgeoisie abroad acquires a base.

The proletariat naturally marched to the revolution with by far the greatest hopes, and in its overwhelming mass, with great illusions. Hence, given a retarded tempo of development, and an extremely low material level of existence, there must inevitably flow a diminution of the hopes in the ability of the Soviet power to alter profoundly the entire social system within the more or less immediate future.

The defeats of the world revolution, particularly during the last few years, when the leadership was already in the hands of the Comintern, have tended in the same direction. They could not fail to introduce a new note into the attitude of the working class toward the world revolution: great reservations in hopes; skepticism among the tired elements; downright suspicion and even surly exasperation among the immature.

These new thoughts and new evaluations sought for their expression. Had they found it in the party, the most advanced layers might perhaps have adopted a different attitude towards the international revolution, and above all towards that in their own country; it might have been less naive and exalted and more critical but, in return, more balanced and stable. However, the new thoughts, judgments, aspirations, and anxieties were driven inward. For five years the proletariat lived under the old and well-known slogan: "No thinking! Those at the top have more brains than you." At first this engendered indignation, then passivity, and finally a circumscribed existence, compelling men to withdraw into a political shell. From all sides the worker was told, until he ended by saying himself, "You, there! This is not the year 1918."

The classes and groups hostile or semihostile to the proletariat take into account the diminution in the latter's specific weight which is felt not only through the state apparatus or the trade unions but also through the day-to-day economic life, and the daily existence. Hence flows an influx of self-confidence that has manifested itself among the politically active layers of the petty bourgeoisie and the growing middle bourgeoisie. The latter has reestablished its friendship, and reconstituted its intimate and family bonds with the entire "apparatus," and it holds the firm opinion that its day is coming.

The worsening of the international position of the USSR, the growth of the hostile pressure on the part of world capitalism, under the leadership of the most experienced and rabid British bourgeoisie—all this enables the most intransigent elements of the internal bourgeoisie to raise their heads again.

These are the most important elements of the crisis of the October Revolution. It had its partial manifestation in the recent grain strike on the part of the kulaks and the bureaucrats. The crisis in the party is its most general and dangerous reflection.

It follows as a matter of course that it is impossible to forecast as yet, at any rate, from a distance, at what time and in what form these processes towards dual power, which are still semi-subterranean, will seek to assume an open political expression. This depends largely upon international conditions, and not only upon internal policy. One thing is clear: the revolutionary line does not consist in waiting and guessing until the ever-increasing enemy seizes a favorable moment to assume the offensive, but in assuming the offensive ourselves before the enemy, as the German saying goes, towers above the trees. There is no returning the lost years. It is a good thing that the CC has finally sounded the alarm about the ominous facts, which are in large measure due to its own policy. But it is not enough merely to sound the alarm, and to issue general appeals. Even prior to the Fifteenth Congress, at a time when the slogan of squeezing the kulak was still invested with a purely literary character by the leading faction, the Opposition wrote in its theses:

"The slogan of squeezing the kulak and the Nepman . . . if taken seriously, presupposes a change in the entire policy, a new orientation for all the state organs. It is necessary to say this precisely and clearly. For, neither the kulak, on the one hand, nor the poor peasant, on the other, has forgotten that in the course of two years (between the Fourteenth and Fifteenth Congresses) the CC held a totally different policy. It is entirely obvious that by keeping mum about their former position, the authors of the theses proceed from the idea that it is presumably sufficient to issue a new decree in order to effect a change in the policy. Yet, it is impossible to realize the new slogan, not in words but in action, without overcoming the bitter resistance of some classes and without mobilizing the forces of other classes."

These words retain their full force even at the present moment. It was no easy matter to turn the party from the Leninist road onto the right-centrist road. In order to create and consolidate within the Bolshevik Party an influential wing that did not "recognize" classes; in order that the party should not take official notice of the existence of this wing and in order for the leadership to be able to deny its existence for years; in order for this wing, which was not exposed by the Fifteenth Congress, to reveal itself officially *not through the party but through . . . the Grain Exchange*—all this took five years of incessant propaganda in favor of the new orientation, plus thousands of Stalinist and Bukharinist cribs on the integration of the kulak into socialism, and in mockery of the parasitic psychology of hungry men; plus pogroms of statistical bureaus simply because they took note of the existence of the kulak; plus the triumph of mindless functionaries all along the line; plus the formation of a new propagandist school of *Katheder-Sozialisten*,[98] sophists in Marxism, and many other things. But above all it took a vicious, unreflecting, rude, disloyal, and arbitrary persecution of the proletarian left wing. Meanwhile, all the Thermidorian elements in the party (who "emerged" according to the winged expression of *Pravda*) took form and consolidated themselves, invested themselves with connections, ties, and sympathies, and shot out their roots far beyond the confines of the party deeply into the soil of great classes. All this cannot be eliminated by means of a tiny circular letter, no matter how snappy its style. It is necessary to reeducate. It is necessary to revise. It is necessary to achieve regroupings. It is necessary to till the field overgrown with weeds with the deep plow of Marxism.

The attempt to lull oneself and the party with the notion the Opposition is weak and impotent cannot be reconciled with the rabid struggle against the latter. The Opposition has a program of action that has been tested in events and cadres that have been tempered in the fire of persecutions and did not waver in their loyalty to the party. Such cadres, expressing the mounting historical line, cannot be uprooted or destroyed. The Opposition is the cutting edge of the party sword. To break this edge is to dull the sword raised against the enemy. The question of the Opposition is the pivot point of the entire left course.

Only a victorious development of the world revolution will bring a real and complete liberation not only from external but also internal crisis. This is ABC for a Marxist. But an unbridgeable abyss yawns between this and the hopeless fatalism dished up to us by Bukharinist scholasticism. There are crises and crises. Capitalist society, by its very nature, cannot free itself from crises. This does not at all mean to say that the policy of a ruling bourgeoisie is of no importance. A correct policy raised up bourgeois states, a false policy either ruined or retarded them.

Official scholasticism is utterly incapable of understanding that between mechanistic determinism (fatalism) and subjective self-will there stands the materialist dialectic. Fatalism says: "In the face of such backwardness, nothing will ever come." Vulgar subjectivism says: "It's a cinch! We have willed it, and we build socialism!" Marxism says: "If you are conscious of your dependency upon world conditions and upon the internal backwardness then, with a correct policy, you will rise, entrench yourself, and integrate yourself into the victorious world revolution."

Crises are inevitable in a transitional Soviet regime, until the proletariat of advanced countries will have seized power firmly and decisively. But the task of the ruling policy lies in preventing crises within the Soviet regime from accumulating to the point when they become crises of the regime as a whole. The primary condition for this is: that the position and self-consciousness of the proletariat as the ruling class be preserved, developed, and strengthened. And the sole instrument for this is: a self-acting, flexible, and active proletarian party.

9. THE PARTY CRISIS

A correct economic policy, as well as a general policy, is not assured by merely a correct formulation, which has not obtained since 1923. The policy of the proletarian dictatorship is conceivable only on the basis of continually feeling out all the class strata in society. Moreover, this cannot be done through the medium of a bureaucratic apparatus which is tardy, inadequate on many points, inflexible, and insensitive. It must be effected through a living and active proletarian party, through communist scouts, pioneers, and builders of socialism. Before the growing role of the kulaks can be registered statistically, before theoreticians can generalize it, and politicians translate it into the language of directives, the party must be able to *sense* it through its countless tentacles, and sound the alarm. But for all this, the party in its entire mass must be sensitive and flexible, and above all it must not be afraid to look, to understand, and speak up.

The socialist character of our state industry—considerably atomized as it is: with the competition between the various trusts and factories; with the onerous material position of the working masses; with the inadequate cultural level of important circles of the toilers—the socialist character of industry is determined and secured in a decisive measure by the role of the party, the voluntary internal cohesion of the proletarian vanguard, the conscious discipline of the administrators, trade union functionaries, members of the shop nuclei, etc. If we allow that this web is weakening, disintegrating, and ripping, then it becomes absolutely self-evident that within a brief period nothing will remain of the socialist character of state industry, transport, etc. The trusts and individual factories will begin living an independent life. Not a trace will be left of the planned beginnings, so weak at the present time. The economic struggle of the workers will acquire a scope unrestricted save by the relation of forces. The state ownership of the means of production will be first transformed into a juridical fiction, and later on, even the latter will be swept away. Thus, here, too, the question reduces itself to the conscious cohesiveness of the proletarian vanguard, to the protection of the latter from the rust of bureaucratism and the pus of Ustryalovism.

A correct political line, as a system, is entirely inconceivable without correct methods for elaborating and applying it in the party. While on this or another question, under the influence of certain impulsions, the bureaucratic leadership might stumble upon the traces of a correct line, there are absolutely no guarantees that this line will be actually followed up, and will not be broken anew tomorrow.

Under the conditions of the dictatorship of the party, such a great power is concentrated in the hands of the leadership as was wielded by no single political organization in the history of mankind. Under these conditions, more than ever before, is it vitally necessary to maintain proletarian, communist methods of leadership. Each bureaucratic distortion, each false step has its immediate repercussion in the entire working class. Meanwhile, the post-Leninist leadership has gradually accustomed itself to extend the hostility of the proletarian dictatorship toward bourgeois pseudodemocracy over to the vital guarantees of the conscious proletarian democracy, upon which the party thrives, and by means of which it is alone possible to lead the working class and the workers state.

This was one of the cardinal cares in Lenin's mind during the last period of his life. He pondered over it in its full historic scope, and all its concrete day-to-day aspects. Returning to work after his first illness, Lenin was horrified by the growth of bureaucratism, especially within the party. This is why he proposed the Central Control Commission; naturally, not the one now existing which represents the direct opposite of what Lenin had in view. Lenin reminded the party that there were no few cases in history of conquerors degenerating, and adopting the morals of the vanquished. He burned with indignation at every piece of news about deliberate injustice, or brutal behavior on the part of a communist in the post of power toward his subordinates (the episode of Ordzhonikidze's fist-work).[99] He warned the party against Stalin's *rudeness* and against internal moral *brutality* which is the blood-sister of perfidy, and which becomes, when wielding all power, a terrible instrument for destroying the party. This is also the reason for Lenin's impassioned appeals for culture and cultural development—not in the sense of Bukharin's present cheap little schemes, but in the sense of a communist struggle against Asiatic morals, against the legacy of feudalism and boorishness, and against the exploitation by functionaries of the innocence and ignorance of the masses.

Meanwhile, during the last five years, the party apparatus has pursued just the opposite course; it has become utterly permeated with the bureaucratic deformations of the state apparatus, superimposing upon the latter the specific distortions—fraud, camouflage, duplicity—elaborated by the bourgeois parliamentary "democracy." As a consequence, a leadership has been formed which, instead of the conscious party democracy, provides: a falsification and an adaptation of Leninism designed to strengthen the party bureaucracy; a monstrous and an intolerable abuse of power in relation to communists and workers; a fraudulent operation of the entire electoral machinery of the party; an application of methods during discussion which might be the boast of a bourgeois-fascist power, but never of a proletarian party (picked gangs of thugs, whistling and jeering to order, throwing speakers from the platform, and similar abominations); and last but not least, an absence of comradely cohesiveness and conscientiousness all along the line in the relations between the apparatus and the party.

The party press has made public the Artemovsk, Smolensk, and other cases in the guise of sensational exposures. The CC has issued appeals to struggle against corruption. And this seems to have exhausted the question. As a matter of fact, it has not even been broached as yet.

In the first place, wide party circles could not but be aware that only a small part has been made public—not dealing with what is generally taking place, but only with what has been exposed. Almost every province has its own "Smolensk" affair of greater or lesser proportions, and, moreover, not for the first day, or even the first year. Long before the epoch of "self-criticism" the affairs in Chita, Khersonsk, Vladimirsk, and many other places flared up, only to be immediately extinguished; 100 percent secretaries of district committees were exposed who secretly and without any supervision wasted enormous sums on the upkeep of their family retinue. Each time such an affair was exposed, it was incontrovertibly established that the crimes were known quite well to hundreds of people, sometimes by a thousand men, a thousand party members who kept mum. Often they kept silent for a year, two, and even three. This circumstance was even mentioned in the papers. But no conclusions were drawn. For it would have been necessary simply to repeat what had been stated very discreetly and mildly in the documents of the Opposition. Without drawing the necessary conclusions, the Smolensk and other exposures remain sensations which arouse the party, do not teach it, but rather, distract its attention.

The crux of the matter lies in the fact that the more independent the apparatus becomes from the party, the more do the apparatus retainers depend upon one another. *Mutual insurance is no local "detail" but the basic trait of the bureaucratic regime.* Some apparatus retainers indulge in abominations, while the rest keep quiet. And what about the party mass? The party mass is terrorized. Yes, in the party of Lenin that achieved the October Revolution, worker-communists are *afraid* to say out loud that such and such a 100 percent apparatus retainer is a scoundrel, an embezzler, a bully. This is the fundamental lesson of the "Smolensk" exposures. And he is no revolutionist who does not blush with shame at this lesson.

Who is the hero, in the social sense of the term, of the Artemovsk, Smolensk, etc., affairs? He is a bureaucrat who has freed himself from the active control of the party and who has ceased to be the banner-bearer of the proletarian dictatorship. Ideologically, he has become drained; morally, he is unrestrained. He is a privileged and an irresponsible functionary, in most cases very uncultured, a drunkard, a wastrel, and a bully, in short, the old familiar type of *Derjimorda*[100] (see Lenin's letter on the national question kept hidden from the party). But our hero has his own "peculiarities": showering kicks and wallops, wasting national resources or taking bribes, the Soviet *Derjimorda* swears not by the "Will of God" but by the "construction of socialism." When any attempt is made from below to point him out, instead of the old cry "Mutiny!" he raises the howl, "Trotskyist!"—and emerges victorious.

An article of one of the leaders of the CCC printed in the May 16 issue of *Pravda* contains the following moral drawn from the Smolensk affair:

"*We must decisively change our attitude toward those members of the party and class-conscious workers who are aware of the abuses and keep quiet.*"

"Change our attitude?" Is it then possible to have *two* different attitudes on the matter? Yes. This is admitted by Yakovlev, a member of the Presidium of the CCC, the alternate of the People's Commissar of Workers and Peasants Inspection. People who know about crimes and keep quiet are considered criminals themselves. The only mitigating circumstance for their guilt lies in their own ignorance, or in their being terrorized. Yet Yakovlev refers not to ignorant people but to "members of the party and class-conscious workers." What sort of pressure and what sort of terror is it that compels worker-party members to keep silent ignominiously about the crimes of individuals whom they themselves presumably elect and who are presumably responsible to them? Can this really be the terror of the proletarian dictatorship? No, because it is directed against the party, against the interests of the proletariat. Does this mean to say then that this is the pressure and the terror of other classes? Obviously it is, for there is no supra-class social pressure. We have already defined the class character of the oppression that weighs down upon our party: the collusion of the retainers of the party apparatus; the amalgamation of many links in the party apparatus with the state bureaucracy, with the bourgeois intelligentsia, with the petty bourgeoisie, and the kulaks in the villages; the pressure of the world bourgeoisie upon the internal mechanics of forces—all this together creates the elements of social dual power, which exerts pressure on the party through the party apparatus. It is precisely this social pressure, which has grown during the recent years, and which has been utilized by the apparatus to terrorize the proletarian core of the party, to hound the Opposition, and to exterminate it physically by organizational methods. This process is one and indivisible.

Within certain limits, the alien class pressure raised the apparatus above the party, reinforced it, and instilled it with confidence. The apparatus did not bother to give itself an accounting of the mainsprings of its own "power." Its victories over the party, over the Leninist line, were smugly attributed by it to its own sagacity. But the pressure, increasing because it has encountered no resistance, has passed beyond the limit where it merely threatens the domination of the apparatus. It threatens something a great deal more important. The tail is beginning to deal blows to the head.

A situation such as makes party members and class-conscious workers in their overwhelming mass afraid to talk about the crimes of the retainers of the party apparatus has not arisen accidentally, nor overnight, nor can it be eliminated by a single stroke of the pen. We are confronted not only with the powerful routine of bureaucratism in the apparatus but also with great encrustations of interests and connections around the apparatus. And we have a *leadership that is powerless before its own apparatus.* Here we have also something in the nature of a historical law: the less the leadership depends upon the party, the more it is a captive of the apparatus. All talk to the effect that the Opposition is allegedly desirous of weakening the centralized leadership is absurd and fantastic. A proletarian line is inconceivable without iron centralism. But the misfortune lies precisely in the fact that the present leadership is all-powerful only by reason of its bureaucratic force, that is to say, it is powerful in relation to an artificially atomized party mass, but it is impotent in relation to its own apparatus.

Seeking to escape from the consequences of their own policy the centrists have pushed to the fore the homeopathy of "self-criticism." Stalin unexpectedly referred himself to Marx who had spoken of "self-criticism as a method of strengthening the proletarian revolution." But in this quotation Stalin approaches a boundary which he is forbidden to trespass. For Marx in reality meant by self-criticism above all a complete destruction by the proletariat of the false illusions from which it must liberate itself, such as the "bloc of four classes"; socialism in one country; the conservative trade union leaders; the slogans: "We must not frighten the bourgeoisie"; the "two-class" parties for the East; and other reactionary rubbish imposed by Stalin and Bukharin during the last period in which, for three years, they slashed away at the Chinese revolution with the scythe of Menshevism until they finally slaughtered it. That is where the scalpel of Marxian self-criticism should really be applied!

But it is precisely here that it is forbidden to apply it, as heretofore. Stalin threatens once again to fight self-criticism of this sort "with all our might and all the means at our disposal." He is unable to understand that there do not exist such forces or means as could prevent Marxian criticism from triumphing in the ranks of the international proletarian vanguard.

◆◆

During one of the plenums in the year 1927, in reply to an Opposition speech which stated that the Opposition had the right to appeal to the party against the leadership, Molotov said, "This is mutiny!" and Stalin made himself clear by saying, "These cadres can be removed only by a civil war." This was the most consummate and candid formulation made in the heat of the struggle of the "supraparty," "supraclass," and self-sufficing character of the ruling apparatus. This idea is directly opposite to the idea lodged in the foundations of our party and of the Soviet system. *The idea of bureaucratic supermen is the source of the present usurpation on a retail scale and of the unconscious preparation of a possible usurpation wholesale.* This ideology has taken shape during the last five years in the process of the interminable fake "reevaluations," tightening up from above, appointments from above, hounding from above, faking elections, brushing congresses and conventions aside for a year, two, or four . . . in short, a struggle "with all our might and all the means at our disposal."

At the summits this was a desperate struggle of views that came into an ever greater conflict with life itself; at the base, in the majority of cases this was a furious gamble for posts, for the right to command, for privileged positions. But the enemy is one and the same in either case: the Opposition. The arguments and the methods are the same: "with all our might and all the means at our disposal." Needless to say, the majority of the retainers of the party apparatus are honest and devoted men, capable of self-sacrifice. But the whole thing lies in the system. And the system is such as makes Smolensk affairs its inevitable fruits.

Well-meaning functionaries see the solution of the greatest historical task in the formula: "We must decisively change." The party must say in answer: "It is not you who must do the changing, but it is *yourselves* who must be decisively changed, and in the majority of cases—removed and replaced."

JULY 12, 1928

Appendix

Introduction to first edition of
'The Draft Program of the Communist International:
A Criticism of Fundamentals'
by James P. Cannon

THE COMMUNIST INTERNATIONAL, which was organized in 1919, first adopted its program at the Sixth World Congress held in July-August 1928, after having previously considered drafts at the Fourth Congress in 1922 and at the Fifth Congress in 1924. The document published here is a commentary by L.D. Trotsky on the draft program drawn up by Bukharin and Stalin before the Sixth Congress and which was subsequently adopted without any important changes. The criticism of Trotsky, written before the Sixth Congress and directed at the Bukharin-Stalin project, thus applies now to the formally adopted program of the Comintern on all essential questions, and his challenge to many of its formulations and conclusions acquires thereby all the greater seriousness.

The question of the program of the Communist International, and the criticism brought against it by one of the foremost leaders of the Russian revolution and the international communist movement, confronts the communist proletariat now as a theoretical and political question of the greatest magnitude with which all practical issues of strategy and tactics are connected.

Communist theories are not abstractions but the guiding line for action. False tactics in the struggle proceed from false programmatic formulations. This axiom of Marxism has been given a fresh and tragic proof, as Trotsky points out, in the enormous blunders committed in recent years since the death of Lenin. Programmatic questions are questions of life and death for the international proletarian revolution.

Trotsky's Criticism of the Draft Program comes to grips with the principal theoretical error which sums up and motivates the opportunist tactics pursued in recent years in the internal questions of the Soviet Union as well as in the international movement: the revisionist theory of socialism in one country. Basing himself on the fundamental teachings of Marx and Lenin, Trotsky turns all his guns on this new revisionism which has been smuggled into the Communist International since Lenin died, to its great detriment. He attacks it from all sides, tearing away the covering of falsely applied quotations from Lenin and reveals its non-Leninist essence, battering down the whole structure of falsification and scholasticism upon which it is built.

Trotsky not only annihilates the new revisionism with the hammer blows of Marxism and Leninism. He also exposes down to their roots the tactical errors connected with it and points the way for their avoidance in the future. His criticism is a searchlight in the fog of official propaganda, scholasticism, and administrative decree which has been substituted for the ideological leadership of the Executive Committee of the Communist International in earlier years. Trotsky restores the best traditions and standards of Marxist and Leninist thought. He applies them to the burning questions of the day and shows the path to which we must return.

With a sure command of the theoretical weapons forged by Marx and Lenin and with an international sweep and perspective equaled by none since Lenin, Trotsky grapples with the key problems of world magnitude. The diverse and knotty questions are tied together and shown as parts of a single whole with the interrelation of the parts explained—and always from the standpoint of revolutionary perspectives and the revolutionary solution of the world contradictions.

The criticism deals with the role of American imperialism and with the prospect of new revolutionary situations arising from its hegemony and growing aggression. The section on the Chinese revolution and its lessons elucidates the problems of the Chinese revolution and enables the American reader, for the first time, to glimpse the actualities of this world historical event. The theses, articles, and speeches of Trotsky and the other leaders of the Russian Opposition on the problems and tasks of the Chinese revolution, which estimated the whole course of events with the most remarkable precision, were suppressed and concealed from the parties of the entire International. This unbelievable and absolutely unprecedented procedure becomes all the more monstrous in the light of the subsequent developments which wholly confirmed the correctness of the position of Trotsky and his colleagues and revealed the Menshevist tactics of Stalin and Bukharin as the source of the cruel defeats of the Chinese proletariat. Trotsky's Criticism of the Program draws the lessons of the period of the Chinese revolution which culminated with the Canton uprising, lays bare the errors of the leadership with all their tragic consequences and the incalculable menace for the future contained in the attempt to conceal or justify these errors in the adopted program.

In the Chinese revolution in 1926–27 the Opposition led by Trotsky proposed the slogan of soviets uniting the workers and the peasants, under the leadership of the former against the bourgeoisie. They wanted to warn the workers and peasants not to trust the leaders of the Kuomintang or of the Left Kuomintang. They wanted the workers and the vanguard of the peasants to arm themselves. They wanted complete independence for the Communist Party and in general a course toward the establishment of a democratic dictatorship through the workers and peasants soviets.

The Stalin-Bukharin leadership rejected all these proposals of the Leninist Opposition in favor of the Menshevik policy of union with the liberal bourgeoisie which in actual practice gave the hegemony to the bourgeoisie, prevented the real development of the independent Communist Party and led to the defeat of the working class. The bourgeois "allies" of the proletariat became the hangmen of the revolution just as the Opposition foretold.

All these questions of the Chinese revolution will arise again in China, India, and other Eastern countries. Consequently the formulation of the questions in the program, from which the tactics of tomorrow are inseparable, becomes a matter of overshadowing importance for the whole of the Communist International.

Trotsky shows how the Bolshevik and Menshevik parties and the left wing of the German social democracy took shape on the estimation of the Russian revolution of 1905 and says the evaluations of the results and prospects of the Chinese revolution will have no less significance for the future. We believe this to be absolutely incontestable and that the communist battalions of the future in America as in other countries will be formed to a very large extent in this indispensable discussion. Trotsky's estimate of the Chinese revolution and its prospects, contained in his Criticism of the Program, is the greatest contribution yet made to this discussion and for that alone his document has a priceless value. In connection with this criticism, however, written after the events, it is necessary to study the other material of Trotsky and other Oppositionists written before the events. This material is now being translated and will soon be published as a companion volume to the Criticism of the Program. The conscientious study of these historic documents of the true defenders of Leninism, in comparison with the official material, shot through as it is with revisionist errors, falsifications, and contradictions, will go a long way toward the enlightenment of the American communists on the outstanding problems of the international communist movement.

The formation of "Farmer-Labor" parties—that source of such exaggerated hopes and unbounded mistakes in the American party—is reviewed at length in this volume. The underlying falsity of the whole idea of a "two-class" party is analyzed from the theoretical standpoint of Marxism and the history of the Russian revolutionary movement, and is condemned in principle—for the West as well as for the East. Trotsky's comment on the "third party alliance" with LaFollette, the fight against which was led by him will be especially interesting to American communists. All of which is a timely reminder of the heavy debt our party owes to Trotsky. His part in saving it from the disgrace and the direct threat to its existence contained in the proposal to support LaFollette is not the only exceptional service he has rendered to it. It was his initiative which brought the assistance of the Communist International in 1922 to the task of liberating the Communist Party of America from the straightjacket of illegality in which it had bound itself. And now it is he, above all others, who is showing the party, and the whole Comintern, the way back to Leninism on the great world problems of the present period.

The publication of this masterpiece of Bolshevik literature, written by the foremost living leader of world communism at the height of his powers, is a revolutionary event of great importance for the American movement. The profound influence it has already exerted on circles of our party who have read it in manuscript is an indication of the stimulus to revolutionary thought its publication will create in broader ranks. It is a document of conflict written in the fires of the struggle to preserve the fundamental teachings of Marx and Lenin and maintain the proletarian dictatorship of the Soviet Union.

The history of this work, which is destined to become a classic of Marxist-Leninist literature, shows up the present internal situation in the Communist Party of the Soviet Union and in the Communist International. Suppression, official say-so, and administrative command have been substituted for the free revolutionary thought and discussion of Lenin's time to such an extent that the present leadership attempted to dispose of this contribution of the co-worker of Lenin by the simple expedient of suppressing it.

Trotsky's Criticism of the Draft Program was sent to the Sixth Congress of the Communist International, but was never distributed to the delegates and was not discussed at the congress. The sole attention accorded it was its distribution to members of the Program Commission and a report on the document to the Senioren-Konvent, a selected group of congress delegates, which immediately "settled" the issue without discussion. A rigid control on the document was established forthwith and the few copies which had been distributed were recalled by the Secretariat. Its "illegal" publication now in America and its simultaneous publication in the various European countries are only another proof of the futility of bureaucratic machinations when they collide with a Leninist political line. These machinations and the false line they represent had a temporary success. They brought confusion and disruption into the ranks of the workers vanguard, and they have not yet finished their course. This regime still maintains a formal control but its foundation is cracking. Its days are numbered. Trotsky's truth is breaking through. The logic of events and the heroic, uncompromising struggle of the Opposition are hastening the day of the victory of Leninism and its exponents in the Communist Party of the Soviet Union and throughout the Comintern.

"The Draft Program of the Communist International: A Criticism of Fundamentals" by L.D. Trotsky is a great contribution to that struggle and victory.

James P. Cannon
NEW YORK
JANUARY 3, 1929

Explanatory notes

From the 1936 edition

Foreword to 1929 French edition*

1. Clara Zetkin (1857–1933) was a longtime veteran of the German labor movement, outstanding in her work as a founder, theoretician, and activist in the women's movement. She was associated with Rosa Luxemburg in the prewar German social democracy and afterwards helped found the Spartacus League. She served as a member of the Executive Committee of the Comintern. After Lenin's death she associated herself with the Stalinist machine.

2. Ernst Thälmann was a leader of the German Communist Party during Hitler's rise to power. He was imprisoned by the Nazis and perished in the Buchenwald concentration camp in 1944. In the period (1921) to which Trotsky is referring here, he headed the left wing of the German party. Later he swung over to the right, in support of Stalin. In the period of Nazism's rise, he unswervingly followed Stalin's disastrous ultraleft line.

Béla Kun, as a leader of the Hungarian Communist Party, headed the short-lived Hungarian soviet republic in 1919. The upsurge was defeated with the Romanian and Czech armies and French experts coming to the aid of the counterrevolutionaries. Béla Kun escaped to Moscow and was later prominent for a while in the Comintern. He was reportedly shot during the purges of the 1930s.

John Pepper was the pseudonym in the United States for József Pogány, a Hungarian Communist who played an undistinguished role in the 1919 Hungarian events. He came to the U.S. in 1922 in the company of a Comintern delegation and remained. He was put

---

* Notes 1–10 were added to the third (1970) Pathfinder edition.

on the American Communist Party's top committee until recalled to Moscow in 1924. He was an ultraleft at the Third Congress of the Comintern in 1921. Later swinging to the right, he became a supporter of Bukharin and was expelled.

3. See notes 42 and 51.

4. Marcel Cachin (1869–1958), as a leader of the French social democracy, supported World War I. He joined the Communist Party in 1920 and became an unswerving Stalinist. He was a longtime editor of *L'Humanité*.

5. In 1929 after Trotsky was exiled to Turkey, he tried, without success, to obtain a residence visa from any of the bourgeois-democratic European countries. The Communist parties of those countries campaigned against their governments' granting him a visa.

6. Events of the next few years caused Trotsky to change his mind about forming a Fourth International.

7. At a conference in Vienna in 1920 an attempt was made to constitute an organization of those center parties that had broken with the Second, or social democratic, International, but which opposed joining the Third, or Communist, International. Derisively labeled the "Two-and-a-Half International," it lasted only until 1923 when it fused back with the Second International.

Friedrich Adler, one of its initiators, was the son of Victor Adler, a founder and leader of the Austrian Social Democratic Party. In 1916 Friedrich Adler assassinated Count Stürgkh, the Austro-Hungarian premier. He received a death sentence that was later commuted to life imprisonment. He was released from prison as a result of the revolutionary developments in 1918.

8. Georg von Vollmar (1850–1922) was a leader of the Bavarian social democracy and a deputy for Munich. In 1879 in an article entitled "The Isolated Socialist State," he advanced and defended the idea of socialism in one country. He also anticipated Bernstein and was a pioneer of German reformism. He was a social patriot during World War I.

9. In the mid-1920s, the Stalinists considered Chiang Kai-shek a great revolutionary leader. Trotsky discusses Stalinist policy in China at length in this book.

10. Trotsky later dropped his characterization of Stalinism as centrist.

The Draft Program of the Communist International
A Criticism of Fundamentals

11. The first draft of a program for the Comintern was submitted to the Fourth Congress (November-December 1922) by Bukharin. Other drafts were submitted at the time by Thalheimer, for the German Communist Party, whose document was distinguished from Bukharin's mainly by its advocacy of Rosa Luxemburg's theory of the accumulation of capital; by Kabakchiev, for the Bulgarian Communist Party; and a critical program of action by the Italian Communist Party. The congress voted against the adoption of a program at its sessions, and for submitting all drafts and documents to a program commission for elaboration and study, with the provision that the Fifth Congress would reach a final decision on the question. At the Fifth Congress (June 1924), motions were adopted on the programmatic report of Bukharin providing for the adoption of the draft presented by the program commission as a basis for subsequent discussion in the parties; for a commission charged with the final editing of the document; for a permanent program commission to make public the draft and to direct the international discussion of it; for a final adoption of a program at the coming congress. At the Sixth Congress (July-September 1928), all the old drafts had completely disappeared and a new one, written principally by Bukharin and submitted in his name and in Stalin's, was presented, which, with minor modifications, was finally adopted by the congress as the program of the Comintern. It is this draft which is the object of Trotsky's critique.

12. August 4, 1914, is generally considered in revolutionary circles

to mark the date of the collapse of the Second International. On that date the social democratic fraction in the German Reichstag voted the war credits demanded by the kaiser and the chancellor, signifying by this action not only support of the capitalist fatherland in the war but also the establishment of *Burgfrieden* (civil peace). The same day witnessed the identical action of the socialist group in the French Chamber of Deputies, who established the *Union Sacrée* (holy union) with their ruling class. The Belgian, Austro-Hungarian, British, and in part, the Italian, Bulgarian, and Russian social democratic parties followed the same course. The International Socialist Bureau, unable, of course, to adjudicate the dispute which was being decided on the battlefields, ceased to exist, to all intents and purposes, during the war.

13. The view that the socialist revolution is "immeasurably closer in Europe than in America" was somewhat conditioned and modified by Trotsky a couple of years after this was written. In 1930, he said: "In my work on the Russian revolution of 1905, I remarked on the fact that Marx had written that capitalism passes from feudalism to the guild system to the factory. In Russia, however, we never knew the guild system, with the possible exception of the *kustari* [handicraftsman]. Or, one might compare the development of the working class in England and Germany with that in Russia. In the first two countries, the proletariat has gone through a long period of parliamentary experience. In Russia, on the other hand, there was very little of a parliamentary system for the workers. That is, the Russian proletariat learned its parliamentary history from an abridged handbook. In many respects, the history of the development of the United States is akin to that of the Russian working class. It is nowhere written, and theoretically it cannot be substantiated, that the American workers will perforce have to pass through the school of reformism for a long period of time. They live and develop in another period, their coming to maturity is taking place under different circumstances than that of the English working class, for instance. . . . It is not at all permanently established that the United States will be last in the order of revolutionary primacy, condemned to reach its proletarian revolution only after the countries of Europe and Asia. A situation, a combination of forces is possible in which the order is changed and the tempo of development in the United States enormously accelerated. But that means that it is

necessary to prepare." (The *Militant*, May 10, 1930.) [Available in *Writings of Leon Trotsky: Supplement (1929–33)*, New York: Pathfinder, 1979, pp. 28–29.]

14. Thus, as late as 1926, the publishing house of the Comintern issued an official pamphlet on the United States of Socialist Europe, which said: "It is very important that we not only have a critical position towards this bourgeois–social democratic slogan ('Pan-Europe'), by demolishing its fraudulent pacifist contents, but that at the same time we set up against it a positive slogan which can actually be the comprehensive political slogan for our transitional demands. For the next period the slogan of the United States of Socialist Europe must serve as the comprehensive political slogan for the *European* communist parties." (John Pepper, *Die Vereinigten Staaten des Sozialistischen Europa*, p. 67, Hamburg, 1926.) The slogan was, however, advanced by the Comintern Executive and the European parties with decreasing frequency and was finally dropped entirely when the exigencies of the factional struggle against the foremost proponent of the slogan—Trotsky—seemed to demand its withdrawal.

15. Revisionism is the tendency in the socialist movement which received its principal initial impulsion in Germany towards the end of the last century. In 1897, Eduard Bernstein, a prominent leader of the German Social Democratic Party and intimate friend of Friedrich Engels until the latter's death, wrote a series of articles for the theoretical organ of the party, *Neue Zeit*, which undertook an *Überprüfung* (revision, thence revisionists and revisionism) of the Marxian doctrines. Counterattacks on Bernstein's position were soon made by such noted Marxists as Plekhanov, Parvus, Kautsky, and Luxemburg, who defended the position of revolutionary socialism. His articles being subsequently rejected by Kautsky, editor of the *Neue Zeit*, Bernstein presented his views in 1899 in systematic form in a book entitled *Die Voraussetzungen des Sozialismus und die Aufgaben der Sozialdemokratie* (Eng. ed., *Evolutionary Socialism*). Bernstein contested the validity of the Marxian "theory of the collapse" of capitalism, the centralization and concentration of capital, the diminishing role of the middle class, the intensification of poverty among the proletariat. For the policy of class struggle he proposed the substitution of class collaboration with the

"progressive" bourgeoisie, and as against the dictatorship of the proletariat he envisaged a peaceful transition to socialism by means of a progressive permeation of democratized capitalism. He rejected dialectical materialism and inclined strongly to a neo-Kantian idealism.

The German party convention at Hanover in October 1899, following a special report by August Bebel who assailed Bernstein's views (the latter, in England because of the old Bismarckian antisocialist laws, had his position stated by David), decided by an overwhelming majority to reject Bernstein's position, stating that "the development up to now of bourgeois society gives the party no cause to give up or to alter its fundamental views on the same," there being "no reason why the party should change either its principles and basic demands, its tactics, or its name, that is, to become a democratic socialist reform party instead of a social democratic party." The Lübeck convention, September 1901, also condemned Bernstein's revisionism by adopting the resolution presented by Bebel and Kautsky, but in so mild a form that the perturbations of the militant and intransigent left wing, led by Luxemburg and Parvus, were fully justified.

Even though the Second International itself, at its 1904 congress in Amsterdam, also condemned Bernsteinism, it became increasingly apparent with the passage of each year that the theories, and to an even greater extent the practices, of revisionism were becoming in fact the theories and practices of most of the important socialist parties throughout the world. This evolution was crowned by the collapse of the Second International at the moment the World War broke out. Revisionism is now the official doctrine of the Second International, having been subscribed to even by one of its original opponents, Kautsky, who made formal amends to its main proponent a short time before the latter's death.

16. The three principal slogans of the Bolsheviks, especially during the period between the first two revolutions, were the democratic republic, the eight-hour working day, and the confiscation of the land for the benefit of the peasants. The three slogans were popularly referred to as the "three pillars of Bolshevism," and sometimes as the "three whales of Bolshevism," after the ancient myth according to which the world rested upon three whales. The Bolsheviks conceived these slogans as realizable only by means of the over-

throw of czarism. The struggle over these slogans revolved to a large extent around the dispute with the so-called "liquidators" who opposed these slogans and advocated in their stead the demands for the right to organize, the right of free speech and press, etc., which were presumably to be realized even within the framework of czarism.

17. The Opposition (or Left Opposition, Moscow Opposition, Opposition of 1923, Bolshevik-Leninists, "Trotskyists") originated in Moscow in 1923 around the questions of workers democracy in the Russian Communist Party and of the decisive role of state-planned industrialization in the social life of the Soviet republic. After a long, muted struggle in the Political Bureau of the party during which Trotsky vigorously advocated the establishment of workers democracy and a struggle against bureaucratism, he finally summarized his standpoint, as against that of the ruling trinity (Stalin, Zinoviev, Bukharin) in a letter to the Central Committee and Central Control Commission on October 8, 1923. Following a vigorous denunciation of his views by the Political Bureau, which marked the opening of the public fight against "Trotskyism," a collective letter of solidarity with Trotsky and his views was received by the Central Committee on October 15, 1923. It was signed by forty-six prominent communists, including Pyatakov, Preobrazhensky, Serebryakov, I. Smirnov, Antonov-Ovseenko, Ossinsky, Bubnov, Sapronov, V. Smirnov, Boguslavsky, Stukhov, Yakovleva, V. Kossior, Rafail, Maksimovsky, Beloborodov, Alsky, Muralov, Rosengolts, Sosnovsky, Voronsky, E. Bosh, Drobnis, Eltsin, etc. Rakovsky and Krestinsky did not sign the letter only because they were on diplomatic missions abroad. Radek sent a separate letter urging reconciliation with Trotsky inside the Political Bureau.

It is this group of prominent old Bolsheviks that formed the base and heart of the Moscow Opposition of 1923. In 1926, it was joined by the so-called Leningrad Opposition, led by Zinoviev, Kamenev, Sokolnikov, Krupskaya, Salutsky, and others, which had arisen in 1925 as a result of the alarm felt by the Leningrad workers over the policy of Stalin and Bukharin towards the kulak and the theory of "socialism in one country." The resultant fusion created the Opposition Bloc of Bolshevik-Leninists. The bloc, which summarized its views in the famous *Platform* presented to the Fifteenth Party Congress in 1927, was outlawed by that congress. Most of the Leningrad leaders, headed by Zinoviev and Kamenev, capitulated to Stalin and were eventually readmitted into the party; thousands of recalcitrants were expelled, imprisoned, and exiled. The general views developed by the Opposition in the first five years of its existence are dealt with in the present volume. For details about the origin of the group, see *Since Lenin Died* by Max Eastman and *Ten Years* by Max Shachtman. [The latter title can be found in *Towards a History of the Fourth International*, Part 5 (New York: Pathfinder, 1974). See also the three-volume Pathfinder series *The Challenge of the Left Opposition* by Leon Trotsky.]

18. The New Economic Policy was adopted, on Lenin's initiative, by the Tenth Congress of the Russian Communist Party, early in 1921, and reinforced at the tenth party conference in May of the same year. Not only had the postwar revolutionary wave in Europe subsided, especially after the failure of the Red drive on Warsaw, but relations with the peasantry in Russia had become strained to the breaking point. The extremely rigorous regulations of so-called war communism (requisitioning and confiscation of grain from the peasant), accompanied by the breakdown of industry consequent upon the ravages of the civil war (in 1920, industrial output was only 18 percent of the prewar level; in heavy industry, specifically, the situation was far worse), had brought the alliance of the workers and peasants to extreme tension. The Tenth Congress met during the Kronstadt rebellion, which reflected the intense discontent of the peasants. Lenin proposed a policy of substituting a tax in kind for requisitions; of allowing the peasant to dispose of his surplus within the limits of "local trade"; of allowing the development of capitalist concessions to a delimited extent, and of state capitalism, on the ground that state capitalism was a higher economic form than that which prevailed in most of agricultural Russia.

The retreat sounded by Lenin was to allow a breathing spell during which, while waiting for the decisive aid of the European revolution, Russia could reconstruct her industries, electrify and modernize them, and establish a more harmonious relationship with the mass of her population, the peasantry. Capitalism, in industry and agriculture, was to be allowed a considerable field of possibilities in which to develop, provided, however, that the workers state retained control of the socalled "commanding heights," namely, the nationalized key industries, state banking, nationalization of the land, monopoly of foreign trade. The New Economic Policy (NEP), despite the inherent dangers of capitalist restoration, greatly facilitated not only the reestablishment of good relations between worker and peasant, but also the reconstruction of Russia's industrial life.

19. It is to be found in the *Jahrbuch für Sozialwissenschaft und Sozialpolitik,* published by Dr. Ludwig Richter, Zurich, 1879, pp. 54–75, and is entitled "Der Isolirte Sozialistische Staat" von G. V[ollmar]. In setting forth his view, Vollmar, prominent spokesman for the right wing of the German social democracy in his time, wrote: "I believe—and shall seek to demonstrate it in the following pages—that the final victory of socialism is not only historically more likely primarily in a single state, but that nothing stands in the road of the existence and prosperity of the isolated socialist state."

20. The State Planning Commission ("Gosplan") is a national body charged with assembling, coordinating, and elaborating the annual and five-year plans for the industrialization of the Soviet Union. It is primarily a technical commission, composed of communists and noncommunists, whose general outline of work is marked out by the Political Bureau of the Communist Party, which also exercises veto power over its conclusions.

21. *Smychka,* the Russian word for alliance or union, is popularly employed in Russian political terminology with reference to the alliance between the working class and the bulk of the peasantry. Lenin and the Bolsheviks laid great stress on the need of preserving this alliance, at least so long as socialism was not yet established and, consequently, classes—the peasantry included—abolished. The *smychka* was therefore considered one of the principal pillars of the dictatorship of the proletariat in Russia.

22. In Lenin's time, congresses of the Third International took place on the average of once a year, despite the extremely difficult domestic and foreign position of the Soviet Republic. The First Congress was held in March 1919; the Second Congress in July 1920; the Third Congress in June 1921; the Fourth Congress in November 1922. With Lenin removed from participation in the leadership, the interval between

congresses steadily increased. Thus, the Fifth Congress was held in June 1924. But four years elapsed before the Sixth Congress was held, in July 1928. Section 8 of article 2 of the constitution of the Comintern adopted at the 1928 congress definitely provided that "The world congress shall be convened once every two years" (Eng. ed., N.Y., 1929, p. 87). Despite this provision, the Seventh Congress did not convene in Moscow until August 1935, that is, more than seven years after the Sixth. No official explanation was ever vouchsafed for this explicit violation by the leadership of the Comintern of the constitution which it had itself adopted in 1928.

23. In his concluding remarks on the report "The Opposition Bloc and the Inner-Party Situation," Stalin, at the Fifteenth Conference of the CPSU in November 1926, made reference to Friedrich Engels's first draft of the *Communist Manifesto* which was subsequently published under the title *Grundsätze des Kommunismus* [Principles of Communism]. Engels listed the points in the program of the communist party of his time, the execution of which would usher in the new order, and he emphasized that these points could not be realized in full except under conditions of a proletarian revolution and victory in several countries. Listing these points, Stalin sought to buttress his theory of "socialism in a single country" by arguing that Soviet Russia alone had carried out virtually all of them. "That, comrades, is the program of the proletarian revolution set up by Engels in his *The Fundamental Principles of Communism*. You see that nine-tenths of this program has already been carried out by our revolution. . . . Engels said that the proletarian revolution with the above program *could not* succeed in one single country alone. The facts, however, show that under the new conditions of imperialism, such a revolution in its most essential parts *has already been carried through* in one single country alone, for we have carried out nine-tenths of this program in our country." (*International Press Correspondence,* vol. 6, no. 78, November 25, 1926, p. 1,350.)

24. The International Workingmen's Association, or First International, was formed in St. Martin's Hall, London, on September 28, 1864, by representatives of British trade unions, French labor organizations, Italian Mazzinists, and individual Poles and Germans. Karl Marx, in attendance, became a member of its first General

Council and drafted its first public address. It was not only supported by Marx and Engels, despite its heterogeneous composition, but by dint of their perseverance and by virtue of their overwhelming intellectual superiority, they soon became its leaders and spokesmen. The defeat of the Paris Commune in 1871, however, presaged the collapse of the First International, which was hastened by the increasingly violent conflict between the followers of Marx and the supporters of the Russian anarchist, Mikhail Bakunin. The Hague conference of the International in 1872 was marked by the victory of the Marxists over the Bakuninists and the vote to transfer the seat of the International to the United States, where the last conference was held in Philadelphia on July 15, 1876. The Bakuninists continued to consider themselves the International for a time longer, held several ineffectual congresses, and then also dissolved.

25. In contrast to the unmistakably revolutionary trend of the First International and its centralized character, the Second International was a loose association of national socialist parties of all varieties. Its date of formation is generally accepted as 1889, when the French and German Marxian groups, together with several others, gathered at a congress in Paris. The International Socialist Bureau, the only central organ of the Second International, was established only in 1900 with headquarters in Brussels. The revolutionary high-water mark of the Second International was the Amsterdam congress in 1904, at which the revisionism of Bernstein and the ministerialism of Millerand-Jaurès were, in effect, condemned. Despite the formal condemnations, and the acknowledgments made to revolutionary Marxism, the practice and theory of reformism was gradually gaining the upper hand in the Second International, coming to its triumphant climax when the World War broke out and the International collapsed into its national constituent parts, most of which came to the support of the imperialist war. After the war, and following the formation of the Third International, efforts were made to revive the Second. This was finally attained at Hamburg in 1923, when the International of the extreme reformist parties fused with the so-called "Vienna International," led by the Austrian social democracy, which had remained outside and to the left of the principal European socialist parties. The Hamburg fusion was effected

entirely on the basis of the classic reformist positions.

26. The Communist, or Third, International was constituted by the congress held in Moscow in March 1919 in reply to a call issued by the Russian, Polish, Lettish, Ukrainian, and similar communist parties. Objections to the immediate constitution of the International were made, under instructions from his party, by the delegate of the German Communists (Spartacus League), on the ground of inadequate representation in Moscow and prematureness. Nevertheless, the International was founded as the "general staff of the world revolution" and the "heir of the First International," accepting as its principles those popularized by the Russian Bolsheviks since their victory. Representation at this congress was indeed insignificant, apart from the Russian and German parties. By the time of the Third Congress in 1921, however, the new International had gained the affiliation of the majorities of the French Socialist Party, the Independent Social Democratic Party of Germany, the Czech social democracy, the Norwegian Labor Party, the British Socialist Party, the American Socialist Party, and substantial minorities in such socialist parties as the Italian, Spanish, and others.

27. Anarchism is the doctrine, popularized by Mikhail Bakunin and Peter Kropotkin, of social organization based upon free, autonomous, loosely associated communes of equal producers. Whatever the differences in anarchist ranks, their general difference from Marxism is their opposition to any parliamentary activities, to any political parties, to any centralized, or "authoritarian" political and governmental bodies, even during the revolution itself when the insurrectionists are faced with the need of coordinated resistance to counterrevolution. *Revolutionary syndicalism*, a manifestation of anarchism in the trade union field (particularly in France and Spain, and partly in the United States in the form of the IWW), also opposes parliamentary action and all political parties and stresses the "complete independence" of the trade unions (in French, *syndicats*) and the conception that they are all that is necessary and sufficient for the working-class struggle for emancipation from capitalism, which is to be replaced by a non-profit-making social order managed by the trade or industrial unions. *Constructive socialism* embraces the conceptions developed by the extreme right wing of the Second International (MacDonald, Vandervelde, Wels) on the gradual, nonviolent integration of capitalism into a socialist order, by eschewing

the class struggle and "permeating" the capitalist state apparatus. *Guild socialism* is a conception developed mainly in England (by Hobson, Cole, etc.) under which "ownership of the means of production is to rest with the community, but the trade unions are to be definitely recognized by the state as the normal controllers of industry," that is, a "democratized state" is to own the means of production in the name of the "consumers," with the cooperation of the national parliament of "guilds" of all crafts, trades, and professions, which are to perform managerial functions.

28. The Estonian insurrection was a putsch, i.e., a conspiratorial adventure behind the backs of the masses, in the fullest sense of the term. Early in the morning of December 1, 1924, a total of 227 armed communists gathered at specified points in the capital, Reval, for an assault upon the officers' school, the armories, airdrome, railroad station, government buildings, etc. Action was begun at 5:15 A.M. and by 9 A.M. of the same morning, the putsch was completely crushed by government forces. "What played the decisive role in the outcome of the insurrection was the fact that small groups of revolutionary workers, militarily organized, having launched the insurrection, remained isolated from the bulk of the proletariat. . . . The working class of Reval, in its mass, remained a disinterested spectator in the struggle." (A. Neuberg, *L'Insurrection armée,* Paris, 1931, p. 77.)

In Bulgaria, the Communist Party had remained completely "neutral" in September 1923, when the extreme reaction of Zankov overthrew the "radical" government of the peasant leader, Stambulisky. After having entirely missed an opportunity to intervene actively in the struggle, the Communist Party ranks came under the influence of adventuristic moods which, in their more desperate manifestations, took the form of acts of individual terror. The assassination of notorious reactionaries and, finally, the blowing up of the Sofia cathedral in April 1925, were some of the signs of the reaction of revolutionists who, infuriated at the passivity and opportunism of the Bulgarian communist leaders in the crucial period of 1923, misguidedly sought a rectification by means of individual action.

As to the Canton uprising of December 1927, see note 64.

29. In his report in November 1926 to the Fifteenth Conference of the Communist Party of the Soviet Union, Stalin said: "How was

this question [of the possibility of socialism in a single country] regarded by earlier Marxists, in the forties of the last century for instance, and in the fifties and sixties? At that time the monopolist development of capitalism had not yet come about, the law of the unequal development of capitalism had not yet been discovered and could not have been discovered, so that the question of the victory of socialism in one country was not so important as it is now. All Marxists, from Marx and Engels onwards, were at that time of the opinion that it was impossible for socialism to be victorious in one single country; they considered it necessary for the revolution to take place simultaneously in a number of countries, at least in a number of the most advanced and civilized countries. And at that time this was right." (*International Press Correspondence,* vol. 6, no. 77, November 20, 1926, p. 1,320.)

30. Early in 1918, Bukharin and his group opposed the signing of the Brest-Litovsk peace with the German imperialists on grounds of principle, and preached instead the revolutionary war to the bitter end. The Left Communists, who included also Radek, Krestinsky, Ossinsky, Sapronov, Yakovlev, M.N. Pokrovsky, Pyatakov, Preobrazhensky, V. Smirnov, Bubnov, Yaroslavsky, and others, published a periodical of their own (the Moscow *Kommunist*) in which Lenin and his supporters were violently condemned as having betrayed the revolution to the Germans and the kulaks. Bukharin not only wrote that the Soviet government (following Brest-Litovsk) was only a formality, but it appears that plans were then afoot for the Left Social Revolutionists, who also opposed signing the treaty, and the Left Communists to put Lenin in jail, constitute a new Council of People's Commissars, and prosecute a revolutionary war against the Germans. A letter published in *Pravda,* December 21, 1923, by nine former Left Communist leaders supports this report by narrating the approaches made to Radek and Pyatakov by the SRs, Kamkov and Proshyan, in 1918, for the purpose of eliminating Lenin and establishing a more "left" government. Though the dispute was extremely sharp, as this incident indicates, the Brest-Litovsk opposition was dissolved within a year.

31. The call of the German Communist Party in March 1921 for an armed insurrection to seize power, in connection with the struggle in central Germany, was a direct manifestation of the so called theory of

the offensive, whose principal inspirers and theorizers in the Comintern were Bukharin and to a somewhat lesser extent Zinoviev. The party leadership not only plunged its membership into what was obviously doomed in advance as a futile military action by a small minority of the working class, but after the collapse of the March action, it declared that it would repeat the action at the first opportunity. These actions, it was stated by the ultraleftists, would electrify the working class and cause them, each time, to mobilize into an ever greater force which would eventually overthrow capitalist rule. "If it is asked what was actually new about the March action, it must be answered: precisely that which our opponents reprove, namely, that the party went into the struggle without concerning itself about who would follow it." (A. Maslow, *Die Internationale,* Berlin, 1921, p. 254.) "The March action as an isolated action of the party would be—our opponents are right to this extent—a crime against the proletariat. The March offensive as the introduction to a series of constantly rising actions, a redeeming act." (A. Thalheimer, *Taktik und Organisation der revolutionäre Offensive,* Berlin 1921, p. 6.) "The slogan of the party can, therefore, be nothing but: offensive, offensive at any cost, with all means, in every situation that offers serious possibilities of success." (Heyder, *Ibid.,* p. 22.)

The Third Congress of the Comintern, confronted with this problem, was almost on the verge of a split. The Bukharin wing was supported by the majority of the delegates and leaders, including Pepper [Pogány] and Rákosi, who had directed the March action, Béla Kun, Münzenberg, Thalheimer, Frölich, most of the Italians, etc. Lenin, who placed himself demonstratively in the "right wing of the congress," threatened it with a split if the supporters of Bukharin and the "offensive" carried the day. Supported by Trotsky, and through the medium of Radek, who played the role of a conciliator, Zinoviev and Bukharin were outvoted in the Russian delegation, with the final result that Lenin's views carried the day. The theses of the Third Congress and the slogan "To the masses!" which introduced the broad policy of the united front adopted shortly afterward, was a definite blow at the leftists and put an effective end for a long period of time to putschistic moods in the International.

32. The Finnish revolution, begun in the middle of January 1918, was finally suppressed in April of the same year. The revolutionists were

concentrated in the south (Helsingfors, Vyborg); the counterrevolutionists in the north. The latter triumphed with aid of German, Swedish, and Russian White forces, the first-named, 20,000 men under the command of General Mannerheim, being particularly notorious for the extensive White Terror that was subsequently inaugurated. The socialist leaders of the revolution preached pacifism and legality to the workers and failed to take any of those measures which insured the success of the Bolshevik revolution in neighboring Russia. Kuusinen, one of the Finnish leaders, managed to escape to Russia from the terror. He eventually became one of the principal functionaries of the Comintern. Upon his arrival in Russia, he wrote an "essay in self-criticism" upon Lenin's suggestion, in which he vigorously excoriated the conduct of himself and his fellow-leaders. "We, who falsely called ourselves 'Marxists,' did not want a revolutionary action and without us the 'revolutionists' of the Central Federation of the trade unions would not act.... In fact we were 'social democrats' but not 'Marxists.' As such, we adopted the point of view of a pacific and progressive class struggle, in no way revolutionary.... We did not believe in the revolution, we put no hope in it and we did not aspire towards it. In this respect we were typical social democrats." (O.V. Kuusinen, *La Révolution en Finlande, Essai d'autocritique sur les luttes de 1918,* Petrograd, 1920, pp 12f.)

33. After Louis Auguste Blanqui, the French revolutionists of the nineteenth century, who stood at the extreme left wing of the turbulent Parisian movement of his time. In contrast to Marxism, Blanquism favored an insurrectionary movement organized conspiratorially and conducted by a small, active minority which, without basing itself upon a broad working-class movement, would seize power by a single, sudden stroke, and, after establishing a proletarian party dictatorship, would inaugurate the new social order by means of communist measures decreed by the revolutionary government. Lenin, accused in 1917 of Blanquism, even by many of his own party friends, dealt in his writings at great length with the distinctions between Blanquism and the Marxian conception of "insurrection as an art" based upon the preparation, guidance, and active participation of a broad mass movement.

34. A reference to the letter of Stalin to Zinoviev and Bukharin,

who were the leading Russian representatives at that time (1923) in the Executive Committee of the Comintern. The letter was read into the official records of the party at the plenum of the Central Committee and Central Control Commission in 1927 by Zinoviev. Stalin wrote: "Should the Communists (at the given stage) strive to seize power without the social democrats, are they mature enough for that? That, in my opinion, is the question. When we seized power, we had in Russia such reserves as (a) peace, (b) the land to the peasants, (c) the support of the great majority of the working class, (d) the sympathy of the peasantry. The German Communists at this moment have nothing of the sort. Of course, they have the Soviet nation as their neighbor, which we did not have, but what can we offer them at the present moment? If today in Germany the power, so to speak, falls, and the Communists seize hold of it, they will fall with a crash. That in the 'best' case. And at the worst, they will be smashed to pieces and thrown back. The whole thing is not that Brandler wants to 'educate the masses,' but that the bourgeoisie plus the right social democrats will surely transform the lessons—the demonstration—into a general battle (at this moment all the chances are on their side) and exterminate them. Of course, the fascists are not asleep, but it is to our interest that they attack first: that will rally the whole working class around the Communists (Germany is not Bulgaria). Besides, according to all information, the fascists are weak in Germany. *In my opinion, the Germans must be curbed and not spurred on."* (*Arbeiterpolitik,* Leipzig, February 9, 1929.)

35. On October 12, 1923, three German communists, Heckert, Brandler, and Böttcher, entered as a minority into a coalition Landtag government in the province of Saxony together with the left socialists, headed by Minister Zeigner. Participation in such a government, the first of its kind in the history of the Comintern, was categorically advocated in a telegram to the Germans from the Executive Committee in Moscow. Presumably, entry was to be made for the purpose of facilitating the arming of the workers in preparation for the uprising throughout Germany. The arming of the workers was not even begun, due to the stiff opposition of Zeigner and the acquiescence of the communist ministers; nor was the uprising carried through, except, as the result of an accident, in Hamburg. The coalition government lasted nine days, after which it was swept away by the intervention of armed

forces sent by the central government which had mobilized them ostensibly for the purpose of dealing with the fascists in Bavaria, but actually for the purpose of nipping in the bud any insurrectionary movement of the workers incipient in Saxony and Thuringia. At the Fifth Congress of the Comintern, devoted largely to the German capitulation, the principal condemnation of the Brandler leadership revolved not around its general conceptions, hesitancy, lack of orientation and preparation for the insurrection, but around opportunistic speeches of communist ministers in the Saxon Landtag, failure to press for the arming of the workers, failure to convene the congress of the factory councils, etc.

36. Early in June 1923, the government of the peasant leader, Stambulisky, was overthrown in an armed struggle against it conducted by the extreme reactionaries. The Bulgarian Communist Party, in its declaration of June 16, stated: "Hundreds and thousands of workers and peasants are being arrested and, on the basis of the exceptional laws against banditry, are being turned over to the courts on the pretext that they offered resistance to the coup d'état. We declare that in the unclear situation which arose at the moment of the civil war between the two bourgeois cliques, a part of the workers defended their lives and families, but did not participate in the struggle for power." The CP of Bulgaria, traditionally rigid and stiff in its conceptions, after having ignored the significance of the peasantry and of the Macedonian question, adopted a position of complete neutrality in the struggle and did not participate in it, independently or otherwise. This did not prevent the triumphant reaction from inaugurating an almost unprecedented White Terror against the communists.

In his report on the Bulgarian events to the session of the enlarged Executive Committee of the Comintern, Radek presented his report against which Kolarov subsequently polemicized so vigorously: "We are of the opinion that the coup d'état in Bulgaria represents a decisive defeat of our party. We like to hope that it will not be an annihilating defeat. But it is certainly the greatest defeat that a communist party has ever experienced. . . . The Bulgarian party does not endeavor to understand its defeat, but on the contrary to adorn it. We have before us the appeals of the Bulgarian party. They are the sorriest feature of the whole defeat. We have the appeal of February 9, the appeal of the 15th and a whole series of articles. The party defended this standpoint in them: two cliques of the bourgeoisie are fighting; we, the working class, stand aside, and we hope and demand that we will be vouchsafed freedom of the press and all sorts of good things. . . . (Karl Radek, "Der Umsturz in Bulgarien," *Die Kommunistische Internationale,* vol. 4, no. 27, Petrograd, 1923, pp. 115, 118.)

37. ". . . We start from the hypothesis that the present international and internal situation of British capitalism will not only not improve, but on the contrary will continue to get worse. If this prognostication were to prove incorrect, if the British bourgeoisie were to succeed in strengthening the empire, in recovering for itself its former position on the world market, in uplifting industry, in giving work to the unemployed, in raising the workers' wages, then the political development would take on an intelligible turn: the aristocratic conservatism of the trade unions would again be strengthened, the Labour Party would fall into a decline, within it its right wing would be strengthened, under which circumstances the latter would draw closer to liberalism, which in turn would experience a certain influx of vital forces. But there is not the least foundation for such a prognostication. On the contrary, whatever may happen to be the particular variation of the economic and political position, everything points to the further intensification and deepening of those difficulties through which Britain is at present passing, and therefore to a further quickening of the tempo of her revolutionary development." (Leon Trotsky, *Where Is Britain Going?*) [Available in *Leon Trotsky on Britain,* New York: Pathfinder, 1973, p. 143.]

38. At the July 1926 plenum of the Central Committee of the Communist Party of the Soviet Union, Zinoviev made the following declaration: "We state that there is no doubt that the main center of the Opposition of 1923, as is proved by the line taken by the leading fraction, gave a justified warning of the danger of deviating from the proletarian line, and of the growing regime of the apparatus." (*International Press Correspondence,* vol. 6, no. 77, November 20, 1926, p. 1,318.)

39. The *Mitteilungsblatt (Linke Opposition der KPD)* was launched at the beginning of 1927 by the former leaders of the Central Commit-

tee of the Communist Party of Germany, who had just been expelled: Ruth Fischer, A. Maslow, W. Scholem, Hugo Urbahns, etc. After a few issues, it became transformed into the *Fahne des Kommunismus*, published as a weekly theoretical supplement to the *Volkswille* of Suhl (later of Berlin). It continued to appear almost uninterruptedly as the organ of the allies of the Russian Opposition organized into the Leninbund, under the leadership of Hugo Urbahns, until Hitler's advent to power.

40. On June 17, 1924, the "Federated Farmer-Labor Party" formed by the Workers (Communist) Party of the United States met in St. Paul for the purpose of nominating presidential candidates. The noncommunist elements present represented whatever mass organizations there were in the FFLP, but they were entirely under the influence of Senator La Follette. The communists nominated two non–Communist Party members, Duncan MacDonald for president and William Bouck for vice president, in the hope of retaining their agrarian–La Folletteist companions within the framework of the communist-controlled party. In the same spirit, the communists also wrote a mild, semi–La Folletteist platform. But within a few weeks it became clear that all the important non-communist contingents in the FFLP had gone over to the La Follette movement and were supporting the Wisconsin senator for the presidency. On July 8, 1924, therefore, the Central Committee of the Communist Party announced that the FFLP candidates had been withdrawn, and that the CP would conduct its own campaign with its own candidates, William Z. Foster and Benjamin Gitlow. For further details, see Alexander Bittleman, *Workers Monthly,* December 1924, and M.S., *The New International,* March 1935.

41. In November 1924, a large delegation of British trade union leaders, headed by the president of the Trade Union Congress, A.A. Purcell, arrived in Moscow and, after making a survey of the Russian situation, returned to issue a report praising the achievements of the Bolshevik government. An exchange Russian delegation to England, headed by the chairman of the Central Council of the Russian trade unions, M. Tomsky, appeared at the Hull congress of the British unions in May 1925. On May 14, 1925, a protocol was drawn up in

which the leaders of the two trade union movements agreed to form the Anglo-Russian Trade Union Unity Committee, with equal representation from both organizations. The purpose of this committee was understood to be the promotion of international trade union unity, the struggle to prevent the triumph of reaction and the struggle against the danger of new wars. The committee continued to exist for a year after its British section had conducted itself so ignominiously in the general strike of May 1926, although the Russian Opposition demanded that the Russians leave the committee demonstratively, so that the British labor leaders should be deprived of the revolutionary covering afforded them by the cordial relationships of the Russians. The committee was finally dissolved, not on Russian initiative, but when the General Council of the British trade unions withdrew from it.

42. The most important of the central committees imposed upon the decisive European parties assumed their functions shortly after the launching of the struggle against "Trotskyism" on an international scale. In France, the leadership of Souvarine, Rosmer, and their associates, which had expressed strong sympathies for the Russian Opposition, was replaced by the "left" leadership of Albert Treint and Suzanne Girault, who supported the Zinoviev regime. In Germany, the Brandler-Thalheimer leadership, which had what Trotsky called "misplaced sympathies" for the Russian Opposition and which the latter refused to join in making a scapegoat of, for the German debacle, was replaced by the Zinovievist supporters, Fischer and Maslow. In Poland, the Warski leadership was replaced by the "left" leadership of Domski. None of these leaderships, which were consecrated at the Fifth Plenum of the Comintern, in 1925, lasted much more than a year. As the preparations were being made by Stalin-Bukharin for the elimination from leadership, especially in the Comintern, of Zinoviev, and as the approaching union of the latter with Trotsky became more discernible, the "left" leaderships of the post–Fifth Congress period were removed with the same dispatch and arbitrariness employed in appointing them. The Domski group was replaced and finally expelled by the Warski-Kostrzewa leadership; Fischer and Maslow were expelled and replaced by the Thälmann-Neumann faction; Treint and Girault were removed, then expelled, and replaced by the group of Doriot-Barbé-Thorez. In each case, the expelled "left" leaderships, after a period of evolution and self-revision, turned to support the Trots-

kyist Opposition, for a longer or shorter period. The removals coincided, of course, with the inauguration of the rightward period of development of the Comintern's policy.

43. The *Platform of the Bolshevik-Leninists (Opposition)* was submitted in 1927 for the discussion period prior to the Fifteenth Congress of the Communist Party of the Soviet Union by Trotsky, Radek, Pyatakov, Rakovsky, Zinoviev, Kamenev, Yevdokimov, Peterson, Bakayev, and a number of other members of the Central Committee and Central Control Commission of the party. It was refused publication in the Russian party press by the Stalinist bureaucracy on the ground that it was an "antiparty document." For taking the responsibility for having reproduced it on a mimeographing machine, several of the leaders of the Opposition, including Preobrazhensky, Serebryakov and others, were expelled from the party, shortly before the expulsion en masse of all the Opposition supporters. [An English edition is to be found in Trotsky, *The Challenge of the Left Opposition (1926–27)*, New York: Pathfinder, 1980, pp. 301–94.]

44. Like most of the articles written in that period by representatives of the Opposition, this one was not permitted publication in the Russian party press and had to be circulated from hand to hand in multicopied manuscript form. Written in 1927, it was printed for the first time in any language only in 1934. It will be found in *The New International*, September-October 1934. [Available in *Leon Trotsky on Britain*, New York: Pathfinder, 1973, pp. 279–98.]

45. Article 58 is that section of the Soviet Penal Code which provides for the punishment to be meted out to those engaged in counterrevolutionary activity directed against the Soviet state. It was never intended by its authors as a factional weapon against innerparty opponents but it was converted into such an instrument by the Stalinist leadership, which used it as the juridical basis for the imprisonment, exile, banishment from the country, and capital punishment of those party members charged with supporting the Opposition.

46. The main body of the letter which has come to be known popularly as "Lenin's Testament" was written on December 25, 1922; the postscript on January 4, 1923. In it, Trotsky is characterized as "the

most able man in the present Central Committee." "Stalin," writes Lenin in his postscript, "is too rude, and this fault, entirely supportable in relations among us communists, becomes unsupportable in the office of General Secretary. Therefore, I propose to the comrades to find a way to remove Stalin from that position and appoint another man who in all respects differs from Stalin only in superiority—namely, more patient, more loyal, more polite and more attentive to comrades, less capricious, etc. This circumstance may seem an insignificant trifle, but I think that from the point of view of preventing a split and from the point of view of the relation between Stalin and Trotsky which I discussed above, it is not a trifle, or it is such a trifle as may acquire a decisive significance." The document, intended for the party by Lenin, who felt that his malady was depriving him more and more of the possibility of intervening actively in the impending party crisis, was suppressed by the party leadership. It is to be found in full, together with commentaries on its origin and surrounding circumstances, in *The Suppressed Testament of Lenin,* New York 1935. [The document is also available in *Lenin's Final Fight,* New York: Pathfinder, 1995, pp. 179–200.]

47. At the July 1926 plenum of the Central Committee of the Communist Party of the Soviet Union, completing their break with Stalin and Bukharin, and consummating their bloc with the Moscow Opposition, Zinoviev and Kamenev recorded the fact that there had functioned for quite some time, apart from the official Political Bureau of the party, a factional Septumvirate of the former anti-Trotskyist group of Zinoviev, Stalin, and Bukharin (plus Kamenev, Voroshilov, Kalinin, and a nonmember of the Political Bureau, Kuibyshev, although the latter, as head of the Central Control Commission, was presumably charged with supervising party morals and propriety). This group had organized a clandestine machine within the framework of the official party apparatus, and effectively directed the latter without either the knowledge or consent of the party.

48. The schism came into public sight at the Fourteenth Conference of the Russian Communist Party in 1925 when the Leningrad delegation came forward with a distinct standpoint of its own, directed at the ruling group of Stalin and Bukharin. The Leningrad delegation was, however, alone in the conference. During its sessions, and especially

after them, the central apparatus of the party was set into motion and the Leningrad organization was ruthlessly, speedily, and systematically purged of the new Opposition. Its leaders were removed and dispersed to the four corners of the Soviet republic. The leaders of the new Opposition included such prominent figures as Zinoviev, chairman of the Comintern and president of the Leningrad Soviet; Kamenev, president of the Moscow Soviet and formerly chairman of the Political Bureau; Sokolnikov, Soviet emissary to London; Sarkis, editor of the Leningrad *Pravda*; Krupskaya, Lenin's widow; Lashevich, vice-commissar of war; Vujović, chairman of the Young Communist International, and numerous others.

49. On the eve of the Fifteenth Party Congress, it was suddenly announced in the Russian party press that the Opposition Bloc had been caught in a counterrevolutionary conspiracy with an officer of the notorious White Guard general Baron Peter Wrangel. Upon investigation by the Opposition, it was discovered that the "Wrangel officer" was an agent of the government police (GPU) who had been sent into the ranks of the Opposition for the purpose of compromising it. His "counterrevolutionary activity" appeared to consist entirely of having suggested to Oppositionists his ability to procure for them machinery required for reproducing documents, such as the *Platform*, which the party leadership had forbidden publication. The acknowledgments made by Menzhinsky, head of the GPU, and Stalin, that the "Wrangel officer" was indeed a Soviet police agent purposely sent into the Opposition group, are of course officially recorded. But the Stalinist press throughout the world actively disseminated the news of the "conspiracy" and continues to refer to it, whereas the actual facts were never allowed to reach beyond a narrow circle.

50. The "new explosion" foreseen by Trotsky actually occurred a short time afterward. Toward the end of 1929, after having denied the existence of any rift whatsoever, much less of a right wing, inside the Political Bureau, Stalin suddenly launched a public attack upon the "right wing" and (capitalist) "restorationist" tendencies in the party. The representative of this tendency was named—an obscure official called Frumkin. Shortly thereafter, it appeared that the representative of the "restorationist" tendency was of greater importance, for the attack was, again suddenly, launched against Uglanov, secretary of the

Moscow Committee of the party, who was promptly removed from his post. In this manner, Stalin not only laid down an "ideological barrage" against his Political Committee opponents of the right wing, but disposed of their support in the apparatus before tackling them directly. Only in 1930 was it made publicly known that the object of Stalin's attacks had always been the three PB members, Bukharin, chairman of the Comintern, Rykov, chairman of the Council of People's Commissars, and Tomsky, chairman of the Central Council of the Russian Trade Unions. All three (and their supporters) were removed from their positions, stripped of all honors, publicly humiliated, and compelled to renounce their views openly before being permitted to retain party membership. Their places were taken everywhere by 100 percent Stalinist supporters.

51. In *Germany,* the Brandler-Thalheimer group was finally expelled from the Comintern in 1929, and attempted to establish an international association of expelled right-wing groups under the name of the International Communist Opposition. Its attempts to get readmitted have thus far failed. Maslow and Ruth Fischer, after breaking with the Leninbund and seeking readmission into the Comintern, reoriented, especially after the capitulation of the German CP in 1933, towards the Trotskyist Opposition. In *France,* Rosmer and Souvarine, after a greater or lesser period of active support of the Russian Opposition, withdrew from political life; Monatte and Loriot (before his death) renounced communism and returned to the conceptions of revolutionary syndicalism; Girault returned to the Stalinist party, while Treint, after a brief period in the Trotskyist organization, withdrew from it to form a small group of his own which shares many of the views of the Bolshevik-Leninists. In *Belgium,* Van Overstraeten withdrew from active political life in 1929-30, but the bulk of his group, which had been removed from the leadership of the Belgian party which it enjoyed in 1928, remained associated with the Bolshevik-Leninists (International Communist League). In *Italy,* Bordiga, upon release from his fascist island prison, was expelled from the Comintern as a "Trotskyist counterrevolutionist," as his supporters had been 2-3 years previously. In the *United States,* Cannon, Swabeck, Abern, Shachtman, members of the Central Committee of the Communist Party, were expelled in 1928, with numerous supporters, for "Trotskyism." In *Canada,* Spector, member of the Executive of the Comintern, met with the same

fate, to be followed shortly afterward by the expulsion of the party secretary, MacDonald.

In 1929 began the expulsion of the so-called right-wing groups throughout the International. In the *United States,* the party leadership of Lovestone, Gitlow, and Wolfe was summarily expelled after having obtained the support of 90 percent of the party membership. In *Mexico,* the party leaders Monzón, Bach, and Rivera were expelled for various political reasons. In *Italy,* Tasca (Serra), the party leader, was expelled as a right-winger, followed by the expulsion for Trotskyism of three other leaders, Feroci, Santini, and Blasco. In *Czechoslovakia,* the principal party and trade union leaders, Hais and Jilek, were expelled, and returned to the social democracy. In *Austria,* the party leader Strasser went with the Left Opposition and Schlamm with the Brandler opposition (for a short time). In *France,* Doriot was expelled as a right-winger, together with Sellier and his group, an action followed by the expulsion of the succeeding leadership of Barbé and Celor. In *China,* the leader and founder of the party, Ch'en Tu-hsiu, was expelled for "Trotskyism." In *Sweden,* the bulk of the party leadership and membership, headed by Kilbom, was expelled as the right wing, associated itself with Brandler for a time, and then organized as a socialist party. In *Spain,* leaders of the party like Nin and Andrade were expelled for Trotskyism, and Maurín, head of the Catalonian communist movement, was expelled for right-wing deviations. The succeeding leadership of Trilla, Adame, and Bullejos was subsequently expelled for obscure reasons.

52. Blue is one of the colors of the official flag of the Kuomintang.

53. The Kuomintang was admitted to the Comintern as a sympathizing party early in 1926, approved by the Politbureau of the CPSU with the sole dissenting vote of Trotsky. Hu Han-min, right-wing Kuomintang leader, participated in the Sixth Plenum of the ECCI, February 1926, as fraternal delegate from the Kuomintang. Shao Li-tzu, a henchman of Chiang Kai-shek, was fraternal delegate of the Kuomintang to the Seventh Plenum, ECCI, November 1926 (*Minutes,* Ger. ed., pp. 403*f.*) In 1925, Hu Han-min was elected as the representative of the Chinese peasants to the presidium of the Peasants International. Hu was at the time in virtual exile from Canton

because of his connection with the murder of Liao Chung-k'ai, a left-wing Kuomintang leader.

54. Chiang Kai-shek struck his first open blow for power on March 20, 1926, when in a sudden coup in Canton he won for himself undisputed political and military control of the nationalist movement, which had then already taken on great mass proportions (Canton-Hongkong strike, Kwangtung peasants movement, etc.). News of this coup was concealed from the sections of the Comintern and even denied in the Comintern press. One foreign account of it was denounced by *International Press Correspondence,* the official Comintern organ, as "a lying report" (Eng. ed., April 8, 1926, p. 415). Voitinsky, one of the Comintern functionaries in China, characterized the reports of the Canton coup as "an invention of the imperialists" (*International Press Correspondence,* May 6, 1926, p. 600). Not until more than one year later did the Comintern press suddenly take cognizance of the Canton coup of March 20, 1926, which revealed Chiang Kai-shek's fundamental course in the nationalist movement.

At the time Borodin and the Chinese Communist Party met the terms imposed by Chiang as his price for further collaboration. At the May 1926 plenum of the CEC of the Kuomintang, the Communist Party was pledged not to criticize the anti-class-struggle ideas of Sun Yat-sen and to limit its participation in key Kuomintang bureaus and committees to one-third. (See note 80.) Chiang was elected chairman of the Central Executive Committee and chairman of the all-powerful Standing Committee of the Kuomintang. He became commander-in-chief of the nationalist armies; and in July, with the full support of the Russian advisers and the vast propaganda machine developed and operated largely by communists, Chiang embarked upon the Northern Expedition. (See note 57.) Having made strikes illegal in Canton, Chiang began in Kiangsi, in February 1927, to suppress trade unions and the peasant leagues.

At Shanghai the workers, who had captured the city themselves in a victorious insurrection on March 21–22, were taught to receive Chiang as a revolutionary leader. Rumors of an impending coup were denounced as "provocations" by the communists in Shanghai and abroad. "Far from dividing, as the imperialists say, the Kuomintang has only steeled its ranks." (*International Press Correspondence,* Fr.

ed., March 23, 1927, p. 443.) "A split in the Kuomintang and hostilities between the Shanghai proletariat and the revolutionary soldiers are absolutely excluded for the moment.... Chiang Kai-shek ... himself declared that he would submit to the decisions of the party.... A revolutionist like Chiang Kai-shek will not go over, as the imperialists would like to have it believed, to Chang Tso-lin [the Northern militarist] to fight against the emancipation movement.... The only danger for the Shanghai proletariat lies in an imperialist provocation." (*Ibid.*, March 30, 1927, p. 459.) Chiang systematically and almost openly prepared his coup for three weeks while the communists waited, paralyzed by orders, "not to provoke Chiang" and "in case of extreme necessity to bury their arms" (Mandalian, a Comintern functionary in Shanghai at the time, in *International Press Correspondence,* Fr. ed., July 23, 1927, p. 1,028). The result was that when Chiang struck on April 12, only a few workers, in defiance of party orders, resisted the physical destruction of the trade unions and the mass movement.

In April and May Stalin-Bukharin and the Comintern defended this course. In his April thesis Bukharin asked, offhandedly, "if it was not better to hide arms, not accept battle and thus not let oneself be disarmed." (*Problèmes de la révolution chinoise,* p. 56, Paris, 1927.) The Eighth Plenum of the ECCI in May declared that any plan to oppose Chiang at Shanghai "was absurd." The workers "would have been exterminated...." (*International Press Correspondence,* Fr. ed., June 15, 1927, p. 885). "Chiang Kai-shek's coup d'état ... could not have been prevented." (*Ibid.*, June 25, 1927, p. 932.) Not until some months later was it discovered that the Communist Party's conduct at Shanghai was an "opportunist betrayal." Meanwhile the flower of the Chinese proletariat was slaughtered by Chiang's headsmen on the streets of Shanghai and the remainder demoralized and defeated.

55. The first Chinese revolution occurred in 1911, resulting in the downfall of the Manchu dynasty which had reigned since 1644. The power of the Ching emperors had practically crumbled away but the Chinese bourgeoisie, politically and economically expropriated by the imperialists, was unable to erect a democratic republic on its ruins. Power fell to regional military satraps whose internecine wars perpetuated and deepened the chaos and misery in the countryside

and whose rivalries often reflected the conflicts of rival imperialist powers. Despite weakness and division after 1911, two attempts at monarchical restorations failed. The war vastly accelerated the growth of productive forces and the nascent forces of Chinese capitalism again raised their heads. (An estimate of China's industrial growth, taking 1913 as 100, gave an index of 226.1 in 1926 as an average for all main fields of industrial activity. Increases in some leading fields, as in cotton goods and tobacco, were as much as 500 percent in the 13-year period). With industrial growth, the influences of the World War and the October Revolution quickly gave form to nationalist political currents. As early as 1915 the new Chinese intelligentsia, led by Ch'en Tu-hsiu, steered a course toward a break with the old traditionalism in politics, morals, literature, philosophy, and the arts. The sensational growth of industry brought a modern Chinese proletariat onto the scene and thrust it almost at once into the midst of political struggle. Japan's attempt to hold Shantung after the war led to the student rising of May 4, 1919. Strikes followed. Trade unions sprang into existence. The successful mechanics' strike in 1920 launched the modern labor movement. The same year saw the founding of the Chinese Communist Party. These events ushered in the epoch of the second Chinese revolution which ended in shattering disaster at the close of 1927.

56. In 1919 Sun Yat-sen issued a detailed plan for "sincere" international collaboration among the powers in the development of China as a "practical solution for international war, commercial war, and class war." He envisaged an idyll of close and friendly and mutually profitable participation in the economic exploitation of China for all the major powers and even believed that foreign capital would help construct a noncapitalist economy for China in which there would be no germs of war, of the international, commercial, or class varieties. Sun's plan was coolly received by the powers. It was published in 1922 under the title *The International Development of China*. See also Sun Yat-sen, *Memoirs of a Chinese Revolutionary,* London, 1927.

57. After concentrating political and military control of Canton in his own hands after the March 20 coup, Chiang Kai-shek took the field in July, 1926, for the conquest of Central and North China,

aided by Russian arms, a staff of Russian military advisers, and a vast propaganda machine lubricated and propelled by communist methods and initiative, but confined programmatically to the Kuomintang slogans of a 25 percent land rent reduction and improved labor conditions. The northward march coincided with the rise of a vast mass movement in the provinces of Kiangsi, Hunan, and Hupeh which drew into its orbit by spring 1927, nearly 10 million peasants and nearly 1 million workers in Hankow, Shanghai, and other urban centers. The Nationalist armies won easy victories with the aid of this movement which swept the northern resistance out of the Nationalist path. By September 1926, the Yangtzse valley was in Nationalist hands. In December, the Nationalist Government moved from Canton to Hankow, which together with the cities of Wuchang and Hanyang at the confluence of the Yangtzse and Han rivers formed the city of Wuhan. Chiang Kai-shek moved more slowly through Kiangsi towards Shanghai.

Back in Canton strikes were prohibited and the mass movement checked. The Canton-Hongkong strike was brought unconditionally to an end in October 1926. Chiang closed up trade unions and peasant leagues as he marched northward. This checked his progress to such an extent that he at one stage stopped the repressions and called the communists back to help him advance. They came unquestioningly. By February 1927, his troops were within striking distance of Shanghai. On February 18, the Shanghai workers rose in a general strike and insurrection in expectation of the arrival of the Nationalists. Chiang ordered his troops not to move and let Li Paochang, the military governor of Shanghai, suppress the uprising with great slaughter. Li was later rewarded with a command in Chiang's army. In March, Chiang launched the terror in Nanchang, Kiukiang, Anking, and Wuhu. On March 21, meanwhile, the Shanghai workers arose, this time victoriously, and with their own forces drove the Northerners from the city, handing it over next day to the Nationalists. Chiang arrived on March 26. Three weeks later, after concluding a deal with the foreign and Chinese bankers of Shanghai, he turned on the workers with unparalleled ferocity. (See note 54.)

58. Trudoviki (the group of "Toilers") were the second-largest grouping in the first imperial Russian Duma, representative largely

EXPLANATORY NOTES / 353

of the radical petty bourgeoisie and especially of the middle peasantry. At first the Trudoviki cooperated with the Constitutional Democrats ("Cadets") but later on a breach occurred, and they frequently cooperated in the Duma with the social democratic fraction. Their extremely loose organizational structure and indefinite social composition went hand in hand with an extremely confused and diffused program and behavior. Characteristic of its leadership was Kerensky.

59. The Chinese tariff was limited to 5 percent *ad valorem* as a result of the Treaty of Nanking of 1842 with Great Britain, signed aboard a British warship at the conclusion of the first Anglo-Chinese war. The "most-favored nation" clause in subsequent treaties made this universally applicable to China's trade relations with all the powers. The treaties also fixed the values upon which the revenues were to be calculated. These were revised only twice, in 1902 and 1918, the 5 percent rate remaining unchanged. China presented demands for tariff revision to the Versailles Conference which went unheeded. Under the pressure of the rising nationalist movement in China, the Washington conference in February 1922 produced a nine-power agreement to hold a conference to readjust the Chinese tariff. This conference did not materialize until December 1925, when the great mass movement opened up the possibility that the Chinese masses might seize what the powers were slow to give. The conference was called to dangle tariff autonomy before the Chinese bourgeoisie to help wean it from the mass movement. Restoration of tariff autonomy by January 1, 1929 was proposed by the conference. Enforcement of this promise, not made effective until the tariff promulgated on January 1, 1931, was one of the prices paid by the imperialists to Chiang Kai-shek for smashing the national-revolutionary movement in 1927. Foreign supervision and rigid foreign control of revenues earmarked for foreign loan payments were preserved. Imperialist pressure, especially Japanese, has compelled the scheduling of tariffs favorable to foreign goods and disastrous for native Chinese industries, particularly in the cotton trade. This has made tariff autonomy more formal than actual.

60. The PPS (Polish Socialist Party), the Dashnaktsutiun, and the Bund were, respectively, Polish, Armenian, and Jewish petty-bourgeois nationalist organizations, with a socialistic coloration, functioning within

the old czarist empire. For a short time the Bund was a part of the Social Democratic Party of Russia, but separated itself from it and led an independent existence, as is the case today in Poland and Lithuania. The Bund frequently cooperated with the Mensheviks, but virtually never with the Bolsheviks. As for the Polish and Armenian organizations mentioned, they were never part of the Russian party or any of its sections.

61. "The Kuomintang is an organization of a peculiar type, a cross between a political party and an organization like the soviets in which different class groupings enter.... The Kuomintang englobes the liberal bourgeoisie (which with us was organized in the Cadet Party and had already become counterrevolutionary in the earlier stages of the revolution), the petty bourgeoisie, and the working class. From the organizational point of view, the Kuomintang is not a party in the customary sense of the term." (N. Bukharin, *Problèmes de la révolution chinoise,* Paris, 1927, p. 50.) At the Eighth Plenum Stalin called the Kuomintang "a revolutionary parliament." In his famous article of April 10, 1927, in *Pravda,* Martynov called it "a bloc of four classes."

62. The Wuhan government consisted of a group of Left Kuomintang leaders led by Wang Ching-wei, supported by T'ang Sheng-chih, a Hunan militarist, and nominally by Feng Yü-hsiang, the "Christian General" in the Northwest. Tan P'ing-shan and Hsü Ch'ien, communists, occupied the posts of agriculture and labor. In April 1927, Stalin characterized this government as the "revolutionary center" which, with the indispensable collaboration of the communists, would carry through the agrarian revolution. (See Stalin's theses, *International Press Correspondence,* April 28, 1927.) "The revolutionary Kuomintang in Wuhan, leading a decisive struggle against militarism and imperialism," wrote Stalin, "will in reality be transformed into an organ of the revolutionary democratic dictatorship of the proletariat and the peasantry." At the Eighth Plenum on May 24, Stalin said: "The agrarian revolution is the basis and content of the bourgeois democratic revolution in China. The Kuomintang in Hankow and the Hankow government are the center of the bourgeois democratic revolutionary movement." (*Minutes,* Ger. ed., p. 71.) The Eighth Plenum resolution declared that the Hankow government "is effectively leading the

revolutionary struggle against the imperialists, the feudal lords, and now also against an important part of the bourgeoisie." This government was urged to turn resolutely toward the masses and "the task of the Communist Party is to assure such an orientation on the part of the Hankow government." (*International Press Correspondence,* Fr. ed., June 15, 1927, p. 884.) Trotsky's demand for the slogan of soviets was rejected because "it is a slogan of struggle against the revolutionary Kuomintang."

Trotsky denied that Wuhan was the revolutionary center and declared that one had to be created: "The Wuhan authorities are not enough for this. . . . Soviets are needed, soviets of the toilers." "We say directly to the Chinese peasants: the leaders of the Left Kuomintang of the type of Wang Ching-wei and Co. will inevitably betray you, if you follow the Wuhan heads instead of forming your own independent soviets. . . . Politicians of the Wang Ching-wei type, under difficult conditions, will unite ten times with Chiang Kai-shek against the workers and peasants." [Speech at the Eighth Plenum, in *Leon Trotsky on China,* New York: Pathfinder, 1976, p. 217.] In order to carry out the Comintern line and forego soviets "which would accelerate the conflict with the generals" (*International Press Correspondence,* Fr. ed., June 29, 1927, p. 949), the Chinese party conceded the ground to the Kuomintang liberals and the generals and tried to check the "excesses" of the workers and peasants. This only emboldened the reaction. Even while the Eighth Plenum sat, the generals seized power in Hunan (May 21). Feng Yü-hsiang, to the consternation of Moscow, came to terms with Chiang Kai-shek (June 22) and the Wuhan government broke with the communists (July 15), capitulating completely to Chiang's "counterrevolutionary center" at Nanking in August. On July 14, when workers' heads were already rolling in Hankow streets, the ECCI formally proclaimed: "The revolutionary role of the Wuhan government is at an end." (Resolution of the ECCI, *International Press Correspondence,* Fr. ed., July 27, 1927, p. 1,041.)

63. Narodniki ("Populists") were an organized movement of the Russian intellectuals of the last century who inclined strongly towards anarchist conceptions. They were violently antimonarchistic, were organized conspiratively, and often employed terrorist methods of combat. Their principal propaganda activities were con–

centrated among the peasants and, in a confused way, they aimed at a communal order of society. Their party, *Narodnaya Volya* (People's Will) was finally destroyed by the czarist government in the eighties, with the aid of spies, and out of it eventually developed two wings, one of which moved towards Marxism and the other towards what became the party of the Social Revolutionaries, that is, a petty-bourgeois peasant party.

64. The Canton uprising took place on December 11, 1927. It was crushed fifty hours later at the cost of 5,700 proletarian lives, among them the best remaining worker cadres of the revolution. The Canton Commune (see note 79) was the culminating disaster of the period of adventurism which followed the collapse of the movement in August. (See note 75) Yeh T'ing, military commander of the rising, put the actual number of participants at 4,200, consisting of 1,200 military cadets and 3,000 workers, most of them poorly armed. (Ch'en Shao-yü [Wang Min]: *The Story of the Canton Uprising*, in the collection *The Canton Commune*, p. 142, Shanghai, 1930.) These forces were hurled into a frontal attack against 50,000 well-armed Kuomintang troops either in or within marching distance of Canton, among whom "we had done no work. . . . We organized no nuclei among them." (Lozovsky: *Lessons of the Canton Commune, ibid.*, p. 5.) "There was not at the moment of the insurrection any serious revolutionary movement among the peasants in the districts near Canton . . ." wrote Heinz Neumann, who helped "lead" the rising. "The Canton insurrection was not supported by any intervention of the proletarian or peasant masses in the other provinces of China. (A. Neuberg, [Heinz Neumann]: *L'Insurrection armée*, p. 124, Paris, 1931.) "Obviously," wrote Lominadze, who with Neumann "advised" the Chinese communists in this period, "we far too greatly exaggerated the extent of the development of the peasant uprisings at that time." (*The Anniversary of the Canton Commune*, in *The Canton Commune*, p. 205.) In the city of Canton itself the party "was not capable of organizing strikes. . . . Only when the roar of guns was already in progress did the working masses know an insurrection was going on. . . . They regarded it as a sudden, accidental thing." (Lozovsky, *ibid.*, p. 6.)

65. "It would be a great error to hand over the flag of the Kuomin-

tang to the Chiang Kai-shek clique." (N. Bukharin: *Problèmes de la révolution chinoise,* Paris, 1927, pp. 59–60.) "The Communist Party will undoubtedly not permit the Kuomintang flag to fall now into the hands of the counterrevolutionists." (A. Stetzki, "La dialectique de la lutte en Chine," *International Press Correspondence,* Fr. ed., May 7, 1927.) "The flag of the Kuomintang, which was the banner of the national emancipation struggle, must not be handed over to those who betrayed it." (*Resolution of the Eighth Plenum, ECCI, International Press Correspondence,* Fr. ed., June 11, 1927.)

66. The total of foreign investments in China was estimated, as of 1931, at US$3.3 billion. Of this total 78.1 percent was directly in business and trade enterprises and 21.9 percent in loans to the Chinese government. Foreign capital controls nearly half the Chinese cotton industry. It directly controls about one-third of China's railways and has a mortgage of more than $200 million on the rest, with a total railway investment of $641.3 million. Foreign bottoms carried 81.31 percent of China's foreign and coastal trade. Trade figures show a total adverse trade balance since 1902 of more than $3.3 billion. There was an unrecorded but enormous drain of silver as a result of the opium trade during the nineteenth century. (For tables see C.F. Remer: *Foreign Investments in China,* N.Y., 1933, p. 58; H.D. Fong: *Cotton Industry and Trade In China,* Peking, 1932; H.D. Fong: *China's Industrialization,* Shanghai, 1931; *China Year Book*). It is interesting to note that the total foreign investment in Russia on the eve of the Great War was $3.882 billion. To protect these investments the imperialist powers maintain military garrisons in key Chinese ports which totaled in 1927, 11,880 American, British, Japanese, French, and Italian marines and soldiers. There are also regularly stationed American, British, Japanese, French, and Italian fleets, patrolling the coasts and rivers. They include cruisers, aircraft carriers, destroyers, submarines, and gunboats. There is also a large foreign police personnel in the foreign concessions. All these forces were increased during 1926–27.

67. In the absence of authentic and complete population statistics in China, there exist only estimates and partial studies. A count of factory workers in 29 cities in 9 provinces in 1931 totaled 1,204,318. Another estimate including transport workers, dockers, construction

workers, and miners, brought the total to 2,750,000. Handicraftsmen, coolies engaged in miscellaneous labor, carriers, shop employees, apprentices, artisans, were estimated at 11,960,000 for all China in 1927, giving an approximate total for proletariat and semiproletariat of about 15 million. This may be compared to the estimated Russian factory population in 1905 of about 10 million. The best estimates and studies of class divisions in the peasantry, who form about three-quarters of the whole population, have been made by Ch'en Han-seng, the noted agrarian economist, who found that in Kwangtung, as typical of the south, poor peasants formed 74 percent of the population and held 19 percent of the land. In Wusih, central China, poor peasant families were 68.9 percent of the total and held 14.2 percent of the land. In Paoting, in the north, poor peasants were 65.2 percent with 25.9 percent of the land. Prof. Ch'en lists 65 percent of China's farm population as land hungry. (For statistical tables and different estimates see: Ch'en Han-seng, *The Present Agrarian Problem in China,* Shanghai, 1933; H. D. Fong, *China's Industrialization,* Shanghai, 1931; Fang Fu-an, *Chinese Labour,* Shanghai, 1931; Lowe Chun-hwa, *Facing Labor Issues in China,* Shanghai, 1933; *Proceedings of the Pan-Pacific Trade Union Conference,* Hankow, 1927.)

68. The distinction between the so-called democratic and the socialist periods of the Russian Bolshevik revolution are described by Lenin as follows: "*First* there was a movement, in conjunction with the entire peasantry, against the monarchy, against the landlords, against medievalism, and to that extent the revolution remained a bourgeois, a bourgeois-democratic one. Then it became a movement, in conjunction with the poorest peasantry, with the semiproletariat, with all the exploited against capitalism, including the village rich, the village vultures and the speculators, and to that extent the revolution became a socialist one. To attempt to put artificially a Chinese wall between the two stages, and to separate them by any other factor than the degree of preparedness of the proletariat and of its unity with the village poor, means completely to pervert and vulgarize Marxism and to replace it by liberalism. It means to smuggle through a reactionary defense of the bourgeoisie against the socialist proletariat, under the cloak of quasi-learned references to the progressive character of the bourgeoisie as compared with medievalism." (N. Lenin, *The Proletarian Revolution and*

the Renegade Kautsky, London, 1920, p. 92 [*LCW,* vol. 28, p. 300].

69. Organized workers in China rose from 230,000 in 1923 to 570,000 in 1925, 1,264,000 in 1926, and 2,800,000 in 1927. (*Pan-Pacific Worker,* no. 2, Hankow, July 15, 1927.) More than 800,000 workers participated directly in the wave of strikes which followed the massacre of students by British police in Shanghai on May 30, 1925. General strikes completely paralyzed Shanghai and Hongkong, the latter strike lasting sixteen months. The peasant movement, which took on modern forms of organization only in 1922, directly embraced 9,720,000 peasants by March 1927, in Kwangtung, Hunan, Kiangsi, and Hupeh provinces alone, where independent seizure of the land was begun by the peasants in 1926 and carried out on a large scale, especially in Hunan, in the spring of 1927.

70. Ch'en Tu-hsiu resigned from the chairmanship of the CC in mid-July 1927, when the "Left Kuomintang"—in which the Comintern ordered the communists to remain notwithstanding—started executing communists and workers in Wuhan. Ch'en was finally driven by these events to demand withdrawal from the Kuomintang. "The International," he wrote, "wishes us to carry out our own policy on the one hand and does not allow us to withdraw from the Kuomintang on the other. There is really no way out and I cannot continue my work." (*Letter to the Comrades of the Communist Party.*) A new leadership, with Ch'ü Ch'iu-pai, Li Li-san, Chou En-lai, and Chang Kuo-t'ao as the principal figures, was set up at the August 7 conference. This leadership, which embarked, under Comintern orders, on a course of adventurist uprisings (see note 73) was declared "to guarantee that henceforth there will be correct, revolutionary Bolshevik leadership." (*Letter to the Comrades of the August 7 Conference.*) On August 9 in Moscow the joint plenum of the CC and CCC of the CPSU, declared itself "in a position to state with satisfaction that this right deviation in the leadership of the Chinese brother party has now been liquidated and the policy of the leadership corrected." (*International Press Correspondence,* August 18, 1927, p. 1,074). This "correct" and "Bolshevik" leadership led the party—to the Canton Commune. (See notes 64, 73.)

71. In his speech at the Eighth Plenum of the Comintern (May

1927) Stalin said: "Now can we say that the situation in Russia from March to July 1917 represents an analogy to the present situation in China? No, this cannot be said. It cannot be said not only because Russia then stood before the proletarian revolution whereas China now stands before the bourgeois-democratic revolution, but also because the Provisional Government in Russia that time was a counterrevolutionary government whereas the present government in Hankow is a revolutionary government in the bourgeois-democratic sense of the term. . . . The history of the workers soviets shows that such soviets can exist and develop further only if favorable premises are given for a direct transition from the bourgeois-democratic revolution to the proletarian revolution, that is, if favorable premises exist for the transition from the bourgeois governmental power to the dictatorship of the proletariat. And didn't the workers soviets in Leningrad and Moscow in 1905 as well as the workers soviets in Germany in 1918 go under just because these favorable premises did not exist at that time? It is possible that in 1905 there would have been no formation of soviets in Russia if there had existed at that time in Russia a broad revolutionary organization of the type of the present Left Kuomintang in China." (*Die Chinesische Frage auf dem 8. Plenum der Exekutive der Kommunistische Internationale,* Hamburg-Berlin 1928, pp, 66f.) This speech of Stalin is not reprinted in either one of his two collected volumes of speeches and writings entitled *Probleme des Leninismus.*

72. The Communist Party of China, according to the organizational report of Ch'en Tu-hsiu to the Fifth Party Congress, had in April 1927, a membership of 57,967 including 53.8 percent workers, 18.7 percent peasants, and the remainder soldiers, students, intellectuals, and others. (*Cf.* P. Mif, *Kitaiskaya Revolutsia,* p. 117, Moscow, 1932.) No reliable or credible figures of the membership total since 1927 have been published, but on social composition there are the following: "The party does not have a single healthy party nucleus among the industrial workers." (Circular of the Central Committee, November 8, 1928.) "At the time of the Sixth Congress [July 1928] the proportion of workers in the party was . . . 10 percent. Now it has shrunk to 3 percent." (Chou En-lai, *Organizational Questions in the Party at the Present Time,* May 15, 1929.) ". . . The industrial workers in the party total 2.5 percent." (*Appeal of the Central Com-*

mittee, etc., Red Flag, March 26, 1930, Shanghai.) ". . . now it is less than 2 percent (Kuchiumov, of the Far Eastern Secretariat of the Comintern in the *Discussion of the ECCI Presidium on the Li Li-san Line,* December 1930, printed in *Bolshevik,* Shanghai, May 10, 1931.)

73. Putschist moods continued to govern the course of the Chinese Communist Party after the Canton insurrection for a period of more than two years under the leadership of Li Li-san. This course completed the divorce of the party from the proletariat. (See note 72.) It oriented itself upon the movements of bands of insurgent peasants and ex-Kuomintang soldiers in Kiangsi, Hupeh, and Hunan provinces. Out of these forces rose the peasant Red Armies which attempted (1930–34) to carry out the agrarian revolution in isolated rural districts of central China, cut off from the cities and the urban labor movement. The proletariat remained in a state of depression and demoralization as a result of the defeat of 1927, the Kuomintang terror that followed, and the "red union" policies of Stalinism's "Third Period." Existing workers organizations remained entirely under the control of the Kuomintang. Most of the workers were left without any organization at all, even of the most elementary type. Out in the countryside the superior armed forces of the Kuomintang, aided by the imperialists and unimpeded by a strong labor movement, finally defeated the peasant forces of central China, reoccupied all the so-called soviet districts in November 1934, and forced the Reds to flee to the distant west and northwest where they are still seeking to establish a new base of operations. (For an analysis of the 1928–34 period see: Harold R. Isaacs, "Perspectives of the Chinese Revolution, A Marxist View," *Pacific Affairs,* September 1935.) Following these defeats and in line with the right turn of the Communist International, the Chinese Stalinists have now reverted sharply to an exact reproduction, on a lower plane, of the opportunist line of 1925–27, again offering collaboration to the Kuomintang and participation in a "united government of self-defense." The myth of "Soviet China" has been shed and the revolutionary peasant forces represented by the Red Armies offered up as a new sacrifice to the "anti-imperialist united front." (For an elaboration of the "new line" see the special Chinese number of *Communist International,* February 1936.)

74. After Chiang Kai-shek's Shanghai coup: "Despite the partial defeat . . . the revolution has been raised to a higher stage." (*Resolution of the Eighth Plenum, ECCI,* May 1927, *International Press Correspondence,* Fr. ed., June 11, 1927, p. 867.) After the "defection" of the Wuhan "Left Kuomintang": "The revolution is striding forward to the highest phase of its development, to the phase of direct struggle for the dictatorship of the working class and the peasantry." (*On the International Situation,* resolution of the Joint session of the CC and CCC of the CPSU, August 9, 1927; *International Press Correspondence,* August 18, 1927, p. 1,075.) After the defeats of the Nanchang and Yeh-Ho uprisings: "The Chinese revolution is not only not on the ebb, but has entered upon a new, higher stage. . . . Not only is the strength of the revolutionary movement of the toiling masses of China not yet exhausted, but it is precisely only now that it is beginning to manifest itself in a new advance of the revolutionary struggle." (Resolution of the November Plenum, CC, CCP, Chiu Chiu-pei: *The Chinese Revolution and the Communist Party,* Shanghai, 1928, p. 136.) After the defeat of the Canton insurrection: "The general situation in China is still a directly revolutionary situation . . . the perspective of the stabilization of Chinese capitalism after the Canton uprising not only does not improve but infinitely diminishes." (*Resolution of the Politbureau of the CCP* of January 3, 1928, given by Chiu Chiu-pei, *op. cit.*, p. 247.)

75. After the collapse of the Wuhan regime (see note 62) the Comintern lurched sharply to the left. "The Communists must immediately begin to propagate the idea of soviets, in order to be able, in case the struggle to win the Kuomintang fails, to call on the masses to create soviets. . . ." (*Pravda,* July 25, 1927.) A new communist leadership was set up at a conference hastily called "by the telegraphic instructions of the Comintern and by its new representative" (Chiu Chiu-pei, *The Chinese Revolution and the Communist Party,* Shanghai, 1928, p. 122), and the party was ordered "to organize uprisings of the workers and peasants under the banner of the revolutionary Lefts of the Kuomintang." (*Resolution of the August 7 Conference of the CCP.*) There was an abortive military uprising in Nanchang on August 1. Forced to flee, the troops commanded by Yeh T'ing and Ho Lung marched to Swatow in Kwangtung and were there dispersed. At the same time the so-called "Autumn Harvest" uprisings took place in

scattered rural localities. All were pitilessly crushed.

On September 19 the Chinese Politbureau finally decided that "the uprisings can under no circumstances be held under the banner of the Kuomintang." (Chiu Chiu-pei, *Ibid.*, p. 134.) On September 30 *Pravda* announced that "the propaganda slogan 'Soviets!' must now become a slogan of action." (*International Press Correspondence,* Fr. ed., October 8, 1927, p. 1,437.) The November plenum of the CCP finally "recognized the bankruptcy of the Left Kuomintang" and affirmed that the blue banner of the Kuomintang "had become the banner of the white terror." The plenum therefore ruled that "the central slogan for all uprisings shall be: All power to the conference of workers, peasants, soldiers, and poor people's deputies (soviets)!" and declared that despite the defeats of the Nanchang and Autumn Harvest uprisings "a directly revolutionary situation exists today throughout China." (Chiu Chiu-pei, *Ibid.*, p. 136.) This led to the catastrophe of the Canton Commune. The Ninth Plenum of the ECCI, in February 1928, while formally decrying putschism, forecast the immediate approach of a new revolutionary wave and placed before the Chinese party "the practical task of organizing and carrying out the armed insurrection of the masses." (*Resolutions of the Ninth Plenum, ECCI,* Fr. ed., p. 49.) It was with this orientation that the decimated Chinese party entered upon the new disasters of the "Third Period" of Stalinism, which in China took the form of putschism under the leadership of Li Li-san, whose course ruled the party until the end of 1930.

76. The Nanchang uprising of August 1, 1927, led by Yeh T'ing and Ho Lung, was conducted under the Kuomintang banner with a "revolutionary committee" composed of Soong Ch'ing-ling, Eugene Chen, and Teng Yen-ta, who were already en route out of China to a European exile, and other Left Kuomintang figures who were similarly unaware of their "leadership" in the Nanchang events. The Yeh-Ho program promised confiscation of land holdings in excess of 200 *mow* (33⅓ acres), which meant protection for most of the Kiangsi landlords. As they marched through the province with their Kuomintang banners, the Yeh-Ho troops appeared to the masses "like the armies of Chiang Kai-shek the Third" (Chiu Chiu-pei, *The Chinese Revolution and the Communist Party,* Shanghai, 1928, p. 124.) Chiu attributes the failure of the uprising to "the su-

perior strength of the enemy" and adds the following "errors of leadership": "(1) Lack of a clear-cut revolutionary policy. (2) Indecisiveness about the agrarian revolution. (3) Lack of connection with the peasant masses and failure to arm the peasants. (4) Failure to crush the old political organizations and set up new ones. (5) Errors in military judgment." (*Ibid*.) The army attacked Swatow in Kwangtung in September, was defeated and dispersed to the hills. Part of it became a nucleus for the later peasant armies in Kiangsi.

77. Nestor Makhno was the leader of small partisan bands of peasants in the Ukraine during the civil war after the Russian revolution. He fought against Ukrainian reactionaries and the German forces of occupation. Under anarchist and often kulak influence, he steadfastly rejected proposals to integrate his forces into the centralized Red Army. As the latter grew in size and effectiveness, Makhno's partisan bands came into conflict with it, both physically and politically. His forces were finally dispersed by Soviet arms. The term Makhnoism is employed to designate isolated, adventuristic, essentially rural warfare of partisans.

78. "Comrade N" was Heinz Neumann, the German communist, who joined Lominadze on the staff of Comintern delegates to China after the departure of the discredited Borodin. Neumann had a direct hand in the planning of the Canton insurrection and was present in Canton when it took place. Yeh T'ing, military commander of the rising, later bitterly told the Comintern in Moscow that Neumann was "the first to flee" when the collapse of the adventure became apparent.

79. The "Canton Council of Workers, Peasants, and Soldiers Deputies" which assumed power in Canton at 6 a.m., December 11, 1927, consisted of fifteen men selected at a secret meeting of the organizers of the insurrection on December 7. Nine men represented the 3,000 workers under communist influence who participated in the uprising. Three were delegates of the cadet regiment of 1,200 which also took part in the uprising, and three were named to represent the peasants of Kwangtung. Two of the latter did not arrive in time. The same meeting decided that on the morrow of the uprising the "soviet" would be enlarged to a

membership of 300. These facts are given by Huang Ping, a leading participant in the Commune and "foreign minister" of the short-lived government, in *The Canton Commune and Its Preparation,* in the collection *The Canton Commune,* Shanghai, 1930, pp. 89–90.

80. Following the coup of March 20, 1926, the occurrence of which was denied by the Comintern press (see note 54), Chiang Kai-shek drove home his political advantage at the May plenum of the Central Executive Committee of the Kuomintang, which adopted a resolution introduced by Chiang which required communists "not to entertain any doubt on, or criticize Dr. Sun (Sun Yat-sen) or his principles." The Communist Party was required to hand over to the Standing Committee of the Kuomintang a list of its members in the Kuomintang. Communists were forbidden to become the heads of any party or government department. Communist membership in municipal, provincial, and central party committees were limited to one-third the total. Kuomintang members were forbidden to join the Communist Party. (For the text of this resolution see T.C. Woo, *The Kuomintang and the Future of the Chinese Revolution,* London, 1928, pp. 176f.) Chiang emerged from the plenum chairman of the Central Executive Committee, chairman of the Standing Committee, chairman of the Military Council (originally headed by Wang Ching-wei and designed as a civilian "check" on the military), and supreme dictator of Canton with all government departments, subordinate to general staff headquarters. In return for Borodin's agreement to these terms, Chiang "expelled" some of his right-wing associates to await his arrival in Shanghai.

81. In contrast to the Russian Bolsheviks who did not hesitate to take over the agricultural program of the Social Revolutionary Party and give the soil-hungry peasants the land, the Hungarian communists proceeded immediately upon the establishment of the soviet republic to socialize all the land, and, without regard to the sentiments and aspirations of the masses of poor and middle class peasants, to inaugurate a large-scale socialist production in agriculture overnight. By thus ignoring the bulk of the peasantry, Béla Kun, Pepper, and the other communist leaders facilitated the work of the counterrevolution among the rural population and thereby sped the fall of the soviet republic. "If this solution of the agrarian

question failed to realize the alliance of the proletariat of town and country, it did, however, consolidate the alliance of the urban bourgeoisie with the peasantry, which began to strangle the rule of the proletariat. . . . The counterrevolution incited the peasantry to resistance which declared quite plainly: the dictatorship only wants to exploit the peasant, it only wants the peasantry to furnish it with provisions this year and thereby to reinforce the dictatorship, so that it shall be able to continue with its socialization next year and rob the peasant of the land." (Béla Szanto, *Klassenkämpfe und die Diktatur des Proletariats in Ungarn,* Vienna, 1920, p. 83.)

82. "We have no illusions about La Follette. We know that he will betray the industrial workers and exploited farmers; even though we pledge ourselves to vote for him in the election we will point out his shortcomings, his compromises and his betrayal of the interests of the industrial workers and poor farmers. We cannot support La Follette as enthusiastic followers, but the situation which we face is such that we are compelled to make an election alliance in support of La Follette because the masses of farmers and industrial workers who are supporting the class Farmer-Labor Party still labor under the illusion that La Follette is the Moses who will lead them out of the wilderness. While supporting La Follette, it is our duty to destroy this illusion." (C.E. Ruthenberg, *The Farmer-Labor United Front,* Chicago, 1924, p. 27.) By decision of the Executive Committee of the Comintern in the same year (1924), the position of the Central Executive Committee of the Workers (Communist) Party of America in favor of supporting the La Follette party and its presidential candidates was reversed.

83. In the early period of the German revolution (1918–19), Rudolf Hilferding, one of the theoreticians of the German social democracy, proposed a constitutional structure for the republic which would provide for a combined form of workers councils and parliamentary democracy, in which the former would function as a prop beneath the latter, which would enjoy the decisive legislative and executive rights. In practice, both in Germany and in Austria, this "combined form" proved to be the easiest way of effecting the dissolution of the existing workers councils in the interests of the final and exclusive domination by the parliamentary republican regime.

84. Krestintern is a combined term made up of abbreviations of the Russian words for the Peasants International, formed under the aegis of the Comintern in Moscow in October 1923. It seems impossible to determine the exact time when it was actually dissolved, for no official notification of its liquidation appears to have been made in the Communist press.

85. The decisions of the February 1928 plenum of the Executive Committee of the Third International, which marked the official registering of the opening of the "leftward" course of the International, are dealt with in greater detail in the following essay, "What Now?"

What Now?

86. Although Trotsky's criticism of the draft program of the Comintern was brought to the attention of some of the delegates to the Sixth Congress, and even then only in heavily edited form, the document "What Now?" was never submitted to the attention of any of the members of the congress, in violation of the constitutional right of appeal against disciplinary action formally enjoyed by Trotsky. It was made available for the first time by Trotsky himself, in the French edition of his book *L'Internationale Communiste après Lénine*.

87. Gregory Zinoviev, chairman of the Comintern since its foundation, and unanimously reelected to that post by the Fifth Congress in 1924, was removed from his functions by the Stalinist apparatus in 1926; forbidden to appear before the Eighth Plenum of the Executive Committee in May 1927; and even though readmitted by the time of the opening of the Sixth Congress, he did not appear at its sessions at all. Other members elected to the Executive Committee at the Fifth Congress who were expelled before the Sixth Congress or shortly thereafter for "Trotskyist" or "Brandlerist" deviations include: Schlecht, Rosenberg, Ruth Fischer, Wynkoop,

368 / EXPLANATORY NOTES

Roy, Bordiga, Ch'en Tu-hsiu, Schefflo, Kamenev, Trotsky, Treint, Sellier, Girault, Doriot, Neurath, Höglund, Kilbom, Samuelson.

88. For dates of the congresses of the Comintern and the progressively longer intervals between them, see note 22.

89. The reference is to the suppressed "Testament of Lenin." See note 46.

90. Together with Kamenev and numerous other leaders of the Bolshevik Party, Zinoviev was a vigorous opponent of Lenin's course towards armed insurrection in the fall of 1917. After the Central Committee had decided conspiratorially, against the votes of Kamenev and Zinoviev, to set the date of the insurrection and put all efforts into effecting it, the two opponents appeared with a public statement in Maxim Gorky's daily paper, *Novaya Zhizn*, dissociating themselves from Lenin's position and appealing openly for a reversal of the course towards insurrection. Lenin, still in hiding from Kerensky's police, thereupon publicly attacked the two as "faint-hearts" and "strikebreakers"; to the Central Committee he proposed that they be promptly expelled from the party.

91. Trotsky's insistence on this score, coupled with his proposals for a long-term industrialization plan which would give industry the upper hand in the country's economic life and enable it to guide agriculture out of its backwardness and onto a socialized, mechanized level, was met with hostility or derision by the rest of the party leaders. In a speech delivered to the Executive Committee of the Comintern on January 6, 1924, on behalf of the Russian party leadership, Zinoviev explained the dispute in the Russian party as follows: "It seems to me, comrades, that the obstinate persistence in clinging to a beautiful plan is intrinsically nothing else than a considerable concession to the old-fashioned view that a good plan is a universal remedy, the last word in wisdom. Trotsky's standpoint has greatly impressed many students. 'The Central Committee has no plan, and we really must have a plan!' is the cry we hear today from a certain section of the students. The reconstruction of economics in a country like Russia is indeed the most difficult problem of our revolution.... We want to have transport affairs managed by

Dzerzhinsky; economics by Rykov; finance by Sokolnikov; Trotsky, on the other hand, wants to carry out everything with the aid of a 'state plan.'" (*Daily Worker,* April 12, 1924.)

92. On November 27, 1927, the Central Committee of the Communist Party of Belgium adopted, by vote of 15 to 3, a resolution, taking note of the measures that had just been taken, against the expulsion of Kamenev, Rakovsky, Smilga, Yevdokimov, and Avdeyev from the Central Committee; the expulsion of Muralov, Bakayev, Sokolovsky, Peterson, Solovyev, and Lizdin from the Central Control Commission; and the expulsion of Trotsky and Zinoviev from the party. The Belgians demanded that the Executive of the Comintern vote a suspension of these measures and convene a world congress immediately for the purpose of judging the situation. Upon order of the Stalinists, the Belgian party convention of March 1928 was thoroughly stacked and the old leadership, including Van Overstraeten, Hennaut, Lesoil, Lootens, Cloosterman, and others, was ousted from its position and from membership in the party. The Van Overstraeten group promptly constituted itself as a separate organization supporting the view of the Russian Opposition and publishing weekly organs (*The Communist*) in French and Flemish.

93. In a proclamation issued in Moscow on August 16, 1926, signed by A.I. Rykov, as chairman of the Council of People's Commissars, J.V. Stalin, as secretary of the Communist Party, and V.V. Kuibyshev, as chairman of the party Control Commission, the standpoint of the official leadership was put forth on "The Successes and Defects of the Economy Campaign in the Soviet Union." Referring to the need of economy for the purpose of saving the funds needed to industrialize the country, the Trotskyist Opposition was attacked despite the fact that the proclamation, by virtue of Rykov's signature, bore an at least partially governmental character. The Opposition scheme for raising the required funds is criticized because it plans presumably "to take away as much from the peasant as possible, and to utilize the means thus exported for the requirements of industry. Some of our comrades urge us to take this way, but we cannot do so, for it would mean a rupture between the workers and the peasantry, the breakdown of the alliance between workers and peasants, an undermining of the dictatorship of the proletariat, the reduction to poverty of the peasantry, and

with this the weakening of industry." (*International Press Correspondence*, vol. 6, no. 60., p. 1,021. September 2, 1926.)

94. The *Chervonetz* was the first effective gold currency established after the Russian revolution under the administration of the then commissar of finance, Sokolnikov. At par, it was approximate equivalent to a United States five dollar gold coin or note. Its Russian equivalent is ten rubles.

95. The 9th of Thermidor (July 27, 1794) was the date in the calendar of the Great French Revolution when the counterrevolution effected its dramatic coup by the execution of the revolutionary Jacobins Robespierre, Saint-Just, Couthon, Lebas, and others, thus opening the period of the Thermidorian reaction. The term is applied by Trotsky to conditions socially analogous in the Russian revolution, meaning the growth of social, economic, and political reaction occurring under old structural forms and banners.

96. After the Russian professor and economist, N. Ustryalov, who changed his position in favor of intervention against the Soviets to a position of working for the Soviet government as an employee in one of its institutions in Harbin. Ustryalov's views were that by working within the Soviet regime, capitalism could be restored by means of a gradual permeation of the Soviet organism. In the struggle between Stalin and Trotsky, Ustryalov supported the former as one step in the direction of his own goal.

97. Towards the end of 1927 and throughout the years 1928 and 1929, numerous cases of sabotage, bureaucratism, corruption, nepotism, and terrorization of workers and rank and file communists were laid bare in a number of regions in the country. The affairs of the Donetz Basin ("Shakhty trial"), Smolensk, and Artemovsk were among the most sensational of those brought to light.

98. *Katheder-Sozialisten* was a term applied by a German writer in 1871 to professors of economics with moderately socialistic leanings. *Katheder-Sozialisten,* or socialists of the chair, "soon passed into other countries as a designation for those who favor a moderate expansion of the paternalistic state, with the least possible disturbance to exist-

ing institutions. Their philosophy, which is at best a diluted form of state socialism, is usually called 'academic socialism' or 'professorial socialism.' "

99. In connection with the dispute over the national question in Georgia (1922–23) Lenin wrote several times to Trotsky appealing to him to intervene jointly on their behalf against the policy of Stalin, Dzerzhinsky, and Ordzhonikidze. At one meeting, when the discussion became intense, Ordzhonikidze struck a young Georgian opponent a blow in the face. On December 30, 1922, Lenin wrote in one of his confidential notes: "That Ordzhonikidze could explode to the point of resorting to physical force, as Dzerzhinsky reported to me, enables me to get an idea of the morass we have fallen into." (B. Souvarine, *Staline,* Paris 1935, p. 289.) Lenin proposed that Ordzhonikidze be immediately expelled from the party. [For further information, see *Lenin's Final Fight,* pp. 193–95, 265.]

100. The name of the inspector in Gogol's classic, *Inspector-General.* Literally, it means: "Hold your snout!" and it has passed into general Russian cant as a term, in part humorous, in part contemptuous, in part hateful, for a policeman or gendarme.

Index

Adler, Friedrich, 18, 324
Anarchism, 93, 334
Anglo-Russian Trade Union Unity Committee, 101, 138, 144, 152, 237, 241, 261, 264, 342–43; political character of, 142–48
Article 58, 162, 166, 239, 281, 344
Austria, Vienna uprising in (1927), 94–95, 102, 156

Bakunin, Mikhail, 333
Baldwin, Stanley, 146
Bauer, Otto, 59–62
Bavaria, 1919 uprising, 156
Bebel, August, 328
Bernstein, Eduard, 93, 327–28, 333
Bismarck, Otto von, 189
Blanquism, 112, 338
"Bloc of four classes," 192, 216, 229, 253, 312. *See also* Chinese revolution (1925–27)
Bolshevik Party (Russia), 167, 191, 231 "granite hardness" of, 154–55; in October Revolution, 101–2, 114, 158; organizational norms of, 168; "Three Whales" of, 48, 328–29. *See also* Communist Party (Soviet Union)
"Bolshevization" campaign, 139–40, 168–69
Bonapartism, 102
Bordiga, Amadeo, 170, 347, 367–68
Borodin, Mikhail, 149, 349, 364, 365
Bourgeois-democratic revolutions: in China, 185–86, 189, 202–3, 350–51; national bourgeoisie and, 184–90; peasantry in, 236; and proletarian dictatorship, 194, 202–3, 205; working class in, 192. *See also* Democratic dictatorship of proletariat and peasantry
Brandler, Heinrich, 110, 111, 117, 118, 170, 343, 347
Brest-Litovsk treaty (1918), 105, 336
Britain, 75–76, 341; 1926 general strike, 102, 143–44, 156; opportunist line in, 101, 137–39, 142–48, 155, 256, 261, 263, 271. *See also* Anglo-Russian Trade Union Unity Committee
Bukharin, Nikolai, 25, 60, 119, 126, 308, 312, 325, 347; on Anglo-Russian Committee, 143; on bourgeois-democratic revolutions, 183, 184, 187; on Brest-Litovsk treaty, 105, 336; on Chinese revolution, 149, 183–84, 187, 209, 221–22, 225–26, 228–29, 239, 350, 354, 356–57; on kulaks, 149, 281, 282, 291, 304; on Opposition, 60, 119, 279–80; on permanent revolution, 104–5, 106–7, 140; scholasticism of, 64, 78–79, 105, 106, 141, 305; on "socialism at snail's pace," 64, 68, 69, 262; on socialism in one country, 44, 56–55, 61–64, 78, 79, 81–82; ultraleftism of, 104–7, 140, 337
Bulgaria: 1923 defeat in, 119, 156, 335, 340–41; 1925 putschist actions in, 132–33, 259, 260, 335
Bureaucratism: in Comintern, 19, 149–50, 248, 252–53; and nonproletarian class pressures, 171, 300–303, 308–12; "socialism in one country" and, 84, 86, 265; in Soviet CP, 161, 172, 252, 308–12; in Soviet state, 301

Cachin, Marcel, 17–18, 324

Cannon, James, P., 317–22, 347
Canton insurrection (1927): adventurism of, 95, 133, 160, 210–11, 212, 218, 356; proletarian character of, 193–95, 212; soviets in, 202, 213, 216, 217, 364–65
Capitalism: in colonial world, 189–90, 351; contradictions of, 25, 41, 71, 77, 97–98, 99; "hopeless situations" of, 82, 83, 108; possibilities for expansion of, 60–61, 83, 98; postwar stabilization of, 27, 29, 99, 100, 106, 118–19, 120, 124, 130, 132, 145–46, 173, 175, 254–55, 260–61, 265; and world economy, 25, 37, 38–39, 38–40, 74, 96. *See also* Bourgeois-democratic revolutions; National bourgeoisie
Center Party (Germany), 227
Centrism, 18, 72, 112, 139, 253, 257, 325
Chamberlain, Austen, 243
Ch'en Tu-hsiu, 199, 251, 348, 351, 359, 367–68
Chervonetz, 282, 370
Chiang Kai-shek: Comintern support for, 149, 150, 155, 197, 198, 231; and fight against imperialism, 185, 186; as hangman of revolution, 192, 193–94, 349–50, 351–52;
China: capitalism in, 189–90, 351; class structure of, 196, 220, 351, 357–58; and imperialism, 185–87, 189–90, 191–92, 196, 353, 357; national bourgeoisie in, 182–92, 196, 197, 202, 209; national liberation and, 186–87; 1911 revolution in, 185–86, 187, 350–51
Chinese revolution (1925–27), 102, 156; agrarian question in, 195, 198, 200, 201, 205, 207, 211; "Autumn Harvest" uprisings, 362–63; bourgeois-democratic tasks, 189, 194, 195–96, 202–3; false perspective on, 101, 256, 261, 264, 271, 319–20; maneuvers with bourgeoisie in, 149, 150, 151, 152, 155; Northern Expedition, 187, 198, 349–50, 351–52; Opposition on, 142; proletariat in, 194, 196, 221, 235; Shanghai uprising, 182, 205, 349–50, 352; stages of, 192–93. *See also* Canton insurrection (1927); Communist Party (China); Kuomintang
Chinese revolution (third): socialist character of, 194, 195–96, 203, 207, 218–24;
Cole, G.D.H., 157, 335
Communist International (Comintern), 139–41, 149; bureaucratism in, 19, 149–50, 160–73, 248, 252–53; expulsion of oppositionists from, 16, 111, 170, 172, 175, 246, 273, 280, 283, 296, 329–30, 332, 347–48, 367–68; gaps between congresses of, 21, 117, 246–48, 252, 331–32; impact of defeats on, 17, 93, 94–95, 242, 255–56, 264; left turn (1928), 132–34, 142, 239–40, 266–67, 367; membership in, 334; missed opportunities by, 100, 102, 132–34, 139; program of, 15–16, 317, 325; removal of leaderships, 16, 111, 139–40, 169–70, 171–72, 248–49, 251, 273, 343–44, 347–48, 367–68, 369; rightward shift (1925), subordination to CPSU, 247; ultracentralism in, 168, 247–48
Communist International congresses:
—First Congress (1919), 15, 331
—Second Congress (1920), 15, 331
—Third Congress (1921), 114, 267, 337; Lenin at, 15–16, 33–34, 105–6, 107, 119, 337; political struggle at, 15–16, 104–7, 119, 337; Trotsky at, 15–16, 105–6
—Fourth Congress (1922), 16, 47, 59–61, 107, 126, 169, 331; Lenin at, 16, 47
—Fifth Congress (1924), 246, 332; on China, 137; on Germany, 109–10, 117–23, 127, 340; misreading of

374 / INDEX

world politics by, 37, 119–20, 123–24, 126–27, 131, 132, 133–34, 139, 175, 254, 259, 267, 269; Zinoviev role in, 118, 120, 249, 250, 251

Communist International Executive Committee (ECCI), 148–49, 160, 180; membership on, 246, 248–49; Seventh Plenum (1926), 31–32, 34, 44, 55–56, 57, 58, 77, 80–81, 81–82, 186, 193, 251–52, 273, 279; Eighth Plenum (1927), 350, 354–55, 359–60; Ninth Plenum (1928), 198–99, 200, 201, 208–9, 211–12, 239, 265–66, 268–69; overcentralism of, 168, 247–48; Presidium of, 116, 124, 168, 210–11, 247

Communist Manifesto (Marx and Engels), 93–94, 188, 226

Communist parties: bourgeois public opinion and, 114; centrality of, 99–103, 138; independence of, 224, 228, 232–34; and maneuvers, 153; organizational norms of, 161–62, 168, 247, 312; as world party, 24, 42

Communist Party (Belgium), 170, 273, 369

Communist Party (Britain), 137–39, 142

Communist Party (China), 114–15, 167; deposing of leaderships in, 199–200, 252, 359; and Kuomintang, 190, 225, 228–29, 349, 365; after 1927, 361–62; workers in, 360–61. *See also* Chinese revolution

Communist Party (Czechoslovakia), 170

Communist Party (France), 169, 170, 343

Communist Party (Germany): election results by, 120–21, 122, 268, 269; factionalism in, 109, 167, 272; and March 1921 action, 104, 272, 336–37; ouster of leaderships in, 16, 111, 170, 272–73, 343; spontaneism of, 157–58; turn after March 1921, 107–8. *See also* Germany, 1923 revolutionary situation

Communist Party (Italy), 170

Communist Party (Norway), 170

Communist Party (Poland), 343

Communist Party (Soviet Union): bourgeois layers in, 253, 293–98, 300–305, 311; bureaucratism in, 161, 172, 252, 309–12; centrist faction in, 18, 72, 112, 139, 254, 257, 297–98, 312; factionalism in, 112, 163, 165–66, 345; growth of apparatus in, 161–62, 164, 247–48, 249, 253, 258, 296–97, 310; left turn (1928), 245, 273–74, 292–99, 303–4; monolithism in, 164, 165–66, 296–97; 1919 program of, 226; reform of, 299; Eleventh Congress (1922), 65, 276; Twelfth Congress (1923), 257–58; Thirteenth congress (1924), 116, 164; Fourteenth Congress (1926), 64, 165–66, 172, 278, 289, 291; Fifteenth Congress (1927), 247, 250, 282, 287, 296, 300, 304. *See also* Bolshevik Party (Russia)

Communist Party (Sweden), 170

Communist Party (U.S.), 170, 321; La Follete/FLP adventure, 135–36, 230–31, 320–21, 342, 366

Constructive Socialism, 93–94, 334–35

Cook, Arthur J., 138, 146

Cooperatives, 51–52

Cornelissen, Christian, 94, 157

Croatian Peasants Party, 134–35

Culture, 52–53, 223, 301, 307, 308

Curve of capitalist development, 83, 105, 122

Defeatism, 90

Democratic centralism, 161–62, 246, 312

Democratic dictatorship of proletariat and peasantry: in China, 192–93, 197, 204, 205, 207–8; in Russia, 203, 206

Dictatorship of proletariat, 72, 81, 167; on agenda in China, 193–96, 203, 207, 218–24; and bourgeois-democratic tasks, 194, 202–3, 205; dangers to, 164–65; and socialism, 45, 73, 218, 219–20, 222
Dombal, Tomasz, 134, 137
Dual power, 192, 203; in Soviet Union, 293, 300, 303, 311

Engels, Frederick, 38, 130, 332
Estonia, 1924 putsch in, 95, 132–33, 156, 259, 260, 264, 335

Factions: communist approach to, 162, 169–70; prohibition of, 105–6, 162–64, 167, 168; secret, 112, 164–66, 345; at third Comintern congress, 106, 107, 168, 337. *See also* Communist Party (Soviet Union), factionalism in
Factory committees, 217
Farmer Labor Party adventure, U.S. (1924), 135–36, 230–31, 320–21, 342, 366. *See also* "Two-class workers and peasants parties"
Fascism, 123–31
Finland, 1918 revolution in, 94–95, 110, 337–38
First International, 93, 332–33
Fischer, Ruth, 119, 139, 343, 347, 367–68
Fourth International, 18–19, 324
France: Left Bloc in, 98, 123, 125; Socialist Party in, 88–89, 124–25
Friends of the Soviet Union, 247

Gandhiism, 160
General strike, 157. *See also* Britain, 1926 general strike
Germany: March 1921 action, 104, 105, 113–14, 271–72; 1918–19 revolution, 102, 156, 271. *See also* Communist Party of Germany; Social Democratic Party of Germany
Germany, 1923 revolutionary situation, 101, 107–11, 114, 127, 156, 263, 264; Comintern evaluation of, 109–10, 115–23, 116–17, 127, 258; CP turn toward, 108–9, 110–11, 272; fifth Comintern congress on, 109–10, 117–23, 127, 340; impact of defeat of, 111, 120–21, 122, 127, 140, 173–75, 242, 256, 260–61, 267; objective conditions in, 108, 109; and Saxon landtag, 118, 127, 270, 339–40; soviets and, 216–17, 217–18; Stalin on, 112, 338–39; Trotsky position during, 110–11, 258. *See also* Communist Party of Germany
Girault, Suzanne, 139, 170, 347, 367–68
Green, William, 135
Guchkov, A.I., 187
Guesde, Jules, 88
Guild Socialism, 93–94, 157, 335

Herriot, Edouard, 126, 127
Hilferding, Rudolf, 231, 267, 366
Ho Lung, 210, 363
Hobson, John, 157, 335
Hu Han-min, 197, 348–49
Hungarian revolution (1919), 94–95, 102, 156, 230, 365–66

Imperialist epoch, 23–24, 96–100, 102–3, 236, 271; revolutionary character of, 98–99. *See also* Capitalism
India, 224
Insurrections: preparation of, 113–14, 156–60, 213–15. *See also* Germany, 1923 revolutionary situation; Russian revolution (October 1917)
Interimperialist competition, 27, 29, 123–24
Italy, 231; September 1920 events in, 94–95, 102

Japan, 224–25
Jews, 191

Kamenev, L.B., 149, 249, 289, 329,

330, 346, 368
Katheder-Sozialisten, 304–5, 370–71
Kautsky, Karl, 28, 327, 328
Kerensky, Alexander, 185, 186, 188, 203, 353
Kolarov, Vasil, 110, 135, 136, 340–41
Korea, 225
Krestintern. *See* Peasants International
Kronstadt uprising (1921), 163, 330
Kuibyshev, V.V., 278
Kulaks, 163, 195, 241, 261, 281, 292–93; 282–91; Bukharin-Stalin on, 149, 278, 279, 280, 282, 283, 291, 304; danger from, 163, 278, 279, 293, 300, 302; enrichment of, 254, 258, 276, 282; and grain crisis, Stalin's maneuvers with, 149, 150, 153
Kun, Béla, 15–16, 323, 337, 365
Kuomintang: Chinese CP and, 190, 216, 225, 228–29, 349, 365; class character of, 186, 227, 228–30, 234, 354; Comintern support for, 185, 198, 208, 225–26, 227–30, 256, 260, 263; dictatorship by, 193; and imperialism, 186; Left, 192, 205, 227, 354–55, 360, 363; maneuvers with, 149, 152, 155; membership in Comintern of, 137, 182, 197, 238, 348–49; workers' break with, 193–95
Kuusinen, Otto, 110, 338

La Follette, Robert, 135–36, 137, 149, 230–31, 237–38, 259–60, 321, 342, 366
Labour Party (Britain), 123, 124
Labriola, Arturo, 94
Law of uneven and combined development. *See* Uneven and combined development
League Against Imperialism (All-American Anti-Imperialist League), 238, 247
Lenin, V.I.: April theses of, 207; 119; on building socialism in Russia, 45–47, 50–53, 54, 204–5, 219, 221, 222, 223; on communist parties, 42, 83; "On Cooperation," 44, 50–53; on democratic dictatorship, 45, 48, 49, 192, 206; on factions, 163, 168; falsification of, 43–44, 176–77; final writings of, 50–53, 247–48, 308, 311, 345, 371; at fourth Comintern congress, 16, 47; leadership role of, 101–2, 114; on NEP retreat, 274–77, 330–31; on oppressed and oppressor nations, 184, 190; on overcentralism, 168, 247–48; on peasantry, 152, 232–33, 237; and socialism in one country, 32–34, 36, 44–48, 53–54; on Soviet Russia and world economy, 65, 66–67, 69; on Soviet Russia and world revolution, 32–34, 53–54, 85; on soviets, 213–14, 215; at third Comintern congress, 15–16, 105–6, 107, on United States of Europe, 30, 31; Testament of, 163, 252, 344–45
Lensch, Paul, 87, 88
Lessons of October, The (Trotsky), 111–12, 113, 114–15, 138
Levi, Paul, 119
"Liquidationism," 119, 131–32, 141, 209–10, 259
Loriot, Fernand, 170, 347
Luxemburg, Rosa, 157

MacDonald, Ramsey, 98, 126, 127, 146, 334
Makhno, Nestor, 211, 364
Maneuverism, 149–56, 270
Martynov, Aleksander S., 137, 149, 204
Marx, Karl, 115–16, 156, 200–201, 312
Maslow, Arkadi, 139, 170, 337, 343, 347
Melnichansky, G.N., 146
Mensheviks, 184, 201
Mikoyan, Anastas I., 280
Milyukov, P.N., 185
Milyutin, V.P., 136

Molotov, V.M., 313
Monatte, Pierre, 170, 347

Narodniks, 192, 231, 355–56
National bourgeoisie, 137, 182–92, 202, 261, 180–82, 183. *See also* Kuomintang
National liberation movements, 184, 185
National socialism, 18, 24, 44
Nations, oppressed and oppressor, 183–84, 190
Neumann, Heinz, 212–13, 343, 356, 364
New Economic Policy (NEP), 51, 60, 105, 163, 274–76, 330–31; social consequences of, 175–76, 258, 284–85
Noske, Gustav, 90, 128

October Revolution. *See* Russian revolution (October 1917)
Opposition, Bolshevik–Leninist, 346; bourgeoisie and, 243–44; expulsion of, 175, 246, 273, 279, 283, 296, 329–30, 347–48, 367–68; history of, 329–30; "liquidationism" of, 119, 131–32, 260; November 1927 demonstration by, 281; official condemnations of, 120, 251–52; "pacifism" of, 125–26; as proletarian wing of party, 176, 305; repression against, 13, 17, 142, 173, 199, 253, 281, 305, 311, 330; on *smychka* and kulaks, 289; social causes of defeat of, 174–76; Social Democracy on, 241–42. "social democratic deviation" by, 59–62, 64; as "superindustrialists," 278; theses of to fifteenth CP congress, 280–81, 289–90, 300, 304; "underestimation of peasantry" by, 234–35, 258; "Wrangel officer" slander against, 166. *See also* Platform of the Opposition
Opposition, Leningrad, 165, 329, 345–46

Orage, A.R., 157
Ordzhonikidze, G.K., 250, 308, 371

Pacifism, 81, 124, 125–27, 184
Patriotism, revolutionary, 89, 90
Peaceful coexistence, 33, 63
Peasant parties, 226–27, 236–38, 259–60. *See also* "Two-class workers and peasants parties"
Peasantry: class alliance with, 48, 51, 52, 54, 152–53, 226, 231–34, 257–58, 285, 331; in China, 195–96; Comintern errors on, 134–35, 136–37, 365–66; proletarian stance toward, 152–53, 226, 235–38. *See also* United States, farmers in
Peasants International (Krestintern), 134–35, 136, 234–38, 259–60, 348, 367
Pepper, John (Jozsef Pogány), 149, 327; in Hungarian revolution, 135, 365; at third Comintern congress, 15–16, 323–24, 337; and U.S. Communist Party, 135–36, 137, 167, 230, 237, 238
Permanent revolution, 58, 200–201; Bukharinist version of, 104–5, 106–7, 140; Stalinist attacks on, 199, 200, 209
Petrovsky, D., 149
Platform of the Opposition (1927), 142, 173, 282, 283, 295, 329, 344
Poland, 190–91
Political parties, bourgeois, 227–28, 237
Productivity of labor, 66, 68–69
Profintern. *See* Red International of Labor Unions
Proletarian revolution: conditions for, 97–100, 102; as international task, 89–90; postwar upsurge in, 103–4. *See also* Chinese revolution; Germany, 1923 revolutionary situation; Russian revolution (October 1917)
Pugh, Arthur, 146
Purcell, Albert, 138, 145, 146, 148,

149, 150, 155, 237, 342
Putschism: in China, 210, 211–12, 363; after 1923, 95, 132–33; in 1921, 105, 113–14

Radek, Karl, 119, 337, 340
Radić, Stefan, 134–35, 136, 137, 149, 238, 259–60
Radicalization: Comintern on, 177–78, 267–72; decline after 1923, 37; and economic crises, 206
Radical Party (France), 124, 228
Rafes, Moshe, 149
Red International of Labor Unions (Profintern), 238, 260
Reformism, 80, 87, 101, 131, 143, 333
Rosmer, Alfred, 170, 347
Ruhr crisis (1923), 36–37, 107
Russia: as capitalism's weakest link, 64, 74–75; February 1917 revolution, 187–88, 189, 201; liberal bourgeoisie in, 184, 185–86, 187, 189; national oppression in, 190–91; 1905 revolution, 180, 184, 189, 214
Russian revolution (October 1917): Bolshevik Party and, 101–2, 114, 158; class character of, 48–50, 78–79, 206, 358; democratic stage of (Oct. 1917–July 1918), 195, 196, 197, 203, 358; Lenin's role in, 101–2, 114; soviets in, 213–14; and world revolution, 32–34, 36, 48–49, 51, 54, 57, 84–85
Rykov, A.I., 278, 280, 290, 347, 369

Second International, 93, 97, 333–34; collapse of, 325–26, 328. *See also* Social Democracy
Semard, Pierre, 267
Septumvirate, 164, 165, 345
Shaw, George Bernard, 94
Shulgin, V.V., 187
Smychka, 69–70, 176, 257–58, 276, 277–79, 282–89, 302, 331
Social democracy, 40–41, 60–61, 143, 228, 234; betrayal of revolutions by, 103–4; and Bolshevik-Leninist Opposition, 60–62, 65, 241–43; and fascism, 128–29, 130–31; revival of after 1923, 27, 124–25, 241–42, 254, 265, 267, 269–70; support for bourgeoisie by, 128, 129, 270. *See also* Second International
Social Democratic Party of Germany: post-1923 revival of, 121–22, 123, 124, 129, 178, 242, 268; prewar, 157, 327–28; in World War I, 88, 325–26
Socialism: material prerequisites for, 50–53, 71, 74–76, 219, 222; "at snail's pace," 64, 68, 69, 262; and world revolution, 32–34, 36, 54, 73–74, 81, 84–85, 85, 86, 257, 260–61, 306
Socialism in one country, 260, 262, 264, 286, 312; in China, 222; Lenin and, 32–34, 36, 43–44, 43–58, 45–47, 53–54; national socialism and, 36, 80, 87–91, 223; as petty-bourgeois theory, 71, 277; role of Comintern in, 79–80; Stalin on, 38, 44, 54–55, 81, 262, 332, 335–36; and uneven and combined development, 40–41, 70, 336; Vollmar on, 62–63; and world economy, 63–70, 71–72, 78
Socialist Revolutionary Party (Russia), 184, 201, 231, 233, 236–37
Social patriotism, 40–41, 87–90
Sokolnikov, G.Y., 249, 329
Souvarine, Boris, 170, 347
Soviet Union: debate on economic growth in, 69, 70, 254–55, 262–64, 274–82; establishment of socialism in, 45–47, 49, 84–85, 332; foreign trade, 65, 67; grain crisis in, 257–58, 274, 280, 281–91; and imperialist intervention, 64, 66, 79, 83; industry lag in, 70, 76–77, 176, 258, 276, 278–80, 281, 283–89, 285, 286, 301–2, 368–69; "90 percent socialism" in, 84–85, 264,

332; relations with capitalist world, 33, 63, 78–79, 151, 263–64, 303; revolutionary patriotism toward, 89, 91; social crisis in, 175–76, 178, 265, 283–92; working-class in, 78–79, 287, 302–3; and world economy, 61, 64–70, 78–79, 262, 289; and world revolution, 32–34, 36, 53–54, 81, 84–85, 86, 257, 260–61, 306. *See also* Communist Party (Soviet Union); New Economic Policy; *Smychka*

Soviets, 213–18; in China, 198, 202, 211, 213, 214, 216, 217–18, 319, 355, 360, 362–63, 364–65; in Russian revolution, 213–14, 360

Spector, Maurice, 347–48

Spontaneism, 157–58

Stabilization. *See* Capitalism, postwar stabilization of

Stalin, Joseph, 16, 82, 174, 312, 313, 346–47; on Anglo-Russian Committee, 143, 147–48; on China, 149, 224, 225–26, 227, 229, 232, 354–55, 360; on colonial bourgeoisie, 187; on fascism, 128–30; on Germany 1923, 112, 338–39; on kulaks, 277, 291, 294, 305; as leader of right turn, 139, 141; Lenin on, 308; as organizer of defeats, 17; on socialism in one country, 38, 44, 54–55, 80–81, 84–85, 262, 264, 332, 335–36; on uneven and combined development, 38, 62, 335–36

State Planning Commission (Gosplan), 66, 331

Strategy and tactics, 92–93, 94, 99; maneuvers and, 150–56

Sun Yat-sen, 185–86, 205, 222–29, 349, 351, 365

Syndicalism, 93, 334

T'an P'ing-shan, 186, 199, 251–52, 273

Tao Tsi-tao, 295

Thälmann, Ernst, 15–16, 17, 18, 266–67, 268–69, 270–71, 273, 323, 343

Thermidor, 293, 295–96, 305, 370

Third International. *See* Communist International (Comintern)

Thomas, Albert, 146

Tomsky, Mikhail, 143, 342, 347

Trade unions: in Britain, 137–38, 143–44; in Soviet Union, 144, 145

Transitional demands, 106, 272, 327

Treint, Albert, 139, 347, 367–68

Trotsky, Leon: as Comintern leader, 15–16, 246; exile of, 324; at Fourth Congress, 16, 59–61, 126; during German 1923 events, 110–11, 259; at third Comintern congress, 15–16, 105–6; at twelfth party congress, 257–58

"Trotskyism": attacks on, 28, 140, 141, 160, 163, 209, 239, 249, 251, 266, 268, 329; condemnation of, 14, 15, 32, 58–59, 252, 259; legend of, 176, 177. *See also* Opposition, Bolshevik-Leninist

Trudoviks, 188, 352–53

Tseretelli, I.G., 203

"Two-class workers and peasants parties," 135–36, 223–35, 312, 320–21

Two-and-a-Half International, 18, 324, 333

"Ultra-imperialism," 228

Ultraleftism: in Comintern (1921), 105, 113–14, 336–37; of 1924–25, 132–33, 137, 139, 140, 242, 257, 259, 261, 264

Uneven and combined development, 34–35, 38–41, 44–45, 59, 70, 74, 76, 77, 97, 197; Stalin on, 38, 62, 130, 335–36

United front, 106, 266, 270

United States of America: as dominant imperialist power, 26, 28, 29, 318–19; and European capitalism, 27, 29, 123–24; farmers in, 135–36, 230, 236, 238; impending crisis in, 28–29; La Follete campaign

(1924) in, 135–36, 149, 230–31, 237, 238, 260, 320–21, 342, 366; Populist movement in, 236; revolutionary prospects in, 27, 28, 326

United States of Europe slogan, 27, 30–37, 87; accepted by Comintern, 30, 35, 37, 327; Lenin on, 30, 31, 35

Unprincipled combinationism, 150, 153, 154, 155–56

Ustryalovism, 293–94, 307, 370

Vaillant, Edouard, 87, 88
Van Overstraeten, Eduard, 170, 347, 369
Varga, Jenö (Eugen), 120
Vollmar, Georg von, 18, 62–63, 324, 331
Voroshilov, Kliment, 148

Wang Ching-wei, 150, 192, 193–94, 197, 198, 354, 355
War communism, 163, 274, 287, 291, 330
Where Is Britain Going? (Trotsky), 138–39
Workers and peasants parties. *See* "Two-class workers and peasants parties"
World War I, 25, 29, 77, 326
"Wrangel officer," 166, 346

Yakovlev, V., 311
Yeh T'ing, 210, 356, 363
Young Communist League, 42, 57, 85

Zetkin, Clara, 14, 119, 323
Zinoviev, Gregory, 125–27, 126, 143, 368, 289; attacks on Opposition by, 119, 125, 368–69; bloc with Stalin by, 112, 329; on Chinese revolution, 142; as Comintern leader, 110, 120, 246, 249–51, 367; as member of Opposition, 120, 249–50, 329, 341, 346; 1927 capitulation of, 112–13, 149, 330; and German 1923 events, 110, 112, 116, 117–18, 120–21; on Peasants International, 134–35, 149

FOR FURTHER READING

The History of the Russian Revolution
Leon Trotsky
The social, economic, and political dynamics of the first socialist revolution. The story is told by one of the revolution's principal leaders writing from exile in the early 1930s, with these historic events still fresh in his mind. Unabridged edition, 3 vols. in one. $35.95

The First Five Years of the Communist International
Leon Trotsky
The early years of the Communist International, documented in articles and speeches by one of its founding leaders. Two volumes, $25.95 each

The Challenge of the Left Opposition
Leon Trotsky
Documents the fight of the communist opposition from 1923 to 1929 against the reactionary political and economic policies of the rising bureaucratic caste in the Soviet Union. Vol. 1 (1923–25), $27.95; vol. 2 (1926–27), $30.95; vol. 3 (1928–29), $27.95

The Revolution Betrayed
What Is the Soviet Union and Where Is It Going?
Leon Trotsky
In 1917 the working class and peasantry of Russia carried out one of the most deep-going revolutions in history. Yet within ten years reaction set in. Workers and peasants were driven from power by a privileged bureaucratic social layer led by Joseph Stalin. This classic study of the Soviet workers state and its degeneration illuminates the roots of the social and political crisis shaking the countries of the former Soviet Union today. $19.95

Collected Works of V.I. Lenin
Writings of V.I. Lenin (1870–1924), the central leader of the Bolshevik Party, the October 1917 Russian revolution, the young Soviet republic, and the early Communist International. 47 vols. $500.00

Alliance of the Working Class and the Peasantry
V.I. Lenin
From the early years of the Marxist movement in Russia, Lenin fought to forge an alliance between the working class and the toiling peasantry. Such an alliance was needed to make possible working-class leadership of the democratic revolution and, on that basis, the opening of the socialist revolution. $17.95

Leon Trotsky on Britain
The displacement of British industry, trade, finance, and diplomacy by its U.S. rival following World War I opened a period of social crisis and class battles across Britain, discussed in these articles by Trotsky. Includes an analysis of the 1926 general strike, betrayed by the labor officialdom. $23.95

In Defense of Marxism
The Social and Political Contradictions of the Soviet Union
Leon Trotsky
A reply to those in the revolutionary workers movement at the close of the 1930s who were beating a retreat from defense of the degenerated Soviet workers state in face of looming imperialist assault. Trotsky explains how the rising pressures of bourgeois patriotism in the middle classes during the buildup toward U.S. entry into World War II were finding an echo even inside the communist movement, and why only a party that fights to bring growing numbers of workers into its ranks and leadership can steer a steady revolutionary course. $24.95

The Communist International in Lenin's Time

Workers of the World and Oppressed Peoples, Unite!
Proceedings and Documents of the Second Congress, 1920
The debate among delegates from 37 countries takes up key questions of working-class strategy and program and offers a vivid portrait of social struggles in the era of the October revolution.
2-vol. set $65

To See the Dawn
Baku, 1920—First Congress of the Peoples of the East
How can peasants and workers in the colonial world achieve freedom from imperialist exploitation? By what means can working people overcome divisions incited by their national ruling classes and act together for their common class interests? These questions were addressed by 2,000 delegates to the 1920 Congress of the Peoples of the East. $19.95

Lenin's Struggle for a Revolutionary International
Documents, 1907–1916; The Preparatory Years
The debate among revolutionary working-class leaders, including V.I. Lenin and Leon Trotsky, on a socialist response to World War I. $32.95

The German Revolution and the Debate on Soviet Power
Documents, 1918–1919; Preparing the Founding Congress
$31.95

Founding the Communist International
Proceedings and Documents of the First Congress, March 1919
$27.95

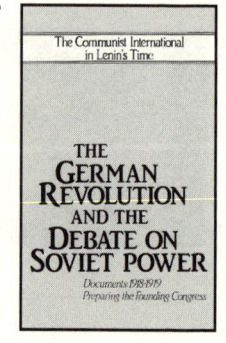

AVAILABLE FROM PATHFINDER

Also from PATHFINDER

The Changing Face of U.S. Politics
Working-Class Politics and the Trade Unions
JACK BARNES

A handbook for workers coming into the factories, mines, and mills, as they react to the uncertain life, ceaseless turmoil, and brutality of capitalism in the closing years of the twentieth century. It shows how millions of workers, as political resistance grows, will revolutionize themselves, their unions, and all of society. $19.95

Woman's Evolution
From Matriarchal Clan to Patriarchal Family
EVELYN REED

Assesses women's leading and still largely unknown contributions to the development of human civilization and refutes the myth that women have always been subordinate to men. "Certain to become a classic text in women's history"—*Publishers Weekly*. $22.95

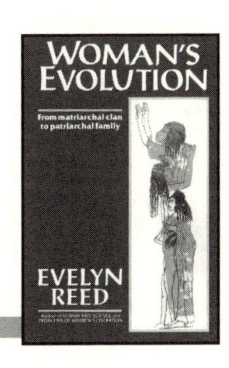

Episodes of the Cuban Revolutionary War, 1956–58
ERNESTO CHE GUEVARA

Ernesto Che Guevara, Argentine by birth, became a central leader of the Cuban revolution and one of the outstanding communists of the 20th century. This book is a firsthand account of the military campaigns and political events that culminated in the January 1959 popular insurrection that overthrew the U.S.-backed dictatorship in Cuba. Guevara describes how the struggle transformed the men and women of the Rebel Army and July 26 Movement led by Fidel Castro. And how these combatants forged a political leadership capable of guiding millions of workers and peasants to open the socialist revolution in the Americas. Guevara's *Episodes* appears here complete for the first time in English. Introduction by Mary-Alice Waters. $23.95

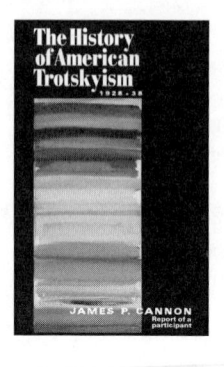

The History of American Trotskyism
JAMES P. CANNON

"Trotskyism is not a new movement, a new doctrine," Cannon says, "but the restoration, the revival of genuine Marxism as it was expounded and practiced in the Russian revolution and in the early days of the Communist International." In this series of twelve talks given in 1942, James P. Cannon recounts an important chapter in the efforts to build a proletarian party in the United States. $18.95

The Politics of Chicano Liberation
Recounts the lessons of the rise of the Chicano movement in the United States in the 1960s and 1970s, which dealt a lasting blow against the oppression of the Chicano people and the divisions within the working class based on language and national origin. Presents a fighting program for those today who are determined to defend hard-won social conquests and build a revolutionary movement capable of leading humanity out of the wars, racist assaults, and social crisis of capitalism in its decline. $15.95

February 1965: The Final Speeches
MALCOLM X

Speeches from the last three weeks of Malcolm X's life, presenting the accelerating evolution of his political views. A large part is material previously unavailable, with some in print for the first time. The inaugural volume in Pathfinder's selected works of Malcolm X. $17.95

Teamster Rebellion
FARRELL DOBBS

The 1934 strikes that built an industrial union and a fighting social movement in Minneapolis, recounted by a leader of that battle. The first in a four-volume series on the Teamster-led strikes and organizing drives in the Midwest that helped pave the way for the CIO and pointed a road toward independent labor political action. $16.95

The Communist Manifesto
KARL MARX, FREDERICK ENGELS

Founding document of the modern working-class movement, published in 1848. Explains why communists act on the basis not of preconceived principles but of *facts* springing from the actual class struggle, and why communism, to the degree it is a theory, is the generalization of the historical line of march of the working class and of the political conditions for its liberation. Also available in Spanish. Booklet $3.95

In Defense of Socialism
FIDEL CASTRO

Not only is economic and social progress possible without the dog-eat-dog competition of capitalism, Castro argues, but socialism remains the only way forward for humanity. Also discusses Cuba's role in the struggle against the apartheid regime in southern Africa. $13.95

The Struggle for a Proletarian Party
JAMES P. CANNON

In a political struggle in the late 1930s with a petty-bourgeois current in the Socialist Workers Party, Cannon and other SWP leaders defended the political and organizational principles of Marxism. The debate unfolded as Washington prepared to drag U.S. working people into the slaughter of World War II. A companion to *In Defense of Marxism* by Leon Trotsky. $19.95

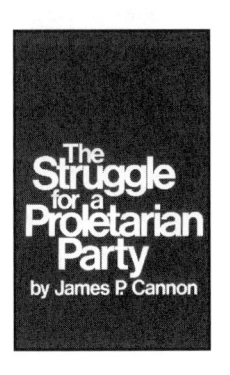

Nelson Mandela Speaks
Forging a Democratic, Nonracial South Africa

Mandela's speeches from 1990 through 1993 recount the course of struggle that put an end to apartheid and opened the fight for a deep-going political, economic, and social transformation in South Africa. $18.95

Write for a catalog

New International
A MAGAZINE OF MARXIST POLITICS AND THEORY

New International no. 10
Imperialism's March toward Fascism and War *by Jack Barnes* • What the 1987 Stock Market Crash Foretold • Defending Cuba, Defending Cuba's Socialist Revolution *by Mary-Alice Waters* • The Curve of Capitalist Development *by Leon Trotsky* $14.00

New International no. 9
The Triumph of the Nicaraguan Revolution • Washington's Contra War and the Challenge of Forging Proletarian Leadership • The Political Degeneration of the FSLN and the Demise of the Workers and Farmers Government $14.00

New International no. 8
The Politics of Economics: Che Guevara and Marxist Continuity *by Steve Clark and Jack Barnes* • Che's Contribution to the Cuban Economy *by Carlos Rafael Rodríguez* • On the Concept of Value *and* The Meaning of Socialist Planning *two articles by Ernesto Che Guevara* $10.00

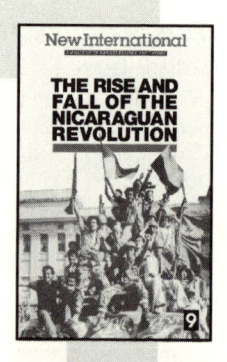

New International no. 7
Opening Guns of World War III: Washington's Assault on Iraq *by Jack Barnes* • Communist Policy in Wartime as well as in Peacetime *by Mary-Alice Waters* • Lessons from the Iran-Iraq War *by Samad Sharif* $12.00

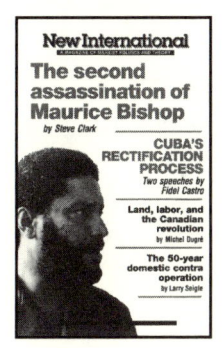

New International no. 6
The Second Assassination of Maurice Bishop *by Steve Clark* • Washington's 50-year Domestic Contra Operation *by Larry Seigle* • Land, Labor, and the Canadian Revolution *by Michel Dugré* • Renewal or Death: Cuba's Rectification Process *two speeches by Fidel Castro* $10.00

New International no. 5
The Coming Revolution in South Africa *by Jack Barnes* • The Future Belongs to the Majority *by Oliver Tambo* • Why Cuban Volunteers Are in Angola *two speeches by Fidel Castro* $9.00

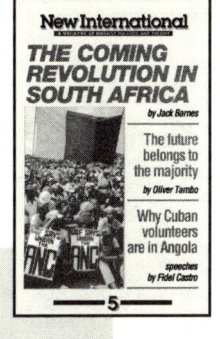

New International no. 4
The Fight for a Workers and Farmers Government in the United States *by Jack Barnes* • The Crisis Facing Working Farmers *by Doug Jenness* • Land Reform and Farm Cooperatives in Cuba *two speeches by Fidel Castro* $9.00

New International no. 3
Communism and the Fight for a Popular Revolutionary Government: 1848 to Today *by Mary-Alice Waters* • 'A Nose for Power': Preparing the Nicaraguan Revolution *by Tomás Borge* • National Liberation and Socialism in the Americas *by Manuel Piñeiro* $8.00

New International no. 2
The Aristocracy of Labor: Development of the Marxist Position *by Steve Clark* • The Working-Class Fight for Peace *by Brian Grogan* • The Social Roots of Opportunism *by Gregory Zinoviev* $8.00

New International no. 1
Their Trotsky and Ours: Communist Continuity Today *by Jack Barnes* • Lenin and the Colonial Question *by Carlos Rafael Rodríguez* • The 1916 Easter Rebellion in Ireland: Two Views *by V.I. Lenin and Leon Trotsky* $8.00

Distributed by Pathfinder
Many of the articles that appear in **New International** are also available in Spanish in **Nueva Internacional,** in French in **Nouvelle Internationale,** and in Swedish in **Ny International.**